KAHLIL
GIBRAN

Man and Poet

RELATED TITLES PUBLISHED BY ONEWORLD:

Gibran: Love Letters, translated by Suheil Bushrui and Salma H. al-Kuzbari, ISBN 1-85168-106-X
Jesus the Son of Man, Kahlil Gibran, ISBN 1-85168-079-9
The Prophet, Kahlil Gibran, ISBN 1-85168-178-7
The Prophet: annotated edition, Kahlil Gibran, introduction and annotations by Suheil Bushrui, ISBN 1-85168-105-1

OTHER INSPIRATIONAL TEXTS PUBLISHED BY ONEWORLD:

God's BIG Book of Virtues, compiled by Juliet Mabey, ISBN 1-85168-171-X
God's BIG Instruction Book, compiled by Juliet Mabey, ISBN 1-85168-170-1
On Sight and Insight, John Hull, ISBN 1-85168-141-8
Words to Comfort, Words to Heal, compiled by Juliet Mabey, ISBN 1-85168-154-X

KAHLIL GIBRAN

Man and Poet

A NEW BIOGRAPHY
SUHEIL BUSHRUI AND JOE JENKINS

Foreword by Kathleen Raine

ONEWORLD

OXFORD

DEDICATION
This book is dedicated to Jean and Kahlil Gibran
in gratitude for their outstanding work,
and in recognition of their leadership
and contributions to Gibran studies
throughout the world.

KAHLIL GIBRAN: MAN AND POET

First published by Oneworld Publications, 1998
Reprinted 1999
First published in paperback, 2001
Reprinted 2003, 2005
First published in trade paperback, 2008

© Suheil Bushrui and Joe Jenkins, 1998

ISBN 978-1-85168-541-7

Cover design by Design Deluxe
Printed and bound by the Maple-Vail Book Manufacturing Group,
Braintree, MA, USA

Contents

Foreword

I was in Lebanon only once, and for less than forty-eight hours. Professor Bushrui had invited me to speak on Blake at an exhibition and conference in 1983 to celebrate the hundredth anniversary of Kahlil Gibran, which I had accepted the more gladly because *The Prophet* had been a book very dear to my mother. Before my plane arrived at Beirut airport the conference had been canceled because of renewed conflict in that war-torn city. The room containing an exhibition of Gibran's writings and paintings remained empty of speakers from America and elsewhere who never arrived. I became Professor Bushrui's guest for the night, the lovely Mediterranean scent of pine and sea violated by the renewal of the conflict destroying that beautiful city with its high level of culture and prosperity.

All was to be seen as on a stage-set. From the mountain-range above the city intermittent bombardment of the airport continued; driving across the city we passed the site of the recently destroyed Palestinian camp. Youths with budding mustaches, proud of their rifles and tin helmets, stopped the car from time to time – hard to know whom they represented. Round one corner we saw a small Israeli encampment. Armored cars carrying U.N. peacekeeping troops from Italy swept past with theatrical panache. At the airport I heard the phrase "They are Sons of Satan!" pronounced by one side or the other, I know not which. I had never before been in a country at war with itself, made the more dramatic by the intimacy of the scale, against its background of lovely mountains where doubtless the age-old "cedars of Lebanon" still kept watch.

Twice Professor Bushrui's house had been destroyed, together with his library, yet he remained with the American University where he taught until, a year later, it became impossible to reach the campus. Only then did he leave his beloved country. I am profoundly grateful to Professor Bushrui whose invitation permitted me to experience in microcosm a glimpse of the many conflicts of this time. Yeats's words about his own Ireland came to mind: "Much hatred, little room."

It was out of Lebanon, already war-torn a generation before he was born, that Kahlil Gibran arose to be the prophet of peace alike to his Lebanese Arab compatriots and to the Western world to which he emigrated with his mother, sisters, and a brother when he was twelve years old. A Maronite Christian by birth, Gibran re-visioned Jesus Christ, not frozen in history but as an ever-living presence in the human heart, Blake's "divine humanity," the divine ground of all life, present to people of all religious traditions and of none.

The end of the nineteenth century might be seen as the final triumph of rational materialism based on natural science as the accepted orthodoxy of the Western and Westernized world; yet in retrospect can we not see that whereas materialist civilization (whether Marxist or capitalist) was in its terminal phase, a powerful counter-current was flowing – not through one mind only but as if some collective spiritual power found agents where it could. In India there were holy men equal to any teachers of her golden age – Ramakrishna, Vivekananda, Ramana Maharshi, Sri Aurobindo, and Mahatma Gandhi's inspired faith in the power of non-violence to change the world; Yeats's friend AE's vision of a world where "the politics of time" would be conducted according to the "politics of eternity"; Yeats himself who totally rejected the materialism of his time and scanned the whole horizon of his world for a learning of the Imagination through which wisdom and poetry might return. Gibran, re-visioning Christianity in the light of Islamic (Sufi) mysticism, is of this group of inspired teachers of the modern world. All these were persecuted in one way or another: Gandhi was repeatedly imprisoned. Yeats himself, great world-poet as he was, was ridiculed by his contemporaries who were ignorant of the great mainstream of civilization from which he drew his knowledge. Gibran was dismissed for the opposite reason, because of his immense following of ordinary men and women, for he answered to a deep need within the Western world, starved as it was of its spiritual food. Communism and capitalism alike have believed that mankind could be fed on "bread alone" but once again the prophets of the ever-living spirit have shown that the "Word of God" is the necessary food of the soul. It is as if one mind had spoken through their several voices, none more eloquent or beautiful than the lonely voice of the Christian Lebanese Arab, Kahlil Gibran.

Professor Bushrui has already published books on Gibran in the East and in the West, and no one could be so well qualified as he is to speak on

Gibran's contribution to Arabic poetry and to the English-speaking world to which Gibran traveled, and was to remain for the rest of his life. In this authoritative critical biography Professor Bushrui has collaborated with Joe Jenkins, an author who represents a new generation of Gibran scholars and it is fitting that this collaboration should give birth to a new biography of a writer who transcended the barriers of East and West.

Kathleen Raine

A NOTE ON TRANSLITERATION

As regards the transliteration of Arabic words I deliberately reject the artful and complicated system, ugly and clumsy withal, affected by scientific modern Orientalists . . . the devices perplex the simple and teach nothing to the learned.

Sir Richard Burton, The Book of the Thousand and a Night (London, 1897), xxix

In transliterating into the Roman alphabet from Arabic script, the authors of this book have adopted a simple system of their own creation. All transliterations for Arabic words in quoted passages are retained as they appear in the text from which the quotation is extracted.

Illustrations and Acknowledgments

ILLUSTRATIONS

COLOR PLATES (*between pages 180 and 181*)

Five early sketches, published here for the first time, *c.* 1907–8
Portrait of Mikhail Naimy, pencil on paper, *c.* 1920 (courtesy of the late
Mikhail Naimy)
Untitled, watercolor on paper, n.d. (courtesy of National Committee of
Gibran)
Autumn, watercolor on paper, (courtesy of National Committee of Gibran)
Untitled, watercolor on paper, n.d. (courtesy of National Committee of
Gibran)
Untitled, watercolor on paper, n.d. (courtesy of National Committee of
Gibran)
The Beholder, watercolor on paper, *c.* 1911 (courtesy of the National
Committee of Gibran)
You are the Bows from which your Children as Living Arrows are Sent Forth,
from *The Prophet,* watercolor on paper, *c.* 1923 (courtesy of the National
Committee of Gibran)
Micheline, watercolor on paper, n.d. (courtesy of the National Committee
of Gibran)

GIBRAN'S ART (*between pages 276 and 277*)

Gibran, self-portrait, pencil on paper *c.* 1910 (courtesy of Telfair Academy
of Arts and Sciences)
Mary Haskell, pencil on paper, 1910 (courtesy of Telfair Academy of Arts
and Sciences)
Two sketches by Kahlil Gibran of himself, ink on paper, Paris, 1910
(courtesy of Youssof Ibrahim Yazbeck)
Sketch by Gibran and Ameen Rihani for an opera house in Beirut; signed
by both, pencil on paper, London, 1910 (courtesy of the Ameen Rihani
Museum)
Sketch of Ameen Rihani, pencil on paper, *c.* 1910 (courtesy of the Ameen
Rihani Museum)
Three book plates, drawn for Ameen Rihani's *Book of Khalid,* 1911
(courtesy of Ameen Rihani Museum)
Gibran's mother, Kamileh Rahmeh, pencil on paper, n.d. (courtesy of the
Telfair Academy of Arts and Sciences)
Auguste Rodin, pencil on paper, 1915 (courtesy of the National Committee
of Gibran)

Portrait of 'Abdu'l-Bahá, pencil on paper, 1912 (courtesy of the Bahá'í International Archives)

Albert Pinkham Ryder, pencil on paper, 1915 (courtesy of the Metropolitan Museum of Art)

The Struggle, reproduced from *Twenty Drawings*, 1919 (courtesy of Alfred A. Knopf Inc.)

The Three are One, pencil on paper, frontispiece for *The Madman*, 1918 (courtesy of Telfair Academy of Arts and Sciences)

Man's Yearning, pencil on paper, *c.* 1920 (courtesy of the National Committee of Gibran)

The Heavenly Mother, pencil on paper, published in *The Forerunner*, 1920 (courtesy of Telfair Academy of Arts and Sciences)

Frontispiece for *The Prophet*, pencil on paper, 1923 (courtesy of Alfred A. Knopf Inc.)

Head of Christ, pencil on paper, *c.* 1928 (courtesy of Telfair Academy of Arts and Sciences)

ACKNOWLEDGMENTS

In the preparation of this volume we have received much valuable help from Miss Beth Hakola, who carefully edited the final manuscript and made many valuable suggestions. We also appreciate the help given at several stages by Mr. David Jeffrey, who assiduously typed the first draft, Mr. Askan Monfared, Mr. Kalim Hanna, Mr. Neil Pigott, Miss Cynthia Gorman, and Mr. John Watson. We owe a special debt to Professor Miles Bradbury, whose warm friendship and advice were indispensable during the time this book was taking shape; and to Miss Susan Reib for her valuable contribution to the bibliography. Finally we wish to record here our special indebtedness to the Kahlil Gibran Research and Studies Project at the University of Maryland for sponsoring the research and the production of the final manuscript.

Introduction

I

When historians look back at the twentieth century they will see human consciousness being stretched upwards toward the heavens and outwards across the earth; an age when East and West finally touched and the peoples of the world awoke to the voices of a larger humanity. They will see the great poets of the West embracing the East – Yeats's translation of the *Upanishads* and Eliot's epiphany as he first read the *Rubáiyát of Omar Khayyám* – the world itself appearing transformed, renewed, painted with "bright, delicious" lines.[1] They will find too the great writers of the East embracing this new global consciousness and embarking upon a voyage of discovery.

At the forefront of this new adventure they will find the "burning genius"[2] of Kahlil Gibran. In his work, as in his thought, Gibran achieved lasting eminence and fame as a writer in two completely disparate cultures and represents the meeting of two worlds. A liberating force in Arabic literature, he became one of the most widely read authors in his adopted tongue – his work possessing a rare and distinctive flavor of ancient wisdom and mysticism, often leaving readers amazed to discover that its creator lived in New York from 1912 to 1931.

As an oriental who wrote his most celebrated work in the major language of the Western world, Gibran's style and philosophy is characteristic of the East, and of the Arab in particular. His constant inspiration was his own heritage, which colored his English and exercised an inescapable hold over his mind, its insistence being upon the wholeness of visionary experience and the perpetual availability of another realm of being. In all his work he expressed the deep-felt desire of men and women for a kind of spiritual life that renders the material world meaningful and imbues it with dignity.

1

He was one of those rare writers who actually transcend the barrier between East and West, and could justifiably call himself – though a Lebanese and a patriot – a citizen of the world. It was, however, as a man from Lebanon that he spoke, and it was a Lebanese mode of thought and belief he ardently expressed. His words went beyond the mere evocation of the mysterious East but endeavored to communicate the necessity of reconciliation between Christianity and Islam, spirituality and materialism, East and West; Gibran in his work and his life refuted Kipling's often-quoted line, written in 1889, "Oh, East is East, and West is West, and never the twain shall meet."[3]

Gibran was born in "a year of transition."[4] While the Ottomans were still in control of his homeland, the British had invaded Egypt and the Sudan, and in 1883 were struggling against the Mahdi. In the same year Sir John Seeley published *The Expansion of England*, arguing that the growth of empire was an inevitable process and the British had an imperial mission. Incited by similar ambitions the French gained control over Tunisia in 1883, adding this to their neighboring colony, Algeria. That same year from India, Kipling proclaimed his concept "the white man's burden"; and in October the Orient Express made its first run: West and East were coming closer together – if not colliding – in the most dangerous of ways.

In the sphere of technology the machine-gun and the first skyscraper were built, while in the realm of ideas Wagner, Marx, and Turgenev passed on and Kafka, Keynes, and Kahlil Gibran were born.

During Gibran's comparatively short life from 1883 to 1931 the Arabic-speaking world came to consider him the genius of his age, while in the West his work has been compared to Blake, Dante, Tagore, Nietzsche, Michelangelo, and Rodin.[5] His popularity too as an oriental writer is unprecedented, and, after the works of T. S. Eliot and W. B. Yeats, *The Prophet* is today the most highly regarded poem of the twentieth century,[6] as well as being the most widely read book of the century.

The more that has been written about Gibran the more elusive the man himself has tended to become as critics, friends, and biographers have built up a variety of unconnected pictures. Gibran himself is partly to blame. He wrote very little about his own life and in recurrent moments of insecurity and "vagueness,"[7] particularly during his first years of recognition, often fabricated or embellished his humble origins and troubled background. This self-perpetuation of his myth – a tendency followed by other literary figures such as Yeats and Swift – was not intellectual dishonesty, but a manifestation of the poetic mind's desire to create its own mythology.

At crucial moments in his early life – when external conditions changed – Gibran was able to rely on his innate qualities of fortitude and resilience. Born as he was into a troubled household often beset by tension between father and mother, the boy sought solitude in the magnificent landscape around his small village in northern Lebanon where he first sketched and scribbled among the mysterious ruins of bygone ages.

When he was ten a severe fracture left him paralyzed for weeks, awakening him to the reservoir of his own inner world. As a twelve-year-old he experienced a fracture of an entirely different kind when he sailed to the New World and encountered a new set of stimuli which he began to interpret through the lens of his unique artistic sensibilities – what he would later call his "madness" – his insatiable urge to create. Throughout these difficult years, and indeed throughout his life, it was always to his pen and brushes that he would turn when tragedy, exile, and rejection hounded him.

The charismatic personality, the burning ambition, and the "rapt spiritual quality"[8] of Gibran needs acknowledging in any account of the poet's life if one is to understand his growth within the West. As early as 1898, when the boy from the Boston ghettoes was just fifteen, Americans were beginning to recognize in him a unique quality: "The boy was made to be one of the prophets;"[9] similar descriptions corroborating this aura occurred throughout Gibran's life: "His face is full of stars. Look at him and you'd know there's not a dead spot in him . . . a peculiar power in him and a peculiar beauty";[10] a colleague wrote of "the delicate boy with chestnut hair, high forehead and large wandering eyes – and here one must stop in describing Gibran – for those large eyes . . . arrested the attention of the beholder so that observation seldom went beyond."[11]

While the young man with the beautiful manners[12] attracted a host of admirers, he was reticent about his humble origins, sometimes alluding to a fortuitous birth in India, a "charmed" childhood, aristocratic relatives "who kept lions as pets,"[13] and ancestor "princes" who were crucified in Antioch in the thirteenth century.[14] He avoided references to the humiliating circumstances when his father became embroiled in a tax-collecting scandal which drove his wife and his children from Lebanon to the United States.

Gibran found himself in America at a propitious time. The benevolent social scientists of Boston – where Kahlil settled with his mother, half-brother, and sisters – were struggling to bring order to the chaos of the seething tenements. Boston was a city where the new showpiece of culture, the Boston Public Library, had recently opened; a city still throbbing from the transcendentalist chords struck by their own Ralph Waldo Emerson – where avant-garde enclaves rebelled against the sentimentality of the "sick little end of the century,"[15] and dabbled with spiritualism and orientalism against an "exotic" backdrop of Turkish carpets, jade bowls, water pipes, fezzes, pointed slippers, and Maeterlinck's Neoplatonic broodings on death and preordained love.

However, to the tens of thousands of immigrants like Gibran and his family living "over the railroad" in an environment compared unfavorably with the notorious slums of East London, life was hard and uncompromising.[16] By the 1890's the city's charitable organizations, realizing that something had to be done to "lighten the burdens"[17] of the poor immigrants, had begun to establish settlement houses run by social workers. It was at one of these centers in 1896 that Gibran's drawings first caught the eye of an art teacher, Florence Pierce. Word moved quickly and two weeks later the young artist found himself entering the world of the colourful avant-garde photographer, publisher, and philanthropist Fred Holland Day.

Over the next few years as he crossed the railroad into the colorful world of "Brahmin Boston," Gibran sensed among Americans a vague spirituality – an inchoate civilization, increasingly looking to the East for the substance and authority lacking at home.

He also sensed that exoticism is ultimately superficial, frivolous, and merely decorative, caring most about its own desires. When its fickle disciples have grown bored of their objects of devotion – and "objects" they have become – they are dropped back into the ghetto and the inherent spiral therein. However, Gibran's unswerving belief in his own destiny – "I came to this world to write my name upon the face of life with big letters"[18] – his innate abhorrence of superficiality, and his weariness with the tendencies of "self-admiration"[19] ensured that this particular "street fakir"[20] escaped from the high priests of pretension.

By 1912, tired of Boston,[21] and her "children of *yesterday*,"[22] Gibran sought change. This need for a fresher, more invigorating environment had been fueled by the two years he spent studying in Paris[23] between 1908 and 1910. It was here that he first came under the spell of *Thus Spake Zarathustra* which was revolutionizing the literary sensibility of the age, and, more importantly for Gibran, was written by an author who convincingly and audaciously adopted the towering figure of a prophet from the East as his mouthpiece. Gibran found in Friedrich Nietzsche, this

4

"sober Dionysus,"[24] a lightning erudition capable of demolishing – with one searing flash – the ancient habits of thought, and moral prejudices; a writer whose breathless blasphemy and ecstatic prose – "Write with blood: and you will discover that blood is spirit"[25] – matched his own deepest needs for artistic authenticity. In Paris Gibran also met Rodin who introduced him to the art and poetry of William Blake. Gibran immediately felt a "kinship"[26] with the visionary Englishman, and the benign shadow of Blake was to fall on virtually all of his English writings as well as many of his Arabic works.

Gibran was one of a long line of writers who were indelibly affected by their origins. For William Butler Yeats it was the sands of Sligo Bay, the emerald loughs and rivers of Western Ireland and the legendary mountains of Ben Bulben and Knocknarea that provided an inexhaustible store of symbol and image with which to fire his poetic imagination. For Kahlil Gibran the land that provided the lasting inspiration for his work was Lebanon, unique in so many ways, particularly in its geographical position and its admixture of ethnic groups. Lebanon of the sacred grove, of the dreaming ruins of the temple of Astarte, of the lofty snow-capped mountains soaring into heaven; Lebanon where the Phoenicians built their great ocean-going vessels which carried the hardy cedar to the pharaohs, and the weaves, purple dyes, glass, sculptures, and alphabets to the Greeks; a land of poets, seers, and prophets who brought their moral revelations to a barbaric world.

The breathtakingly beautiful countryside around the village of Bisharri, where Gibran was born, was untouched by the polluting forces that were robbing the America of the early 1900s of her countryside. Reminiscences of the Lebanese countryside fill the emigrant's letters and conversations and color all his work. Among the mountains, hills, streams, waterfalls, and copses the little boy played, rejoicing in the delights of freedom that stimulated his dreams and reveries.

Trees, and particularly the cedars of Lebanon, had a special place in Gibran's heart – ". . . poems that the earth writes upon the sky. We fell them down and turn them into paper that we may record our emptiness."[27] In his long Arabic poem *al-Mawakib* (*The Procession*), published in 1919, he uses the image of the tree to suggest the peaceful continuity of nature contrasted with the clamor and confusion of urban living. In another of his Arabic pieces the poet pictures himself as having "fled from the multitude" and taken refuge in a quiet valley in Lebanon where he is able to enter the "temple invisible,"[28] expressing his lifelong yearning for the sanctuary of the

Cedar Mountain, a yearning that intensified as he became more embroiled in life in America.

Much of what Gibran gave to the world he owed to his homeland, particularly his acute awareness of the interchange of cultural and artistic influences by which Lebanon is so enriched, a land which provided the social and geographical context for so many of his works. Perhaps most of all he was indebted to Lebanon for his awareness of the inestimable blessings that flow from the harmonious coexistence of differing peoples and faiths, as well as his vivid apprehension of the catastrophes that must inevitably result from the breakdown of such religious and social harmony. During his lifetime he witnessed the consequences of such breakdowns – the terrors of reciprocal destruction and the horrors of famine in his native land – a period when he became, in one observer's eyes, "shattered like a Belgian Cathedral."[29]

Although at the forefront of efforts to awaken the West to the plight of his people,[30] Gibran believed that ultimately the root of all conflict was not political but a psychological "sleep" lying heavy on the human heart. Like his contemporaries Rilke, Yeats, and Eliot, and like Blake before him,[31] Gibran challenged what René Guenon called "The Reign of Quantity," and reaffirmed in the face of ascendant materialist ideologies the reality of the living Spirit as the true agent of liberation and peace – what the Irish mystic poet and painter George Russell (AE) called the "politics of eternity."[32]

II

From an early age Gibran, although brought up as a Maronite Christian, was conscious of the exalted place of the Qur'an in Arabic literature and its simultaneous potency as a spiritual, social, and literary source of inspiration.[33] He once declared that he "kept Jesus in one half of his bosom and Muhammad in the other,"[34] and constantly expressed his belief in the fundamental unity of religion and the many ways to truth. His desire to reconcile Christianity and Islam, as well as being instinctive, was practical in that he foresaw the dangers of sectarianism in Lebanon as well as the insidious Western interventionist policies that such division would provoke.[35]

When Italy declared war on Turkey in 1911 and tensions mounted in the Middle East, Gibran began to speak out against the divisive habits of his countrymen in the past, whereby the Druze adhered to England, the Orthodox to Russia, and the Maronites to France. He implored the Muslim community to understand that the war was not a conflict between Islam and Christianity.[36] During the same period that Mahatma Gandhi expounded his teaching of *satyagraha* in South Africa, Gibran, at a gathering of Arab immigrants in Boston in 1911, propounded his own program of non-violent reform. He implored his people not to rely on religious or political partisanship, or the constitution, or the "putrefied corpse"[37] of state, but work toward a change of heart, whereby, shackled by worldly chains or not, true freedom could still prevail. He published too, in the Arab press, "The Voice of the Poet", condemning violence as a means of conflict resolution;[38] and in his writings he urged the people of the Middle East to exercise caution and discrimination in their dealings with Western powers:

> The Spirit of the West is our friend if we accept him, but our enemy if we are possessed by him; our friend if we open our hearts to him, our enemy if we yield him our hearts; our friend if we take from that which suits us, our enemy if we let ourselves be used to suit him.[39]

There were times, especially during the war years, when Gibran found life in the West uncomfortable, even intolerable: "The *normal*, educated, polite, moral man . . . is so thin . . . hanging in the air between heaven and hell – but he is so comfortable there that he is always smiling at you!";[40] and often he felt "tortured" and estranged in a distant land where "life is as cold as ice and as grey as ashes."[41]

The hermit in Gibran became more "determined" around this time,[42] and a quality of "aloneness" became a characteristic of his life and a feature of his writings. In some of his letters he portrays a "solitary traveller,"[43] wandering in Central Park until nightfall, an artist quietly sketching, or a man thoughtfully jotting down his thoughts in his notebook.[44] Although he could be the most sociable of men,[45] he *ached* for solitude[46] – sometimes wearing his "aloneness" around him like a carapace, calling himself "a stranger among men," entirely on his own even while "possessing seventy thousand friends of both sexes."[47]

Despite his popularity – particularly in his early years in New York – Gibran could be insecure, "crippled and diminished under discord,"[48] yet, if the disagreer was an enemy, "cocksure, lofty, dogmatic, almost contemptuously blunt."[49] The paradoxes of his personality – the asperity and warmth, the vanity and modesty, the self-protectiveness[50] and openness, the man "so readily agitated and depressed . . . so soon rested and refreshed,"[51] the temper and the self-possession – remained an enigma even to those who came closest to him, riddles in part written by Gibran himself who held that those who understand us enslave us.[52] Although during this period Gibran felt "chaotic inside,"[53] characteristically, he had the will to transform his traumas through the "mystic pain"[54] of his creativity, concurring with Nietzsche who wrote: "One must still have chaos, to give birth to a dancing star."[55]

From the furnace of Gibran's alienation *The Madman* emerged – his first English work. Published just as the war ended in 1918, and for all its oriental garb, the anxious mood of *The Madman* could be understood by a generation who had known the horrors of the epoch just past. Although some critics called it "destructive and diabolic stuff,"[56] it was not an inopportune work with which to introduce himself to the English-speaking world. The impact was immediate and within a year *The Madman* had been translated into French, Italian, and Russian.[57]

The Great War reactivated Gibran's deep concerns for Lebanon, and, although at heart he was a rebel, he had difficulty in finding the right outlet for his energy. He might have enlisted and helped liberate his country from the Turks – his pacifism lapsing as stories of atrocities reached America – but, never benefiting from a strong constitution, he decided instead to act as a mouthpiece for the Arab cause in the West.

In 1914 he published an "Open Letter to Islam" calling on the various native sects in Ottoman-occupied lands to cease their internecine struggles and unite in opposition to the Turks, as well as writing other articles highlighting the plight of his people and appealing for aid. He also helped organize a League of Liberation, and was instrumental in the formation of a relief committee which raised funds to combat the famine that was sweeping the Middle East during those terrible years.

His health deteriorated markedly during this time and, despite the worthiness of his aims, Gibran was "apolitical";[58] many years later he received an invitation to join the government of Lebanon – an offer he refused.[59]

The tone of Gibran's writings changed dramatically during these years – striking a sombre, even nihilistic, note – the confident affirmations replaced by gloomy prophecies of the fall of civilization. This disillusionment is apparent in an anthology of his various journalistic writings in Arabic, collected from 1912 to 1918 and published under the title of *al-'Awasif* (*The Tempest*). In the book he portrayed civilization as "an old corrupt tree" and liberty as a cadaverous specter defeated by the savagery of the "new primitives"[60] – themes captured in "The Grave Digger," where the chief character, a giant ghost, buries the hordes of spiritually dead people with apparent relish; a piece that earned Gibran the title "the Grave-Digger" in the East.[61]

Coming from a part of the world that only twenty years before his birth had been convulsed by religious strife, Gibran constantly expressed his conviction that beneath the various forms of religion was an underlying unity. As a student he drew up plans for a Beirut opera house with two domes symbolizing the reconciliation of Christianity and Islam. Although his dream never bore fruit, his writings through the years reflect his desire to merge the Sufi Muslim tradition with the Christian mystical heritage of his background – a dream realized in his portrayal of Almustafa, the eponymous prophet, both a Christ figure and the universal man of Muslim civilization – representing the literary and philosophical meeting-point between the spiritual traditions of East and West.

Every nation has as part of its heritage an inspirational heroic myth. The Irish have the figure of Cuchulain, whose name and mighty deeds are a symbol of national consciousness and aspiration. Christians in Lebanon have Jesus Christ who, as a leader of men, refuses to combat ignorance and intolerance with weapons other than peaceful ones. For Gibran Jesus was the supreme figure of all ages: "My art can find no better resting place than the personality of Jesus. His life is the symbol of Humanity. He shall always be the supreme figure of all ages and in Him we shall always find mystery, passion, love, imagination, tragedy, beauty, romance and truth."[62] Gibran saw Christ as a "raging tempest,"[63] a depiction that appears in many of his early Arabic writings. The poet's vision of the Nazarene was crystallized too in his English work *Jesus, the Son of Man* (1928), a book which some critics thought was imbued with an inspirational intensity that even exceeds *The Prophet*.

While many of his opinions were modified over the years, his fascination with Christ continued throughout his life, and any understanding of Gibran the man and poet will fail unless it explores the deep kinship the man from Lebanon felt with the "commander" from Galilee.

The template for his unique portrayal of Jesus was inspired by his meetings in 1912 with 'Abdu'l-Bahá, the Bahá'í leader, whom he drew in New York, a man whose presence moved Gibran to exclaim: "For the first time I saw form noble enough to be a receptacle for the Holy Spirit."[64] His meetings with 'Abdu'l-Bahá left an indelible impression on the poet, surpassing in its influence many propitious acquaintances Gibran made during his years in New York, including Carl Gustav Jung and W. B. Yeats.

III

Gibran's first published writings, which were exclusively in Arabic, made him the foremost exponent of Romanticism in Arabic literature. As a founder-president of "al-Rabita al-Qalamiyyah" ("The Pen Bond," or "Arrabitah") much of the credit must go to Gibran for the dissemination of that society's pioneering and innovative ideas. Arrabitah, by liberating Arabic poetry from stupor and decadence, transformed the literary art in every sphere of its activities[65] and instigated a renaissance in Arabic creativity.[66] Just as Gibran's incantational prose-poems influenced writers of the thirties and forties, his fierce rebellion against ecclesiastical and political corruption inspired writers and artists of the fifties and sixties.[67]

Arrabitah was composed of "a small and rather select group of avant-garde men of letters"[68] who, under the guiding spirit of Gibran, became "an accomplished school in action",[69] embarking on an adventurous literary experiment that effected a historic shift of emphasis in hitherto accepted Arabic literary excellence.[70] William Catzeflis, himself a member of Arrabitah, remembered Gibran's influence on the New York Arabs: "Arrabitah, with Gibran in the lead, threw a bombshell by saying, 'if the meaning or beauty of a thought requires the breaking of rule, break it.'"[71] As a result of such a radical and liberating approach there was a "greater purity of attitude and practice," a new truthfulness, and a greater flexibility of language, meter, and rhythm.[72] Contrary to some interpretations, Gibran was no escapist but deeply involved, "even obsessed," with contemporary history and realities.[73] Although the voice of his early rebellion was at times the cry of an *émigré* artist, as he grew in confidence, his expression became the roar of an artist tempered by "the harsh discovery of a freer way of life."[74]

Gibran's Romanticism was a health-restoring revival of the instinctual life in contradistinction to the constraints that sought to sublimate human freedom in the united name of social tradition or religious conformity; in many ways his rebellion was akin to the beginnings of Romanticism in England a century earlier, when Blake, Wordsworth, and Shelley strove to explore the literature of internalized quest and Promethean aspiration.[75] These English writers drew much of their inspiration from ideas that filtered indirectly from the East – Arabic and Persian poetry, the Indian Sanskrit classics – and in turn inspired Gibran, who reinforced his own native mysticism with their visionary vocabulary.

In his "outpost" of New York, Gibran initiated a Romantic movement and school in Arabic literature that echoed a generation's instinctive call for change and renewal. Living five thousand miles away from the stern and sanctimonious gaze of those whose vision could not transcend the inherited and inhibitive methods of their age, this first true rebel in Arabic literature[76] enjoyed an unparalleled freedom that allowed him to revolutionize the literary sensibility of the time.[77]

The Arab Romantic movement never acquired a poetic creed or formulated any defined principles after its development. It was directed from the outset by an ardent desire to acknowledge poetry as an expression "of the heart and not just the tongue,"[78] an unconscious belief in the inner freedom of the individual and a rejection of the fossilized traditions of the East. Its viewpoint was primarily subjective and more self-consciously emotional than neo-classical poetry, so presenting itself as a "religion of the heart."[79] One of its central themes is the high estimation given to the "self," this subjectivism being the mainspring of Gibran's creative position.[80] His whole life has been described as a "Romantic quest" – a progressive evolution from innocent childhood to disillusioned experience, and, finally "Higher Innocence borne out of knowledge" – a life often caught between Nietzschean rebellion, Blakean pantheism, and Sufi mysticism.[81] Yet Gibran's creative imagination fused and fired this apocalyptic mix into "one grand design"[82] perhaps unmatched in its profundity since the utterings of the great medieval mystics.

His conscious concern was an artistic one, capable of answering the forces within the field of poetry itself, which in the early part of the century yearned for a change in form, language, attitude, and content. Its time had come, and although the Arab Romantic movement came into being with the rise of Arab nationalism, it could not be identified with it.[83] Nevertheless, both movements arose as more Arabic-speaking people began to realize the disparity between acquired ideals and the realities of life around them – an intense acknowledgment of the urgent need for liberation.[84]

For Gibran, liberation in artistic terms meant challenging the authority and ideals of classicism. Unable to harness himself to the yoke of traditional meter, he was rarely able to translate his poetic vision into the outworn forms of traditional verse. In this we find a parallel with James Joyce who, like Gibran, found himself unable to write in traditional form – his experimentation with the language of prose allowing him to create a new form and a new poetic style, represented in *Ulysses* and *Finnegan's Wake*.

Likewise Gibran's inability was providential in the extreme. His experimentation in prose rather than poetry allowed him to perfect the prose-poem as a new genre, freeing him from the established poetic diction of the decadent period in Arabic literature. He was therefore able to create a totally new rhythm with a life of its own, emanating from within the syntactical framework, and, as such, his poetic prose, or prose poetry, constitutes a unique contribution to modern Arabic literature.

Aesthetic or literary technique aside, Gibran's presence acted as a renovating influence on the Arab world, which had already begun to aspire to a healthier and more just society. This deep social concern – although remaining pervasive and even becoming more politically significant in the pan-Arab dimension of his colleague Ameen Rihani's work – became diluted in Gibran whose writings over the years took on a more universal aspect.[85] The expression of alienation became not merely geographically oriented but evolved into the expression of an exiled soul descended into the foreign realm of matter; his vitriol directed not just at the corrupting influences in his homeland but the universally defiled image of man – a spiritual emigrant in the "heart of darkness,"[86] the universality of his experiences resonating with a Western audience reeling under the pernicious reign of materialism and militarism and quaking before the merciless idol of "Progress."

Such was the impact of *The Prophet*, the quintessence of Gibran's universalism, that the *New York Times* was reminded of "Gautama, the philosophers of the *Upanishads* . . . and the best of the old Hebrew prophets," the "epigrammatic pithiness of utterance" recalling "the older sages of the Orient."[87]

IV

The response to Gibran's English works was sometimes marked by bewilderment or hostility: "meaningless mysticism";[88] "Is it a source merely of psychological indulgence?"; "Gibran's appeal probably lies in the nearness of his imagery to the symbolism of the subliminal consciousness";[89] "taken directly out of Jung's revealing 'Wandlungen und Symbole der Libido.'"[90] Such contrived responses were inevitable given what Jung himself called "the assiduously cultivated credulity of the West in regard to Eastern thought";[91] but in an age when it was impossible to generate by intensive publicity the kind of sales modern best sellers enjoy, it became strikingly obvious that the English-speaking public was genuinely moved by Gibran's impulse to sing from the heart. Not since *The Arabian Nights* had a writer of Arab descent enjoyed such universal appeal and *The Prophet*, the "strange little book,"[92] went on to outsell all others in the twentieth century except the Bible.

It took the poet more than eleven years assiduously to perfect the unity of a message he mirrored through text and pictorial medium. It was, he once said, an expression of the "sacredness" of his "inner life,"[93] and it came as no surprise to those around him when Gibran, the "Bard of Washington Street," was mentioned in the same breath as his "God-man," William Blake.[94]

For some critics *The Prophet* represented the height of Gibran's literary career:[95] "This prophet," he once said, who had "already 'written' me before I attempted to 'write' him."[96] Given the importance of *The Prophet* in Gibran's oeuvre, it is not surprising that some critics thought his works leading up to *The Prophet* were exploratory, even rudimentary, the products of "an extremely sensitive soul groping its way towards a goal whose contours are yet wrapped in mist."[97]

Another view however takes his Arabic works such as *Iram, City of Lofty Pillars*, published two years before *The Prophet* in 1921, and his English works such as *The Madman* on their own terms, giving due regard to Gibran's profound exploration of the Sufi principle of the unity of being (*wahdat al-wudjud*) in *Iram Dhat al-'Imad (Iram, City of Lofty Pillars)*, and to his trenchant criticism of social values and the elevation of the outsider-poet-seer in *The Madman*.

Gibran awaited his moment before publishing *The Prophet*. As World War I drew to a close, he wrote: "Human beings have changed remarkably during the past three years. They are hungry for beauty, for truth."[98] The receptiveness Gibran sensed for his healing message was well attuned. Within a month all 1,300 copies of the first edition had been sold. He told an interviewer: "America represents the bud just pressing at its sheath, just ready to blossom, still hard, still green, and not yet fragrant, but vigorous and full of life."[99]

Although the sensational success of *The Prophet* brought its author universal acclaim, Gibran's latter years were marked by sickness and burdened by fame. As more self-appointed devotees of "Gibranism" learnt that the "Lebanese savant"[100] was living on West Tenth Street, he began to be inundated with visitors. While some came to "confess" or seek counsel,[101] others came simply out of curiosity. Gibran himself, always aware of his own shortcomings, however, had no desire to wear the mantle of a "prophet."[102]

Increasingly tiring of life in "New Babylon,"[103] he returned to his sister

Marianna and the Syrian community in Boston. Even here, however, there were conflicts of a different kind – the "orderly life" pulling Gibran away from creative writing and forcing him to concede that "chaotic living is the best sharpener for my imagination,"[104] and the mysterious illness, which eventually killed him when he was forty-eight, feeding his self-doubt: "I am filled with regret because I remained a chatterbox until my jabbering weakened my strength."[105]

As we follow this man from Lebanon, sometimes in his Irish homespun suit,[106] sometimes in Dervish robes splattered with paint, and sometimes attired like a cultured Frenchman,[107] we find the life of a man struggling against his weaknesses and trying to construct something permanent and holy out of his private failures and disappointments. From the small dreaming boy who planted bits of paper in the hope of growth on the thin soils of northern Lebanon, to the mature writer in Manhattan, we are confronted by a consummate artist, who believed "there is nothing more tiresome than laziness."[108]

Less than twenty years after his emigration to the New World, the youth from Bisharri found himself moving among the elite literary and artistic circles of America, where he would seemingly slip on new personas – masks that enchanted, fascinated, and sometimes beguiled his American acquaintances. Astounded by Gibran's chameleon-like ease of adaptiveness one journalist in New York wrote, "Gibran is Broadway or Copley Square or The Strand or the Avenue de L'Opera – a correctly dressed cosmopolitan of the Western world . . . a sensible denizen of Greenwich Village – for such there be";[109] while another onlooker thought the dapper man of five foot three with the white suit, hat, and cane "the spitting image" of another immigrant of the time, Charlie Chaplin.[110]

Beneath the masks, however, was a man whose gestures were those of "the unhurried courtesy of the East,"[111] one friend writing: "The odour of the Sacred Grove seemed somehow still to cling to him."[112] Gibran, however, as a poet from the East, had no illusions about the moribund state of its literature and consciously set out to change it forever. His vehicles of expression – the epigram, the parable, the short essay, poetry, the apophthegm, and the prose-poem – were sometimes interspersed with powerfully symbolic artwork.

The combination of his Rousseau-like belief in the innate goodness of an unshackled humanity and his personalized interpretation of the Christian message of universal love led him to launch a radical assault on church and state in his two early works 'Ara'is al-Muruj (Nymphs of the

14

Valley, 1906) and *al-'Arwah al-Mutamarridah* (*Spirits Rebellious*, 1908). Such assaults represented the wildest insubordination to the status quo, and he was vilified and condemned as a heretic.[113] Gibran's severe criticisms of the church have still not been entirely forgiven – understandable perhaps given such vitriolic denunciations of the priest as a "betrayer" of Christ and "a hypocrite whom the faithful girded with a fine crucifix, which he held aloft above their heads as a sharp sword."[114] By 1910 apocryphal stories abounded around anathemas, the public burning of Gibran's books in Beirut, and his excommunication from the Maronite church.

In addition to attacking both church and state for their obsession with self-glorification, power, and wealth, throughout his writings – right up to his last work, *The Wanderer*[115] – Gibran attacked fanaticism, extremism, and injustice in all its forms. Although often scathing and bitter, Gibran's early works subtly manifest a masterful interpretation of the mystical ontology, reforging Sufi thought to express the poetic realities of his own creative vision.[116] His aphorisms, parables, and allegories closely resemble Sufi wisdom – the themes of paradox and illusion turning on the unripeness of a sleeping humanity attached to the ephemeral. His reverence for Sufi thought too finds clear expression in his Arabic book *al-'Awasif* (*The Tempest*), which contains short essays on three of the greatest figures in Sufi literature: Ibn al-Farid, al-Ghazali, and Ibn Sina (Avicenna) who, on Gibran's own admission, was nearer his own "spiritual inclination" than any other.[117]

Although Gibran's first English work, *The Madman*, did not appear until 1918 the intervening period was one in which the poet imbibed, assimilated, and brought to fruition the manifold cultural influences to which he was exposed – guided by his American benefactress, Mary Haskell.

In Gibran's early days in America – which saw the tragic deaths of his sister, only brother, and mother and his ostracism by many in his community for his single-minded obsession with art rather than the more traditional forms of work expected of a young immigrant – it was Mary Haskell, a schoolteacher from South Carolina, his "guardian angel,"[118] who reassured him that he was "not a stranger in a strange land,"[119] and who became his patroness and confidante. He once told her: "Three things in my life have done most for me: my mother, who let me alone; you, who had faith in me and in my work; and my father, who called out the fighter in me."[120]

Mary Haskell's role is so crucial to Gibran's development that at times biographers find two destinies woven as one.[121] Although it was not until

1917 that her protégé's art was finally acknowledged, Mary's faith in, and generosity towards, "the Syrian genius" never wavered. She paid for him to live and study in Paris and on his return the patroness and poet fell in love. Unlike the many women who were merely drawn to the poet's striking looks Mary's relationship with Gibran was an intellectual, yet warm and tender, "kinship." Although not without difficulties, Mary helped transform his dreams into realities and remained a loyal friend right through his life.

A radical headmistress, Mary was drawn to the passionate young writer, "electrifying . . . mobile like a flame . . . *The Pulse* visible,"[122] whose volcanic outpourings against tyranny and corruption sent a shudder through the power-possessing beings of Syria, and whose upbraiding of the complacency he sometimes found in America resonated with her own native perceptions. Mary was also attracted to the gentle romantic being "longing simply to be allowed to love," to his "unspeakable sensitiveness"[123] that expressed itself in such tender love stories as *al-'Ajnihah l-Mutakassirah* (*The Broken Wings*), a semi-autobiographical work in which Gibran tells the story of a love that beats desperately against the taboos of oriental tradition. Magnetized too by the ethereal paintings that she first saw at a small exhibition in Boston in 1904, Mary felt drawn to Gibran's art, which some critics years later thought challenged "the present to a recapitulation of its standards".[124]

Mary's intense relationship with Gibran, meticulously recorded in her journal, shows Gibran's evolution from a provincial Arab writer to an American artist expressing universal concerns – a man who, in 1911, declared to her: "I know I have something to say to the world that is different from anything else."[125] During his years in New York, Gibran worked incessantly, often until dawn, bringing his twin crafts to perfection, and under Mary's guiding hand the apocalyptic blend of Western and Eastern influences merged insensibly into his psyche.

Gibran's punishing working habits, usually fortified with little else but strong coffee and cigarettes, sometimes left Mary, and in later life medics, concerned for the state of his health. Early in February 1912 after an intense bout of work he wrote to Mary: "It seems that I was born with an arrow in my heart, and it is painful to *pull it* and painful to *leave it*."[126] But for Gibran the role of the poet was a holy one – "the wire that transmits the news of the world of spirit"[127] – always striving, searching against all odds for the *essence* and the spirit of all things.

Although writing in two languages Gibran made an easy shift in his "double psyche,"[128] choosing a vocabulary less idiomatic than writers more conscious of modernism in language. The disparities between the linguistic consciousness of East and West should have created the problem of "root words" but, because Gibran's sensibility had been influenced and tempered by the language of the Bible – a book belonging to both East and West – he was able to bridge what seems, at first glance, to be unbridgeable.[129]

Although his appearance on the Arabic literary scene was timely in that it satisfied a great need, the critic Salma Khadra Jayyusi felt it was "his personal tragedy" that he did not appear thirty years later, in an age unhindered by the peculiarities of Arab poetic history and the ignorance and timidity of its literary arbiters:

> He was restricted by the poetic needs of the time to follow a career of liberating both the form and the spirit of literature, but with all these handicaps he could not be both the liberator and the creator of literary works that would transcend his time and yet remain in the lead among a sophisticated reading elite that was constantly growing in number.[130]

Nevertheless it must also be acknowledged that many of his Arabic works possess a lasting appeal. This is nowhere more obvious than in his many aphorisms and epigrams, which, even when translated into English, retain a vividness and effectiveness – transcending temporal or cultural barriers – as well as reflecting the pithiness of their author's wit.

Although Kahlil Gibran's name is widely known throughout the world, his achievements in the West have, to date, received only scant attention by scholars. It is doubtful whether any other writer who has attained such global popularity has been so neglected.

The failures of the past to acknowledge Gibran may be on account of *The Prophet's* reputation for appealing to the young, or to only "late romantics" and seekers of "the exotic"[131] . . . "a creed for the vaguely well-meaning."[132] Despite Gibran's contributions to such publications as the influential *Seven Arts* as early as 1916 – alongside the likes of Robert Frost, D. H. Lawrence, and Amy Lowell – none of the leading journals in the West reviewed his books when they were published. They invariably omitted Gibran from surveys of modern American literature – reflecting an inability to come to terms with literature that falls outside conventional terms of reference.

Unlike his contemporaries Eliot, Pound, and Yeats, Gibran had no wish to refine the English language to meet the realities of the age, but yearned to inject into it the priceless values of the mysticism of the East. Gibran was indifferent to the dictates of an age in which creativity becomes mere reaction to the shifting sands of the fashionable milieu; he was intent instead on expressing a timeless and universal literature: "I'll make a tree and pick the fruit for six hundred years ahead."[133]

If critics persist in regarding Gibran as an English writer to be considered and measured against his contemporaries, they will find that the existing criteria of evaluation do not apply. Driven by a mechanistic *Weltanschauung*, the Western mind has often been arrogantly unresponsive to mysticism, blatantly rejecting any vision of the unity of culture. Furthermore, Gibran's experiences of vision cannot be adequately represented, as most Western critics demand, in the language of philosophy or in the framework of materialistic logic.

Over recent decades, however, this piecemeal consciousness of the Western mind has begun to wither. A vision of the universe as a dynamic web is emerging, in which each is seen as being a part in the whole and the whole being in each part; physicists perceiving that the "quintessential religious experience, the experience of mystical oneness and 'supreme identity' might very well be a genuine and legitimate experience of this implicate and universal ground."[134]

For those academics still cloistered by their own one-dimensional ethnocentric attitudes and their analyses of the particular as against the universal the literature of Gibran will pass them by as it transcends global dualities, cultural barriers, and academic one-dimensionalism. Those who dare to embrace and evaluate a literature such as Gibran's, both deriving from, and unified by, two separate traditions will find in the poet from Lebanon a literary pioneer bound by little save the beauty of his words: "And how shall you rise beyond your days and nights unless you break the chains which you at the dawn of your understanding have fastened around your noon hour?"[135] The Irish mystic poet George Russell (AE) was one of the first critics to glimpse the possibilities therein:

> If Europe is to have a new renaissance comparable with that which came from the wedding of Christianity with the Greek and Latin culture it must, I think, come from a second wedding of Christianity with the culture of the East. Our own words to each other bring us no surprise. It is only when a voice comes from India or China or Arabia that we get the thrill of strangeness from the beauty, and we feel that it might inspire another of the great cultural passions of humanity.[136]

It is not surprising that it was an Irishman who was one of the first critics to acknowledge the importance of Gibran's work. Himself a key player in the Irish literary renaissance – which occurred during the same period as Arrabitah – AE's perceptions highlight the affinity that undoubtedly exists between Celtic and Arabic poetic genius. There is a certain affinity of spirit and sentiment toward language; a common devotion to the manner of expression; a heady delight in the hypnotic rhythm of the music of speech and a deep awareness of the mystical elements that permeate the landscape of mist and mountain, desert and moonlit night.

Gibran's vision was not that of an academic or a philosopher, but of a poet whose raw materials came from his own psychic life, "the final form of what he had been able to prove from his knowledge, and the last word arising from the influence of his suffering."[137] The grief and acute sense of alienation experienced by the hypersensitive youth laid its stamp on him, attuning his subconscious to the "most delicate light and shade" and prompting him to sing with the eloquence of Isaiah and the sorrow of Jeremiah.[138] One critic described Gibran's work as being "dipped in blood . . . a cry bursting through a wounded heart", asking of those who wish to understand Gibran to "imagine for themselves what a degree of pain it would require to inspire them as did that suffering which so inspired Gibran."[139]

By an evolution that testifies to the nature of his character, Gibran's appearance grew more commanding, more resolutely masculine and illumined as his health declined. The reticent youth matured into a man deemed by others to be "the captain of his soul and the master of his fate,"[140] his early experiences of death somehow deepening his concentration towards a passionate affirmation of life: "I want to be alive to all the life that is in me now, to know each moment to the uttermost."[141]

V

Writing as he was when Darwinism was at its height, Gibran's extraordinary receptiveness to the appeal of nature may in many ways be seen as offering a positive counterpoise to the Darwinian metaphor. The most powerful imagery in his work he borrowed from nature, her rich and beautiful store of symbols providing him with the emotional and intellectual apparatus of his poetry and intensifying his most dreamlike moods with the "unfathomable mystery of Nature's secrets."[142]

In his last Arabic work, *Iram Dhat al-'Imad* (*Iram, City of Lofty Pillars*), which he published in 1921, Gibran's visionary perception of nature becomes apparent:

In one atom are found all the elements of the earth; in one motion of the mind are found the motions of all the laws of existence; in one drop of water are found the secrets of all the endless oceans; in one aspect of *you* are found all the aspects of *existence*.[143]

It was Einstein who encapsulated the Western malaise as "separation-delusion," a view echoed by Gibran when he wrote: "The heart is drunken with overmindfulness of self[144] . . . The image of the morning sun in a dewdrop is not less than the sun . . . You and the stone are one. There is a difference only in heart-beats. Your heart beats a little faster, does it, my friend? Aye, but it is not so tranquil."[145]

Throughout his work with both pen and brush Gibran expressed his belief in the sanctity of the living earth and our duty to protect her and ennoble her, revere and celebrate her, learn from her and commune with her. His views represented a significant new departure in Arabic literature which previously had usually treated the natural world as either a force to be reckoned with or as an ornament evoking little save aesthetic appreciation. Gibran, however, in "mystical fusion,"[146] identified in nature a universal source of creative energy. To observe the cumulative affect of this oeuvre is to recognize him as a powerful advocate of the unity of being in the West on the one hand, and a pioneer in the transformation of the Arab mind's perceptions of the planet on the other, becoming one of the first major ecological poets of the twentieth century both in the East and in the West.

For Gibran everything separate and closed within itself must perish for lack of a principle of renewal. This renewal requires mutuality and within this matrix human destiny is irrevocably linked with that of the cosmos; only by the giving and receiving of energies can cosmic harmony be maintained. In Gibran's words, "We live upon one another according to the law."[147] He perceived the natural world to be a living being: "If you sing of beauty though alone in the heart of the desert you will have an audience";[148] "the body and its environment are linked together"[149] – the foresight of his environmental message striking in its anticipation of modern theories in physics which are internally consistent and in perfect harmony with the views of Eastern mysticism.[150]

In Gibran's imagery, the metaphors and similes are closely interwoven "like brilliantly coloured dyes" evoking a highly emotional and "new but familiar way of describing" nature.[151] In the processional of the year – the spring breezes nursing the awakening buds, the iridescent leaves of autumn with their memory-laden smells – the poet acknowledges the thoughts and emotions of some great consciousness. The reader senses the impassioned conviction of a poet who felt "the most god-like thing in man is his wonder at life"[152] and feels they are listening to one whose senses are heightened by an irrepressible fascination with, and reverence for, a planet conceived as a living being, speaking "in the tongues of brooks and streams."[153]

Gibran's writings – reverberating as they do with the language of the King James Authorized Version of the Bible – reveal the incantational tone of the Song of Solomon and the rhythm of the Psalms. Using wisdom stories in several works from his first English book, *The Madman*, to his last, *The Wanderer*, it is in the "esoteric, figurative, imaginative style . . . not new in Arabic literature"[154] that they are expressed. Such tales should be seen as Arab meditations recast in the English idiom, albeit one that is in itself a translation from an oriental original. It is for these reasons that any ethnocentric evaluation of Gibran according to the standards of purely Anglo-American literary tradition is inherently deficient.

There is an extraordinary diversity of critical opinion as to the literary and philosophical worth of Gibran's English works in particular. There are those who have criticized him as being effusive, sentimental, and melodramatic: "He [Gibran] writes sentimental, corny, sloppy, semi-erotic, tasteless but popular stuff . . . . To be popular one does not have to be good. They are almost mutually exclusive."[155]

There are those too, who, in blindly worshiping Gibran, as if one only needed to read *The Prophet* for life's problems to vanish away, have done him as much disservice as those who have pilloried him for his unfashionable emphasis on tolerance and compassion. Few have appreciated the essentially Lebanese character of the man and acknowledged the influences that shaped his art and poetry – the blend being no amalgam but a visionary phenomenon entirely his own.

The existing critical apparatus of Western literary criticism lacks the relevant criteria by which to judge Gibran, and opinions of his work have swung violently from the eulogistic to the condemnatory. *The Prophet* does indeed hold an ambiguous position in the field of English literature – it is neither pure literature, nor pure philosophy, and as an Arab work written in English it belongs exclusively to a unique tradition – and some critics suggest that it is time to adopt a new critical mechanism for assessing this type of literature deriving from two separate cultural traditions and bound by the prejudices and restrictions of neither.[156]

VI

All of Gibran's writings express a passionate urge to improve the lot of an exploited humanity. Some exhibit a prevailing melancholy for the cruel waste of life lost to poverty, injustice, and institutionalized violence. In an age when it was not fashionable to do so Gibran became one of the most fervent and outspoken champions of human rights. He waged a long, ferocious, and sometimes bitter battle against the vicious inequalities that exist between men and women, religious extremism, feudalism, and the sublimation of love in the name of tradition. His early works are tales of courage, stories in which the downtrodden struggle for liberty and proclaim a message of justice – a whip in Gibran's words as he unleashes his vituperation on those who exploit the poor. There is also a message of conciliation for those who struggle to be free from the shackles of nationalism, sectarianism, and medievalism.

With the moving intensity that characterizes truly significant utterances Gibran's writings project timeless universal truths, expressing passionately the deep human yearning and hunger for true liberation. Like his contemporary P. D. Ouspensky – whose book *Tertium Organum* (1912) Gibran recommended to the Arab world – he conceives the emotions as organs of knowledge, the "stained-glass windows of the soul."[157]

Early interpretations of Gibran's character have sometimes tended to denigrate the poet as a naive outsider who, besieged by melancholy and blunted by introspection, ceased to be "nourished by reality."[158] However, since the publication of the Haskell–Gibran papers in 1972 a very different picture has emerged.

We find a man at ease with others – war years aside when he felt he was "becoming like" a madman;[159] a humorous man: "never a time have we met – even when we were sad – that he has not made me laugh and laugh, at something that the moment suggested to his flashing mind";[160] a man with "gentle tact" sometimes belying the "fighter" within;[161] "intensely practical";[162] who cast lead as a lad of eight[163] and later designed jewelry, sculptured wood carvings and earned his living as a portrait painter – 'Abdu'l-Bahá, Debussy, Rodin, Jung, Maeterlinck, Masefield, W. B. Yeats, Lady Gregory, Laurence Housman, Sarah Bernhardt, Ruth St. Denis, the young Garibaldi, and Albert Pinkham Ryder being just a part of his eminent portfolio.

We find too a blundering businessman who once provoked an exasperated partner to cry: "Mr. Gibran this isn't any Christ-like matter – this is just plain business";[164] a self-possessed man who lived an "inner life, despite the world" about him;[165] a man who consciously went out of his way to shatter people's images of "the kind gentle Mr. Gibran";[166] a poet who felt himself a wheel turning against all other wheels, a "human chaos" moving "amongst finished worlds";[167] and a man who strove to be open in all his relationships: "Let it be foolish, if foolishness is my best today, and let someone hit me hard. That I may be a little less foolish next time . . . there is too much of the closed heart."[168]

Unlike some writers and artists whose lives have been blighted by complex sexual liaisons – who took "sex love as it came"[169] – Gibran's love life was, on the whole, uncomplicated. He had "no code about sex except honesty,"[170] and he found in his adopted land an unhealthy attitude where people had become "slaves" to sex.[171] As a young man Gibran sometimes found the "forwardness" of Western attitudes to sexuality alien,[172] particularly when as a fifteen-year-old such a woman had "initiated" the beautiful boy into manhood – an event that quickened his return to Lebanon, as his mother struggled to shield him from further "sin and temptation."[173] Coming as he did from a culture that cherished the virtues of "honour and cleanness and decency,"[174] Gibran himself, described as "fastidiously reserved,"[175] was not the young man sometimes depicted as being "full of affairs . . . because he is passionate and is lightly regarded as freely at feast."[176] Before his long-term relationship with Mary Haskell Gibran had let only four[177] women into his private life, among these the aspiring young French actress "Micheline" and a poetess, Josephine Preston Peabody.

We find too, a man who strove for genuineness and sensed that many "virtues" are merely "social things," "reaction mechanisms," emanating from acquired personality and not true "being"[178] – which is manifest more in the likes of the "shepherd" rather than the "sophisticated" dweller in the city.[179]

Gibran became the most successful and famous Arab writer in the world. Despite our technological achievements, our "analysis galore,"[180] the modern psyche has still been left with a wound in its soul. Gibran's message is a healing one and his quest to understand the tensions between spirit and exile anticipated the needs of an age witnessing the spiritual and intellectual impasse of modernity itself. His atmospheric writings reveal the penetrating vision of a seer, who, without crusading or preaching, warns of the terrible dangers that befall an epoch intent on border consciousness, material greed, and blistering yet blind change. His work, set forth in the form of a simple lyrical beauty and a profound depth of meaning for all who endeavor to seek it, applies dynamically and with striking timelessness to the momentous challenges of today.

1

Beginnings
(1883–1895)

I

Gibran Khalil Gibran, who became known as Kahlil Gibran,[1] was born in the far north of Lebanon on 6 January 1883.[2] The village of his birth, Bisharri, is perched on a small plateau at the edge of one of the cliffs of Wadi Qadisha, known as the sacred valley. Towering above is Mount Lebanon.

Khalil Gibran, the poet's father, whose name the child inherited as his middle name according to Arabic custom, was a tax collector in Bisharri. A strong, sturdy man with fair skin and blue eyes, he had received only a basic education, yet was a man of considerable charm who liked to cut a dash. Although he owned a walnut grove Khalil Gibran's meager income soon evaporated as he fed his extravagant habits – alcohol and gambling. Regarded by some as "one of the strong men of Bisharri," he was by all accounts a hard man to live with, and his wife and children feared him.[3]

The son in later life expressed filial feelings toward his father – an attempt to disguise the harsh reality of what was undoubtedly a difficult relationship:

> I admired him for his power – his honesty and integrity. It was his daring to be himself, his outspokenness and refusal to yield, that got him into trouble eventually. If hundreds were about him, he could command them with a word. He could overpower any number by any expression of himself.[4]

However, in truth Kahlil's relationship with his father was difficult and often strained. The boy never felt very close to this autocratic, temperamental man who was hostile to his artistic nature[5] and was not a loving person.[6]

His mother, on the other hand, evoked in the child feelings of deepest affection and admiration. Kamileh Rahmeh was the daughter of a Maronite clergyman named Istiphan Rahmeh. She is described as a thin, graceful woman with a slight pallor in her cheeks and a shade of melancholy in her eyes.[7] Kamileh had a beautiful singing voice and was a devoutly religious person. When she reached marriageable age she was married to one of her own clan, her cousin Hanna 'Abd al-Salaam Rahmeh. However, like many Lebanese of his time, he emigrated to Brazil to seek his fortune, but while he was there he died, leaving Kamileh with a son Boutros (or Peter). Some time after Hanna Rahmeh's death, the young widow married Khalil Gibran. After the birth of her son Kahlil, two daughters were born to the couple, Marianna[8] in 1885 and Sultanah[9] in 1887.

In contrast to her husband, Kamileh was an indulgent and loving parent, and ambitious for her children. Although without formal education, which at the time was considered useless, if not dangerous, for women,[10] she possessed an intelligence and wisdom that had an enormous influence on her younger son, who later said of her: "It is her mothering me I remember – the inner me."[11] Fluent in Arabic and French, artistic and musical, Kamileh ignited Kahil's imagination with the folk tales and legends of Lebanon, and stories from the Bible.

In one of his earliest Arabic works, *al-Ajnihah al-Mutakassirah* (*The Broken Wings*), the son's deepest respect for motherhood is revealed:

> The most beautiful word on the lips of mankind is the word "Mother," and the most beautiful call is the call of "My mother." It is a word full of hope and love, a sweet and kind word coming from the depths of the heart. The mother is every thing – she is our consolation in sorrow, our hope in misery, and our strength in weakness. She is the source of love, mercy, sympathy, and forgiveness.[12]

Coming from a family steeped in the Maronite tradition, Kamileh had contemplated joining the nunnery at Saint Simon in northern Lebanon before her first marriage.[13] Maronite Christianity, an ancient sect, emerged in the fifth century when the early Christians of Syria pledged their allegiance to a hermit, Marun, whose gifts and virtues brought him many disciples. Using a ritual alive with the Aramaic tongue of Jesus and a liturgy that is among the oldest and most moving in the Christian Church, the Maronites were able to protect their traditions due to the physical remoteness of the mountain region. The spiritual nature of Gibran's mother and the impressions that the child received from the mystical ceremonies of the Maronites remained with him all his life.

Under the huge shadow of Mount Lebanon, Kamileh, the priest's daughter,[14] and her handsome husband reared their family. Although life was hard it was not unendurable, and the rugged and resourceful villagers eked out a living on the thin crust of the soil.

II

However, the people of Lebanon faced a threat more terrifying than poverty. Only a generation before, the country had been propelled into a terrible civil war. Sectarian violence which broke out in 1845 reached shocking proportions in 1860, in one of the most terrible religious massacres in history.[15] Thousands of Christians were slaughtered, many at the altars of their churches. Pillage, plunder, and the burning of villages and towns were common occurrences, resulting in streams of refugees. In all more than 30,000 Christians, mainly Maronites and Greek Orthodox, were massacred in this dark age by the Druze, with the encouragement of the Ottomans.[16]

In a region that perhaps more than any other had been a meeting-point of East and West, as well as a rich melting-pot of religions, the utter turmoil generated by this explosion of sectarian violence and political upheaval etched a deep scar on the consciousness of Khalil and Kamileh's generation. Up to the 1840s Shi'ite and Sunni Muslims, Greek and Syrian Catholics and Orthodox, Armenians, Assyrians, Chaldeans, Maronites, Nestorians, Jesuits, Jacobites, Jews, and Druze, had all lived together in relatively peaceful coexistence.

Of all the provinces living under the oppressive rule of the Ottoman empire – which stretched from Hungary to the Arabian Peninsula and up to North Africa – Lebanon seemed to be the most modern. Over the centuries it had opened up to Western influences, and the people of Lebanon possessed a high level of literacy because of a variety of schools founded by European missions. Since the Turks had extended their empire to include Lebanon in 1516, under the illustrious Sulayman I, Lebanese history had been dominated by two rulers, whose attempts over the years to impose political unity and secure national autonomy failed with the tragic events of 1860.

The first of these rulers was Fakhr-al-Din, a Druze feudal lord who ruled from 1585 to 1635. The Druze constituted one of the major confessional groups in Lebanon. They had emerged from Egypt during the eleventh century, synthesizing Eastern ideas about reincarnation with Islamic and

Hellenic thought. Unlike the Maronites, who were considered second-class citizens under Ottoman rule, the Druze enjoyed full civil rights, although they too were not universally accepted in the Muslim world.

Fakhr-al-Din, realizing the economic and political potential associated with cultivating Maronite links with Europe through their historical connections with Rome, granted them full civil liberty and religious freedom. He was thus able to pursue his own ambitions, commanding, for the first time in Lebanese history, a united front of Christian and Druze leaders. At the same time, a wave of westernization swept the country, with European merchants and technicians bringing their skills to the feudal country. Fakhr-al-Din's policies also paved the way for a more integrated society, with the hitherto segregated Maronites of the north migrating southward, and Fakhr-al-Din came to be considered "the first modern man of Lebanon."[17]

The second influential ruler was Bashir II, who came in and out of power between 1788 and 1840. By the beginning of the nineteenth century European influence had already penetrated into the Arab world. In 1798 Napoleon had captured Egypt, bringing with him cherished Western ideals such as social justice, the scientific method, and individual liberty. However, Napoleon compromised such ideals of the French Enlightenment in favor of building French imperialistic glory. Along with the European invasion came missionaries whose aim was to spread their own particular faith which they believed to be the only true one – although they did contribute significantly to society in the building of schools, hospitals, and clinics. However, bitter theological disputes and controversies erupted, instigated by the very people who purported to preach the gospel of love. As a consequence, the gulf between Christians, Muslims, and Druze widened, as did divisions between the various Christian communities.

Under Bashir II a second period of westernization began. Machinery and modern engineering were introduced and new roads were built connecting the villages with the coast and its ports. In 1820 the Turkish overlords demanded extra levels of taxation. Bashir, not wishing to offend the Druze, demanded more tax from the Maronites. This led to the emergence in the 1820s of a peasants' movement known as the General Uprising. Over the years, some of the Maronite hierarchy – its metropolitans and bishops – had become worldly, greedy, and corrupt as their secular power had increased. The General Uprising, organized by Maronite priests and monks, openly challenged entrenched privilege, both feudal and ecclesiastical. Although Bashir managed to outmaneuver the peasants, the egalitarian ideals espoused were firmly sown in the consciousness of a new generation, and later inspired Gibran in his early Arabic writings.

Westernization, meanwhile, led to the emergence in the towns of wealthy middle-class Christian communities who controlled commerce and industry. The Druze, untouched by progressive influence, were easily exploited by their leaders, who, desiring to fulfill their own ambitions, encouraged and fueled sectarianism whenever possible. Thus arose the confused situation in which economic and political unrest could not be distinguished from religious strife, and in which the latter, combined with feudalism, was ultimately able to derail the country from its path toward progress.

Hoping to capitalize on the growing unrest, the European powers – who were greedily competing for the spoils of a disintegrating Ottoman empire – cynically promoted bloody civil war in Lebanon. The Ottomans themselves also encouraged division and enmity, believing that ultimately their own self-interests would be furthered. The Western powers availed themselves of pretexts for intervention, thus furthering their own expansionist policies. The Maronites looked to France for protection; the Greek Orthodox to Russia for patronage; and the non-Christian communities, including the Druze, enjoyed the support of Britain, which, on the whole, played the role of the sultan's friend in order to forestall French and Russian ambitions in the region.

When the growing mistrust flared into open hostility in 1845, the Ottoman policy was to aid the Druze by promising the fleeing Christians safe haven. Disarming them thus, the Druze were free to butcher them, young and old together.[18] In one period, lasting less than four weeks during 1860, an estimated eleven thousand Christians were killed. The Protestant missionaries and their converts, antagonistic to the Maronites and Orthodox, were not a threat to the Druze, Ottoman, or Muslim authorities, and largely escaped the persecution.

During this destruction the villagers of Bisharri relied on their ancient instinct for survival and retreated to the impregnable fortress of the mountain. Even though Gibran's father escaped the bloodshed, the stories and haunting memories of his older relatives remained in the poet's mind all his life. In *Spirits Rebellious*, published forty-eight years after the massacres, Gibran laments the terrible suffering endured by his people:

We stand now before your terrible throne
Wearing the blood-smeared garments of our fathers;
Covering our heads with the dust of the tombs
    mingled with their remains;
Drawing the swords which have been sheathed
    in their entrails;
Raising the spears that have pierced their breasts;
Dragging the chains that have withered their feet;
Crying aloud cries that have wounded their throats,
And lamentations that have filled the darkness of
    their prisons;
Praying prayers that have sprung out of the
    pain of their hearts –
Listen, O Liberty, and hear us!

In order to secure their power and rest at
    heart's ease they have armed the Durzi to
    fight the Arab;
Have incited the Shi'i against the Sunni;
Have incited the Kurd to slaughter the Bedouin;
Have encouraged the Mohammadan to fight
    the Christian –
How long is a brother to fight his brother on the
    breast of the mother?
How long is a neighbor to threaten his neighbor
    near the tomb of the beloved?
How long are the Cross and the Crescent to
    remain apart before the eyes of God?[19]

Although brought up as a Maronite Christian, Gibran, as an Arab, was influenced not only by his own religion but also by Islam, and especially by the mysticism of the Sufis. His knowledge of Lebanon's bloody history, with its destructive factional struggles, strengthened his belief in the fundamental unity of religions.

His parents set an example, refusing to perpetuate religious prejudice and bigotry in their daily lives. A story is told of how one afternoon the small boy saw a stranger driving a mule with two skin bottles on its back, selling olive oil. An old woman with a rosary in her hand asked for some oil. After bartering over the price, the old woman asked the stranger what denomination he was. When she was told Greek Orthodox, she snatched the bottle from his hand, crossed herself profusely, and stormed into her house mumbling indignantly. Kahlil's father, in contrast, went up to the man, bought a bottle of olive oil, and insisted that the stranger eat supper with them that evening.[20]

III

From an early age Kahlil was consumed by a love for drawing. If there was no paper to be found in the house he would go outside and spend hours sketching shapes and figures on the fresh snow. In his fourth spring he busily dug some holes in the ground and carefully planted tiny scraps of paper, hoping that the summer harvest would provide him with a plentiful supply of paper.[21] When he was five he was given a corner in their small house which he quickly filled – "a perfect junk shop" – with clear stones, rocks, rings, plants, and a collection of colored pencils. If he ran out of paper to draw on, the young artist would improvise and continue his drawings on the walls.[22]

One of his greatest delights was to cast images in lead using old sardine tins. He used to put the lead on the fire to melt and then fill the two halves of the can with fine moist sand. Then pressing the image in between the two, he would scrape away the sand that squeezed out, put the two halves together again and pour the lead into the mold until the image had cooled[23] – the innovative and curious little boy always inventing, planning, creating.[24]

When he was six he was entranced by some old Leonardo da Vinci prints given to him by his mother.[25] He was never to forget this definitive moment – the child moved by a passion that "possessed him from that hour."[26] The discovery of this "incredible man" acted for Kahlil "like a compass needle for a ship lost in the mists of the sea,"[27] awakening in him a yearning to become an artist. Gibran, throughout his life, remained fascinated by both the personality and the art of Leonardo[28] – a man described by Leonardo's biographer as embodying superhuman qualities: "Celestial influences may shower extraordinary gifts on certain human beings, which is an effect of nature; but there is something supernatural in the accumulation in one individual of so much beauty, grace, and might."[29] Gibran himself, thirty-five years later, wrote: "I have never looked on any of Leonardo da Vinci's work without experiencing deep within my self the awareness that a part of his soul penetrates my own"; the pictures he had seen as a child, particularly da Vinci's *The Head of Saint Anne*, plunged him into a "longing for the unknown."[30]

Despite the arguments that often erupted at home Gibran later remembered happier days when he would accompany his parents on their journeys in northern Lebanon. When he was eight they took him to the sea for the first time. He remembered the impressions vividly: "The sea was before us. The sea and the sky were of one colour. There was no horizon and the water was full of the large Eastern sailing vessels with sails all set. As we passed across the mountains, suddenly I saw what looked like an immeasurable heaven and the ships sailing in it."[31]

When he was nine his parents took him to the ruins of Baalbek, the City of the Sun, the city of Ba'al.[32] In a forest near the towering ruins and amidst the haunting silence of the holy place the family made camp for four days. One morning in the portico of an ancient temple Kahlil met "a solitary man" sitting on the drum of a fallen column and staring into the east. At last he grew bold enough to address the stranger and asked him what he was doing.

"I am looking at life," was the answer.

"Oh, is that all?"

"Isn't that enough?"[33]

Memories of such incidents remained with Gibran all his life and the "City of the Sun" featured in many of his early writings. In "Dust of the Ages and the Eternal Fire" he conveys a pervading sense of the timelessness of the sacred ground which revealed to him "that which has passed with the ages and that which yet remained";[34] and with a strange echoic quality he describes a vision he saw while walking through the ruins:

> The moon drew a fine veil across the City of the Sun and stillness enveloped all creation. And the awesome ruins rose like giants mocking at nocturnal things. In that hour two forms without substance appeared out of the void like mist ascending from the surface of a lake.[35]

From an early age the small boy was spirited and single-minded. As a child of three, he would tear off his clothes and run out into the fierce storms that lashed the mountain. His mother, fearing for his safety, would run out after the ecstatic boy, lift him into her arms, and carry him back to the house where his frozen body would be rubbed with alcohol. But the child was irrepressible, and time and time again he would run out into storms, instinctively drawn to the awesome majesty of nature.[36] The spectacle of thunder and lightning overwhelmed the young boy and developed in him a reverence for the moments in which nature exhibits her fierce power. To his tender imagination it seemed as though he was sharing in nature's roaring laughter with the gods – nature's own way of awakening the dormant spirit of all things. Later in life Gibran expressed much of this love for storm and tempest in the images he used in his writings and paintings. In one of his Arabic works called *The Tempest*, set amidst a raging storm, a hermit reveals his wisdom to a young man:

"And among all vanities of life, there is only one thing that the spirit loves and craves. One thing dazzling and alone . . . It is an awakening in the spirit; it is an awakening in the inner depths of the heart; it is an overwhelming and magnificent power that descends suddenly upon man's conscience and opens his eyes, whereupon he sees Life amid a dizzying shower of brilliant music, surrounded by a circle of great light, with man standing as a pillar of beauty between the earth and the firmament. It is a flame that suddenly rages within the spirit and sears and purifies the heart, ascending above the earth and hovering in the spacious sky. It is a kindness that envelops the individual's heart whereby he would bewilder and disapprove all who opposed it, and revolt against those who refuse to understand its great meaning."[37]

Years later in New York, during a mighty snow storm, he wrote:

A storm is the only thing in nature that frees my heart from little cares and little pains . . . A storm always awakens whatever passion there is in me. I become eager – and eagerness in me must always seek relief in work. I often picture myself living on a mountain top, in the most stormy country (not the coldest) in the world. Is there such a place? If there is I shall go to it someday and turn my heart into pictures and poems.[38]

In the Gibran household, however, there were storms of a domestic kind. Khalil the father, whose heavy drinking fueled his imperious temper, showed little inclination to shoulder the responsibilities of a young family. He frittered away his small income, preferring the gambling games of *domma* and *taoula* to the backbreaking labor of a peasant. In an atmosphere of distressing poverty and bitter recriminations between a drunken father and intimidated mother, the young boy had to draw upon his own inner wellsprings of strength. The sources came from the beauty of the natural world that lay all around him, and from a deeply innate creative urge.

This ingenious mind and precocious intelligence were allied with an intense love of solitude. Among the mountains, hills, streams, waterfalls, and little copses, the child rejoiced in "savouring the delights of freedom" that stimulated his boyish dreams and reveries. For him this was a period "when man's teacher is nature, and humanity is his book and life is his school." Everything revealed a message: "the distant caves echoed their songs of praise and victory"; mist, cloud, earth, snow, bird, beast, flower, tree, and leaf "sent forth the Word of Life." He was thus invited to life's splendid feast where "the villages reposing in peace and tranquillity upon the shoulders of the valley rise from their slumbers; church bells fill the air with their summons to morning prayer. And from the caverns echo the chimes as if all Nature joins in reverent prayer."[39]

Young Gibran would take his precious pencils and pieces of charcoal with him to Mar Sarkis, an ancient monastery hewn out of the side of the mountain near his home. Here he would sit for hours sketching. This love of solitude, which marked Gibran out from many of his peers, fired his artistic, emotional, and spiritual life. Many years later he explained the relationship between "aloneness" and his art:

People say such complicated things about my drawings. An English critic has written about my book of drawings, and oh! such meanings and such significance as he finds intended! – things I never meant at all! For when I draw, if it happens that I do something a little nice or with some worth, I'm unconscious. Three or four hours after it's done I can't tell you anything about what it looks like. I'm not that way when I write. I do know what I'm writing, but I don't know what I'm drawing or painting. And actually when I read all these things that are sometimes said, I feel almost as if I were cheating. For I worked as simply as a child and I don't recognize at all much of what I'm given credit for.

The only way to work is to do everything with the best that is in you. With the deepest heart of the heart and with the Eyes that are the fountain of the tears. I know living poets who never write from their inmost selves. They fear to be alone. And it hurts to be alone with themselves. They will not face that pain. If there is anything in my work that draws people, it is probably that something that speaks to the aloneness in each one of us. I love to be alone. And it is when I am alone and far away, whether I'm in the physical company of people or not, that I love them best. Then they are dear to me. But just let even a thumb's pressure be put upon me to tame the wild something in me, and I feel it like a fetter. It rouses something bitter in me.[40]

This "wild something" would at times put the unfettered child in serious danger. When he was ten years old he was climbing in the mountains with a cousin when the handrail broke and the boys fell about one hundred and fifty feet onto rocks below. His cousin fractured a leg, and Kahlil broke his shoulder and suffered deep cuts to his head. His shoulder "healed crooked" – too high and too far forward – so it had to be broken again. The child was too weak at the time to be given ether and had to endure the excruciating pain – "if it had hurt less [he] should probably have cried out."[41] The agonizing experience of this injury left a deep impression on Gibran, and he later described how the episode made him aware of the kindness of the villagers of Bisharri.[42]

One of these people he later remembered was a local man named Selim Dahir, "a poet-physician" who had the insight to sense the boy's thirst for knowledge and the erudition to satisfy the young inquiring mind. Gibran, who was denied formal schooling for the first twelve years of his life, later recalled Selim Dahir's influence on him.

> But some people are so wonderful that I wonder whether their life isn't creation after all. You remember Selim Dahir? He was a poet, a doctor, a painter, a teacher, yet he never would write or paint as an artist. But he lives in other lives. Everybody was different for knowing him. All Becharry [sic][43] was different. I'm different. Everybody loved him so much. I loved him very much, and he made me feel very free to talk to him.[44]

As he grew older Kahlil began to accompany his tax-collecting father on business,[45] meeting the nomads, shepherds, and goatherds of Lebanon. These men and women, living in the free air of the mountain, possessed a dignity that left a deep impression on Gibran. He was particularly drawn to the young shepherds who, despite their lack of formal schooling, captured his imagination with the brilliance of their extemporaneous verse, the melody of their songs, and the music of their flutes. Gibran never forgot the evenings he spent under the star-studded sky and in many of his writings expressed the mystic beauty of his homeland and her people:

> My god-state is sustained by the beauty you behold wheresoever you lift your eyes; a beauty that is Nature in all her forms. A beauty that is the beginning of the shepherd's happiness as he stands among the hills; and of the villager's in his fields; and of the wandering tribes between mountain and plain. A beauty that is a stepping-stone for the wise to the throne of living truth.[46]

Indeed it was these hills, plains, and mountains that stirred the soul of the boy and fired his imagination. Amidst this breathtakingly beautiful countryside the seeds of his beliefs and visions were sown. He saw the body of the world as an outward manifestation of the divine essence. To Gibran, boy and man, nature was invested with a life of its own, with spiritual, emotional, and intellectual dimensions; for him it was the link that binds us one to another, within it flowing a divine energy which is the perfect expression of the internal rhythm of all being. To commune with nature was for him akin to a religious experience.

Among the cliffs, gorges, and groves, drenched with the incense of the cedar forests, the boy rejoiced in the sounds and silence of nature. Like the mountain itself, the sacred groves of the cedars are a symbol of life. Since ancient times their shadows have fallen on the profusion of cultures that have enriched Lebanon. The hardy trees were used by the pharaohs of ancient Egypt to furnish their tombs, by King Solomon in the building of his great temple in Jerusalem, and by the Phoenicians in the building of their mighty boats which brought such gifts as the phonetic alphabet to the world. For thousands of years they had inspired the mystics and poets of Assyria, Chaldea, Greece, and Rome. All around the young Gibran the cedars stood in silent majesty, echoing his own words: "The cedars upon thy breast are a mark of nobleness, and the towers about thee chant thy might and valour, my love."[47]

The lengthy branches of the trees spread to encompass within their shade Wadi Qadisha, the sacred valley, with its groves of oak, willow, poplar, and walnut. Every springtime the sacred valley would welcome Tammuz (Adonais), a Phoenician god of death and resurrection, and young girls would wander among the flowers that carpet the valley floors, looking for the handsome young god. It was also in this sacred valley that St. Marun, the patron saint of Lebanon, first began to teach. The legends surrounding St. Marun, St. George, and St. Anthony were palpable to the young Maronite Christian wandering in this landscape with its secret caves and mysterious grottoes. He could never forget with what reverence the prophet Isaiah had spoken of "the glory of Lebanon,"[48] nor how the sunburnt girl in The Song of Songs, portrayed as of unsurpassing beauty, is attested by the author as a shepherdess from Lebanon. The vivid images of this mystical landscape would manifest and weave themselves into his dreams throughout his life.[49]

The boy intuitively sensed the holiness of an environment that nourished and awoke within him a deep spiritual longing. The magnificence of the landscape, and the many sacred places he had known, provided him too with the solitude that he craved, nurturing in him an inner strength that would remain with him until the end of his life. Reminiscences of his homeland would fill his letters, color his work, and cast his thought. He was never to forget the dramatic beauty of the places he had known as a child; a landscape which after 1895 became the object of his yearning and a constant source of his inspiration.

> The things which the child loves remain in the domain of the heart until old age. The most beautiful thing in life is that our souls remain hovering over the places where we once enjoyed ourselves. I am one of those who remembers such places regardless of distance or time. I do not let one single phantom disappear with the cloud, and it is my everlasting remembrance of the past that causes my sorrow sometimes. But if I had to choose between joy and sorrow, I would not exchange the sorrows of my heart for the joys of the whole world.[50]

A letter to his friend Ameen Guraieb, written many years later while he was living in America, epitomizes the longing Gibran carried in his heart for his homeland:

> Remember me when you see the sun rising behind Mount Sunnin or Fam El Mizab. Think of me when you see the sun coming down toward its setting, spreading its red garment upon the mountains and the valleys as if shedding blood instead of tears as it bids Lebanon farewell. Recall my name when you see the shepherds sitting in the shadow of the trees and blowing their reeds and filling the silent field with soothing music as did Apollo when he was exiled to this world. Think of me when you see the damsels carrying their earthenware jars with water upon their shoulders. Remember me when you see the Lebanese villager ploughing the earth before the face of the sun, with beads of sweat adorning his forehead while his back is bent under the heavy duty of labour. Remember me when you hear the songs and hymns that Nature has woven from the sinews of moonlight, mingled with the aromatic scent of the valleys, mixed with the frolicsome breeze of the Holy Cedars, and poured into the hearts of the Lebanese.[51]

IV

The seeds of the exile referred to in this letter had been sown over a period of fifteen years by a father who had frittered away his income, and by a mother intent on improving her children's future. The family had been obliged to move to one floor of a house whose owner they paid in political allegiance rather than rent. Amidst intrigue and corruption the elder Gibran found himself facing charges of embezzlement. Long afterwards, Kahlil remembered the morning when the summons was served and how the crowd rode into the courtyard, and his mother stood bravely smiling. Although Kamileh tried to clear his name, her husband was found guilty after three years and all his property was confiscated.[52]

Apart from these domestic pressures there were other, larger, forces at work that were provoking mass emigration. The serious economic situation, exacerbated by a corrupt feudal system, prompted many Lebanese to seek a New World. The exploitation of the people by the governing feudal lords made life extremely difficult for ordinary men and women. The system suffocated any hope of economic growth and, in addition, an unfair taxation system meant that the weak and the impoverished were caught in a cycle of despair. Gibran in one of his early Arabic works highlighted the reality of life for the poor:

In our narrow streets
The merchant barters his days only to pay the thieves from the West,
And none is there to advise him!
In our barren fields
The peasant ploughs the earth with his finger-nails,
And sows the seeds of his heart and waters them with his tears,
And nothing does he harvest save thorns and thistles,
And none is there to teach him!
In our empty plains
The Bedouin walks bare-foot, naked and hungry
And none is there to have mercy upon him –
Speak, O Liberty, and teach us . . .

How long are we to build castles and palaces
And live but in huts and caves?
How long are we to fill granaries and stores
And eat nothing but garlic and clover?
How long are we to weave silk and wool
And be clad in tattered cloth?[53]

Emigration was also fueled by the global events of the 1860s. During the terrifying massacres of this period thousands of refugees fled to Egypt. After the Suez Canal opened in 1869, Lebanon and Syria ceased to be the only crossroads of trade; the silk industry which had traded with Europe suddenly found itself in competition with Japanese and Chinese silk, and the economy went into further decline. The first wave of emigration to the New World began. The first Lebanese immigrant to arrive in North America settled in Boston in 1854,[54] the first family[55] settled in 1878, and the first emigrant to South America arrived in Rio in 1880 after an arduous journey by sailing-ship.[56]

In Bisharri the arguments intensified in the Gibran household. One afternoon Boutros, the oldest son, came home to find his mother in tears. Like many thousands before her, Kamileh found herself faced with a stark choice: either to endure a life of increasing poverty at home, or to embark on an arduous and epochal journey of many thousands of miles to seek a better life for her children in America.

2

The New World

(1895–1898)

In the year that Guglielmo Marconi achieved radio communication and the Lumière brothers gave a first public showing of motion pictures, the exhausted Gibran family stepped into the reception center at Ellis Island, New York, after a 5,000-mile sea voyage. They were among 30 million immigrants who poured into the United States during the nineteenth century. By 1895, the year of the Gibrans' arrival, the country was experiencing intense urbanization and industrialization. Railroads linked the populous East Coast with the rest of the continent, and the revolutions in communications and transportation were beginning to gain momentum with the invention of the telegraph, soon to be followed by the telephone and the automobile.

Americans of the nineteenth century believed in progress and in the unique mission of their nation. For the millions of immigrants like Kamileh and her four children, this was a land born free, a land pregnant with opportunities. The "American Dream" inspired people from around the world with the ardent hope that life in the New World could be different, their spirit elevated by a belief that by economic endeavor humankind could achieve the good life, both individually and collectively. Indeed, as a state of mind and a dream, America had long existed before its "discovery." From time immemorial, peoples had dreamed of a lost paradise, characterized by abundance. With the first accounts of the New World, it was felt that these dreams and yearnings had become reality – a geographical fact. For many the implication was clear: this infant land presented to a senescent world another chance, perhaps the last one, to build anew.

The first immigrants had the will to conquer these vast territories although the brutal insensitivity of their methods destroyed an entire ancient culture and desecrated lands long held to be sacred. In the 1780s the immigrants created a republic which they hoped would guide and inspire them in the building of a new world. A process of democratization began, eventually resulting in a variety of reforms, including property rights for women, public education, prison reform, and the abolition of slavery. In time a spreading Romantic movement contributed to this optimism, finding an eloquent spokesman in Walt Whitman, who captured the ebullient mood of nineteenth-century America in his poem *Song of Myself*:

> I do not know what is untried and afterward,
> But I know it will in its turn prove sufficient,
>   and cannot fail.[1]

Whitman's work epitomized the collective achievement of writers such as Ralph Waldo Emerson and Henry David Thoreau who, freeing themselves from European models, helped American literature attain the quality of world literature. Under their influence, the New England Transcendentalist movement emerged between 1815 and 1836, the first date marking the maturing of the ministry of William Ellery Channing, and 1836 marking the publication of Emerson's *Nature*, the original and most potent expression of Transcendentalist philosophy.[2] Thereafter the movement grew into a profound exploration of the spiritual foundations and moral implications of the new democracy; its vitalizing effect upon American art and literature, and indeed upon the development of American democracy, remaining unrivaled.

In *Nature* Emerson transmitted a new vision to the immigrants of humanity's relationship with the surrounding world – a vision that would influence and inspire the young Kahlil Gibran. The land, to Emerson, expressed the same living spirit as the human body; rather than struggling to impose their own historically determined consciousness onto the natural world, men and women should recognize their profound living relationship with the land. Emerson's views, which are still visionary today,[3] were that American history could be the history of the return of alienated man to nature, rather than his rape of her:

> To speak truly, few adult persons can see nature . . . The lover of nature is
> he whose inward and outward senses are truly adjusted to each other; who

has retained the spirit of infancy even into the era of manhood . . . In the woods . . . a man casts off his years as the snake his slough, and at what period soever of life is always a child. In the woods is perpetual youth. Within these plantations of God, a decorum and a sanctity reign, a perennial festival is dressed, and the guest sees not how he should tire of them in a thousand years. In the woods we return to reason and faith. There I feel that nothing can befall me, in life, – no disgrace, no calamity (leaving me my eyes), which nature cannot repair. Standing on the bare ground . . . the currents of the Universal Being circulate through me; I am part or parcel of God.[4]

Emerson's disciple Henry David Thoreau too sensed the threat of "progress" to the natural world: "The Anglo-American can indeed cut down, and grub up all this waving forest . . . but he cannot converse with the spirit of the tree he fells, he cannot read the poetry and mythology which retire as he advances."[5]

However, for most Americans, as a self-conscious awareness of the "new" country's economic potential created among them an atmosphere of buoyancy and faith in their way of life, the visions of Emerson and Thoreau were irrelevant. The moral and virtuous character of the American Republic was an inherent cultural assumption among its citizens, and despite those such as the dispossessed Native American Indian, the African snatched from his homeland and sold into slavery, and the hungry immigrant who sensed that rhetoric and reality were worlds apart, most Americans assumed that Thomas Jefferson had been right in 1776 when he had stated that life, liberty, and the pursuit of happiness in America were self-evident truths.

This mood of optimism and trust in the future was manifest in the high Victorian architecture that had begun to appear in the 1860s. Cast-iron spires, mansard roofs, abundant pillars, and stained glass appeared on government and university buildings, railway stations, and even town houses. The splendor of buildings such as A. B. Mullett's State, War, and Navy building in Washington and Henry Hobson Richardson's Trinity Church in Boston reflected the people's vision of the grandeur of their God-given institutions.

These elegant manifestations of industrial success, however, cast a shadow on the streets of the booming cities. Industrialism, something of which Americans were proud, did not come without a price. Soulless square tenement buildings appeared in expanding urban areas, sucking in immigrant families such as the Gibrans. With their ugly uniformity, these drab uncompromising buildings, overcrowded, unventilated, and lacking in sanitation, brought gloom and misery; any aspirations the tenement dwellers might have had were quickly eclipsed by infectious diseases, despair, and neglect. An estimated ten million Americans lived in conditions of poverty, barely eking out an existence on family incomes of less than $500 per year.[6] Alongside the struggling working classes were the masses of people living in absolute poverty – the paupers, the disabled, the drifters, the consumptives, the victims of industrial accidents, the orphaned, the exploited, the beggars, the homeless – all helpless and beaten by the harshness of an economic system that had no place for failure.

II

By their own testimonies most immigrants came to America to improve their economic opportunities. For Lebanese immigrants, an ancient tradition strengthened their resolve as they waited nervously for entrance visas at Ellis Island. In Lebanese tradition the Arabic word *al-mahjar* describes a "place" to which pilgrims traveled in search of a new and better life, and for those immigrants in 1895, among them the Gibran family from Bisharri, *al-mahjar* was America.

After spending an uncomfortable night at Ellis Island, the Gibrans journeyed northward to their last port of call, Boston. It was here that, among relatives and friends, in what was then the largest Syrian community outside New York, they settled in Olive Place at the edge of Boston's populous and notoriously impoverished South End. Surrounded by tall tenement buildings, Olive Place was reached by a narrow brick entrance, giving it the feel of a casbah-like retreat. The area, housing people from all corners of the world, was a wretched and overcrowded neighborhood – one that had been compared unfavorably with the notorious slums of East London.[7] Despite these harsh conditions, Kamileh, Boutros, Sultanah, Marianna, and Kahlil were filled with amazement at the lighted streets, street cars, enormous buildings, and the plethora of consumer goods and mechanical gadgets that assaulted their senses at every street corner. The bazaar-like street life, although at times tough and brutal, intrigued the twelve-year-old Kahlil, and youthful curiosity would take him from the ghetto into the colorful world of vaudeville shows, shooting-galleries, waxwork shows, and fairgrounds, which, with their glaring electric lights, presented a stark contrast to his own "dimly lit, squalid neighborhood."[8]

Kamileh, resilient and diligent, began to earn a living by pack peddling during the day and working as a seamstress at night to support her young family. By the time she arrived in America, pack peddling was a way of life for Lebanese and Syrian immigrants. Requiring little capital or knowledge of English, it was an opportunity to earn good profits by introducing the poor immigrants into the homes of more affluent Americans. A supplier, usually a veteran pedlar, would teach new pedlars the value of American currency, a smattering of colloquial English phrases, and a few tricks of the trade. Ready for business, pedlars would greet housebound urban homemakers with a "Buy something, ma'am" before exhibiting suitcases that weighed as much as 200 pounds and contained a bazaar of goods: jewelry, icons, ribbons, gingham, laces, notions, linens, crocheted tablecloths, and handmade children's clothes. With their "exotic" Eastern ways and their olivewood trinkets from the Holy Land, the pedlars excited their customers' imaginations and on the whole were warmly received.

However, for many traveling pedlars, life on the road consisted of trudging for months over half a continent working their way westward, struggling against racist attacks, robberies, and rabid dogs.[9] For Kamileh, based in a city, life was on the whole less perilous, although no less exhausting as she sold her wares across the railroad tracks to the white folks in the leafy suburbs of Back Bay and Cambridge.

While Kahlil's mother was carrying her heavy loads of linen and lace to the privileged classes of Boston, her youngest son was sent to the Quincy School for Boys. It was here that his name was misspelt and shortened from "Gibran Khalil Gibran" to "Kahlil Gibran." He was placed in the ungraded class reserved for immigrant children with no knowledge of English. His quick wit helped him survive, and from his first days in Boston he became well aware that few were likely to succeed in America without a good command of English. He learnt quickly, particularly impressing his teachers with his unique drawings and sketches.

These first two years in Boston, however, were overall an unhappy time for Kahlil. The demoralizing environment of poverty, engendering as it did prejudice, racism, and bullying, jarred with the boy's pride. He later confessed that this period in Boston was "miserable" and save for the teachers' kindness and understanding would have been unbearable.[10]

His sisters Marianna and Sultanah did not go to school; they helped in the family's newly acquired monument to Kamileh's perseverance and thrift: a dry goods store on Beach Street which she had bought within a year of arriving. Later Sultanah and Marianna worked in a dressmaking shop. The young girls adored their dashing older brother Boutros – extrovert, charming, musical, and easy-going. In contrast, Kahlil was withdrawn, introspective, and solitary. He missed Bisharri and craved the wild freedoms of his previous life in the beautiful Lebanese countryside – his acute sense of alienation in the teeming streets of Boston exacerbating his unhappiness. In his first English work, *The Madman*, published twenty-one years later, echoes of this confusing period of his young life can be discerned: "I, a human chaos, a nebula of confused elements, I move amongst finished worlds – peoples of complete laws and pure order, whose thoughts are assorted, whose dreams are arranged; and whose visions are enrolled and registered."[11]

During this period, like so many times in his young life, it was his mother who gave him succor and instilled in him some hope. Despite her own heavy burdens of single motherhood and long working hours, she remained sensitive and sympathetic to the boy's needs: "My mother understood [my remoteness] . . . sometimes she would smile at someone who came in and look at me and lay her finger on her lip and say, 'Hush, He's not here.'"[12] Kamileh strove selflessly to nurture within her son a spirit of independence and a desire to develop outside the family's limiting existence, and Kahlil later said of her:

> My mother was a most remarkable being . . . she was always doing little things that put me on the way to love others besides myself – always, as it were, pushing me away or out a little. She freed me from herself. And she said things to me when I was twelve years old that I'm just realizing now – prophetic things. She knew things very wonderfully.[13]

III

In addition to his mother's influence there were other forces at work that would change and shape the boy's destiny. Since the 1870s some of the residents of Back Bay, acutely aware of their struggling neighbors on the other side of the tracks, involved themselves in charitable projects. At first, their philanthropic endeavors took the form of outdoor relief work and the maintenance of the poorhouses that dotted the city. By the 1890s their contributions were geared toward the construction of settlement houses where social workers living communally endeavored to attract the needy families of the neighborhood to their social and cultural activities.

One of these settlement houses, Denison House, had a liberating atmosphere that encouraged children to attend arts and crafts classes and drama and social studies groups. In the winter of 1895 Kahlil's teachers at the Quincy School, with little persuasion, suggested to Kahlil that he attend one of the drawing classes. His talents were quickly recognized by one of the art teachers at Denison House, a woman called Florence Pierce. Observing an original spark in the intense boy, Florence brought him to the attention of a social worker called Jessie Fremont Beale. Miss Beale, whose work involved the introduction of home libraries in the poorest communities, was influential in Boston's artistic and literary establishment. She was particularly impressed by the twelve-year-old's drawing of a bacchante statue that, before the prudish elements of Victorian Boston protested at its nude sensuality, had stood in the courtyard of the public library. Intuitively sensing the boy's potential, Jessie Beale wrote to a man she felt sure could guide the young boy.

Fred Holland Day, one-time bibliophile, publisher, man of letters, and devotee of Oscar Wilde, was a leading light in bohemian Boston. During his thirty-six years he had explored many of the alternative fashions of his time. Flamboyant in appearance, Day had spent his working life challenging the conformist attitudes of his peers. He was infatuated with English literature and on his many visits to England had ardently collected literary and illustrative material, a pastime that was to earn him a reputation as an artistic bridge between American and English letters. In 1893 he had set up a publishing house with Herbert Copeland, which, during its five-and-a-half-year existence, introduced to American readers poetry from the English and Irish literary scene. These offerings to the American public included Dante Gabriel Rossetti's *The House of Life*, Francis Thompson's *Poems*, Oscar Wilde's *Salome* and the work of William Butler Yeats. American contributions included those of his friend Louise Imogen Guiney, and Stephen Crane, whose grim realism would significantly affect a whole generation of young writers.

Day's greatest love in 1896, when Kahlil was introduced to him, was the emerging art form of pictorial photography. While helping to introduce the children of the South End slums to English literature, Day had become increasingly excited by the possibilities of developing his new art. Faces from every corner of the world provided him with a host of exotic models for his camera. Elegantly clad in a large hat and dashing cape, he scoured the streets in search of the perfect face that would fit his current photographic project. To the children of the street, his endeavors must have all seemed like a sophisticated game, but the more sensitive among them became aware of the transforming effect of the camera lens. With his knowledge of composition, light, and proportion, Day was capable of transfiguring the Armenian, Arab, Celtic, Ethiopian, and Chinese waifs into princes, sheikhs, chiefs, and mandarins.

Kahlil was one of the many children who underwent this magical transformation and during the first year of his acquaintance with Day often posed in the photographer's studio. Here Gibran absorbed the new and exciting set of literary and artistic impressions generated by the eccentric photographer's unbridled energy and enthusiasm. Although he was basically unhappy at this time, the transformational power of the camera portrayed a glossy image of "nobility and lineage" – an image that sparked in Gibran a desire to live up to "the grand illusions caught."[14]

Amidst this intensely creative atmosphere, punctuated by photographic exhibitions, book productions, and literary discoveries, Gibran found himself in a new and enthralling world. The bohemian elements of the Boston of the 1890s were dabbling with orientalism against a backdrop of Turkish carpets, water pipes, fezzes, and Burne-Jones' paintings;[15] an atmosphere still throbbing with the Transcendental legacy of their own Emerson. Increasingly Gibran began to sense that Americans here, weary of materialism, appeared to be looking to the East for the spiritual sustenance they felt they lacked at home.

Day, who was fascinated by Gibran's background and impressed by the boy's quenchless thirst for knowledge, carefully guided him in his new environment. Sensitive to the boy's reverence for his homeland, he encouraged Kahlil to nurture this pride in his heritage. In 1894 his firm had published Bliss Carman and Richard Hovey's *Songs from Vagabondia*, which, alluding as it did to Lebanon, provided Gibran with an early awareness of how his origins might help him realize his own literary ambitions. Day also introduced him to the wider world of literature – Keats, Shelley, Blake,[16] Emerson, Whitman, and the work of the Belgian symbolist Maurice Maeterlinck, whose masterpiece, *The Treasure of the Humble*, published in 1897, was firing the hearts and minds of Day and his contemporaries. For a time Gibran felt a deep affinity with the Belgian's intuitive meditations, brooding speculations, and universal visions. Maeterlinck had written:

> A time will come, perhaps, – and many things there are that herald its approach – a time will come perhaps when our souls will know of each other without the intermediary of the senses. Certain it is that there passes not a day but the soul adds to its ever-widening domain. It is very much nearer to our visible self, and takes a far greater part in all our actions than

was the case two or three centuries ago. A spiritual epoch is perhaps upon us; an epoch to which a certain number of analogies are found in history. For there are periods recorded, when the soul, in obedience to unknown laws, seemed to rise to the very surface of humanity, whence it gave clearest evidence of its existence and its power. And this existence and this power reveal themselves in countless ways, diverse and unforeseen. It would seem, at moments such as these, as though humanity were on the point of struggling from beneath the crushing burden of matter that weighs it down. A spiritual influence is abroad that soothes and comforts; and the sternest, direst laws of Nature yield here and there.[17]

Gibran, whose English was improving all the time, was awestruck when he heard the utterings of the great English poets, and his reverence for them remained with him all his life. He saw in Keats one of the "very few true worshippers of true Beauty – Beauty which is the only Truth . . . .[a] flame dancing in the immeasurable sky";[18] in Shelley: "a world by himself. His Soul is that of an exiled god who, being sad and weary and homesick, passed the time singing his memory of other planets";[19] and in Blake the "God-man," whose work represented for Gibran "the profoundest things done in English – and his vision . . . the most godly."[20]

Gibran's passion for the written word was complemented by his love of art. Inspired by the weekly visits he made to the exhibitions at Boston's Copley Square library he sketched and drew constantly. Day, by now impressed with Gibran's talent, encouraged him to develop his own style, even permitting him to work on bookcover designs for some of Copeland and Day's publications. He also began introducing his young protégé into the homes and salons of the affluent literati of Back Bay, inviting him to attend his own photographic exhibitions which featured the young Gibran in a number of the pictures.

Within these lofty circles, the fifteen-year-old boy from the South End slums met established artists and writers, such as the painter Lilla Cabot who gave him his first paints,[21] and the poetess Louise Guiney. With his modest manners, his artistic promise, and striking good looks, the boy from Lebanon quickly endeared himself to the intellectual and artistic elite of Boston; and at one stage he found himself being seduced by an older woman.[22] Gibran's artistic gifts were quickly recognized and a distinguished author Nathan Haskell Dole and the publisher L. C. Page chose one of Gibran's pictures for the cover of *Omar Khayyám*.[23] This honor, bestowed on one so young, left its mark on Gibran. Here was poetry *par excellence* – the lines expressing the magic and majesty of Eastern language and style – and here he was adorning the cover of the book that contained the most frequently quoted lines of Eastern poetry:

> Awake! For Morning in the Bowl of Night
> Has flung the Stone that puts the Stars to Flight:
> And Lo! The Hunter of the East has caught
> The Sultan's Turret in a Noose of Light.[24]

Aware of his artistic ambitions and the single-mindedness with which he pursued these goals, Kamileh and Boutros, despite their financial struggles, loyally supported Kahlil in his endeavors. Kamileh, Boutros, Marianna, and Sultanah were all invited to the opening of Day's photographic exhibition at the Boston Camera Club on March 8, 1898, and the family spared no effort in presenting Kahlil to his best advantage at an event which the Gibrans saw as his own private triumph. The exhibition was "an event" and Kamileh ensured that Kahlil was well attired: "I was all velvet – knickerbockers – with silk stockings."[25]

Kahlil was amazed to find seven or eight studies of himself in Day's portfolio, but his greatest delight was his introduction to a twenty-four-year-old poetess called Josephine Preston Peabody, who was later to prove a benign and inspirational influence on him. She said to Gibran: "I see you everywhere . . . But you look so sad," asking him, "Why are you so sad?"[26]

Gibran's introspection – interpreted as sadness by Josephine – was rightly understood by the family as his ever-present longing to return to Lebanon. Kamileh too, was growing increasingly concerned about the boy's sudden projection into the unconventional world of bohemian Boston, especially when word reached her about his experiences with the American woman.[27] Alongside these concerns was her ardent hope that her son's talents should be enriched by a deeper understanding of his own heritage and that he must return to Lebanon to complete his education and develop his knowledge of the Arabic language and its great literature.

In August 1898, the fifteen-year-old boy, enriched by his newfound insights into the Western soul, sailed eastwards to Beirut, in search of the soul of both his people and the land of his birth.

3

Returning to the Roots

(1898–1902)

W hen he stood on the deck and saw the first winter snows on Mount Sannin and Famm al-Mizab towering above Beirut, Gibran knew he was home. He enrolled as a student at the Maronite college Madrasat-al-Hikmah, which had been founded in 1875 by Yusuf al-Dibs, a Maronite priest. The curriculum, supported by the highest quality of teaching, earned the college a reputation as the foremost Christian secondary school in the Arab world.[1]

With its methodical teaching techniques and its openness to Western ideas al-Hikmah generated much of the spirit that led to the creation of a Romantic school of Arabic poetry and the development of new genres and innovative literary styles – a literary revolution inspired by Gibran, who would become the college's most illustrious son.

Gibran's teacher at al-Hikmah, Father Yusuf Haddad, was a well-respected senior member of staff. Although Gibran could read Arabic, he could not write it, and for a year Father Haddad became "a tongue and a pen" to the attentive pupil whose "heart followed its own passions." Haddad saw in Gibran "an alert and dynamic soul with a radical and rebellious intellect. His eye rejoiced in whatever it saw. He had only a few friends, cultivating his mind within his own self."[2]

Gibran singled out one particular classmate as his friend – Yusuf Sa'dallah Huwayyik – who, years later, was to meet up with Gibran in Paris. Huwayyik, the nephew of the Maronite patriarch, was an amiable and sociable young man who became one of Gibran's closest friends. Haddad observed that Gibran "was often critical, obstinately holding to his viewpoint. He was pensive, seldom with a smile on his face . . . mercilessly spurred on by ambition – often gazing into the distant horizon."

The young pupil undoubtedly left a vivid impression on his teacher, who remembered his first meeting with the young man with the "sleepy eyes," the "dropping eyelids," and the long hair which "almost covered his ears." Gibran told Haddad that he had completed his studies in English and had come to Lebanon to study "the literature and the language of my country and to be able to express my thoughts about these subjects" before complaining to the teacher that he had been "relegated" to the elementary class. Haddad explained that learning was like climbing a ladder: one must climb each rung, one at a time. The young man's subsequent response gave Haddad "goose-pimples": "Does not the teacher know that the bird does not ascend a ladder in its flight?"

Haddad, seeing in the young man "a distinct intellect" and "the wisdom of an older man," listened closely as Gibran told him that he wished to attend his classes, adding: "I shall not ask any questions and equally I shall be spared from answering any." He then told Haddad that he was independent and would pay his own school fees. He continued: "If my request is refused I'll have no alternative but to look for another school – one that is not a stickler to bureaucracy and understands its pupils."

Haddad, by now obviously impressed with the youth's determination, went to see the principal to argue Gibran's case. Finally, after much persuasion, the principal conceded and accepted Gibran into the school on his own terms. The following day, as Gibran began his studies at al-Hikmah, Father Haddad found a note left on his desk: "For three months don't ask anything of me, after that you may ask what you wish."

Gibran, at first, did not open any books in class but was "all eyes, and all ears . . . thirsty, unquenchable, ever curious and hungry" for knowledge. Occasionally he would approach Haddad for guidance on what books he should choose from the library. Haddad referred him to *Kalilah wa Dimna*, *al-Aghani*, *The Prologomena of Ibn Khaldun*, *The Epistles of Badi 'al-Zaman al-Hamathani*, and *al-Durrar* by Adeeb Ishaq, and recommended the poets al-Multanabi, al-Baha' Zuhayer, and the Torah. He also studied natural sciences and histories of peoples, their customs, their character, and their ethics.

Soon the brilliant student was submitting essays to the teacher. Haddad found them "coherent with a touch of beauty," although he sometimes felt the student's earliest attempts "incongruent" in their meaning. The teacher began to coach Gibran carefully in his writing, but there was some unique quality in his student that made Haddad view Gibran "as more than just a pupil." He gave Gibran a rule: "Think long and hard and write less. In this way you will gain a lot and become immensely creative." Haddad later recalled: "From the first essay he gave me I realized who Gibran was. I told him you're becoming a genuine poet and a writer of imagination – so fear God and go forward. Gibran's style was blossoming as the white poplar and flowing as a fountain. It was a style that lent strength to an impetuous, mocking and rebellious soul." At the end of the academic year Haddad left the school and lost contact with Gibran. Then much later he received a book sent by his former pupil inscribed with the words: "You should be the first to receive my first." When Gibran had first met Father Yusuf Haddad and revealed his desire to express his "own thoughts" the teacher had little known that the long-haired and determined youth before him would one day change the very face of Arabic literature forever.

II

From the sixteenth to nineteenth centuries Arabic literature had been suffocated by the allied forces of despotic Ottoman rule and reactionary orthodox dogma. In such an authoritarian atmosphere literary creativity and originality were subdued, reducing literature to little more than a decorative art or an attempt to display linguistic skill. Imprisoned by a predetermined content, Arabic literature lacked the two elements productive of literary greatness: the quickening of a higher culture and the inspiration of a free and vigorous national life.[3] Writers were forced to neglect content and substance for form, and in the process the intimate relationship between the writer's inner world and what was written was severed. During this age the minds of writers were enfolded by an anesthetic lethargy out of which they were awakened only by the cannons of Napoleon in Egypt.[4]

When Napoleon captured Egypt in 1798 he shattered any illusions held by the Muslim world about its unchallengeable superiority.[5] Addressing his soldiers on the eve of the invasion Napoleon said: "You are going to undertake a conquest, the effects of which upon commerce and civilization will be incalculable."[6] Meanwhile in Beirut Western missionaries challenging traditional Muslim theology were undertaking a conquest of a different kind. The Arab world could either ignore these Western military and religious challenges and consequently be submerged under Western domination, or revolutionize itself in a process of cultural reexamination and regeneration which would restore to the Arabs a genuine living character of their own.

However, bitterly conscious of the sectarianism exploited by Western interference, potential Muslim reformers believed that the helplessness of the Muslim world in the face of Western intervention was not so much due to Western strength as it was the inevitable result of a departure from true Islam in its purest form. The subsequent call of the Arab revivalists was for a return to Muslim principles corrupted over the centuries, they believed, by a succession of ruling authorities.[7] They called for a reinstatement of the past and a rejection of Western ideas, hoping to reform the present by adhering to the all-civilizing principles of religion as manifested in the glorious age of Islam. Likewise Arabic writers looked back to the golden days of Arabic literature. They saw the work of this period as the embodiment of all great literature, and it thus became the measuring-rod by which all contemporary works were judged. Again, as in the past, theology supplied the intellectual, philosophical, and literary framework for Arab writers who looked to the past, and not to the West, for models of technique and expression.

For Christian Arab writers of the nineteenth century, however, the growing tide of Western influence, especially in their colleges, could not be ignored. Nineteenth-century writers such as Nassif al-Yazijji and Faris al-Shidyaq, unbounded by supra-literary religious ideologies, remained receptive to the renovating impact of the modern age. Yazijji's work marks the first steps toward the revival of a more high-minded literary tradition, and the quality of his writing is manifest in the Jesuit Bible which he translated between 1872 and 1880. Acutely aware of his Arabic heritage, Yazijji saw Arabic literature, which is the common inheritance of both Christians and Muslims, as a means of achieving national unity. Springing from this was his involvement with the nationalist movement and his denunciation of Turkish rule and church corruption.[8]

Yazijji's Christian contemporary, Faris al-Shidyaq, fused his Arabic heritage with the European ideas he had assimilated from the West, drawing up a practical program of reforms, condemning the iniquity of feudal privileges and calling for the emancipation of women and justice for the working classes. For these Christian writers, mastery of the Arabic language could not be conceived of as an end in itself. Rather, liberated from a dogma they did not worship, they were able to sow the seeds for later Christian Arab writers such as Gibran to pursue excellence while embracing modern ideas.

Genuine traces of this new drive are to be found in the work of the journalist, translator, and scholar Butrus al-Bustani. In a speech delivered in

Beirut in February 1859 he had traced the development of Arabic science and learning from pre-Islamic times to the decline of Arab civilization, indicating the majestic heights this civilization had once reached. The readiness and openness of the Arab mind, argued Bustani, had enabled it to embrace, absorb, and revitalize other cultures with which it had come into contact, thereby acting as a mediator between the old and the new.

> Just as the Westerners did not, in their days of ignorance, scornfully neglect the literature of the Arabs for the mere fact that it was attributed to the Arabs, it does not likewise become the Arabs to neglect scornfully the learning of the West for the mere fact that it is western. In fact, it is becoming of us to welcome the sciences irrespective of whoever presents them to us, whether they come from China, India, Persia or Europe.[9]

Bustani, a Protestant convert who was educated at Ayn Warqah College in Lebanon, a Maronite institution modeled on European lines, was characteristic of a new generation of Arab-Christian writers who, receptive to Western literature and ideas, sought to reform the Arab world in accordance with the needs and demands of the modern age. Bustani's greatest contribution to modern Arabic literature was the significant role he played in translating the Bible from the Hebrew, Greek, and Syriac into Arabic, completing the work in 1865.

This translation, called the "*American*", in contrast to the "*Jesuit*" translation of a few years later, emerged as the first book of real importance in modern Arabic literature.[10] Apart from the boundless literary treasures it introduced to modern writers, it presented Bustani with a living example of how great literature can still be achieved without rhetorical affectation, stylization, and literary embellishment. For the first time the poetic summits of the Psalms, the Song of Solomon, and the New Testament, where poetry and language express the sweet melody of an inner thought and the feeling with which that thought is charged, were made available in modern Arabic. The American, and later the Jesuit translations of the Bible, quickened and galvanized a whole generation of writers in their determination to explore Western culture, inspiring them in their own search for creativity. At the hands of writers such as Marun al-Naqqash, Najib al-Haddad, Salim al-Bustani, Farah Antun, and Francis Marrash, all of whom were graduates of the missionary schools or had studied in Europe, Arabic literature in the nineteenth century entered, at least in kind, its modern era.[11]

Marun al-Naqqash, a Maronite who was educated in Lebanon, came back to Beirut from a short visit to Rome in 1848 and, on a stage he erected at his house, presented his Arabic version of Molière's *L'avare*, an event that marked the beginning of dramatic art in Arabic literature.[12] It was followed by the pioneering work of Najib al-Haddad, who among his many plays translated the work of Hugo, Molière, Racine, Shakespeare, Sophocles, and Voltaire.

This active process of opening the Arab world to Western literature expanded to include other Western genres such as the novel, the story, the essay, the article, and, at a later stage, genuine Arab drama. Arab-Christians greatly contributed to the development of journalism, remaining throughout the nineteenth century its undisputed masters.[13] Newspapers and magazines, such as *al-Jinan* and *Lisan al-Hal*, gave the novel and the short story special attention, with the result that the works of numerous Western writers were translated into the Arabic language. Many, encouraged by such translations, attempted to create the Arabic novel along Western lines. Salim al-Bustani, son of Butrus, wrote the first real novel in the Arabic language.[14] The journalist, novelist, and essayist Farah Antun introduced the Arab world to the insights of Tolstoy, Ruskin, and Rousseau, and helped translate Nietzsche's *Thus Spake Zarathustra* – a book that was to have a profound effect on Gibran.[15]

In his own writings, Antun expressed his concern that the Arab world would only progress if the union between civil and religious authority were dissolved and Arab thought allowed to function freely and independently – a view he encapsulated in his book on the twelfth-century Andalusian philosopher Ibn Rushd (Averroes). In it he writes that theological orthodoxy was responsible for the persecution of the learned Averroes, and thus marked the discontinuation of original thought in the Muslim East.[16]

With the influx of Western literature came Western ideas and ideologies. The Christian Francis Marrash, who was influential in introducing French Romanticism, provided the Arab world with new ways of thinking and exciting modes of expression. His writings on human rights and the inevitable triumph of liberty over tyranny were couched in a new and fresh style, and many of his expressions became stock images for writers in the twentieth century.[17] Marrash's originality of thought shines through in his poetico-philosophical notion of love, as expressed in his greatest work *Ghabat al-Haqq*, asserting that biological procreation, social interrelationships, and the attraction between atoms which makes possible the creation of stars and planets are all manifestations of love.

It is by Love that the world is maintained, by Love each creature perpetuates itself separately, and by Love the whole preserves its parts . . . He who calls Love the goddess of human society is not wrong, because of the strange effects and miraculous impressions produced by her among men.[18]

Marrash's philosophy of universal love marked the first creative expression of the Christian spirit in Arabic. He transcended the concept of that school of love poetry known among the Arabs as *al-'uthreyoun* (platonic-love poets), extracting out of the essence of Christianity the concept of love that was Sufi in nature yet interpreted in realistic terms, becoming love in action, love visibly reflecting the divine in man. Every action is thus measured by the purpose it serves while action and purpose must be dynamically propelled by the power of love. The quality of his style and the visionary and allegorical interpretation of his thoughts were to leave a profound impression on the young Gibran as he explored and assimilated his literary heritage at al-Hikmah.

Christian writers accepted that their language, Arabic, and their civilization were permeated by Islamic values and ideals, and never questioned their cultural identity in the context of Islamic civilization. As long as political and religious freedoms were guaranteed within the framework of a secular state these writers not only applauded their Islamic cultural heritage but were indeed its most jealous defenders against non-Arabic Muslim communities which represented a cultural and linguistic threat. The Ottoman Turks ousted Arabic as the official language, replacing it with Turkish. The Christian writers not only defended the purity of the Arabic language – the language of the Holy Qur'an – but also applauded the noble ideals of Islamic civilization.

Another writer whose radical works Gibran read widely at al-Hikmah was Adeeb Ishaq, a contemporary of Marrash. Basic to Ishaq's doctrine of reform was his concept of nature, as opposed to society, history, and culture. To Ishaq, humankind, stripped of convention and tradition and reduced to its essentials, is good, free, and tolerant.[19] Human morality is one and universal, untarnished in its essence by external phenomena which are "like ashes which hide the embers but do not extinguish them."[20] With his belief that human rights and liberty are permanent natural qualities of existence, he vehemently denounced the tyranny of societies that deprived people of their natural rights by imposing inequality and slavery on them.[21] His denunciation of Arabic society, based on observation of the despotic hierarchy that bound the people of his own age, could not have been more dramatic. His heroic efforts to awaken the Arab world to the need for change marked him as a great reform writer. Although he possessed a tremendous capacity to assimilate and apply Western ideas his greatest achievement was his literary style, which later influenced the writings of his successors, including Gibran.[22]

The Arabic syllabus at al-Hikmah included selections from ancient literature and the literature of the revival with special emphasis on al-Shidyaq, Marrash, and Ishaq.[23] During his studies at al-Hikmah Gibran also first met the majestic poetry of the great Sufi poets, such as Avicenna, and the soaring ideas of al-Ghazali, Ibn 'Arabi, and al-Farabi, all of whom would have a profound effect on his spiritual and literary development. He was also introduced to French literature, particularly French Romantic literature, and even before he attained sound knowledge of the French language he read those French works that were available in translation, such as *Atala*, by Francois René Chateaubriand[24] and *Les Misérables* by Victor Hugo.[25]

III

Gibran's tendency to choose for himself a seminary-like course of studies, suited to his own needs, temperament, and literary aspirations, and his reluctance to submit to formal discipline, may have arisen from an innate distrust of authority, which he feared would suffocate his originality.[26] Whatever the reason, it meant that Gibran was able to concentrate his attention on Arabic and French and develop his talents for creative writing.[27] His unease around authority may also have been the result of his earlier childhood experiences at home where his father's harsh discipline jarred with his own free-spirited nature, and during his time at al-Hikmah he sometimes clashed with the authoritarian regime. Wearing his hair long and lacing his conversations with stories about his American experiences, he was remembered for his extravagant style and forthright attitudes long after he had left.

During these formative years at al-Hikmah certain qualities emerged: a gift for intellectual leadership; a single-minded ambition; a rebellious nature; and a self-assurance belying his years. In his last year at the college Gibran established a literary circular called *al-Manarah (The Beacon)*, in collaboration with two classmates, Yusuf Huwayyik and Bisharra Khuri.[28] Despite Huwayyik's superior social standing, Gibran's experiences at the publishing firm of Copeland & Day in Boston enabled him to adopt a position of leadership in this literary venture. As well as providing him with a vehicle to express himself openly in the written word, the magazine allowed Gibran to apply his artistic talents in illustration. Huwayyik later recalled that his friend, "lonely, obstinate and strange in appearance,"[29] was passionately involved in the innovative venture.

Despite Gibran's unconventional attitudes his teachers were open-minded enough to acknowledge the boy's talents and award him the college poetry prize. The prize meant a great deal to Gibran and although it was "just school work" the honor made him ecstatic and he declared: "in all my life I shall never know such an uplift again."[30]

These uplifting experiences, however, were very different from the reception the poet received when he returned to Bisharri for the summer holidays. He found that his father had not mellowed with age. If anything, his self-indulgent obduracy and harshness had been exacerbated by his tarnished reputation and the loss of his family, and he had become a complete drunkard whose loneliness fed his bitterness.[31] The schism between the arrogant father and the adolescent son grew and Kahlil, as in childhood, found his unsympathetic father's insensitivity difficult to bear.

One evening at a gathering of friends at his father's house a guest asked Kahlil to read from one of his poems. This was his first ever "public recital" and a special moment for the sixteen-year-old. His father, however, treated the whole affair with undisguised "contempt" and after Kahlil's rendition said: "I hope we shall never have any more of this sickmindedness."[32] The incident precipitated the son's departure, and he went to live with an aunt and his cousin N'oula Gibran, an apprentice carpenter.[33] The family was poor and Kahlil found himself in dismal, damp, and vermin-infested lodgings. Fastidious about his personal hygiene, he hated the skin-crawling degradation of his new environment, and, as in childhood, sought refuge in the majestic countryside around Bisharri with his cousin:

> We'd make camp by the spring and sleep under the stars. How the heavens are there, with the stars so brilliant and the sky so full of many depths! We'd wake early in the morning and Venus would come up – she casts a shadow there. The brook and every flower, the birds and even the rocks seemed to sing.[34]

He also found respite in a rekindled friendship with the teacher-poet and physician Selim Dahir, who would recount colorful legends and local tales to the aspiring young writer who would carefully record them. These evenings spent sitting by the hearth[35] nourished Gibran's desire to learn all he could about his homeland. As well as enriching his intellect and imagination, his relationship with Selim Dahir provided Gibran with new acquaintances, and he began visiting the influential family of Tannous Asad Hanna Dahir. Dahir, charmed by the youth's courteous and gentle manner,[36] allowed him to help his daughters, Sa' idi and Hala, with their chores. The elder daughter, Hala, who was two years older than Gibran, fell in love with the passionate and intelligent young man, and he with her. Their relationship, however, was to end in anguish and separation.

During the summer of 1899, Gibran's second and last summer in Bisharri, Hala's brother, a town official, realized that the attachment between his sister and "the son of a goat-tax farmer" as he called Gibran, was more serious than he had suspected. Hala was forbidden to see Gibran, and the couple had to meet secretly in a forest near the Mar Sarkis monastery.[37]

The difficult situation made Gibran aware of the contrast between the forest where he would meet Hala and the state of society where he was misunderstood by his father, despised by Hala's brother, and unable to express publicly his love for a young woman whose life was controlled by patriarchy. These adolescent experiences, like those of his childhood, drove Gibran to the harmonious forest which later became in his writings a symbol for liberty and freedom,[38] a sanctuary beyond good and evil.[39]

In his Arabic novella *The Broken Wings*, written thirteen years after his love affair, Gibran tenderly recalls Hala as Selma Karamy,[40] forced into marrying a bishop's nephew. As well as exploring the iniquities of misogyny and clerical corruption, *The Broken Wings* established Gibran as one of the first defenders of women's rights in the Middle East.

Gibran also reveals the nature of his adolescent temperament "torn by two forces. The first force elevates him and shows him the beauty of existence through a cloud of dreams; the second ties him down to the earth and fills his eyes with dust and overpowers him with fears and darkness."[41] In *The Broken Wings*, this inner conflict is only eased when his love for Selma is reciprocated. However, true love is thwarted by a society in which a woman "is looked upon as a commodity, purchased and delivered from one to another,"[42] and where men look upon women "from behind the sexual veil and see nothing but externals."[43]

During this period when he was reexploring his heritage Gibran's mind's eye did not turn just to the majestic forests and mountains of Lebanon, but also fell upon the human despair caused by the corrupt and exploitative attitudes of those in power in Lebanon. His ears did not only hear the sounds of the whispering winds in the cedar trees of Lebanon, but heard too the sighs and lamentations of a people oppressed.[44]

Inspired by the nineteenth-century reform writers of Lebanon, Gibran in his early Arabic works was vehemently to attack the tyranny and injustice perpetuated by traditional laws and customs. His rebellion, no doubt in this instance fired by his own bitter rejection by Hala's powerful family, is evident in *The Broken Wings*, in which he follows the plight of a woman forced into a union dictated by wealth and power:

> Human society has yielded for seventy centuries to corrupted laws until it cannot understand the meaning of the superior and eternal laws. A man's eyes have become accustomed to the dim light of candles and cannot see the sunlight. Spiritual disease is inherited from one generation to another until it has become a part of the people, who look upon it, not as a disease, but as a natural gift, showered by God upon Adam. If those people found someone free from the germs of this disease, they would think of him with shame and disgrace.[45]

Significantly, all of Gibran's early writings were set in Lebanon. This land of mystic beauty became his solace, his source of imagination, and in later years his object of yearning. The places of his childhood and adolescence, the mountains and valleys of northern Lebanon, became for him the epitome of beauty and unity, evoking in him a profound sense of reconciliation far away from the sad cries of humanity. The heroes in his early writings who fearlessly challenge the ecclesiastical and political status quo, although their names and situations vary, in essence unmistakably represent Gibran himself[46] and in *The Broken Wings* the author makes no attempt to conceal his identity. Although Gibran was to revisit Lebanon briefly again as a guide, his departure in 1902 effectively marked the beginning of his life-long exile. On his return to America his struggles were to be of a different kind when disease would cruelly tear at the very heart of his family.

4

Overcoming Tragedy

(1902–1908)

I

Boston had been a relatively healthy city before the 1840s, a city in which life-span was long and disease rare.[1] However, as the century progressed, pollution, poor diet, and overcrowding took their toll. Year after year contagious maladies like cholera returned to haunt the depressed areas of Boston's South End, sweeping through the congested tenements, especially in the hot summer months. More vicious in the long run than the spectacular ills were those that, conceived in squalor, quietly ate away resistance before delivering their final blow. Of these, tuberculosis in particular ravaged the lives of the young and the weak.

Preventive measures – fresh air, wholesome foods, and the avoidance of contaminated sputum – were impossible for the poor of the South End. The streets at dawn would find despairing mothers walking with babies, trying to stir a cooling breeze to fan their young brows. The rooftops at dusk would find young and old alike huddled together, struggling to inhale the cool evening air in vain efforts to ease bloody coughs and burning fevers. With the first hot nights of summer police reports would record the deaths of men, women, and children who had rolled off the roofs while asleep. In the stifling July nights when the crowded rooms were like fiery furnaces – their very walls giving out absorbed heat – people would lie in restless, sweltering rows panting for air and sleep, every crowded fire-escape becoming a bedroom infinitely preferable to any a house could afford.

The Gibrans moved from tenement to tenement within the Syrian quarter, almost as if they were consciously trying to distance themselves from the lethal diseases that stalked their neighborhood. There was, however, no escape.

Sultanah, who resembled Kahlil in physique and manner, and who possessed a beautiful singing voice like her mother, had been seriously ill since she was twelve years old. Glandular swellings had appeared on both sides of her neck and the doctors could do very little, fearing that the sick child would not survive a major operation. Sultanah grew steadily weaker and was bedridden when consumption of the bowel set in. Two months before she died she showed her swollen legs and feet to her younger sister Marianna, crying, "Now I can never get up at all."[2] The whole family nursed and cared for her, but the illness defeated them, and on April 4, 1902, Sultanah, aged fourteen, died.

On the death certificate the official cause of death was recorded as "chronic diarrhoea and interstitial nephritis," a disease of the urinary system. Kahlil was not present during the harrowing days of Sultanah's death. It is unclear whether he was still studying in Beirut, or whether he was away traveling.[3] What little evidence that does exist points to him returning from Lebanon to the United States by way of Paris, where he read in an Arab paper of Sultanah's death.[4] It *is* clear, however, that he returned to the family two weeks after she died.

Boutros, who had worked long hours struggling to make a success of the family store, was particularly shattered by the death of his sister, and fell into a deep depression, neither eating nor sleeping.[5] Although suffering from consumption, his responsibilities as the "head" of the family drove him to continue working. But the death of Sultanah was too cruel a blow for him to bear. His health deteriorated and his body, once robust and strong, quickly weakened with incessant coughing and debilitating fevers. Although driven to exhaustion he was careful about guarding the family from contagion.[6] In the autumn of 1902 the doctor told him to return to Lebanon, to the healing power of the sun, away from the polluted atmosphere of the South End. He decided to go to Cuba instead where he had friends in business, and he left on December 13. Although his health continued to deteriorate his letters home concealed the fact that he was beginning to lose more and more weight.[7]

The years of struggle and hardship had taken their toll on Kamileh too. Her resilience had been worn down and her body weakened by the years of carrying heavy bundles and packs. The death of Sultanah had been a dreadful blow, and concerns about the deteriorating health of her oldest son affected her own. Two days after Boutros left for Cuba, she was admitted to hospital where she was diagnosed as having a tumor. After six weeks the doctors operated, but held out no hope. Kahlil and Marianna "cried together and consoled each other" the night they realized that their mother was going to die.[8]

Before this trial, fate had destined that the beleaguered family would have to endure yet another death-watch. When Boutros returned home he was so wasted by disease that Marianna did not recognize him when he rang the doorbell. His trip to Cuba had failed to restore his health. He was by now so weak that Kahlil had to help him up the stairs. Boutros took to his bed, but four weeks later, with Kahlil at his side, he died, aged twenty-five.[9] He was buried at Mount Benedict cemetery in Boston. Kahlil and Marianna's grief was compounded by the agonizing realization that their mother would not be long in following her oldest son "beyond the blue horizon."[10]

With Boutros gone Kahlil had to take full responsibility for the family store while Marianna nursed their mother in the dingy back room. The family must have wondered if they had made a terrible mistake in coming to America. Kamileh lingered until June 28 when she became incessantly restless. When Marianna tried to spoon-feed her some chicken broth, after a week without eating, she couldn't swallow. Marianna called the doctor who gave Kamileh something to ease her pain and she slept. Unaware of the imminence of their mother's death Marianna and Kahlil felt relieved to see her, at last, sleeping peacefully. Kahlil went out, but five minutes before he returned, Kamileh died. When he saw that his beloved mother had died he fainted.

He was later to write of his mother: "Ninety per cent of my character and inclinations were inherited from my mother (not that I can match her sweetness, gentleness and magnanimity)."[11] He described her last days thus: "Her face gave never a sign that she suffered. Her mind was clear; her soul commanded her body, and she lived her real life to the very end. The day before she died she was talking with me about the mysticism of Thomas Aquinas and of St. Thérèse."[12]

The memories of his mother remained indelibly etched on his mind, and in later years his reminiscences expressed not only the influence she had on him, but the profound love and admiration that the mention of her name stirred in his heart:

> I never saw her when to the least being she was less than a sister or to the greatest less than master. She gave me to understand, even when I was three years old, that the tie between us was as between any two other people, a tie of liking each other – and that we were two separate beings brought

together by life and by shame. She was the most wonderful being I have known – I can see her face now, so thin; and yet it grew only more beautiful. The bony structure was so fine – the nose seemed even more fine. Her enormous eyes grew even larger.[13]

After the funeral Gibran, now twenty, was faced with the awesome task of putting the family affairs in order. The store was heavily in debt and he took two of the largest creditors on as partners. Just over a year later the debt had been cleared but Gibran decided that he had had enough of shopkeeping and left the business.[14]

Of the five brave souls who had left their homeland eight years earlier only two remained. During this period the grief and the sense of loss – sharpened and intensified by being cut off from the consoling presence of relatives back home in Lebanon – brought Kahlil and Marianna closer together. Their deep friendship was "of two souls that suffered much together" and in many ways was born out of fear of losing each other. After the successive deaths of their dear ones neither sister nor brother could "trust life any longer," making them fearful of "shadows and dreams and thoughts,"[15] fears not without foundation, for medical science until the turn of the century regarded consumption as a hereditary disease.[16]

Marianna worked hard to provide the necessities of life for her brother and herself, having no other wish but to see her brother happy and healthy and free to pursue his interests. She became the chief breadwinner, and spent her days and evenings sewing for $60 a month, as well as doing the housework and cooking Kahlil his favorite Lebanese dishes.

After disposing of the family business Gibran reluctantly let his sister's work provide for them. Many in the closely knit Lebanese community saw his behavior as an unforgivable violation of their cultural values, and he was despised by many and ridiculed by some.[17] However, an observer later recounted that restraint and courtesy ruled Gibran's behavior toward his fellow countrymen,[18] and, undaunted, he persevered with his art despite the hostility he sometimes faced. Prepared to give up a secure life in commerce in order to pursue his literary and artistic dreams, he was no idle dreamer. His utter devotion to pen and brush was not a sign of deluded ambition but rather revealed an enormous capacity for work and an originality of expression that caught the eye of some outside the ghetto.

One such person drawn to his art was the beautiful young poetess Josephine Preston Peabody. By the age of twenty her verse had already been published in the prestigious *Atlantic Monthly*; later she had published a collection of poems, *The Singing Leaves*, and a full-length play, *Marlowe*. Brilliant, defiantly independent, and possessing an irrepressibly exuberant spirit, the charismatic Josephine left an impression on all who met her.

The fifteen-year-old Kahlil had been briefly introduced to the twenty-four-year-old poet at Fred Holland Day's photographic exhibition at the Boston Camera Club in 1898. Memories of her physical radiance and winsome beauty remained with him and he felt moved to make a sketch of this remarkable young woman with the shock of brown hair and bright brown eyes. Two weeks after Gibran had returned to his studies in Lebanon, Day gave the drawing to a surprised, yet delighted, Josephine. A few months later he showed her some of Gibran's drawings and told her something of his life. Intrigued by his background and clearly impressed by the boy's unique talent, Josephine decided that she would write to Gibran in Beirut and in her letter told him that she felt his art "pointed out the beautiful inwardness of things."[19]

When Gibran returned from his travels some three years later, no doubt preoccupied with the family tragedy unfolding before his eyes, he waited six months before he made contact with Josephine. By this time she was holding a regular Sunday salon which attracted many of the leading thinkers and artists of contemporary Boston. The nineteen-year-old youth from Lebanon was not in the slightest intimidated or overawed by the eminent group who orbited around the effervescent nature and incandescent beauty of Josephine Preston Peabody. Self-assured and refreshingly open-minded he quickly endeared himself to the group. Gibran obviously impressed Josephine, for he was invited back a week later. This time he brought a portfolio of his drawings and the couple were able to talk alone.

Josephine felt drawn to the young man with an intensity that surprised her. As well as being convinced that he was "an absolute genius"[20] she was intrigued by his colorful background. She came from a world of gentility and sophistication, whereas Gibran, in contrast, had experienced first hand the ravages of poverty and the slum. She had spent her life in the West, whereas Gibran had already experienced both Western culture as well as the mysterious and magic world of Arabia and the East. Josephine's relationship with the man from Lebanon excited her imagination and provided her with insights into new realms of thought; whereas for Gibran Josephine stimulated within him profound emotions inspired by her beauty and the brilliance of her mind. Their relationship was described by Josephine in mystical terms:

There were other remarks of this young mystic that set me thinking much: What ever-lasting symbols women are! I know so well, now, when these beautiful moments happen, that it is none of it for me. I know so well that I am a symbol for somebody; I am a prism that catches the light a moment. It is the light that gladdens, not the prism. And yet for that moment, the prism, the symbol, the bringer of tidings, the accidental woman, becomes perforce an αγγελος , a messenger of God, an angel truly, wonderfully, most humbly. And if she stops to know it, she knows how and why and for how long, and she must choose between the humbleness of real angelhood or the bitter pride of self-love that is bound to hurt sooner or later.[21]

As she considered herself a muse for Gibran she also found that he inspired her. Around this time she wrote a short poem which she called "His Boyhood" and then changed it to "The Prophet." It was eventually published in her collection *The Singing Man*.[22] According to some observers the seeds of the final title of Gibran's own most illustrious work, *The Prophet* (published twenty-one years later), were probably sown during these days[23] when he was in the company of this gentle and gifted young woman. However this is too simplistic an analysis. The whole concept of prophecy and poetry had lingered in the consciousness of Gibran from his earliest days when he had heard the majestic utterings of the Old Testament prophet-poets, the Psalms, and the Song of Songs; perceptions that were later strengthened when he discovered the poet-prophet *par excellence* William Blake and consolidated when he discovered Friedrich Nietzsche's *Thus Spake Zarathustra*.

II

The gulf between the sophisticated drawing-room atmosphere of Josephine's salon set and the harsh realities of life in Boston's slums was enormous. Although the drawing-room and the dark tenement were only a few blocks apart, they were in reality worlds apart. Gibran, however, bridged this apparently unbridgeable chasm with the drawings he would present to Josephine. She was enchanted by such pieces as *Love and Hunger* and *Consolation*, and began to make preparations for his work to be included in an exhibition at Wellesley College where she lectured on English literature.

Throughout the winter, Gibran never disclosed the awful conditions of his home life where Boutros and Kamileh lay dying. His secrecy, rooted in a deep insecurity, was borne of a fear that he would be rejected if Josephine knew that his household was plagued by disease. Throughout the exceptionally cold winter of 1903 Josephine provided the young artist with a refuge and a sweet means of escape from the unbearable burdens of the ghetto. Even when his mother was admitted to hospital Gibran said nothing. Although unaware of the exact nature of his burden, Josephine began to suspect that all was not well, observing that he often seemed preoccupied and self-absorbed.[24]

During February they became publicly identified, attending concerts together and visiting Josephine's acquaintances. With Gibran only slightly taller than Josephine, the elegant socialite and the handsome young Arab must have looked an interesting couple as they strolled through the Back Bay streets of Boston. Toward the end of the month, however, Gibran could not conceal his tragic secret any longer and told Josephine about the disease that was slowly destroying his family. Josephine wrote to a friend about Gibran's grief, describing him as "Pegasus harnessed to an ash-wagon."[25]

Perhaps in an attempt to ease his anguish, Josephine did Gibran the unique favor of allowing him to peruse her private journal. This gesture, allowing him an insight into her innermost self, gave him some solace and, alongside their intimate times spent alone, distracted him from the agony of his home life. Some in the Lebanese community continued to condemn his behavior openly, believing that his social outings during his family's crisis were unforgivably thoughtless in the extreme. Gibran, however, undaunted as ever by the views of others, was essentially striving for self-preservation. Aside from his natural inclination to seek impressions of a different kind than those afforded by tenement life, he was acutely aware that the contacts he was making in his life over the railroad tracks provided the passport to his artistic survival, and, thus, his only hope for a meaningful existence.

He felt justified in his behavior when, on 21 May, his drawings were included in an exhibition at Wellesley College. It was his official debut as an artist, a debut greeted in the college society's *The Iris* with a warm review: "Mr. Gibran's work shows a wonderful originality in conception and an exquisite delicacy and fineness in execution."[26] Five weeks later Kamileh died, her pain no doubt very slightly eased by the knowledge of her son's small success.

For Josephine, the summer brought difficulties of a lesser kind when her once wealthy family began descending into genteel poverty and had to move home. Two days after Kamileh's death Josephine went to New Hampshire. Preoccupied with family affairs and concerned about the unpredictability of her future she had little time to console Gibran. The intensity of their relationship subsided, and although Josephine and Gibran continued to correspond during their separation, their former intimacy was never to be regained.

When Josephine returned to Cambridge, Gibran continued to visit her. However, Josephine's ardor was cooling fast. He clung stubbornly to the relationship and occasionally escorted her to cultural events such as W. B. Yeats's lecture on Irish poets at Wellesley College. Despite his efforts to regain her favor, Josephine had, for reasons only known to herself, consciously decided that their relationship was destined to end. Both retreated into their respective private worlds and Gibran began writing almost exclusively in his native Arabic tongue.

Around this time he began experiencing a "grippe"-like malaise that would reoccur every year for the rest of his life. Even the slightest cough or cold would become a cause of deep consternation to Marianna and Kahlil. Fred Holland Day, sensing his young friend's need to escape from the suffocating air of the South End, invited him out to his seaside property at Five Islands, Maine. Gibran stayed there for nine days recuperating, spending much of his time walking in the pine forest and sitting by the sea. On returning to Boston, Day, whose faith in his protégé's talents had never waned, invited Gibran to exhibit his paintings in his Harcourt Buildings studio on Irvington Street in Boston.

That winter the young artist worked feverishly, his depression slightly lifted as he focused his attention on the exhibition, which finally opened on April 30, 1904 and ran until May 10. Day's faith in his "Syrian genius"[27] was confirmed when a positive review appeared in the *Boston Evening Transcript*:

> The ponderous beauty and nobility of certain of his pictorial fancies are wonderful . . . All told, his drawings make a profound impression, and, considering his age, the qualities shown in them are extraordinary for originality and depth of symbolic significance. The series of drawings entitled "Towards God" (20), recently executed, is perhaps as remarkable as any of the works in the exhibition. In spite of some crudity in the draughtsmanship, the drawing called "Earth Takes Her Own" (20f), in this series, is fairly majestic in its meaning and expression. It reminds one of William Blake's mystical works.[28]

This publicity caused considerable interest. Two of Gibran's paintings were sold and some people who had seen the exhibition encouraged their friends to view this "remarkable vein of individual invention."[29] One of these visitors came on the recommendation of Lionel Marks, a professor in mechanical engineering at Harvard, who two years later was to marry Josephine. The visitor's name was Mary Elizabeth Haskell, a woman whose relationship with Gibran was to be crucial in his development as both man and poet. Gibran later recalled his first encounter with Mary:

> I was drawn to you in a special way the first time I saw you . . . I knew many people in Boston at that time . . . The others found me interesting. They liked to get me to talking, because I was unusual for them. They liked to watch the monkey. But you really wanted to hear what was in me. You kept making me dig for more.[30]

III

Headmistress at Miss Haskell's School for Girls at 314 Marlborough Street, Boston, Mary Haskell was always searching for fresh stimuli that might enlighten her teenage students. The daughter of a distinguished confederate officer, she had inherited a strong sense of justice and a passionate yearning for reform – ideals she espoused as a teacher. Showing the works of a young *émigré* artist to her pupils reflected her pedagogical inclinations to introduce those under her charge to the outside world. She arranged for Gibran's paintings to be exhibited at her school: "it would be good for the girls to see the work of a man of promise before he won recognition."[31] Although the students, staff, and visitors admired his work, he sold no paintings. Returning to work at Day's studios he was depressed – Josephine finding him "in a low state of mind"[32] – painfully aware that apart from Marianna's meager income as a seamstress, there was no other money coming into the household.

However when Gibran heard that the editor of a New York Arab-*émigré* newspaper was visiting the Syrian community in Boston he quickly made himself known. Ameen Guraieb, editor of *Al-Mohajer (The Emigrant)*, was impressed by the articulate young man's boldness and opportunism. He was particularly interested in the fact that Gibran's drawings had been "admired in the newspapers of Boston, the esteemed city of arts and sciences."[33] Won over by Gibran, Guraieb offered him two dollars a week for a series of Arabic essays. Gibran, quietly ecstatic, gratefully accepted.

Gibran's first published piece in the newspaper appeared under the title of "Vision," in which he describes a caged bird, dead from lack of food and water. As the poet looks closer he sees the cage becoming the dry skeleton of a man, the dead bird a human heart; a poignant expression of the despair he was experiencing at the time:

> I am the human heart, that is imprisoned in the darkness of the multitude's edicts and fettered by illusion until I am arrived at death's point. I am forsaken and abandoned in the corners of civilization and its seduction. The tongue of mankind is bound and its eyes are dry the while they smile.[34]

In November Fred Holland Day suffered a tragic loss. A devastating fire completely gutted his Harcourt studio, with an estimated one thousand paintings, by forty artists, being lost. Interviewed by the *Boston Sunday Globe*, Day described the enormity of the catastrophe: "It was practically the work of twenty-five years. And I have not the slightest conception of the value of the collection."[35] The papers gave the story front-page headlines recording the forty artists who had studios in the burnt out building. Kahlil Gibran's name was not among them. Tragically his whole portfolio like those of the better known artists had been lost, including *Consolation*, a drawing that Josephine Peabody had only so recently called the "picture of the divine heart of youth."[36]

Mary Haskell wrote to Gibran expressing her sorrow at his loss – a letter that initiated a remarkable correspondence between them that would last for twenty-five years.[37] Gibran replied, in possibly the first letter he ever wrote to her:

> My dear Miss Haskell.
> It is the sympathy of friends that makes grief a sweet sorrow. And after all, the perishing of my drawings – the years of Love's labor – the flower of my youth – must be for a beautiful reason unknown to us. Few days ago I thought of seeing you but I had not the strength, but I shall try to come sometime soon. I do not know what to do with my coloured pencils at present; perhaps they will be kept in the chest of forgetfulness. But I am writing. Your sweet letter is indeed a consolation. Your friend, Kahlil.[38]

Gibran's letter left a considerable impression on Mary and from the outset of their acquaintance she found herself intrigued and enchanted by the young man. After the fire, Gibran began painting and writing with renewed resolution. Perhaps in recognition of his indebtedness to Fred Holland Day he wrote "Letters of Fire", beginning his soliloquy with the lines inscribed on Keats' grave in Rome: "Here lies one whose name was writ in water."

In the prose-poem the melancholic pessimism that had gripped Gibran during the nightmare years becomes painfully apparent:

Shall death destroy that which we build
And the wind scatter our words,
And darkness hide our deeds?
Is this then life?...
Shall all that is joy in our hearts
And all that saddens our spirit
Vanish ere we know their fruits?[39]

However, characteristically the poet rises above his negative emotions:

If that sweet singer Keats had known that his songs would never cease to plant the love of beauty in men's hearts, surely he had said:
"Write upon my gravestone: Here lies the remains of him who wrote his name on Heaven's face in letters of fire."[40]

Gibran's Romanticism, his simple Arabic style capturing as it did the rhythm of everyday speech familiar to him from childhood, appealed to the immigrants for whom he was writing. His passionate belief in the inherent potential of all that exists began to inspire a whole generation of fellow immigrants. In a profound sense, immigrants are the personification of the Romantic vision, a vision which posits the interconnectivity of all people; for the immigrant is a living link between his native land and language and his adopted culture. Immigrants of all generations, and from all corners of the globe, found much in Romantic philosophy that was relevant to their own new experiences. Indeed, to succeed in an alien environment, optimism and faith in the highest ideals are prerequisites for harmonious survival. Romantic dedication to the unity and oneness of people, its universalistic and cross-cultural ethos, and its implicit rejection of the nativist strain of nationalism reflected the hopes and aspirations of the immigrant soul.

A central feature of the Romantic philosophy was a transcendent view of life, whereby reality is understood only by transcending the world of the senses. The American Transcendentalists, with whom Gibran was familiar, unceasingly emphasized the spiritual foundation of all existence. These views were supported by organicism which defined reality as a living state in which all elements are intrinsically interrelated, a view that was later to be supported by modern physics. The hallmark of organicism and its Romantic adherents, then, was a belief in the unity of existence and the oneness of being. For Gibran, the ideas of writers such as Emerson must have reminded him of the Sufi tradition, with its theme of *tawhid*, the doctrine of divine unity, which flowered in his native Arabia. Sufis too over many centuries had expressed their insights through literature, developing an exquisitely beautiful style of symbolic poetry which "can speak without hindrance not only to learned believers, but also to the simple man of the people; the craftsman and the Bedouin."[41]

By the spring of 1905 Gibran's articles had become popular with his immigrant readers, learned and unlearned alike, his articles first appearing on April 1, 1905 in a column entitled "Reflections." Many of his prose-poems – conveying as they did the joy of physical and spiritual union – contained references to a muse:

> And when my mind had fled from the prison of matter to the realm of imagining, I turned my head and beheld, standing by my side, a maiden. It was a nymph of paradise. On her was neither garment nor adornment save a branch of the vine that concealed part of her, and a crown of poppies that bound her hair of gold. And when she perceived my glances of surprise and wonderment, she said: "I am a daughter of the forests. Fear me not."[42]

Gibran's muse, whom four years previously had been Josephine, was probably still the mainspring of his inspiration in these early works. Although his relationship with Josephine was by now entering its final phase, the poet was never to forget her companionship during his most heart-breaking years. On her thirty-first birthday he presented her with a parable he had written, beautifully illuminated with Arabic calligraphy, dedicating it to her. Josephine adored the exquisite gift but was adamant in her decision not to pursue a relationship with Gibran.

In the summer of 1905 a pamphlet by Gibran, *al-Musiqah* (*Music*), was published by *al-Mohajer*. The piece, regarded by many as his first Arabic book, was a lyrical eulogy of the art of music, and was probably inspired by his visits to the Boston symphony orchestra, to which he had been introduced by Fred Holland Day. Shortly after publication Gibran brought a copy to Josephine and read her the opening lines:

> I sat by one whom my heart loves, and I listened to her words. My soul began to wander in the infinite spaces where the universe appeared like a

dream, and the body like a narrow prison. The enchanting voice of my Beloved entered my heart.
This is Music, oh friends, for I heard her through the sighs of the one I loved, and through the words, half-uttered between her lips.
With the eyes of my hearing I saw my Beloved's heart.[43]

Al-Musiqah, as a work of art, betrayed all the characteristics of neophyte apprenticeship. There was no lack of passion, but the fire of his imagination was dampened by an ornate style, a languid tone, and uncertain rhythm. This was Gibran's first book after all, but once he was out of the "twilight" staring into the full blaze of "noon," his style became more robust and his poetic expression gained a masculine quality which was all his own.

IV

His relationship with Josephine ending, and Fred Holland Day becoming increasingly reclusive after the fire, Gibran began to spend more time among his compatriots on account of his rising popularity as a writer. For the previous three years he and Marianna had moved between various apartments in the South End, but at last they were settled. Marianna, now twenty-one, kept the tiny apartment immaculate, no doubt associating dirt and dust with disease. She also had become an excellent cook, yet still remained the chief breadwinner. Although loyal and selfless, she also manifested a rigid stubbornness, especially when it came to learning how to read and write. Despite her brother's coaxing she preferred to spend the evenings cooking, sewing, and listening to Kahlil recount his day's experiences.

Gibran's contacts with the Arab literati were increasing and among those he met was Saleem Sarkis who worked on the emigrant newspaper *Mira't al-Gharb* (*Mirror of the West*). His acquaintance with Sarkis led Gibran into a liaison with a twenty-six year-old woman called Gertrude Barrie in 1906. The petite Irish Protestant pianist and the diminutive Christian Arab poet immediately felt a strong attraction to each other and soon became lovers. Gertrude, a graduate from the New England Conservatory and one-time concert pianist, lived at 552 Tremont Street opposite the National Theater and only five minutes walk from Gibran's neighborhood. Although their relationship lasted for nearly two years, by 1908 the intensity of their "moon-struck love" had waned. However they continued to remain friends and very occasionally corresponded with each other right up to 1922 when Gertrude married the Italian violinist Hector Bazzinello.[44]

Given the stability of life in Boston, Gibran began to focus all his attentions on his writing. His column in *al-Mohajer*, called "Tears and Laughter," was becoming increasingly popular among its readership and also the Arabic literati in America.[45] Evident in these early writings is the poet's belief that nature is a living being. In personifying nature, Gibran was not merely making use of a convenient literary device but was actually expressing the way he perceived her.[46] In expressing his ideas of a living world Gibran sometimes uses the imagery of erotic and maternal love, conceiving nature as a teacher who preaches "the gospel of the Spirit:"

At the hour of dawn, before the sun's rising from beyond the horizon, I sat in the middle of a field communing with Nature. At that hour filled with purity and beauty I lay on the grass, what time men were yet wrapped in slumber, disturbed now by dreams, now by awakening. I lay there seeking to know from all that I looked upon the truth of Beauty and the beauty of Truth. And when my reflecting had set me apart from the flesh, and my imaginings lifted the covering of matter from off my inner self, I felt my spirit growing, drawing me near to Nature and revealing to me her hidden things and teaching me the language of her wonders."[47]

For Gibran the immigrant living in an urban jungle, nature had become the realm of freedom, a holy sanctuary in stark contrast to the social oppression he saw in the "City": "I beheld the city squatting like a daughter of the streets holding to the hem of Man's garment. And the beautiful wild parts I saw standing from afar and weeping for his sake."[48] During this period, the poet was also increasingly growing aware of the destructive attitudes toward the environment that he witnessed in the cities of eastern America, comparing it with the harmony he had experienced in his homeland, Lebanon. He began to express a vision of the world as a manifestation of the divine, deploring – as Emerson and Thoreau had done before – the rapacious way that modern man treated the natural world:

Thus I was as the breeze passed through the branches of the tree, sighing plaintively like an orphan child. I sought understanding and said: "Why do you sigh, gentle breeze?" And it answered: "Because I am going to the city away from the sun's warmth. To the city, where the germs of sickness and disease will cling to the hem of my clean garment, and the poisoned breath of flesh breathe on me. Because of this do you behold my sadness."[49]

Writing, as he did, when Darwinism was at its height, Gibran's work may, in many ways, be seen as offering a positive counterpoise to Darwinian science and scientific materialism. His depiction of nature represented a new direction in Arabic literature.[50] In classical Arabic poetry, influenced by the desert way of life, nature was a force to be reckoned with, but when the Arabs moved to the more fertile regions of the north and across North Africa to Spain, nature was treated as an ornament. Gibran however, saw nature as invested with a divine energy, and in his Arabic prose poem "A Glimpse into the Future" he writes:

> I saw that Man was knowing of his place as the cornerstone of creation, lifted above smallness and raised above little things; tearing the veil of deception from off the eyes of the Spirit that it might read what the clouds had writ on Heaven's face, and the breeze on the surface of the water; and know the manner of the flower's breathing and the meaning of the songs of the thrush and the nightingale.[51]

As well as his ecological vision Gibran explored another theme close to his heart: the oneness of humankind. To his countrymen, still haunted by their recent history of bloody sectarianism, such sentiments as "You are my brother and we are the children of one universal holy spirit"[52] made a profound impression. Unconcerned about those who saw his writings as being naive or sentimental, Gibran felt compelled to speak out for unity and the essential oneness of religion.[53] Sometimes sectarian violence would spill out onto the streets of the South End, with ancient feuds between Maronite Christians and Orthodox Christians being reenacted. In an effort to ease this explosive situation the editors of *al-Mohajer* ran a front-page drawing by Gibran, depicting an angel extending both hands to the conflicting factions.[54]

As well as espousing unity, Gibran was fearless in his condemnation of the tyranny of church and state. His fresh and passionate stories held an immediate appeal to his readers. The familiar settings, the working-class heroes, the strident anticlerical tones, were a breath of fresh air, in sharp contrast to the formalistic Arabic writings of the day. Three stories written during this period, "Martha," "Yuhanna the Mad," and the "Dust of the Ages and the Eternal Fire," were later published together under the title *'Ara'is al-Muruj (Nymphs of the Valley)*.

The story "Martha" deals with the oppression of women in the Middle East, and the contrast between nature and the city, or more precisely between the village and the city. Consistent with his earlier views was a Wordsworthian belief that an awakened humanity would realize that nature is a teacher: "Shall there come a day when man's teacher is nature, and humanity is his book and life his school? Will that day be?"[55]

Martha, an orphan, is brought up in a small isolated village amidst the beautiful valleys of Lebanon. Despite a desperate life of fearful exploitation at the hands of her guardians she finds harmony, joy, and freedom in the natural world. When she reaches adolescence Martha is raped by a stranger, a horseman, who takes her to the city and makes her his mistress. When she becomes pregnant, however, the man throws Martha out of his home. Driven by abject poverty and the need to feed her newborn son, Fouad, she turns to a life of prostitution on the seedy back streets of Beirut. The brutal and humiliating life takes its toll, and after a few years she succumbs to disease. Gibran, the narrator, comes across Martha after seeing Fouad, now only five years old, begging on the streets. As she lies dying in a gloomy room he says:

> You are oppressed, Martha, and he who has oppressed you is a child of the palaces, great of wealth and little of soul. You are persecuted and despised, but it were better that a person should be the oppressed than that he should be the oppressor; and fitter that he should be a victim to the frailty of human instincts than that he should be powerful and crush the flowers of life and disfigure the beauties of feeling with his desire . . . Ay, Martha, you are a flower crushed beneath the feet of the animal that is concealed in a human being. Heavy-shod feet have trodden you down, but they have not destroyed that fragrance which goes up with the widow's lament and the orphan's cry and the poor man's sigh towards Heaven, the fount of justice and mercy. Take comfort, Martha, in that you are the flower crushed and not the foot that has crushed it.[56]

Martha dies, but the priests prevent her body being buried in consecrated ground, and Gibran and Fouad are left to bury her in a deserted field far away from the town.

In "Yuhanna the Mad" Gibran continues to attack the corruption, exploitation, and hypocrisy of the Middle East. While reading his Bible, Yuhanna, a poor herdsman, allows his oxen to stray into a wealthy pasture owned by the monastery. The monks refuse to return the herd to Yuhanna unless he pays. Yuhanna is furious: "From his pocket he drew out his Bible as the warrior draws his sword to defend himself, and cried: 'Thus do you make a mockery of the teachings of this Book, O hypocrites, and use that which is most sacred in life to spread the evils therein.'"⁵⁷ The monks throw him in prison, releasing him only when, unbeknownst to Yuhanna, his elderly mother hands over her precious locket to the head priest. At Easter time Yuhanna stands in a crowd with his fellow poverty-stricken villagers watching the rich and gluttonous priests celebrating the construction of an elaborate church. When the pomp and pageantry has ended, Yuhanna speaks out on behalf of the oppressed:

> These people, O Jesus, have raised temples and tabernacles to the glory of Thy name and adorned them with woven silk and molten gold. They have left naked the bodies of Thy chosen poor in the cold streets; yet do they fill the air with the smoke of incense and candles.⁵⁸

His passionate tirade continues amidst increasing murmurs of approval from the crowd, and the priests have him arrested a second time. The governor, condemning Yuhanna's sermons as the words of one deranged, but aware of the growing support he is gaining, finally pardons the young man, who lives out his days as a madman – a figure Gibran increasingly used in his writings – beleaguered by the jeering people of his village.

Such stories represent the poet's early condemnation of the powerful and their avaricious exploitation of the poor, of women and children. His stories were to have a profound effect on the Arabic world – their themes and style hitherto untouched in Arabic literature.

The other story in the trilogy, "Dust of the Ages and the Eternal Fire," deals with the themes of reincarnation and preordained love. The hero appears first as Nathan, the son of a Phoenician priest in Baalbek, and then in his new incarnation as Ali al-Husaini,⁵⁹ a Bedouin nomad. Nathan is promised by his lover, who is dying, that they will meet again in nineteen centuries. This remarkable vow is fulfilled when, amongst the ruins of the ancient city temple of Baalbek, the shepherd Ali experiences a vision which awakens him to the cause of his "spiritual hunger," a hunger that has haunted him all of his young life. He begins to remember his past life. Consumed by memories of the distant past he returns to his sheep when suddenly he sees a beautiful maiden drawing water from the stream. Their eyes meet and they begin to experience "vague remembrances" of their past lives.⁶⁰ The lovers "commune," and awaken to the realization that they have been reborn – and the reader glimpses the joy of eternal youth.

In "Dust of the Ages and the Eternal Fire," love is the immortal fire. In his early works Gibran often refers to reincarnation and many years after this piece was written told Mary Haskell: "I feel sure we have lived before. In myself I have experiences that indicate previous lives to me."[61] Gibran also wrote a story, seven years later, entitled "The Poet from Baalbek," dealing with the theme of reincarnation. In it, the emir of Baalbek in the year 112 B.C.E. is visited by an Indian sage who "preaches the doctrine of the transmigration of souls and the incarnation of spirits which move from one generation to another seeking more and more perfect avatars until they become god-like." The wise old man explains to the emir "how the spirits pass from one body to another, elevated by the good acts of the medium which they choose, and influenced by their experience in each existence." The emir asks if his spirit will be reincarnated, to which the sage answers: "'*Whatever the soul longs for, will be attained by the spirit.*' Remember, oh great Prince, that the sacred Law which restores the sublimity of Spring after the passing of Winter will reinstate you as a prince." The emir is reborn 1,800 years later as a prince, who remembers "images of forgotten days."[62]

Gibran's references to reincarnation in these early works portray a romantic view of rebirth – the stories concealing the precise nature of his own views.[63] He seems in his early writings to suggest that the soul, in essence a part of the Unity of Being, *will* return again because of the bonds of eternal love. Gibran felt that this life was not his first and years later spoke to Mary Haskell of his being an incarnation of "a being and a work," but failed to elucidate exactly what he meant.[64]

The influences on Gibran's belief in reincarnation would have come from a wide variety of sources. Perhaps most immediate to him as a young man in Beirut were the beliefs of the Druze, who believed that the souls of the righteous immediately pass at death into progressively more perfect embodiments, until they reach reabsorption into the Godhead. No less influential for Gibran were the views of the Sufi poets; in particular Jalal al-Din Rumi, honored among many as the greatest mystical poet in history,[65] who wrote in his masterwork, *Mathnawi-i-Ma'nawi* (*Spiritual Couplets*): "I am but one soul but I have a hundred thousand bodies . . . Two thousand men have I seen who were I; but none as good as I am now."[66]

Sects of Christian gnostics, many of whom, contrary to the orthodox viewpoint, taught the doctrine of reincarnation, spread from Lebanon through Asia Minor into Europe where their esoteric teachings had a profound influence on Western thought and on Gibran. In the nineteenth century, Transcendentalism, which influenced him too, fired by oriental thought had a reincarnationist streak running through it – scarcely an American writer of note being untouched – Emerson inspired by the *Bhagavadgita*, and Thoreau asserting that he had lived in Judea at the time of Christ.[67]

V

Mary Haskell, in the summer of 1906, experienced her own spiritual awakening. After a lapse of "several prayerless years"[68] she was suddenly overwhelmed by the need for "religious devotion."[69] She had recently lost a close friend, Sarah Armstrong, a retired school principal, a woman who had almost been a spiritual guide to her, a bereavement that deeply affected Mary, leaving her in a state of depression.

Slowly she nurtured new friendships: Charlotte Teller, a freelance journalist and active suffragette whose first novel *The Cage*[70] had documented the explosive labor situation in America – a brilliant mind who later became a Jungian analyst; Emilie Michel (known as Micheline), a beautiful, intelligent, and popular young French teacher who worked at Mary Haskell's school; and Kahlil Gibran.

Gibran, aware that he needed artistic guidance, was now attending life classes in the winter of 1908 at Mary Haskell's school. His first model, Micheline, nursed ambitions to be an actress. The artist and the model felt a strong attraction and fell in love. However, they both realized that ultimately, because of their respective ambitions, any affair could not last. Despite this awareness their relationship was a passionate and a caring one, inspiring Gibran to write a piece called "The Beloved," in which he describes "The First Kiss":

> A soft touch like the finger-tips of the breeze in their passing over the rose, bearing a sigh of gladness and a sweet moaning.
> The beginning of disturbance and trembling that separate lovers from the world of matter and transport them to the regions of inspiration and dreams.
> And if the first glance is as the seed that the goddess of love sows in the field of the human heart, the first kiss is as the first blossom on the first branch of the Tree of Life.[71]

Gibran was drawn to the mademoiselle whose beauty he likened to radium – "burning without being burned."[72] Conscious of her beauty and assured that she was a transparently instinctual actress, "Micheline" was sure a glittering stage career lay before her. Her greatest passion thus, as yet, was unconsummated, and her new love affair in Boston did not mitigate her restless desire for the fame of Broadway.

Mary Haskell's own relationship with Gibran was just what was needed at this juncture of her life. At thirty-four she yearned for fresh acquaintances and new interests after years of selfless dedication to her school. Quickly realizing that Gibran was by far the most talented of her protégés she began to record every aspect of his life in her journal:

> There is a rapt, spiritual quality about him when he is released in mind – the gentleness of a child, the nobility of a prince, the order of flame, a limpid gravity. These things are apparent whenever he is happily at work and conscious that love is about him, but the bared neck and throat brought out all the warmth and glow of them. His eyes have the longest, silkiest lashes I have ever seen – and a sudden scoop in the lower lid when opened which he has not yet got into any of his pictures of himself. They are truly like stars reflected in deep water – so radiantly soft in quality. His face changes like the shadows of leaves with every thought or feeling. I have seen it redden, contract, grow drawn and unfold like a broad beam of light, all within a few moments. It is a study in living beauty.[73]

Aware of Gibran's hunger for guidance and technical training in the fine arts, Mary, by now captivated by Gibran, offered to send him to Paris to study art. He was ecstatic at the offer and wrote exuberantly to his editor Ameen Guraieb about his unexpected and thrilling news:

> The twelve months which I am going to spend in Paris will play an important part in my everyday life, for the time which I will spend in the City of Light will be, with the help of God, the beginning of a new chapter in the story of my life . . . after my return from Paris to the United States, my drawings will gain more prestige, which makes the blind-rich buy more of them, not because of their artistic beauty, but because of their being painted by an artist who has spent a full year in Paris among the great European painters . . .

He told Guraieb that it was "the presence of a she-angel" that brought him such opportunities and assured his editor that the "capital of capitals" would help in the development of his writings as well as his art.[74]

A few weeks before his long voyage to Paris Gibran brought his poem "The Beauty of Death" to Mary; her translation of it marked the beginning of a collaboration that would be of increasing significance over the years. The poem, published in *al-Mohajer* and dedicated to "MEH,"[75] poignantly reveals Gibran's struggles to find some hope in a life scarred by tragedy; yet in almost psalmist style announces the poet's renewed sense of optimism:

> Dry then your tears, my friends,
> Raise aloft your heads
> As flowers lift up their crowns at dawn's breaking,
> And behold Death's bride standing as a pillar of light
> Between my bed and the void.
> Still your breath awhile and hearken with me
> To the fluttering of her wings.[76]

The tragic chapter of his youth ending, on July 1, 1908 Gibran sailed to Paris, "the City of Light," to begin anew.

5

The City of Light

(1908–1910)

I

Paris, "the City of Light," the "capital of the nineteenth century,"[1] "le pivot de la France,"[2] "l'axe du monde,"[3] the city "sans égal dans l'univers,"[4] enraptured Gibran – the unique light cascading onto the sacred architecture of the Sacré Coeur and Notre Dame – a feast for the senses of one who had spent such heartbreaking years in the dark streets of Boston.

By the time of Gibran's arrival in 1908 Parisians were proudly basking in their recently acquired electrical power which was shedding light in abundance on their boulevards, theaters, and cafes. Only eight years previously the 1900 World Fair had as its centerpiece "the Palace of Electricity," which, radiantly clothed in the light from incandescent bulbs, had inspired its promoter to write: "The fairy goddess of electricity, the modern counterpart of Apollo Phoebus, has become an almighty sovereign, endowed, thanks to the genius of man, with infinite powers."[5]

This "City of Light" had attracted, too, unique artistic genius in a group of painters who, meeting at the Académie Suisse, near the Pont Saint-Michel, were to revolutionize the history of art.[6] Inspired by Edouard Manet, these young artists experimented with the interplay of light and shadow in their paintings, their aim to paint light by the contrasted use of pure, instead of mixed, colors. They believed that the artist has to become conscious of and reproduce his or her own impressions resulting from light, for through these impressions each person lives and is acquainted with reality. By capturing the changing effects of light and exploring these effects on color and form, they were able to capture the light that danced around their objects. Light, they contended, was "the principal person in a picture,"[7] thus instigating a revolution in the rendering of vivid colors which some of the more sympathetic observers compared with the revolution in the representation of form brought about by the Greeks.[8]

In later years the term "school of Paris" was applied to those movements in modern painting that followed the impressionists, indicating the intense concentration of artistic activity, supported by critics, connoisseurs, and dealers, which made Paris the world center of advanced aestheticism during the first decades of the twentieth century[9] – an environment that intoxicated Gibran. Over the years the city produced and attracted some of the world's greatest artists, their names a roll-call of honor: Bonnard, Carrière, Degas, Delacroix, Delaunay, Gaugin, Klee, Matisse, Millet, Much, Picasso, Rousseau, Seurat, Toulouse-Lautrec, Van Gogh, Whistler, and Auguste Rodin, whom Gibran was later to meet.

The extraordinary interest taken by men and women of all classes in the visual arts gave the Lebanese painter a profound awareness of the wider public; the novelist Emile Zola writing of the excitement that greeted an exhibition:

> The Champs-Elysées, cheerful in the bright morning sunlight, are full of a long stream of people on foot walking smartly along. At the entrance doors of the Palais de l'Industrie two turnstiles click incessantly, sounding like the sails of a windmill in a furious gale. You walk up a monumental stairway and into the galleries already full of visitors, and you blink, to start with, blinded at the sight of several hundred pictures jumbling together all the colours of the rainbow . . . There are 25 galleries here: several kilometres of painting to be examined, in other words, if the pictures were put end to end. A labour of Hercules! For seven or eight hours you are obliged to struggle in a crowd which is growing all the time, and to elbow your way painfully to reach the pictures, stretching your neck, suffocated by the dust, the heat, and the lack of air . . . And yet, in spite of everything, in spite of the back-breaking fatigue, the opening day of the exhibition is a great attraction. It represents the pleasure of novelty, something people are prepared to pay dearly for in Paris.[10]

The Parisians' instinctive love of art made Gibran aware of the awesome responsibility of the artist, humbling him when he saw the exceptional quality of those around him. This intense climate created a mood of liberation and a conscious acceptance and glorification of existence – echoed in the words of a young poet called Henri Alain-Fournier: "I can involve myself with everything surrounding me, ecstatic, silent, accepting everything that exists with the word: 'behold.'"[11]

After disembarking from the S.S. Rotterdam, Gibran was fortunate in meeting up again with Micheline, who had recently returned to France to visit relatives. She was able to show him around Paris and help him find temporary accommodation in a fifth-floor room on the avenue Carnot. Full of *joie de vivre* the lovers devoured the sights of Paris before Micheline left to visit relatives in Nevers. The couple, though still in love, knew in their hearts that their respective burning ambitions made a long-term relationship unlikely; and their inevitable parting in Paris marked the end of their love affair. Despite Micheline's departure Gibran, enthralled by Paris, wrote to Mary: "This is Paris, my dear Mary: This is the heart of the world. This is the world of arts. Oh what a joy to breathe this air and drink this light . . . Never have I been so thirsty for work – work – work."[12] He found a small studio in Montparnasse at 14 avenue du Maine, enrolled at the Académie Julien on the rue du Cherche-Midi, and excitedly anticipated

> the Palace of the Louvre [to] look upon the paintings of Raphael, Michelangelo, and Da Vinci . . . the Opera [to] hear songs and hymns revealed by the deity to Beethoven, Wagner, Mozart, and Rossini . . . These names, whose pronunciation is rather difficult to an Arab-speaking person, are names of great men who founded the civilization of Europe; these are the names of men whom the earth has swallowed, but whose deeds it could not fold or engulf.[13]

II

Gibran had not been long in Paris when a collection of four narratives that had appeared originally in *al-Mohajer* were published in book form. *Al-'Arwah al Mutamarridah* (*Spirits Rebellious*), like his earlier work *'Ara'is al-Muruj* (*Nymphs of the Valley*), took as its central theme the oppressive social conditions in Lebanon. However, it dealt with this theme in still more outspoken and defiant tones, and unlike *Nymphs of the Valley*, which so graphically highlighted the iniquitous abuses of power, attempted to offer positive alternatives.

The story entitled "Khalil the Heretic" portrays the saintly hero in a similar vein to Yuhanna the madman, except that whereas Yuhanna was crushed by corrupted power, Khalil is strong enough to resist it. As an orphan of seven, Khalil, the protagonist of the piece, enters the wealthiest monastery in northern Lebanon, where he works as a cowherd before becoming a monk. After long meditations in the fields, he becomes conscious that the other monks are violating the teachings of Christ, and he feels an overwhelming compulsion to speak out. The monks, outraged by

Khalil's audacity, have him flogged with rope ends and imprisoned in a dark, insect-infested cell. On his release, his spirit unbroken, Khalil preaches again to the monks, and is again beaten before being thrown out of the monastery.[14] In a state of near collapse, Khalil is saved by a widow, Rahel, and her daughter Maryam. Sheikh Abbas, the governor and prince of the village, on hearing that "a heretic" is living with two women in the village, and afraid that the man's revolutionary utterings might turn the sheikh's serfs against him, has them all arrested. At the trial Khalil defiantly defends himself against the false charges and vehemently attacks his detractors – a sermon that was to make Gibran many enemies among the ruling classes of Lebanon:

> He is a betrayer to whom the followers of Christ gave a holy Book that he made a net to catch that which belongs to them; a hypocrite whom the faithful girded with a fine crucifix, which he held aloft above their heads as a sharp sword; an oppressor to whom the weak delivered up their necks, which he bound with a halter and held with an iron hand and gave not up till they were broken like earthen pots and scattered as dust. He is a ravening wolf who enters the enclosure, and the shepherd thinks him a sheep and sleeps in peace. And when darkness descends, he falls upon the flock one by one. He is a glutton who reveres the well-laden table more than the altar; and a covetous one who pursues a farthing piece even to the caves of the jinn. He sucks the blood of his congregants as the desert sands suck up drops of rain. He is avaricious and watches after his own needs and stores up wealth. He is a trickster who enters through the cracks in the wall and goes out only when the house falls. A thief hard of heart who steals the widow's mite and the orphan's piece. He is a creature strange in his creation, with a vulture's beak and a panther's claws and a hyena's fangs and a viper's touch.[15]

Inspired, and with growing authority, Khalil implores his listeners to remember the message of the gospels. Sensing the crowd's increasing restlessness and their growing respect for the young man, Sheikh Abbas goes to kill Khalil with a sword. A sturdy villager blocks his way with the words: "Sheath your sword, master, for he that draws the sword shall by the sword perish."[16]

The crowd turns against the sheikh and demands that Khalil be appointed as the new master of the village. The hero, however, asks that he be accepted just as a fellow villager, "for if I be not like one of you I shall be naught save as one that preaches virtue but practices evil."[17] The story ends with Khalil and Maryam living happily amidst the florabundant beauty of their village, which sits " . . . like a bride on the side of the valley."[18]

Using "Khalil the Heretic" as his mouthpiece, Gibran's own views on spirituality become apparent in *Spirits Rebellious*: "True light is that which radiates *from within* a man."[19] Taking the New Testament teaching that it is the inner person who must be transformed, Gibran teaches that compassion is the guiding light of a person's actions: "A word of comfort in the ears of the feeble and the criminal and the harlot is worthier than prayers recited in the temple."[20]

For Gibran true religion was joyous and liberating: "teachings that free you and me from bondage and place us unfettered upon the earth, the stepping place of the feet of God";[21] a God who has given men and women "spirit wings to soar aloft into the realms of love and freedom"[22] – a religion of justice, which "makes us all brothers equal before the sun."[23]

Gibran's views on liberty and the essential components of democracy also became apparent in these stories. In "The Cry of the Graves," the second story in *Spirits Rebellious*, he deals with the iniquities of a corrupt and exploitative judicial system.

The tyrannical emir of "The Cry of the Graves," sitting in judgment on the poor, metes out his cruel justice. The accused, described as "criminals" by the emir even before they have been tried, appear one by one. The first is a young man who, charged with killing a commander in the emir's army, is condemned to be beheaded. The second, a young woman accused of adultery, is condemned to be stoned to death, the ancient penalty of Mosaic law. The third is an old man, who is condemned to be hanged for stealing a sacred vessel from the monastery.

However, the reader soon discovers that these "crimes" are not what they might at first appear. The young man killed the commander while defending his fiancée from an attempted rape; the young woman had merely been talking to a lover; and the old man had been driven to stealing by the monks who had employed him while he was fit and strong, yet rejected him when he was old and sick. The three innocents are then cruelly put to death. The youth is beheaded; the young woman, dragged naked outside the city, is stoned to death; and the old man is hung from a tree. Their broken bodies, forbidden by the ecclesiastical overlords to be buried, are left in the wilderness, "so that the vultures and prowling beasts may pick [them] clean and the winds carry the stench of [their] rottenness to the nostrils of [their] kith and kin."[24]

The author, who participates in the action as an observer and commentator, asks:

> Shall we meet evil with greater evil and say: this is the law; and fight corruption with more corruption and proclaim it moral? Shall we overcome a crime with one greater and call it justice? . . . And the law – what is law? Who has seen it descend with the sunlight from the heavens? What human being has seen the heart of God and known His will in mankind? In what age have angels walked among men, saying: "Deny to the weak the light of existence and destroy the fallen with the edge of the sword and trample upon the sinner with feet of iron?"[25]

The other two narratives in *Spirits Rebellious*, "Warde al-Hani" and "The Bridal Couch," deal with the rights of women in the Middle East and the strictures of a bigoted, oppressive, and patriarchal system. "Warde al-Hani" examines the tragedy of a forced marriage. Although Warde al-Hani's husband, Rashid bey Nu'man, is a good and kind man, he is unable to ignite her passion "with the living flame of love."[26] Warde, who is in love with another man, grows weary of sharing her bed with a husband she does not love.[27] In the eyes of the world she is a good wife but Warde knows in her heart of hearts that this is illusory, and she leaves her husband to live with her lover. Although shunned and vilified the woman is liberated as she follows the "cry of the heart."[28]

In the other narrative dealing with the rights of womankind, "The Bridal Couch,"[29] Laila, who is in love with a young man called Selim, is deceived by a rival who tells her that Selim no longer loves her. On the evening of her wedding day Laila sees Selim, her beloved, and asks him to run away with her.[30] The young man, however, a prisoner of social expectations, tells Laila to return to her new husband, and pretends that he loves another woman. Laila, however, does not believe him, and "like a lioness bereaved of her cubs,"[31] draws out a dagger, and stabs Selim. As he dies he cries: "Death is stronger than life, but love is stronger than death . . . You have delivered me, Laila, from the harshness of that discord and the bitterness of those cups. Let me kiss the hand that has broken my bonds."[32] The bride condemns those who sublimate true love to social customs,[33] before stabbing herself to death, saying, "It were better that we go to another land beyond the clouds."[34]

Gibran, in a manner hitherto unknown in Arab writing, expresses the whole problem of the oriental woman in these stories – the lives ruined by misogyny and arranged marriages which serve only the interests and desires of patriarchy: "It is tragedy writ in the blood and tears of womanhood, which a man reads and laughs at because he understands nothing of it."[35]

Gibran's passion for freedom, his quest for justice, and his efforts to highlight the plight of women in the Middle East all come surging up in *Spirits Rebellious*. Such scorching stories would have shocked a more settled age. Gibran's Arab readers had, however, already embarked on a voyage of discovery, laying themselves open to new and challenging ideas and influences. Gibran's stories, reaching as they do to the very core of individual liberty, reflected the hitherto unspoken concerns of a generation.

The passionate ideals of *Spirits Rebellious* were not, however, well received by some and years later Gibran claimed that he was shot in the arm around this time – "a Turkish attempt" on his life; the shot was fired too close and had been "a failure."[36] He wrote to his cousin Nakhli Gibran:

> The apparition of enmity has already appeared. The people in Syria are calling me heretic, and the intelligentsia in Egypt vilifies me, saying, "He is the enemy of just laws, of family ties, and of old traditions." Those writers are telling the truth, because I do not love man-made laws and I abhor the traditions that our ancestors left us. This hatred is the fruit of my love for the sacred and spiritual kindness which should be the source of every law upon the earth, for kindness is the shadow of God in man. I know that the principles upon which I base my writings are echoes of the spirit of the great majority of the people of the world, because the tendency toward a spiritual independence is to our life as the heart is to the body.[37]

Such controversy was nothing new for Parisians. Indeed, the tradition of the poet as a rebel, a mantle that Gibran happily wore, was well established in France. Ten years previously, in 1898, and fifty years before that, in 1848, two French writers, Emile Zola and Alphonse de Lamartine, had taken it upon themselves to intervene decisively in the country's affairs – historical events that had not gone unnoticed by the man from Lebanon. In 1848, Lamartine, amidst the clamorous demands of huge revolutionary crowds gathering in a torchlit square in Paris, appeared on the balcony of the Hôtel de Ville and proclaimed the establishment of the Second Republic. In 1898, Zola published in the newspaper *L'Aurore* an open letter to the president of the Third Republic entitled "J'Accuse," asserting that the Jewish officer Alfred Dreyfus had been wrongly sentenced four years previously by an army court, a letter that precipitated a confrontation between the forces of racism and tolerance which was to polarize political thought and action in France right up to the outbreak of World War I.[38]

Although the publication of *Spirits Rebellious* passed relatively unnoticed among Parisians, its effect on the consciousness of the Arab world was considerable, and Gibran's themes began to inspire a whole new generation of Arab writers.[39] Viewing himself as one of a long line of poet-rebels in the tradition of Zola and Lamartine, he was not surprised by the suppression of his work by the authorities in Syria.[40] The church considered excommunicating Gibran, but the sentence was never actually pronounced. However, two representatives of the Maronite patriarch came to Paris to meet the author of *Spirits Rebellious*, hoping to silence the young rebel. Gibran, however, was in no mood for compromise and "let himself go – furiously and with intent." He told them that he was working on a new book, *The Broken Wings*, which would illustrate "how he entirely disagreed with them" and "he hoped the Holy Patriarch would read it."[41]

III

By the winter of 1909, worried about Marianna's ill health, and feeling unwell himself, Gibran found the gray European winter depressing.[42] His concerns for Marianna, however, were unfounded, her "illness" nothing more than "sheer loneliness,"[43] her unhappiness compounded by her brother's absence so far away. His own health improved when some Syrian friends let him recuperate in their peaceful home at Le Raincy.

Gibran's relationship with Micheline now well and truly over, Mary Haskell's letters became his chief solace. He wrote to her: "When I am unhappy, dear Mary, I read your letters. When the mist overwhelms the 'I' in me, I take two or three letters out of the little box and reread them. They remind me of my true self."[44] Gibran, always restless for new experiences, had by now grown dissatisfied with his tutors at the academy and felt he had reached a point were he had learnt as much as he could from them.[45] During December he came into contact with Pierre Marcel-Béronneau,[46] a visionary painter and a disciple of Gustave Moreau who had been professor at the Ecole des Beaux-Arts and whose pupils had included Rouault and Matisse. Gibran felt an affinity with Béronneau whom he found to be open, direct, and sympathetic. The Frenchman advised Gibran to forgo any self-expression for the time being and concentrate on studying the "*Dictionary* of painting."[47] A few weeks later Gibran met Auguste Rodin, the most celebrated sculptor of the French Romantic school. Gibran thought he had "the expression of an honest Christian" and was awestruck by the work he saw: "Rodin is indeed a creator. His work is a very great step towards the unknown."[48] Rodin talked to Gibran about William Blake, "a sane man in the company of madmen."[49] Although memories of his meeting with Rodin would remain with Gibran[50] to the end of his life, it was his awakening to the majestic figure of Blake that was to prove cathartic.[51]

After leaving Rodin's studio Gibran found a copy of Blake's works in an English second-hand bookshop. In the gardens of the Luxembourg Museum he read: "I thought me a lonely wanderer; now is Blake with his torch lighting my path. What kinship is there between me and that man?"[52] Gibran was magnetized by Blake's uniqueness and his vision: "how free he is from all the thoughts that come before him . . .[53] But no one can understand Blake through intellect. His world can only be seen by the eye of the eye – never by the eye itself."[54]

The impact of Blake's inimitable lyric gifts and the beauty of his illuminated books had a profound effect. After that January day in 1910, Gibran felt that he had "come upon a soul who is sister to my soul."[55]

By early 1909, Gibran was working exclusively with Béronneau, who was trying to teach him "the values of colors," studying rather than beginning new paintings,[56] and continuing to write. In a poem entitled "On my Birthday," which he sent to Mary at the beginning of 1909, we sense a less restless man, one more reconciled with existence:

> I perceive the limitless firmament with its worlds floating in space, and the brilliant stars and the suns and the moons. And the planets and the fixed stars, and all the contending and reconciled forces of attraction and repulsion do I see, created and borne by that Will, timeless and without limit. Submitting to a Universal Law whose beginning has no beginning and whose end is without end.[57]

Mary, who had been working to further Gibran's career back in America, was overjoyed by the poem which he had dedicated to her. In May she organized a second exhibition of his works at Wellesley College which received a warm review.[58]

In June, Gibran's idyll in Paris was shaken when he received news that his father had died at the age of sixty-five.[59] Although their relationship had always been fraught, Gibran was devastated by his lonely death in Lebanon. Although often ambivalent about his authoritarian and temperamental father, Gibran also acknowledged that despite everything, he had "called out the fighter" in him;[60] and, now as in the past, "the fighter" re-emerged when his life was beset by grief. He threw himself into his work.

As well as painting, he began studying the mystical paintings of Eugene Carrière, who had died only three years previously. Carrière, whose style was influenced by Rubens and Velázquez, was particularly noted for his portrayals of motherhood, and the reverential nature of these images made a strong impression on Gibran. Rodin too had been moved by Carrière's art, calling him "one of the greatest of painters,"[61] and Gibran said of him:

> The work of Carrière is the nearest to my heart. His figures, sitting or standing behind the mist, say more to me than anything else except the works of Leonardo da Vinci. Carrière understood faces and hands more than any other painter. He knew the depths, the height, and the width of the human figure. And Carrière's life is not less beautiful than his work. He suffered much, but he understood the mystery of pain: he knew that tears make all things shine.[62]

Gibran was by now beginning to develop his own unique style of painting, a style undoubtedly betraying Blakean influences. He wrote to Mary:

> I have learned from other artists' work how to use pure colours. I have also found out that any logical person can be a draughtsman, but an artist must be something else, beside being logical, to be a colourist. Each colour seems to have a "spiritual" nature by itself, and it also seems that no artist can teach the other how to find or understand that spiritual nature. Each one of us must find it out in his own way; and no two people find it alike.[63]

In July he was delighted to hear that some of his paintings, already cited at two *concours* since he had been working with Béronneau, had received a silver medal. During this period he also met up with his best friend from al-Hikmah, Yusuf Huwayyik, who was studying art and sculpture in Paris. The two young artists began to share models, and within a few months Gibran had left Béronneau's classes to work alone, feeling that he had "taken from the man all he can give"[64] – a decision reflecting Gibran's intensely independent nature, and his abhorrence of any shackles or constraints. Yusuf, following Gibran, also left. In an attempt to compensate for their departure from formal training the Lebanese artists began visiting the great galleries of Paris. Every Sunday, when admission was free, they would go to the Louvre like "pilgrims visiting a holy shrine,"[65] and gaze at the works of Puvis de Chavannes, Carrière, Moreau, Michelangelo, and Leonardo da Vinci who had ignited Gibran's first artistic epiphany: "Leonardo was the most wonderful personality in the world . . . His picture of S. Anna, Mary,

Jesus and the Lamb is . . . the most wonderful picture in the world . . . Leonardo painted *mind*. He wanted to paint what men could not understand."[66] They also visited the Pantheon, built on the ancient church of Sainte-Genevieve, where Gibran was magnetized by Puvis de Chavannes' depiction of Genevieve's face as she meets the barbarian hordes of Attila: a face of such "solemn tranquility."[67]

As well as the works of the past the two Arabs came across the innovative cubist movement. Cubism represented the most rigorous exploration of a conceptual art at the opposite pole from Romantic emotionalism and impressionist techniques. Consciously negating emotional empathy, excluding the representation of atmosphere and light, and dismissing naturalistic perspective and three-dimensional illusionistic picture space, its conceptual realism was the outcome of intellectualized, rather than spontaneous, vision. Although Gibran attempted to understand cubism, he felt no affinity with it. His own artistic ideal, "to give a *good* expression to a beautiful *Idea* or a high *thought*,"[68] was at variance with the realism of the cubists. However, he acknowledged the influence of such movements which firmly established the notion that a work of art exists as an object in its own right and not merely as a reflection of a reality outside itself.[69]

Gibran viewed the currents of artistic activity in Paris as the "mad revolt which is in full swing," and discussed with his friends the revolution that was dividing artists into different camps, acknowledging that "art which is not so easily understood – after much effort – produces great joy."[70] He also acknowledged that these modern movements represented the human hunger for creative freedom, and some years later expressed an appreciation of similar works of modern art at an exhibition in Boston: "The pictures, individually, are not great; in fact, few are beautiful. But the spirit of the exhibition as a whole is both beautiful and great . . . the spirit of the movement will never pass away, for it is as real as the human hunger for freedom."[71]

By the summer of 1909 Gibran's life was full. He moved to a studio "high and dry and warm with good light,"[72] on the rue de Cherche-Midi, and began teaching composition to five pupils twice a week. His painting *Autumn* was accepted at an exhibition held by the Société Nationale des Beaux-Arts, and later that year he received an invitation from the Union Internationale des Beaux-Arts to contribute six of his paintings. He also continued to do portrait studies – a skill that over the years would lead him to meet many of the leading thinkers and artists of the age. In Paris he drew Claude Debussy, Marie Doro, a beautiful young American actress, the

American sculptor Paul Bartlett, and made plans to draw Sarah Bernhardt (whom he finally "captured" in New York in 1913).[73]

At the same time as his reputation as an artist was growing, a Parisian publishing house included his "Martha" in a series of volumes of short stories by leading writers from around the world.[74] Although the translators failed to include the ending of the story, in which Martha is buried in an unconsecrated grave, Gibran was honored to see his name alongside the likes of Anton Chekhov in the collection.

These were happy days for Gibran, and he reveled in the "City of Light,"[75] "l'axe du monde,"[76] befriending Syrian and French poets; English and American painters; German and Italian musicians;[77] Dr. Casper – the Belgian doctor who showed them around the Pasteur Institute and with whom Gibran had heated and intense argument over the ascendancy of science over religion; Olga the Russian student, committed to Tolstoy and revolution, who shared their studio and played Beethoven sonatas; the Romanian interpreter and his two beautiful nieces Susanne and Leah; strolling on the boulevard Montparnasse, drinking coffee at the Cafe du Lilas, sitting by the pond in the Jardin Observatoire. Huwayyik later wrote:

> Now when I close my eyes, how quickly the memory of Gibran comes to my mind – his affectionate smile, warm voice, and expressive hands. I can see us walking to the Luxembourg Garden, turning left and sitting on the roof which overlooks the Palace and a part of the garden. I can hear the echo of Gibran's voice in my ear, "We are in Paris, Yusuf! In this rich garden and on this road stretching before us walked many great learned men and artists. I can feel the presence of Puvis de Chavannes, Carrière, Balzac, Alfred de Musset, Victor Hugo, Pasteur, Curie, Taine and Renan. I feel as if I can trace their footprints on this road."[78]

As well as the aesthetic delights, Gibran and Huwayyik enjoyed the throbbing Parisian nightlife. Gibran threw a cafe party and discovered his large capacity for wine[79] – the carefree and high-spirited qualities of his nature reemerging after the nightmare years in Boston.

Despite the social whirl, however, Gibran's unremitting passion for work began to dominate his life. Increasingly he began to feel restless when he was not painting, sketching, or writing. He wrote to Mary:

> When I am not working I feel so restless. I run away from all things that give joyless pleasure to men and women. I am really tired of all those fantastical lies which people call pleasures. My soul seems to find rest in

strange, silent places . . . And now it is time to go and make a drawing of an old man who looks so much like Renan. I found him yesterday in the street gazing at little children.[80]

IV

While Huwayyik enjoyed sitting in the Dôme Cafe in the *Quartier Latin* soaking up the *zeitgeist* of the era – the late-night discussions on Fauvism, Rodin, free love, revolution, and Nietzsche – Gibran began to spend more time alone, walking by the banks of the Seine or strolling through the old streets of Paris.[81] He began studying the literary heritage of Europe, being particularly drawn to the works of Voltaire and Jean-Jacques Rousseau.[82] He said of both men that they were "the conscience of France toward the end of the eighteenth century,"[83] especially relishing Rousseau's ideas on the innate innocence of the natural man, his revolt against materialism and injustice, and his belief that nature was a teacher.[84] He felt in tune with Rousseau's vision, his rapturous identification with the "inexpressible ecstasies" of mystical union,[85] and his sense of the unity of being.[86] His most exciting discovery came, however, when he read the work of the German philosopher Friedrich Wilhelm Nietzsche, a man Gibran later described as "probably the loneliest man of the nineteenth century and surely the greatest."[87]

When Gibran first discovered Nietzsche's writings, specifically the intoxicating *Thus Spake Zarathustra*, the German philosopher was already regarded as a pioneer in the demolition of ancient habits of thought and moral prejudices[88] – and the concept of the poet as prophet became strengthened in Gibran's imagination. Nietzsche's impact on European thought was to become greater than any other nineteenth-century thinker, with the exception of Karl Marx and, not without justification, he was hailed as one of the greatest psychologists among philosophers in recent times.[89]

Although many of the students and artists of Paris's *Quartier Latin* felt it was merely fashionable to read Nietzsche, the truth was that his influence on modern literature was already considerable, with many of the leading writers of the day acknowledging their debt to this "strange enchanter," and his most influential work, *Thus Spake Zarathustra*, becoming to most of the poets of Gibran's time "a sacred book."[90]

Nietzsche had entered the stage at a time when speculative philosophy was a spent force and Darwin's theories were conquering the world. At the same time, Prussian arms established Germany's political supremacy in Europe; science and technology were making the most spectacular advances; and a mood of optimism prevailed. Nietzsche, however, stigmatized the age as nihilistic. All the material improvements of his time meant as much to Nietzsche as the luxuries and comforts of their generation had meant to the prophets Amos, Isaiah, and Jeremiah; they repulsed and disgusted him. Only one thing seemed to matter, and it seemed incomprehensible that modern man failed to realize the enormity of the truth that "God is dead!"

Nietzsche's message in *Thus Spake Zarathustra*, that "God is dead!," expounded with such desperate passion, shook Gibran's oriental sensitivity – if there is no God what is the possible meaning of our notions of morality, love, or truth? However, Nietzsche's metaphysical nihilism demanded a reinterpretation of civilization and corresponded to his hope for a new humanism. The leitmotiv for this new humanism, this "new man," he symbolized in his "*Ubermensch*", or Superman – the ultimate value, in relation to which everybody and everything has to be seen and everything has to be reinterpreted.

Nietzsche believed that humanity had the potential to affirm itself in such a way as to transform the contingent nature of its activity into an intentional, essential one. Through the exercise of this kind of willing, *the will to power*, humankind can embrace their fate and thus become a maker of their own true self. The idea of Superman had existed in many ancient cultures which have always understood that beings exist who, although human, have overcome psychological dysfunction. It was Nietzsche who revived the idea of Superman in the West, the idea of *definite* movement, *definite* evolution. In his conception of Superman, Nietzsche portrays his own passionate longing for true morality as against the old petrified morality which had long since become anti-moral.[91]

In his smoothly ecstatic prose Nietzsche, through the mouthpiece of his poet-prophet Zarathustra, delivers his searing attacks on morality, nationalism, institutionalized religion, and in particular Christianity. Mesmerized by Nietzsche's fiery style Gibran exclaimed:

> What a man! What a man! Alone he fought the whole world in the name of his Superman; and though the world forced him out of his reason in the end, yet did he whip it well. He died a Superman among pygmies, a sane madman in the midst of a world too decorously insane to be mad . . . And

what a pen! With one stroke it would create a new world, and with one stroke it would efface old ones, the while dripping beauty, charm and power.[92]

Years later Yusuf Huwayyik recalled the impression *Thus Spake Zarathustra* had on Gibran, and remembered saying: "Oh Gibran, . . . I am afraid that reading of Nietzsche has too much affected you. I don't enjoy this stern philosopher who ended in madness."[93] Gibran, however, was so dazzled by the iconoclasm and imagery of Nietzsche that no one could deflate his enthusiasm. He wrote to another friend from Paris:

Yes, Nietzsche is a great giant – and the more you read him the more you will love him. He is perhaps the greatest spirit in modern times, and his work will outlive many of the things we consider great. Please, p-l-e-a-s-e, read "Thus Spake Zarathustra"[94] as soon as possible for it is – to me – one of the greatest works of all times.[95]

Nietzsche's appeal lay not so much in his philosophical treatise as in his pulsating style and form. Gibran found in Nietzsche an ally who, like him, raged against the corruption of institutionalized religion and the hypocritical control it exercised over society.

However, unlike Nietzsche, who totally rejected religion, Gibran's natural impulse was to attempt to reform it, as exhibited in his earlier Arabic works. Despite the divergent ends to which they used their creative powers, Gibran felt an affinity with Nietzsche's general trend of philosophy which opposes vital energy to frozen concepts.[96] He was also fascinated by Nietzsche's blistering attacks on the degenerate condition of modern humanity's inner world, the blind slavery to custom cloaked as morality, and the soporific ignorance of a world which in Gibran's words is "obscured by the mists of falsehood and tyranny."[97] Like Nietzsche, he contrasted the inherent gentle power and wisdom of the forest with the shackled materialism of modern civilization.[98] Although as a lover and worshiper of beauty Gibran could not accept the content of Nietzsche's nihilistic philosophy, we can detect subtle echoes and hints of Nietzschean phraseology in many of his writings.

A good example of this influence is the opening line of Gibran's *The Forerunner*, his second English work, published in 1920. His opening words in the book, "You are your own forerunner,"[99] clearly recall Zarathustra's statement, "Mine own forerunner am I."[100] Another is the image of the grave-digger which both Gibran and Nietzsche utilized. In his first English work, *The Madman*, published in 1918, Gibran writes with Nietzschean irony:

> Once, as I was burying one of my dead selves, the grave-digger came by and said to me, "Of all those who come here to bury, you alone I like." Said I, "You please me exceedingly, but why do you like me?" "Because," said he, "They come weeping and go weeping – you only come laughing and go laughing."[101]

Also in this same book there are discernible Nietzschean influences, when for instance the "Perfect World" of "Complete laws" is contrasted ironically with the madman himself, who is a "human chaos,"[102] reminiscent of Nietzsche's assertion that "one must still have chaos in one, to give birth to a dancing star."[103] Although Gibran's style and his use of parables are occasionally reminiscent of Nietzsche's masterpiece, the overall message is very different from Nietzsche's. Gibran was too steeped in the spiritual acquiescence of the East to be fundamentally disturbed by Nietzschean thought, and his trust in the reality of timeless, eternal values was too firm to be shifted, even by the bouts of pessimism that sometimes gripped him.

Although Gibran, like Nietzsche, was a rebel, his rebelliousness never extended to challenging the cosmological order or to questioning the nature of divinity itself. It was an affinity with Nietzsche's form rather than his formulations, with his passion rather than his philosophy, that most captured Gibran's imagination when he came across this "sober Dionysus"[104] in Paris; and when he wrote his own masterpiece *The Prophet* years later, he turned to a form similar to Nietzsche's.

From 1913 onwards, mention of Nietzsche all but disappears from the correspondence of Gibran and Mary Haskell and from her journal. The clear inference is that Gibran was moving on, and although Nietzsche's influence in Paris "was so strong that it carried him off his feet and almost uprooted him from his oriental soil",[105] many years later Gibran was to write: "Nietzsche took the words out of my mind. He picked the fruit off the tree I was coming to. But he is three hundred years ahead – I'll make a tree and pick the fruit for six hundred years ahead!"[106]

V

In June Gibran met a remarkable man called Ameen Rihani,[107] a writer whose influence on him would be profound and lasting. Gibran was immediately fascinated by the thirty-four-year-old with the "fine face and good soul,"[108] a man who had also been born in Lebanon as a Maronite

Christian. Gibran found in the older man a kindred spirit, describing him as "a great poet,"[109] and in later correspondence referred to him as "*al-mu'allem*" which means "teacher,"[110] addressing him as "my brother in art and my co-worker in the realm of God's law."[111]

Both men had emigrated to America at the age of twelve, returned to Lebanon in 1898 to pursue their cultural studies, and were earning growing reputations as writers who challenged the political, social, and ecclesiastical status quo.

Rihani, a bright yet truculent pupil, had left school at fourteen to work as chief clerk, salesman, and interpreter in his uncle's business in New York. Quickly bored by the work, he sought solace in literature, particularly Shakespeare, Hugo, Rousseau, and the Scotsman Thomas Carlyle, whose essay *On Heroes, Hero-Worship and the Heroic in History* (1841) first alerted him to the glorious history and heritage of Arab civilization. He developed an interest in the theater and played a variety of roles including Hamlet and Macbeth in a traveling theatrical troupe called the Jewett Theater Company. This shift from business to art, from a seeker of wealth to a seeker of truth, was indeed the first break on record with the tradition of Syrian emigrants in America.[112] Having opted for the life of an artist in contradiction to all previous emigrant norms and practices, Ameen Rihani established a new precedent, one that later was to be followed by Gibran. In a letter to his obviously shocked father Rihani had to go to great lengths to explain the economic advantages of his unprecedented step in order to secure the old man's blessing.[113]

Rihani began writing for the emigrants' newspapers, but instead of mechanically regurgitating the sectarian attitudes that abounded in these columns in the early years of the twentieth century, he challenged the predictable moral, cultural, and intellectual values therein, using pen-names such as "Son of the Awake Syrian."[114] The writings of this non-conformist journalist began to attract considerable attention, and in 1902 Rihani's first book – on the French Revolution – was published.[115] Throughout his literary career, the remarkably versatile Rihani addressed himself to a wide variety of topics including history, politics, social affairs, literary criticism, mysticism, theater, oratory, music, painting, and travel writings set in the little-known territories of the Arabian peninsula which were on the verge of being catapulted into the twentieth century by the discovery of oil.

As a young man Rihani had been a talented artist and as early as 1901 he had illustrated his own first significant work, *al-Mouhalafa Athulathiyya fil-Mamlaka al-Hayawanniya* (*The Triple Alliance in the Animal Kingdom*), a Blakean practice that was to be later used by Gibran. A chronic ailment in his right hand, however, prevented him from pursuing this gift, but he had many other talents and in 1903 his translation of the poetry of the eleventh-century blind Syrian poet al-Ma'arri was published. Like Edward Fitzgerald's famous *Rubáiyát of Omar Khayyám* published fifty years previously, al-Ma'arri's verses strongly advocated the unity of all religions. This theme of reconciliation between Islam and Christianity, the crescent and the cross, was a theme that permeated Rihani's later writings – the universality of vision propagated by Gibran in his own writings deriving its dynamic origins from the thought of Rihani. In Rihani's translation of al-Ma'arri's words, we read:

> Now mosques and churches – even a Kaaba stone
> Korans and Bibles – even a martyr's bone,
> All these and more my heart can tolerate,
> For my religion's love and love alone.[116]

In both Arabic and English, prose and verse, Rihani attempted to express something more than the mere ambience of the East. He felt compelled to communicate to the readers his views with regard to humanity's place in the universe. As a Sufi he accepted all religions yet remained unbound by religious dogma. Sufism, belonging as it does to both East and West, appealed to Rihani, for he was acutely aware of the tension between his own cultural background and native tongue on the one hand pulling him towards Islam, and his religious upbringing on the other, which directed him toward Christianity. This tension he felt could only be resolved by taking the Sufi path, which promised reconciliation between East and West. In "A Chant of Mystics" he expressed this theme of reconciliation thus:

> Nor Crescent Nor Cross we adore;
> Nor Buddha nor Christ we implore;
> Nor Muslim nor Jew we abhor:
> We are free . . .
> We are not of the East or the West;
> No boundaries exist in our breast:
> We are free.[117]

As the first Arab traveler of modern times to discover the heart of Arabia, Rihani communicated to the world the great spiritual, moral, intellectual, literary, and material treasures of what he called "the most fertile region in history." He firmly believed in his homeland, Lebanon, and like Gibran saw the Arab world in the context of the family of nations. He regarded himself as the heir to the rich synthesis of Christian–Muslim tradition, and was fully aware of the larger perspective of a global culture and civilization in which peace prevails and harmony exists between East and West.

Rihani demonstrated great foresight in his choice of political and social issues upon which to focus – issues that are still crucial in world affairs today. He appealed to Arabs to be wary of the wealth that was about to descend on them through oil revenue. He warned his people that the only way they could maintain their natural integrity and political independence was to modernize their society without compromising their great spiritual and cultural heritage – themes echoed by Gibran in his Arabic writings.

Of specific significance for Gibran was the fact that Ameen Rihani was the first Arab to write English verse and the first to write a novel in English. This novel, called *The Book of Khalid*, was published in 1911. To illustrate this book Rihani chose Gibran – the artist with whom he felt the closest affinity. The book's influence on Gibran was considerable and may well have encouraged and even implanted in Gibran the idea of writing in English himself.

The Book of Khalid, a philosophical and largely autobiographical work, employs an unusual narrative technique and somewhat florid language. For all its flaws, the book carries a message of continuing relevance today and has been unjustly neglected. The influence it exercised on other Arab writers, notably Mikhail Naimy[118] and Gibran, is more important than the quality of its writing. Full of arresting and innovative ideas the eponymous hero in *The Book of Khalid* is clearly a prophetic figure. While the form of the book was too complex and confusing for Gibran's own purposes, the idea of a sage dispensing wisdom among the people of a foreign land no doubt appealed to him. Although not as strong an influence as Nietzsche's *Thus Spake Zarathustra*, Rihani's book may be said to have foreshadowed Gibran's *The Prophet* in that it conveys the teachings of the East in the language of the West, and was written by an Arab who appreciated the best of both worlds.

The year before *The Book of Khalid* was published, Rihani found himself in the company of his compatriots Yusuf Huwayyik and Kahlil Gibran visiting London. While they were there during June 1910 the three men laid plans for nothing less than the cultural renaissance of the Arab world. The cornerstone of their program was reconciliation, to be symbolized by the construction of an opera house in Beirut. They drew up rough plans for the opera house, the outstanding feature of which was to be two domes symbolizing the reconciliation of Christianity and Islam. Although the plans never materialized, the proposed construction was a manifestation of a deeper, more essential aspect of the men's identities as both artists and Arabs. Half church and half mosque, the opera house sketch was intended to represent the marriage of the essential values of the two world religions in a harmonious and unified whole, where each constituent complemented and balanced the other, drawing on a shared Arab mystic heritage.

In London they visited the art galleries. Gibran was particularly impressed by the work of William Turner:

> Among all the English artists Turner is the very greatest. I place him among the mighty spirits of all ages. His vision is as remarkable as that of Shakespeare, and his imaginations are as wonderful as those of Beethoven. His work fills several rooms of the Tate Gallery, and one must go there many times in order to study him well.[119]

As well as enjoying the aesthetic delights of the Tate, they met up with the Irish nationalist leader Power O'Connor and discussed the parallels between the Irish and Syrian struggles for liberation and home rule. They visited the Houses of Parliament, Windsor Castle, and a costume dinner and recital at the Poetry Society where Gibran, Rihani, and Huwayyik proudly dressed up in Arabic costume. Gibran liked England, particularly "the great treasures of London," and felt that the country was "like the grandmother who keeps in her old closet the jewels of the family."[120]

Soon after their visit Rihani left for New York. Inspired by his trip to England, Gibran refocused his attentions on his drawings. He wrote to Rihani:

> Since my return from London I have been entangled between lines and colours as a bird who has broken free from its cage and flown through fields and valleys. The exercises that I have done are better than anything I have done in Paris. I feel now that an invisible hand is polishing off the dust from the mirror of my soul and is tearing the veil asunder from my eyes and showing me pictures and images more clearly, nay more beautifully and gloriously. Art, Ameen, is a great god. We cannot touch the hems of his robes save with fingers purified by fire and cannot look upon his face save from behind eyelids bathed in tears.
>
> I shall leave Paris in a few weeks and my joy will be great to find you recovered, strong as the sacred tree that grows before Astarte's temple and

joyful as the whispering pond in Kadisha [Qadisha] valley. Until we meet, beloved friend, until we meet, and may God keep you for your brother,

Gibran Khalil Gibran.[121]

Yusuf Huwayyik – who had recently painted the American dancer Isadora Duncan[122] – had also left Paris to continue his travels. Gibran met up with Micheline again, but the initial attraction had now dwindled to a friendship. Micheline, whose acting dreams remained unfulfilled, had not been well but despite this was still "thinking of the stage and its glory," even though she knew "too well the darker side of it."[123] Although Gibran felt isolated as most of his friends had left the city for the summer, he began to prepare himself for his return to Boston.

In August he wrote to Mary, telling her that the Union Internationale des Beaux-Arts had asked him to send six pictures to an exhibition later in the year.[124] However, he decided against showing his pictures, because he did not want to stay on in Paris any longer than was necessary. The invitation, however, illustrated to him how much his work had developed during his two-year stay in the "City of Light."

His departure in October was delayed by a week because of a rail strike but finally on October 22, 1910, he sailed for New York on the *S.S. New Amsterdam.*[125] He returned to America with a new self-confidence, enriched by the impressions of the artists and writers of Europe who had made such an indelible mark on his soul.

VI

Of all the impressions absorbed by Gibran during his Parisian sojourn none had a greater and more lasting influence on him than his discovery of William Blake. In Blake's visionary work Gibran found the support and confirmation for his own early ideas, and he owed more to the Englishman than to any other poet, artist, or philosopher.

Both men believed in impulse and creativity as opposed to conditioning; in prophetic vision as opposed to scientific materialism; in the spirit as distinct from the law; in freedom as distinct from repressive morality; in the Unity of Being as distinct from fragmentation; in the "larger consciousness" and imagination as opposed to reason; and in the need for humanity to awaken.

Both men too strived to keep clear, pure intuition and awareness in their work, an affinity observed by Mary Haskell when she wrote to Gibran: "Blake is mighty. The voice of God and the finger of God are in what he does . . . He really feels closer to you, Kahlil, than all the rest . . . and he feels more beyond and apart than all the rest, as if he moved in a larger consciousness."[126] Blake's aim was to awaken "the lapsed Soul of humankind,"[127] thence to found a new world order based on truth and unity. His poetry, by inducing recognition and affirmation, communicated to Gibran a profound delight engendered by the sheer perfection of Blake's words – a joy and rapture that made Gibran's soul vibrate like a musical note with echoes of shared truth. Almost involuntarily, from deep within, came the response "This I have always known."

He was captivated by Blake's "strange and wondrous soul,"[128] a soul that "was energy itself . . . a man without a mask,"[129] whose "aim was single, his path straightforward, and his wants few . . . free, noble and happy."[130] Gibran felt Blake's presence and power resonating in his visionary paintings and poetry: "The light of stars that were extinguished ages ago still reaches us. So it is with great men who died . . . but still reach us with the radiations of their personality."[131]

The influences that Blake acknowledged form an apocalyptic mixture of vast power: Paracelsus, Plotinus, Porphyry, Hermetic literature, Boehme, Plato, Swedenborg, the Bible, the *Bhagavadgita*, Milton, and Shakespeare whose words in *A Midsummer Night's Dream* chimed with Blake's own ideas on creative imagination and the divine vision:

> The lunatic, the lover, and the poet
> Are of imagination all compact.
> One sees more devils than vast hell can hold:
> That is the madman. The lover, all as frantic,
> Sees Helen's beauty in a brow of Egypt.
> The poet's eye, in a fine frenzy rolling,
> Doth glance from heaven to earth, from earth to heaven;
> And as imagination bodies forth
> The forms of things unknown, the poet's pen
> Turns them to shapes, and gives to aery nothing
> A local habitation and a name.[132]

If Blake is the prophet of the "God within," he was realizing and dramatizing the teachings of the Swedish visionary Emanuel Swedenborg.[133] Like Swedenborg he affirmed that eternity is not in space, but is within the self, and, long before Carl Gustav Jung, recognized the motion of psychic energies.

Blake's views on Jesus too were remarkable for his time, and made a profound impression on Gibran. In his own exposition of Jesus, Blake attacks the orthodox view of a "Creeping Jesus,"[134] gentle, humble, and chaste, portraying instead a passionate, rebellious figure who forgives the woman taken in adultery,[135] reverses the rigid law of Moses, praises "the Naked Human form divine," elevates forgiveness above the "Moral Virtues," and sees sexuality as the means whereby "the Soul Expands its wing."[136]

Gibran's depiction of Jesus, published as *Jesus, the Son of Man* in 1928, 110 years later, bears the imprint of Blake's powerful portrayal. In Gibran's portrayal, Jesus was a "man mindful of his own strength,"[137] who could be "filled with wrath,"[138] like a "tempest that scourged,"[139] or like "a torrent pouring from the heights to the plains to destroy all things in its path."[140] Like his predecessor Blake, Gibran depicts Jesus as having a rebellious yet gentle nature, a man who said, "Remember this: a thief is a man in need, a liar is a man in fear";[141] who absolved the prostitute with the words "You have loved overmuch. They who brought you here loved but little";[142] and who would have his followers "live the hour in passion and ecstasy."[143]

Ultimately Gibran depicts Christ as the "Master Poet,"[144] reflecting Blake's own view that "Jesus & his Apostles & Disciples were all Artists,"[145] reaffirming both men's vision of the poet-prophet. There are detectable Blakean influences too in another of Gibran's English works, *Sand and Foam,* published two years before *Jesus, the Son of Man,* in 1926:

Long ago there lived a Man who was crucified for being too loving and too loveable. And, strange to relate, I met Him thrice yesterday. The first time He was asking a policeman not to take a prostitute to prison; the second time He was drinking wine with an outcast; and the third time He was having a fist-fight with a promoter inside a church.[146]

The similarity of intention is evident too in their view that Jesus abides in the hidden portals of the human heart. Gibran in one of his aphorisms expresses this view with exquisite poignancy:

Crucified One, you are crucified upon my heart; and the nails that pierce your hands pierce the walls of my heart. And tomorrow when a stranger passes by this Golgotha he will not know that two bled here.[147]

In *Jerusalem*, Blake writes:

I am not a God afar off, I am a brother and friend;
Within your bosoms I reside, and you reside in me:
Lo! we are One, forgiving all Evil, Not seeking recompense.[148]

Blake's influences are also present in Gibran's Arabic works, such as *al-Mawakib* (*The Procession*), published in 1919, which mirrors Blake's view of an unclouded and unhindered life – a youth dwelling in the forest – symbolizing a world of unity, harmony, and innocence – and an old man who is trapped in the dualism of good and evil and spirit and body. By choosing the boy to express the unity of existence, Gibran follows in the footsteps of Blake, and the child becomes a symbol of equilibrium and perceptiveness.

In his *Songs of Experience* Blake describes the consequences of conditioning, whereby the human spirit is restricted by the institutions of established religion and law. In this dualistic state vital energy becomes frozen and crystallized by blind conformity and suffocating convention. The poet speaks of "mind-forg'd manacles";[149] the "slumberous mass";[150] "stony dread";[151] kings "who make up a heaven of our misery";[152] priests who bind "with briars my joys & desires";[153] society which in its obsessive drive to control pathetically attempts "to frame" the tiger's "fearful symmetry."[154] In many of his writings too, Gibran echoes Blake's sentiments that the constraints of convention poison the divine essence, lamenting that earthly laws are not those of the spirit.

In *Visions of the Daughters of Albion*, Blake attacks the cruelty of sexual morality whereby the law, and not love, is the bond. In Gibran's novella *The Broken Wings* (1912), borne out of his own bitter experiences in Lebanon, Gibran writes of "the miserable procession of the defeated";[155] "the dim light" of "corrupted laws";[156] and of innocence defiled.[157]

Both Gibran and Blake rejected reason in the name of imagination, the world of vision. Blake's assertion in *Milton* that there is "a false Body, an Incrustation over my Immortal Spirit, a Selfhood which must be put off & annihilated alway"[158] appealed to Gibran's own views, and in his first English work, *The Madman*, he explores the dichotomy between form and essence. For both poets this conditioned veil, dominated by reason alone, must be "cleansed" by the spirit of "Self-examination," and the human soul awaken to the "grandeur of Inspiration," to reject materialist philosophy and became clothed "with Imagination":[159]

> To bathe in the Waters of Life, to wash off the Not Human . . .
> To cast off Rational Demonstration by Faith in the Saviour,
> To cast off the rotten rags of Memory by Inspiration,
> To cast off Bacon, Locke & Newton from Albion's covering,
> To take off his filthy garments & clothe him with Imagination,
> To cast aside from Poetry all that is not Inspiration.[160]

Gibran, whose own vision of the Unity of Being was in stark contrast to the fragmented and mechanistic view of reality of Bacon and Locke, viewed inspiration as "seeing a part of the whole with the part of the whole in you,"[161] and poetic vision as the "understanding of the whole."[162] He believed that "Everything in Creation exists within," and "everything in you exists in Creation,"[163] for, "if the Milky Way were not within me, how should I have seen it or known it?"[164] Blake warned against dwelling on the phenomenal, external form of things, but rather aimed to inspire in the reader an inner perception. If the human eye could achieve this, "and the doors of perception [be] cleansed", then "every thing would appear to man as it is, Infinite,"[165] seeing

> a World in a Grain of Sand
> and a Heaven in a Wild Flower,
> Hold Infinity in the palm of your hand
> and Eternity in an hour.[166]

The interior search is, for both Blake and Gibran, the means by which truth will be discovered. Blake wrote, "O search & see: turn your eyes inward,"[167] for "All deities reside in the human breast."[168] Gibran wrote: "A traveler am I and a navigator, and every day I discover a new region within my soul."[169] For Gibran: "Imagination sees the complete reality," where "past, present and future meet":[170]

> Imagination is limited neither to the reality which is apparent – nor to one place. It lives everywhere. It is at a centre and feels the vibrations of all the circles within which east and west are vitally included. Imagination is the life of mental freedom. It realizes what everything is in its many aspects. – Imagination does not uplift; we don't want to be uplifted, we want to be more completely aware. I want to be alive to all the life that is in me now, to know each moment to the uttermost.[171]

Gibran's identification with the imagination as pure awareness has much in common with Blake, and for both men imagination is the essential faculty by which not only the world, but also the self, can be redeemed. For Blake, imagination is the divine humanity, "the Holy Ghost";[172] it is "the real & eternal World of which this Vegetable Universe is but a faint shadow, & in which we shall live in our Eternal or Imaginative Bodies when these Vegetable Mortal Bodies are no more."[173] Blake's writings are a proclamation of the primacy of the imagination, identifying it with the "God within," naming this inner presence, "Jesus the Imagination," the innate creative spirit from which knowledge derives. Imagination for Blake is more than the limited sense of the poet's "muse," but rather creates the inspiration and knowledge of not the arts alone, but of all deeper intuitions. Blake held the belief, dangerously heterodox at the time, that these deepest intuitions, expressed through the religious impulse, meant that all religions are fundamentally one: "The Religions of all Nations are derived from each Nation's different reception of the Poetic Genius, which is everywhere call'd the Spirit of Prophecy . . . As all men are alike (tho' infinitely various), So all Religions &, as all similars, have one source."[174] Gibran likewise, in an age still poisoned by sectarianism and fanaticism, expresses an identical view: "Your thought advocates Judaism, Brahmanism, Buddhism, Christianity, and Islam. In my thought there is only one universal religion whose varied paths are but the fingers of the loving hand of the Supreme Being."[175]

Blake wrote: "One power alone makes a poet: Imagination, The Divine Vision."[176] He held that the primary imagination was the living power and prime agent of all human perception, writing: "All Things Exist in the Human Imagination."[177] He perceived imagination as signifying the principle of reality itself. In his poetry he explored the imagination, or what more recent explorers would call the unconscious and subconscious,[178] more thoroughly than any other poet before him.[179] For Blake then, the imagination is God working in the human soul, and any creative act executed by the imagination is holy. He believed that by practicing this divine gift humanity's true nature would be fully and finally realized.

He knew the exact nature and responsibilities of the poet in this task, and defined it in his great poem *Jerusalem:*

> I rest not from my great task!
> To open the Eternal Worlds,
> to open the Immortal Eyes
> Of Man inwards into the Worlds
> of Thought, into Eternity
> Ever expanding in the Bosom of God,
> the Human Imagination.[180]

Gibran also believed that the poet's task is to open the eyes of humanity inward, and into eternity. For him the poet is "a link Between this world and the hereafter"; "An angel sent by the gods to teach man the way of gods"; and "A shining light unconquered by the dark:"[181] and in *The Prophet*, Gibran wrote: "Trust the dreams, for in them is hidden the gate to eternity."[182] Both Blake and Gibran viewed the inspired poet as a prophet, a person of vision, insight, and imagination, the mediator between God and humankind, the spiritual and the temporal. Indeed, the role of the poet-prophet was for both men deemed a holy one.

Seeking to address at a profound level the issue of how, in a fragmented existence, individuals can attain reconciliation between matter and spirit, Gibran and Blake perceived humanity to be in a psychological state akin to sleep. Gibran wrote: "Man is asleep in light,"[183] and Blake constantly invokes man to wake up: "Awake! awake O sleeper."[184] For Gibran the poet is a spiritual healer, a prophet who offers up art and life for the redemption of humanity. Viewing his own poetry as an "extension of vision,"[185] the "daughter of inspiration,"[186] and "a flash of lightning"[187] he demanded that it be a journey toward self-knowledge: "Every poem is an autobiography – every discovery a self-discovery. We are not radiators of light – but radiations – from the great light. We are light from the Source."[188]

As mediators between the two worlds, Gibran and Blake were acutely aware of transmitting their message in an accessible way. Gibran said: "True Art should be made practical . . . because anything that adds to our world of vision is practical,"[189] and Blake likewise believed that his aim was to give even the vastest issues the coherence and simplicity of single events.[190] Since the poet communicates spiritual truths through the medium of language, both artists felt that their task involved the transformation and re-creation of language to bring these truths to a sleeping humanity. In what seems a defense of poetry as the soul of language Gibran wrote:

> The means of reviving a language lie in the heart of the poet and upon his lips and between his fingers. The poet is the mediator between the creative power and the people. He is the wire that transmits the news of the world of spirit to the world of research. The poet is the father and mother of the language, which goes wherever he goes. When he dies, it remains prostrate over his grave, weeping and forlorn, until another poet comes to uplift it.[191]

Both poets were extraordinarily sensitive about the nature of language and found in the Authorized (King James) Version of the Bible an inexhaustible source of inspiration. Blake believed that "every Poem must necessarily be a perfect Unity[192] – every word and every letter is studied and put into its fit place . . . all are necessary to each other." Gibran wrote: "Poetry is the inevitable word in the inevitable place."[193]

However, no one could possibly suggest that Gibran was a replica of Blake, for there are a number of differences between the two especially in their respective views of nature. For Blake, nature is external and hostile, a projection of the fallen man: "Where man is not, nature is barren."[194] For his part, Gibran identifies with the Romantic view of the individual and nature, familiar to him through his reading of the New England Transcendentalists, especially Emerson, and of poets such as Coleridge and Wordsworth. "I am trying to find myself *through* nature," he wrote to Mary Haskell from Paris in 1909: "Nature is only the body, the form of God and God is what I seek and love to understand."[195] This Romantic vision of nature is very much in evidence in *The Prophet*, above all in the sermon "On Reason and Passion":

> Among the hills, when you sit in the cool shade of the white poplars,
>   sharing the peace and serenity of distant fields and meadows – then let
>   your heart say in silence, "God rests in reason."
> And when the storm comes, and the mighty wind shakes the forest, and
>   thunder and lightning proclaim the majesty of the sky, – then let your
>   heart say in awe, "God moves in passion."
> And since you are a breath in God's sphere, and a leaf in God's forest, you
>   too should rest in reason and move in passion.[196]

Another major difference is that Gibran visualized the self evolving and eventually realizing the greater self through reincarnation.[197] Nowhere in Blake's poetry can one find anything remotely like the following from Almustafa's farewell:

> A little while, and my longing shall gather dust and foam for another
>   body.
> A little while, a moment of rest upon the wind, and another woman shall
>   bear me.[198]

Nevertheless, the influence of Blake is unmistakable in many of Gibran's works. The expression "a tear and a smile," which Gibran used as a title for one of his books,[199] seems to have been inspired by Blake:

> What to others a trifle appears
> Fills me full of smiles or tears.[200]

The sermon "On Joy and Sorrow" from Gibran's "testimony", *The Prophet*, may have its roots in Blake's "The Mental Traveler." Thus Gibran writes:

> When you are joyous, look deep into your heart and you shall find it is only that which has given you sorrow that is giving you joy.
> When you are sorrowful look again in your heart, and you shall see that in truth you are weeping for that which has been your delight.[201]

echoing Blake's words:

> For there the Babe is born in joy
> That was begotten in dire woe;
> Just as we reap in joy the fruit
> Which we in bitter tears did sow.[202]

As Blake and Gibran explored the depths of the psyche, both poets were able to return from these deep regions with their sanity intact. Unlike writers such as Nietzsche who became overwhelmed by the symbols of the unconscious, both Blake and Gibran were able to counterpoise their "mystic pain"[203] with their artwork,[204] balancing their intense intellectual and emotional adventures with an innate ability to root themselves in their drawings and paintings.

In Gibran's *magnum opus The Prophet*, there are strong parallels with Blake's work. Gibran's prophet, Almustafa, is in some ways comparable with Los, the prophet of eternity in Blake's epic poems *Milton* and *Jerusalem*. Blake himself certainly identified with Los as Gibran at times appears to have done with Almustafa.

In *The Prophet* Gibran writes: "Oftentimes in denying yourself pleasure you do but store the desire in the recesses of your being,"[205] recalling Blake's aphorism in *The Marriage of Heaven and Hell*: "He who desires but acts not, breeds pestilence."[206] Elsewhere in *The Prophet*, Gibran makes use of Blakean imagery, for instance in these lines about clothes[207]:

> Some of you say, "It is the north wind who has woven the clothes we wear." And I say, Ay, it was the north wind,
> But shame was his loom, and the softening of the sinews was his thread.
> And when his work was done he laughed in the forest,[208]

putting us in mind of Blake's "Tyger" in its use of personification, and the image of the forest as being the abode of the spiritually awakened:

. . . & what art
Could twist the sinews of thy heart?...
When the stars threw down their spears
And water'd heaven with their tears,
Did he smile his work to see?
Did he who made the Lamb make thee?

Tyger! Tyger! burning bright,
In the forests of the night . . .[209]

6

The Poet-Painter in Search

(1910–1914)

Mary Elizabeth Haskell, strongly built with a tall, slender, athletic frame, subscribed to a regime of exercise, fresh air, and mountain climbing – following a more ascetic lifestyle than many of her bohemian contemporaries. As a popular headmistress of a girls' boarding school she attended to her duties with a compassionate desire to impart all that was good and true to her students. With her flowing dresses, long strings of beads, and large deep-set eyes, her warmth and graceful bearing, she inspired her students to make their best efforts.[1] In her illustrious career she introduced field trips into the curriculum, encouraged her pupils to develop their own student body, initiated an open-air school for girls in the third grades, and began teaching sex education.

As a student at Wellesley College, she had been an active member of the Agora Society which encouraged the discussion of contemporary political issues: a woman "must be broad enough to have a place in her heart and in her life not only for her home but for her country and for the world."[2] At twenty-one she had begun to meticulously keep a diary with the idea of writing "something that might serve years hence to furnish me with a setting of the customs and circumstances and ideas of my youth, if such a setting should ever be sought by some writer or chronicler."[3] Indeed it is, and any account of Gibran, man and poet, finds at times two destinies – that of Mary and that of Gibran – woven inextricably as one.

Throughout her life, her desire for reform and her belief that young people should have the best available opportunities to extend their horizons fired her instinctive generosity. In many ways she personified the city of Boston during the first years of the twentieth century, a city, according to William Dean Howells, the "dean of American letters," where "right thinking" and "high thinking" begin, and where the "good causes . . . are first befriended."[4] Among Mary's protégés were Charlotte Teller; Jacob Giller, a disabled Russian Jew whom she set up in a bookstore in New York's East Side; Aristides Evangelus Phoutrides,[5] a young Greek who embarked on a brilliant career as a classical scholar; and of course, recently returned from his Parisian adventures, Kahlil Gibran.

Only a few were to know of the nature of the relationship between the headmistress and the artist, and no one actually knew the extent, intensity, or enduring quality of their mutual affection.[6] Throughout her journals and letters Mary's devotion to Gibran and her wish that he express his innermost self through his work are evident: "I want for you what you want for yourself."[7] "Nothing you become will disappoint me; I have no preconception that I'd like to see you be or do. I have no desire to foresee you, only to discover you."[8] Gibran said of Mary:

> You've given me my life in a literal sense. I could not have lived – except that you gave me life. So many actually die for lack of some such person as you to save them. It was not just the money but the way you gave it, the love you gave with it and the faith, the knowledge that there was somebody that cared. I wonder sometimes whether ever in history one soul has done for another what you have done for me.[9]

He called their "kinship"[10] "the most wonderful thing that I have known,"[11] feeling "wholly at home"[12] in a relationship that "enlarged his consciousness."[13]

On his return from Paris and determined to move away from the oppressive atmosphere of the South End with its heartbreaking memories, Gibran found accommodation for himself and Marianna, away from the ghetto, at 18 West Cedar Street. The new arrangement was not a success. Marianna, although overjoyed at her brother's return, missed the familiar sights and sounds of the Syrian enclave and felt insecure in the more ordered and genteel surroundings of their new address. Kahlil found his sister's single-minded devotion and dedication to him at times overpowering. He felt claustrophobic after the independence of Paris, suffocated by Marianna's presence in the small two-room apartment, and frustrated by his sister's obsessive tidiness when she would fuss over the state of his room.

However, despite the constraints of space Gibran was soon painting again. His greatest joy during these days back in Boston was to show his work to Mary: "I was bringing you my heart all the time," he later told her. "I'd work in that little room and then hurry to you with whatever I had – whether it was wet or dry."[14] At last his studies arrived from Paris and, excitedly, with quick, ardent movements,[15] he opened the crate in Mary's kitchen. Of all his efforts he was proudest of his "Temple of Art" series in which he had captured among others, Rodin, Debussy, Rostand, and the critic Henri Rochefort.

By December Mary and Gibran were spending an increasing amount of time together. Forever the teacher, she was keen that he perfect his spoken English, and he spent many an evening reading aloud to her the poetry of Swinburne.[16]

Realizing that she knew very little about Gibran, Mary began coaxing him to reveal something of his background. His response, as recorded by Mary in her journal, shows a character trait that was often to resurface in his life when confronted by such demands. He was prone to exaggeration, and would consciously fabricate his biographies, depicting his paternal grandfather as "a man of leisure – wealthy, aristocratic, athletic, brilliant – who kept lions as pets" and elevating his maternal grandfather from a poor priest to a bishop of the Maronite Church whose meager land became "properties . . . immense – whole towns, vineyards, fields."[17] Such embellishments reflect the young man's uneasiness with, and desire to compensate for, his humble origins,[18] perhaps exhibiting an element of insecurity in his otherwise confident character; a need to be seen as a man of social standing in his own culture as he mixed with the "cultured classes" of American society. Mary, sensitive and astute, and acutely aware of Gibran's ambivalent attitude toward his past, desisted from challenging him, but rather let him allay his insecurities through this tortuous art of embellishment.

Their relationship, which was reaching a new intensity, and their growing affection for each other, is reflected in Mary's journal. Gibran, recognizing in Mary a kindred spirit, told her on December 10, 1910 that he would marry her "if he could." Without hesitation, seemingly expecting such a proposal, Mary answered that her age "made it out of the question," fearing "to spoil a good friendship with a poor love-affair." Her swift response, with its apparent dispassionate objectivity, deeply hurt Gibran's pride. However, the next day, on Mary's thirty-seventh birthday, she recanted and "told him yes."[19]

Mary's journal, over the next few years, meticulously records the intimacy of their relationship.[20] Gibran's "fastidious reserve" had meant that during his youth he had experienced few sexual liaisons. He offered to tell Mary how many, but she declined.[21] The type of woman physically attractive to him was rare. He had found that what is not attractive is extremely repellent in physical intimacy. There had been times when women had approached him sexually but his physical reserve and sense of privacy had made these sexual approaches unwelcome. It was his "temperament" rather than imposed "virtue" that had kept him comparatively chaste. He had no preconceived code about sexual morality, but rather he believed in personal liberty and honesty, "honor and cleanness and decency."[22] Once Mary asked him if he thought it right "if a man or woman loved seven and lived sexually with seven," to which Gibran replied, "If the seven were all willing, yes."[23]

Mary recorded that at times "Kahlil takes me so near: without intercourse he yet gives me the joy of being desired, loved, caressed," with "a new completeness of touch,"[24] and how he kissed her "with a tenderness beyond dreams, as God might kiss a child in his arms."[25]

Many women found the handsome man with his shock of dark hair and clear brown eyes very attractive: "Women naturally long for him," she wrote, "each wants to appropriate, to become the chief object of attention";[26] yet the object of their desire wrote, "I am not inclined, just as certain other men are inclined, to indulge in the sexual athletics known to many by mellifluous adjectives and given seductive-sounding names."[27]

At times Mary's passion for Gibran nearly overcame her,[28] and she felt their abstention meant they were "missing so much!"[29] They agreed, however, that despite abstention, their relationship had "proved itself not dependent on intercourse,"[30] and although they "suffered intensely from this sex-longing and abstinence,"[31] they still kissed, embraced, and touched one another, finding that every "sex-stirring" brought them closer together,[32] – their love giving them a unique insight into what they called "the greater love."[33]

Gibran believed that men and women possess three "centers" – the head, heart, and sex centers, whereby "one or another or two of them lead, in each person – not in the same equilibrium at different times perhaps in a given person."[34] He said "physical things have their day. They pass. I don't want anything between us to pass – anything great."[35] This relationship later inspired many of Gibran's writings, and the essence of his kinship with Mary has echoes in his depiction of the relationship between Mary Magdalene and Jesus in his *Jesus, the Son of Man*, published in 1928: "Other men love themselves in your nearness. I love you in your self."[36]

Secure in his love life, Gibran's life revolved around his work and visits to Mary's home. Keen that Gibran should practice his art, she arranged for him to draw Dr Richard Cabot, who was about to be appointed chief of the medical staff at the Massachusetts General Hospital, and Charles Eliot, president of Harvard.

On Mary's thirty-eighth birthday, Gibran gave her a prose-poem, "We and You," published on January 6, 1911 in the emigrant newspaper *Mir'at al-Gharb* (*Mirror of the West*).[37] The poem is a litany of contrasts between "we" – the poets, prophets, and musicians who "fill the hands of the Angels with the seeds of our inner selves"[38] – and "you" (a pronoun representing the social, political, and ecclesiastical supporters of the status quo), the "sons of the pursuit of 'earthly Gaiety' ", who "place your hearts in the hands of Emptiness."[39] Like his other work of the time, "We and You" is laden with overtones of social protest – the outspoken intensity of the poem reflecting Gibran's own increasing self-confidence within American society, his "reposeful power,"[40] described by Mary as "the big lines of his character" which she sensed were becoming "more pronounced, more dominant, steadier."[41]

Mary's perceptions of Gibran begin to fill her journal: "His face . . . expands and glows, or contracts and ages and sharpens," losing "all blood color, [it] takes on metallic hues, narrows from the brows down and becomes channeled and rent looking . . . his color is warm ivory, eyes large and velvety – hair like black plumy shadow. All the lines and lights are those of power and dignity. Yet only five minutes before he may have been pinched and perplexed or tormented looking." When he is happy his "upper face expands most if affection or feeling predominates; the lower expands equally with the upper if thought predominates. When he draws, he contracts the face a good deal . . . His smile is a regular combustion – it ripples and flashes from the eyes all over the face."[42]

The most remarkable of these "expression storms" occurred when he spoke about his work. He told Mary he was "a worshiper of the word," and revealed that sometimes he would wait weeks for one little phrase: "But always there is something so far ahead I never reach it." His face would change every moment and across it Mary would see "drifts of blue and olive . . . The eyes appeared to smoke. And always the circling of the waves of color – passing swiftly like cloud shadows on a windy day."[43] Gibran was never satisfied with what he had written: "At the time – yes . . . But even a little while after, if I read it again it disgusts me; for by that time I would say it differently – and, I think, better. I work very hard – and work is often the greatest pain . . . for I cannot do what I would."[44] He felt conscious of something in him that must be done – a restlessness that remained with him all his life, even after he had written his masterpiece, *The Prophet*:

> I don't know what – I don't know when. It may be either poetry or picture. But it is more than anything I have yet done. I try to see it – but I cannot. Yet I feel it there – in me. I long for it. It is some great change. I foresee it but I do not understand it. I know I have a something to say to the world that is different from anything else.[45]

Mary observed his extraordinary sensitiveness, "so aware of the most latent or even unconscious hostility or critical disagreement, so boundlessly free under accord"; how he became "crippled and diminished under discord", "readily agitated and depressed and strained" yet "so soon rested and refreshed and relaxed" – the paradoxes of personality openly expressed, seemingly unconcerned about the masks that so many wear to hide the inner perplexities of contradiction and multiplicity.[46]

In January 1911 they spoke of financial arrangements, and Mary told him that she had sent him to Paris as a "test" of his stability and that she felt "bound" to continue this test for at least two more years. The financial question between artist and patron remained a source of anxiety and misunderstanding between them, and ultimately was to prove to be a formidable obstacle in any proposed marriage.

However, in February Mary told Charlotte Teller of their plans, indicating that at this stage she was still seriously considering betrothal. In February, while Charlotte posed for Gibran, Mary came to his studio to watch him at work, brewing up his coffee between sittings, "delicious but devilish stuff," and eating a salted mixture of pistachio nuts, melon seeds, and chick peas.[47]

Mary continued her plans to bolster Gibran's career as an artist, and invited the Copley Greenes, who belonged to the influential art association's St. Botolph Club, to dinner. The evening was a great success, provoking Mary to write: "I think his future is not far away!"; but alongside her delight came another, sadder, emotion, a new awareness, that "there waits a very different love from that he bears me – an apocalypse of love – and that shall be his marriage. His greatest work will come out of that – his greatest happiness – his new full life."[48]

The next day, after spending the night wrestling with the realization that she could not marry Gibran, she prepared herself to tell him of her decision. On hearing her words "I've stopped thinking that I shall ever be your wife,"

Gibran went white. Mary told him how, since December, whenever she thought about their marriage, she felt "obscurely" that it was wrong. Although she knew she still possessed a certain youthfulness and "great vigour" she would soon be on "the downward path" while he was still climbing upwards.[49] Little did she know that he was destined to die young and she would outlive him.

Despite the tensions of the evening, Mary felt that although she had given up the idea of marrying Gibran, it had not parted them but rather brought them closer together. She interpreted, too, Gibran's comparative acquiescence as proof that he never really wanted marriage, but his later remarks of her "coldness" that evening, like "an indifferent spectator,"[50] made Mary wonder how badly he had been hurt.

By the spring of 1911 Gibran was becoming restless and indifferent to living and working in Boston. After the cultural delights of Paris he found Boston stifling,[51] a sentiment echoed by the American writer Van Wyck Brooks, who bewailed early twentieth-century Boston as "congested with learning . . . hyper critical, concerned, self-conscious . . . filled with a sad sterility, the fruit of emotional desiccation."[52]

Gibran had grown tired of the paternalism of the Bostonian aesthetes, many of whom were more interested in his "orientalism" than in himself, and as such he wished to escape from those who considered it fashionable to aspire to the seductive trappings of *Omarkhayyám-culture*.[53] Increasingly weary of the label "Syrian genius," Gibran wanted to exchange the stasis and sterility of Boston for the flux and fluidity of cosmopolitan New York.

His chance came when Mary, sensing his growing dissatisfaction, laid plans for a studio to be found for him in New York, and in April 1911 he stayed at Charlotte Teller's Greenwich Village apartment while Charlotte went on tour with a repertory group.

II

Gibran immediately loved the city, which seemed to express "Might and Force,"[54] and he spent his days exploring New York like a "solitary traveler,"[55] a notebook always at hand.[56] He sensed in New York the spirit of an America whose "Destiny is strong and healthy and eager,"[57] and began to acquaint himself with the artists of Greenwich Village, finding many who had "a saintly respect for art – people who are hungry for the beautiful and the uncommon."[58]

Greenwich Village was a revelation for Gibran. The neighborhood's tangled web of streets had provided an almost continuous haven for those seeking to effect change – artistic, literary, political – as well as a refuge for those pursuing more personal visions, serious or frivolous – and as such opened his vistas to new possibilities. Described as the "Gypsy-minded Latin Quarter" of New York,[59] the village attracted those eager to embrace cosmopolitanism and escape the provincial mind. As a magnet for radical creativity, it had attracted a pantheon of the greatest minds in American literature, including Thomas Paine, Herman Melville, Walt Whitman, Henry James, Eugene O'Neill, Edgar Allan Poe, and Mark Twain.

Gibran found himself in Manhattan at a propitious time. The anarchist Hippolyte Havel called the village during the first two decades of the twentieth century "a spiritual zone of mind";[60] the diverse cultural highlights reminding Gibran of the energy of Paris and the *Quartier Latin.* He heard the young intellectuals of the village discussing politics, culture, sexuality, syndicalism, Freudianism, Isadora Duncan's modern dances, psychoanalysis, Harlem jazz, the Provincetown Players, as they met in the Liberal Club, Polly's restaurant, Albert Boni's bookstore, and Petitpas where John Butler Yeats assured them that "the fiddles were tuning up" all over America.[61]

Gibran made contact with the Syrian community and reestablished his friendship with Ameen Rihani, whose poem "The Song of Siva" had recently been published in the prestigious *Atlantic Monthly.* He also came into contact with political activists who rekindled his fears and concerns for the Lebanese and Syrians in their struggle for freedom. Even in New York, thousands of miles from Lebanon, he found the omnipresent shadow of his country's oppressors, "the dark shadows of these human vultures."[62] He met the Turkish ambassador, Zia Pasha, at a dinner given by Naum Mokarzel, an editor of the *émigré* newspaper *al-Hoda* (*The Guidance*). Gibran made a little speech on "Self-Reliance," yet, despite the superficial pleasantries of the evening, he felt depressed as his mind turned to the suffering of his people at home.[63]

On his return to Boston, inspired by the nationalist cause, Gibran attempted to give his loyalties semi-political expression. In 1911, after Italy had declared war on Turkey, hope for home rule was revived in Turkish-occupied countries. During this period of intense political activity in the Middle East, Gibran formed a Boston branch of the Golden Circle (*al-Halqa al-Dhahabiyyah*). The aim of this group was quite simply to combat Ottoman oppression. The Boston branch of the Golden Circle was one of many groups that existed in Constantinople, Egypt, Lebanon, London, New York, Paris, Syria, and elsewhere.

In his inaugural speech to the Boston group Gibran stressed that the Ottomans' intention was to retain absolute rule over the Arabs and the Arabic-speaking peoples. He told the Syrian emigrants in America to reject the belief that by acquiring American citizenship they could save themselves, and not to be deluded by "the promises and the ambitions of the foreign [i.e. European] states." Gibran urged them not to repeat the political habits of their fathers when the Druze adhered to England, the Orthodox to Russia, and the Maronite to France. Moreover, he considered the Syrians' reliance on local government to be "foolishness itself," for the state was nothing but "carrion, a putrefied corpse": "Knowledge, wealth, rectitude, freedom of speech and work and all that makes man the image of the Gods come from the struggle and diligence of the individual and cannot be obtained by political partisanship, by belonging to the State or by relying on the Constitution."[64] He went on to say to his increasingly bewildered audience, "be without patriotism" and let "your children" be liberated from "the slavery of imitation and traditions and they will remain free in chains and prisons."[65] The audience, however, found such sentiments as his emphasis on endurance rather than action contradictory to their perceived aims, even though Gibran had told them that the Golden Circle's aims were ultimately moral not political. The inaugural meeting was to be the only meeting, as Gibran's seemingly paradoxical message failed to impress his audience.

Shortly afterwards, intent on improving his connections with American society, he returned to New York with a letter of introduction from Mary to visit her old friend the composer and musicologist Arthur Farwell. He drew Farwell, who was impressed with the work, saying it expressed his "whole inner being."[66] In return Farwell took him to some galleries and introduced him to William Macbeth, an art dealer who specialized in contemporary American painters.

Gibran made a drawing of Rihani, which he thought to be his best work since he had returned from Paris. When Charlotte returned to New York, he moved into a rooming-house at 28 West Ninth Street, where Rihani was lodging, and met Rihani's friends, including the editor of *Papyrus*, Michael Monahan, the critic Richard Le Gallienne, and the poet Edwin Markham, whom he drew.

In June, when she visited New York, Mary found that Gibran had "gained some flesh" and was in good spirits."[67] She was excited to see his new portrait of Charlotte, who had posed nude amidst "green, apricot and orange veils" and holding a "brazen jewelled bowl of incense."[68] He also introduced her to Ameen Rihani – the first time she had met any of his Lebanese friends. Around this time, a relationship developed between Rihani and Charlotte Teller which lasted for a number of months. The relationship was not a success, Charlotte finding that they were both "too highstrung to be mated,"[69] and within a year she married Gilbert Hirsch, a young Harvard graduate.

While Charlotte Teller and Ameen Rihani struggled to come to terms with each other's powerful personalities, Mary and Kahlil spent their days wandering carefree through New York, eating out, visiting the cathedral of St. John the Divine, Columbia University, and the Metropolitan and Brooklyn museums. After the intensity and upset of the spring these were happy and relaxing days for the couple. Mary told him that she had decided that rather than send him monthly cheques she would provide him with a lump sum of $5,000, the amount bequeathed him in her will, provoking Gibran to make his own will.[70]

In June he returned to his sister in Boston where he worked on his novella al-'Ajnihah al-Mutakassirah (The Broken Wings),[71] and was thrilled to receive $50 from the publishers Dodd & Mead for illustrating Ameen Rihani's The Book of Khalid. By the end of the month, however, he had been taken ill again by "the Grippe," and the dull weather added to his feeling that he was "in prison."[72]

In September his prose-poem "Slavery," exploring the theme of exploitation, was published in Mir'at al-Gharb. This was a theme close to Gibran's heart; once, on seeing a noon stream of workers in New York, he had said to Mary: "This procession is of slavery. The rich are rich because they can control labor for little payment."[73]

In his prose-poem he wrote that slavery exists in both East and West, placing "man's neck under the domination of the tyrant" and submitting "strong bodies and weak minds to the sons of Greed for use as instruments to their power."[74]

Although Gibran had a great respect for the American way of life, "her ideal of health, her power to organize, her institutions, her managements, her efficiency, her ambition,"[75] he also nursed reservations about "this false civilization."[76]

The Americans are a mighty people, indefatigable, persistent, unflagging, sleepless and dreamless. If they hate someone, they kill him with indifference; if they love someone, they smother him with kindness. He who wishes to live in New York should keep a sharp sword by him, but in a sheath full of honey; a sword to punish those who like to kill time, and honey to gratify those who are hungry.[77]

In September he finally settled in New York. His new studio apartment at 51 West Tenth Street in Greenwich Village had a small balcony, good light, and a low rent of only $20.[78] Designed with a Parisian flair by Richard Morris Hunt and completed in 1858, the imposing redbrick structure had the distinction of being the country's first centralized facility for artists constructed to serve their needs for light, space, privacy, and showrooms. It became a magnet that lured influential critics, affluent patrons, and the curious public alike to its well-publicized exhibitions and "visiting days." The "Tenth Street Studio" had housed some celebrities including Bartholdi, the creator of the model for the Statue of Liberty, and over the years had been the venue for innumerable meetings, including that of the Music Club, whose visitors had included such dignitaries as Paderewski.[79]

On returning to Boston on September 26 Gibran presented Mary with a painting which she named *The Beholder*. She stayed up all night studying the painting, writing four pages of interpretation. Later she told him that she thought the painting marked "the beginning of another ascent"[80] in his artistic progress. They went to see "The Irish Players under Yeats" perform Synge's *The Well of the Saints* and Lady Gregory's *The Workhouse Ward*; heard Yeats address the Drama League at the Plymouth Theater, where he spoke of Synge (saying that a creative imagination is the greatest glory possible to a nation and true art the highest service that can be rendered to a nation;)[81] and afterwards went backstage, where Gibran made an appointment to draw Yeats.[82] Gibran was much taken with Yeats, saying he "is capable of work of absolute quality,"[83] but had reservations about how the patriot in him was spoiling his work: "He ought to be simply an artist. He knows it. I believe he will work out of it."

On October 1, at the Hotel Touraine, the Arab drew the Irishman. Mary, after seeing the portrait, thought that Gibran had brilliantly captured Yeats's complexity, his "practico-aeriality," and the "elusiveness" of "one still hovering."[84]

Although the portrait had only taken about fifty minutes, Gibran and Yeats found themselves deep in conversation for three hours.[85] They had much in common, not least the plight of their respective nations, both suffering under the tyranny of foreign rule. They also found they shared a striking affinity in matters spiritual. Yeats's vision, like Gibran's, was much influenced by Eastern thought, and during his life he had made contact with such figures as Tagore, Chatterjee, Shri Purohit Swami, and Madame Blavatsky.[86] Although Yeats accepted the Christian revelation he could not accept it as exclusive, and, like Gibran, was fascinated by esotericism.

Twelve days after the portrait was drawn, Lady Gregory, who had been impressed with Gibran's drawing, sat for the artist. While he drew her, again at the Hotel Touraine, other admirers, including a young poet called Ezra Pound, flocked to see the great Irish woman and patron of the Abbey Theatre.

Mary's last evening with Gibran before his departure to New York was again spent at the theater, Lady Gregory having expressed her pleasure with Gibran's work by giving him tickets to see her play *The Image*, and George Bernard Shaw's *The Shewing up of Blanco Posnet*.

On his last night with Mary, Gibran told her: "I work with thought of you, and . . . if you like what I do that is the greatest thing I ask."[87] After he had gone, Mary made arrangements for his work to be shown at the prestigious St. Botolph Club. She invited Frances Keyes, who had connections with the club, to view Gibran's work. However, Mary's plans were foiled when Miss Keyes verbally tore Gibran's work to shreds.

Mary had thought Gibran's later paintings marked "a very great step" in his craft,[88] but Miss Keyes thought otherwise. The technique of almost everything dissatisfied her;[89] she criticized the figures, the relation of heads to the paper, the colors and shadows lacking in the study of "complementary colors."[90]

As bitter as Miss Keyes' denunciation of his work was, Mary recorded every devastating word. Finally, after four days, she summoned up the courage to tell Gibran of the criticisms, and wrote a fifteen-page letter. Gibran wrote back from New York, saying that Miss Keyes had a "conventional" view of art,[91] and that she would still be critical even when he had perfected his technique and style. He felt, however, that when the critic had thought his pictures suggested the beginning of another picture, she was actually unwittingly complimenting him. He hoped that he would always be able to paint pictures "that made people see other pictures." Gibran felt that had he been a well-known artist, Miss Keyes would not have dared to criticize, and people like her tried to appear "well informed before the others."[92]

Mary, although generally agreeing with his comments, supported Miss Keyes' right to dissent, calling her a "Concord Soul" who would criticize him not less loudly were he famous, but more.[93] Gibran was unabashed and replied that as for Miss Keyes being a "Concord Soul," he had fought against such "souls" in the Arab world for the last seven years: "Some of them were converted and some are silenced and the others are crushed to oblivion!"[94] – the tone of his reply suggesting self-protective arrogance. It was also a reaction to hurt pride, and, although aware that he still had much to learn, his self-confidence continued to grow.

When Mary visited New York for Thanksgiving she found Gibran happily settled in Greenwich Village. He had made his small studio warm and cheerful, decorating it with tapestries bought in Paris, and hanging lamps and oriental rugs sent to him by Mademoiselle Marie El-Khoury, a gem dealer and a new friend. He had never felt more at home anywhere, sensing in his studio "a great spirit that once dwelt" there.[95] Feeling that he had finally found a center of gravity he said: "I am firm, firm as the Kaaba in the heart of Arabia . . . I have simply found myself . . . my heart burns and I love it."[96] He felt that he could now put his own "House in Order", let go of all the "shadows,"[97] declaring: "The days are filled with burning ideas."[98] He told Mary: "My only desire, Mary, is to be a *live wire*. I want to *be*."[99]

III

In January 1912, after much delay, Gibran's Arabic novella *al-'Ajnihah al-Mutakassirah* (*The Broken Wings*) was published.[100] He sent Mary a copy in which he had translated the dedication:[101]

> TO THE ONE who stares at the sun with glazed eyes and grasps the fire with untrembling fingers and hears the spiritual time of Eternity behind the clamorous shrieking of the blind. To M.E.H. I dedicate this book. – Gibran[102]

The publication of this book enhanced Gibran's reputation in the Arab world but more importantly for him attracted the attention of a critic called May Ziadah who was later to forge a profound and unique relationship with Gibran.

During the winter of 1912 Gibran reveled in his solitude: "While one's heart is being transformed into a little world, one wants to be alone."[103] Often his work so absorbed him that he hardly ate, enjoying these unconsciously self-imposed periods of fasting.[104] In the periods of his life when he was taken out to dine by friends, he would afterwards give himself "a spot of fasting," to "overcome what they, in their affection," had done to him.[105] Work and food together, as far as he was concerned, did not appeal

123

to his constitution[106] and during these periods of abstinence he felt he was able to work "with burning hands."[107] Throughout his life, however, his working habits did little to improve an already weakened constitution. Sometimes he would hardly eat anything all day, only drinking strong Turkish coffee and smoking heavily. Other days he might have an orange for breakfast or a piece of fruit for lunch, never eating anything between these meager pickings. His sleeping patterns too, were sporadic, sometimes from four in the morning to eleven, finding he did his best work between midnight and four.[108]

These habits, however, took their toll on his health and by February his "old friend the Grippe" had returned.[109] He found his body heavy and subject to intense fevers, making him mentally restless:

> I simply can't relax. My mind is like a brook, always running, always seeking, always murmuring. I was born with an arrow in my heart, and it is painful to *pull it* and painful to *leave it* . . . I live so much within myself, like an oyster. I am an oyster trying to form a pearl of my own heart. But they say that a pearl is nothing but the disease of the oyster.[110]

The coming of spring in 1912 lifted his malaise. He began to reacquaint himself with New York's bustling social life. Small groups of people began visiting his studio to view his work, including the artist Adele Watson, sculptor Ronald Hinton Perry and patron of the arts Marjorie Morten. These fellow artists were appreciative of Gibran's paintings and drawings, and one, Juliet Thompson, proclaimed that his work made "her heart weep." Gibran appreciated such a remark by this talented woman who had once been commissioned to paint a portrait of the American president Woodrow Wilson.

Juliet Thompson, a Virginian by birth, was related to Edward Fitzgerald, translator of *The Rubáiyát*. A Celt, from a long line of Irish bards, Juliet's charismatic personality attracted many visitors of all races, creeds, and colors to her nearby apartment at 48 West Tenth Street. Her father, Ambrose White Thompson, had been a close friend of President Abraham Lincoln, and Juliet's beauty, charm, and artistic gifts later carried his daughter too into the White House.[111]

Juliet was a follower of the Bahá'í faith, with which Gibran was acquainted. She had lent him some of the Arabic works of the founder Bahá'u'lláh,[112] whose message of unity and the essential truths common to all the world religions struck an answering chord with Gibran's own beliefs.

Gibran later declared that Bahá'u'lláh's Arabic writings were the most "stupendous literature that ever was written."[113] Auspiciously, the spiritual leader of the Bahá'ís and chief expounder of the faith, 'Abdu'l-Bahá,[114] was due to visit New York that April and Juliet asked Kahlil Gibran to paint his portrait.

In later years Juliet spoke of Gibran's paintings as being "mysterious and poetic," and said of him: "He had a high, delicate voice and an almost shyly modest manner, until he came out with something thundering . . . he was the spitting image of Charlie Chaplin, I used to tell him so. It made him frightfully mad . . . He was very modest and retiring in his personal life."[115] The honor of being given the commission to draw 'Abdu'l-Bahá (referred to by Baha'ís as "the Master") can only be appreciated by observing the devotion Juliet felt toward "the Master."

> No words could describe His ineffable peace . . . For at last we saw divinity incarnate. Divinely He turned His head from one child to the other, one group to another. I wish I could picture that turn of the head – an oh, so tender turn, with that indescribable heavenly grace caught by Leonardo da Vinci in his Christ of the Last Supper (in the study for the head) – but in 'Abdu'l-Bahá irradiated by smiles and a lifting of those eyes filled with glory, which even Leonardo, for all his mystery, could not have painted. The very essence of compassion, the most poignant tenderness is in that turn of the head.[116]

Over the coming days Juliet observed how, as 'Abdu'l-Bahá walked among the people or addressed the poor at the Bowery mission,[117] all eyes would follow "His scintillating power" and "strange, unearthly majesty."[118] Those who met him perceived no more than their capacity could register, and even the skeptical Turkish ambassador Zia Pasha toasted him as "the Light of the age, Who has come to spread His glory and perfection among us."[119]

It was with great anticipation then that Gibran awaited the fruition of Juliet's plans to arrange a sitting, and he wrote to Mary: "I must draw 'Abdu'l-Bahá. His portrait is as necessary to my series as that of Rodin."[120] Mary reassured him: "He will be drawn by you – he will understand your series and you, and it will be his pleasure as well as yours."[121]

Gibran met and talked with 'Abdu'l-Bahá three times before the sitting, even acting as his interpreter for the many visitors who flocked to see their Master.[122] Gibran said of him: "He is a very great man. He is complete. There are worlds in his soul. And oh what a remarkable face – what a beautiful face – so real and so sweet."[123]

Finally a sitting was arranged on Friday April 19 at seven-thirty in the morning, yet despite the "early hour," Gibran felt sure he was capable of "making a great drawing of him."[124] The artist slept badly the night before, sensing the air charged with the horrible sea tragedy of the White Star liner *Titanic* which had sunk on April 14–15[125] off the Grand Banks of Newfoundland with the loss of 1,513 lives.[126] He began his work at eight, and after an hour the twenty-five people in the room began to shake his hands, saying: "You have seen the soul of the Master." 'Abdu'l-Bahá then spoke to Gibran in Arabic: "Those who work with the Spirit work well. You have the power of Allah in you," and, quoting Mohammed, said: "Prophets and poets see with the light of God," Gibran recording that in 'Abdu'l-Bahá's smile "there was the mystery of Syria and Arabia and Persia."[127]

Juliet Thompson later recalled that when Gibran wrote his portrait of Christ, *Jesus, the Son of Man*, he had told her that his meetings with the Bahá'í leader had profoundly influenced his work.[128] These meetings left an indelible impression, and Gibran wrote that he had "seen the Unseen, and been filled";[129] Mary, on seeing a smaller sketch he had made of 'Abdu'l-Bahá's face, wrote: "In it you have set the timeless light and the eye at rest on Reality. Men will see there what they desire: that real things are; and they will be comforted and strengthened."[130]

In the days that followed his meeting, Gibran experienced what he called "something cyclonic . . . something moving as the mighty elements move." His life felt full and expansive: "Models to be studied, poems to be written, thoughts to be imprisoned, dreams to be gazed at and gracious people to whom I must show my work."[131]

These were exciting times for Gibran. His recently published *The Broken Wings* was receiving glowing reviews in the Arab world: "a wonderful work of art," "perhaps the most beautiful in modern Arabic," "a tragedy of subtlest simplicity."[132]

Some reviewers, however, were ambivalent about the character of Selma Karamy, the beautiful girl thwarted in her love by social convention. Mikhail Naimy in *al-Funoon* (*The Arts*)[133] said he thought that the heroine of *The Broken Wings* was not "Syrian in mind or heart" and, stripped of the superficial jasmine blossoms and lemon scents, could have easily been "French, English, Russian, Italian or Austrian." However, the critic, who was later to become a close friend of the author, also identified Gibran as the first authentic voice of his exiled countrymen and the first Arab novelist to employ successfully native themes in his work, detecting in his style and form "the beginning of a new movement in Arabic literature."[134]

The publication was hailed as an event of some importance by the Arabic press[135] and Gibran began to receive correspondence about the book. One such letter was the beginning of one of the most remarkable correspondences in world literature. May Ziadah lived in Cairo and was a regular contributor to *al-Mahrousah* and the leading newspapers and periodicals of her age. The previous year she had published her first major literary work, *Fleurs de rêve*. Written in French and under the pseudonym of Isis Copia, this early work demonstrated the influence, not only of her French education, but particularly of Lamartine, and pointed to the exploratory and creative mind she possessed.[136] Her restless life, desire for experience, and rebellion against convention were remarkable in the context of her environment and of her age, and May was a leading light in the women's emancipation movement, then at its height in Egypt, led by the Egyptian suffragette Huda Sha'rawi.

May praised Gibran's style but expressed a lack of sympathy with the heroine. While Gibran felt that ultimately the individual's only path to self-realization lay in love, May was all too conscious of the inescapable position of Eastern women. She respected the freedom and individuality to which women aspired, but she could not disregard the bonds that subjugate women:

> I myself feel the pangs of the strings that tie the woman down – those fine silky strings are like those of a spider's web, but they are as strong as golden wires. Suppose we let Selma Karamy, the heroine of your novel, and every woman that resembles her in affections and intelligence, meet secretly with an honest man of noble character; would not this condone any woman's selecting for herself a friend, other than her husband, to meet with secretly? This would not work, even if the purpose of their secret meeting was to pray together before the shrine of the Crucified.[137]

Others who had by now read *The Broken Wings* began to visit Gibran in "his Hermitage" in New York City. One of the most colorful of these visitors was Pierre Loti,[138] whom Gibran had met in Paris in 1909. The eccentric French writer was in town to see the production of his play *The Daughter of Heaven*. He said after reading *The Broken Wings* that he thought Gibran was "becoming more brutal and less Oriental" and implored him to return to the East to "save [his] soul."[139]

Another visitor whom Gibran was delighted to see was Micheline. She had by now given up all aspirations to be an actress and had returned to teaching. Micheline found that her one-time lover had changed – his face no longer had "that indefinable expression made of illusions, of longings and hopes for a radiant future . . . that only belong to Youth!" Micheline saw before her a man whom life had touched, confessing that the boy in Gibran had appealed to her "tremendously," but the man brought a "vague feeling of fear."[140] Gibran unwittingly reflected these observations when he wrote to Mary: "There is something so solid and so real about her [Micheline], which I did not see years ago when I was so much of a poet and so little of a man."[141]

In May 1912 Gibran visited the Metropolitan Museum and was thrilled to see the newly acquired work of his artistic mentor, Rodin: "It expresses the two sides of his genius; the exquisite loneliness and the powerful strangeness." The two heroic figures of Adam and Eve particularly impressed him, and he felt that Rodin was under the direct influence of Michelangelo when he modeled his Adam.[142]

Although Gibran would have wished once more to meet 'Abdu'l-Bahá, who was visiting Boston at the time, his own work in New York held him there – finishing new pictures and trying to arrange for Thomas Edison ("he is so representative of America")[143] to pose for him.

In June he wrote to Ameen Rihani, who, suffering from ill health, was returning to Lebanon for a holiday. Hearing of his friend's departure, Gibran, as of old, was flooded with waves of nostalgia:

> I would have wished to accompany you to that land, the rocks and valleys of which I love and the priests and rulers of which I hate. But what dreams portray, wakefulness erases; and what hope clarifies, powerlessness hides. On the morrow you are travelling to the most beautiful and the most sacred country in this world and I shall remain in this distant exile. How fortunate you are and how unlucky I am. If you were but to think of me on Sannin or near Byblos or in the valley of al-Fouraika, you will minimize the torment of exile and reduce the pain of separation. There may be no one in Syria who is interested in me but there are a few individuals in whom I am interested. These are those who think a lot, speak little and feel always. To all those I send my greetings and salutations. But to those who swell like drums and croak like frogs I send nothing – not even an iota of my contempt.[144]

This intense period of work and his longing for Lebanon began to take its toll and again Gibran was haunted by illness. He wrote to Mary: "I am not well . . . and my whole being is aching for a green silent spot . . . Perhaps I need a rest. But I will never get any rest before they lay me in my grave – there among the hills of Lebanon."[145] His health remained a cause for concern throughout the summer. As well as his recurrent attacks of the grippe he contracted a severe stomach virus that incapacitated him to such an extent that he could not even smoke.[146] In September, after excruciating toothaches, he had to have six decayed teeth, including a wisdom tooth, extracted.[147] Mary, recognizing that his being consistently "under par" meant "constant leakage" of his energy, implored him to try and improve his lifestyle[148] and tried, unsuccessfully, to get him to go to the Caribbean and the sun.

Gibran unexpectedly revealed some other concerns that had been eating away at him. He told Mary he could not attend to his health because he was trapped by financial and artistic worries, feeling torn apart by his constant attempts to align the two worlds he was living in:

> Were I in Syria, my poetry would ensure notice to my pictures, were I an English poet, it would ensure them English notice. But I am between the two – and the waiting is heavy. I want to be independent – to have enough to fulfil my work – to help my sister.[149]

Mary saw too how he had "suffered inexpressibly" about money, realizing that if he stopped taking her money he disappointed her desire for his career for which it was designed and that repayment might take longer than if he kept on and became a profitable artist.[150]

This anxiety over his financial dependence on Mary was natural for she had helped support him for six years. By articulating his concerns Gibran felt he had cleared the air. He realized that although he was *dependent* on Mary's patronage, he was also *independent* and in the fortunate position of being able to pursue his work uncompromisingly.

Nevertheless his anxieties ran deep, and before the year was out, the "money relation" reemerged, threatening to destroy their relationship. Despite these awkward feelings, Mary not only sensitively attempted to relieve Gibran's worries over her patronage but continued to equip him linguistically to bridge the disparate worlds that at times caused him such anxiety. By the autumn, relieved that he had expressed his concerns openly, and acting on Mary's advice to cultivate a more balanced lifestyle, he began to feel better.[151]

In October he was invited by his friend the Lebanese scholar Saleem Sarkis[152] to attend a conference organized by the Arab League of Progress in

Beirut.[153] The event was to honor the great Lebanese poet Khalil Mutran, who a few years later was to become the poet laureate of Egypt and Syria. Gibran was, however, too caught up in New York to contemplate a long voyage, and instead sent Sarkis a prose-poem entitled "The Poet from Baalbek,"[154] with instructions that it be read on his behalf before the poet on the day of the event.

As winter approached, however, Gibran's health deteriorated again, and he became in Mary's words "a candidate for consumption."[155] She observed that the youthful good looks that had once turned many a head were beginning to fade and his features showed signs of strain and fatigue.[156] Gibran, however, told her, "I may lose health – but my work will go on." Mary wrote: "Till he sells, [freedom] must gall; his strength leaks while his heart aches."[157]

Sharing Christmas Day with Mary, Gibran disclosed that he had never really looked after himself and from the age of fourteen had done little else but work. He never felt able to plan his day regularly; such a habitual lifestyle seemed "dead" to him and he had to "let details happen as they happen." He told Mary that ultimately he was attending to "one big thing in life" which, if it could "open a new corner in a man's own heart," would mean that he had not lived in vain. He said to her: "Live for yourself – live *your* life. Then you are most truly the friend of man. – I am different every day – and when I am eighty, I shall still be experimenting and changing."[158] Mary wondered whether he would ever see such an old age, the various strains of his life beginning to take their toll on his slight frame of five feet three.[159] His shoulders were starting to stoop, his once full plumy head of hair was beginning to thin, and, at the age of thirty, middle age was creeping up on him, and he was beginning to look much older than his years.[160]

Gibran was increasingly aware that despite his ailments if he wanted to make a name for himself in New York, he had to devote some of his precious energy to establishing new contacts. Early in 1913 the tonic of success came quickly when the Mortens, patrons of the arts, arranged for the painter Arthur Bowen Davies, president of the Association of American Painters and Sculptors,[161] to visit Gibran's studio. Davies felt that Gibran's work was unlike anything that existed in America at that time. "This man is going to surprise the world as he surprised me,"[162] he said to Alexander Morten.

In February 1913 Gibran told Mary there was a possibility of renting a larger studio in the same building: "It is three times as large as mine and it has north light, south light (sunshine) and sky light – very cheerful and very good for work. The rent is $45.00."[163] Mary implored him to take it "before it escapes."[164] She then proposed that she would give him $1,000 toward what they would call the Haskell–Gibran collection. With this latest gift, she proposed that all her previous "loans" to him be canceled. In return she was to receive ten of his paintings which would mean that there would never be more lending to him, "but only buying from" him. She also decided to transfer some securities to him to assist his finances until he became fully independent. Gibran consented to the arrangement, revealing that one of his dearest dreams was, one day, to have an exhibition of all his works together in a large city.[165]

Gibran decided to move to the larger studio, thinking that it would mean a great deal to his work. On a more practical level he felt that in the fickle world of art, people are more likely to avoid a starving artist who lives in a "dark little hole."[166]

During the spring he urged Mary to visit the "Armoury Show" or, as it was officially called, the International Exhibition of Modern Art. He had seen the show, which had received a sensational reception in New York before it had moved on to Boston.[167] The exhibition was enormous, with over sixteen hundred works, containing every variety of contemporary non-representational untraditional experimentation: post-impressionists, expressionists, primitives, cubists, and abstract sculptors mixed judiciously with French traditional and even classical figures. The violence of the reactions to these new movements, the charges of "insanity, degeneracy, anarchy," although fierce, could hardly match the expression of rage that had greeted the Salon des Fauves in Paris in 1905. Quite as vehement as the outraged conservatives were the show's defenders. Both sides knew that the exhibition was more than just an art show, but rather symbolized and affected the whole complex movements of early twentieth-century culture. Some, like the socialite Mabel Dodge, called it the most important event in America since 1776,[168] and Gibran hailed it as "a revolt, a *declaration of independence.*"[169]

Mary was refreshed and delighted by the exhibition, feeling that it "sang alive," and was particularly impressed by the works of the Frenchmen Redon and Gauguin, the American Arthur B. Davies, the Romanian sculptor Constantin Brancusi, and the "utmost visionary beauty" of the Irish–Welsh artist Pritchard.[170]

As always, keen to help the career of her own visionary protégé, she made contact with Walter Pach, one of the organizers of the show. He invited her to lunch where she met members of the Association of American Painters and Sculptors. Afterward she toured the studios of Arthur B. Davies, whose enthusiasm for the Armoury Show was largely responsible for the force of its impact. Two days later she brought Pach to Gibran's studio.

Her hopes of a fruitful encounter were dashed when Gibran's reactions to Pach's presence were "cocksure, lofty, dogmatic." This was a side to his character that Mary had not encountered before, and although she justified his "childish" behavior as nervousness, she was nevertheless genuinely shocked. Gibran's reaction can in part be attributed to a distrust of critics which had been exacerbated by Frances Keyes' recent annihilation of his work. His pride wounded, Gibran was wary of the likes of Pach, who moved in similar critical circles to Frances Keyes. In such situations his sensitivity, "as if raw edges were being touched," fed his insecurity, and he appeared to strangers as "contemptuously blunt."[171]

Despite this outburst his social outings intensified and, according to Mary, the friends Gibran was making were becoming "legion." He said: "If you talk about anything real, to an issue, you are spoiling the dinner party, unless you are so remarkable a mind that you can dominate a table of twenty. And perhaps you do succeed in holding the twenty: it means twenty more dinners . . . It is an endless chain."[172] Spring found him meeting and drawing the eminent Swiss psychiatrist Carl Gustav Jung, who was so taken with Gibran that he invited him to visit him in Zurich.[173] In some of his later works Gibran applied many of Jung's ideas to his poetry and paintings.[174] Jung considered that the individual's most urgent task was to deflect his or her gaze from the conquest of the external world toward the study of his or her own inner world. He was particularly fond of the saying: "He who looks outwardly, dreams, But he who looks within, awakes,"[175] echoing the inner work that Gibran was attending to, when only weeks before he had told Mary: "My life is an inner life,"[176] and Mary had observed, "Most of us live in but two or three rooms of the house of our being. Khalil lives in *all* of his."[177]

For Jung, 1913 was a cataclysmic year. He had broken with Freud and was having to deal with a psychic bombardment of dreams, visions, and symbols, all demanding that he return with them to whatever fathomless depths they had come from. In his autobiography, *Memories, Dreams, Reflections*, he named this period of his life as the beginning of a "confrontation with the unconscious."[178] His nights were troubled by the strangest dreams and his days made terrible with explosive visions that shattered his calm at the most unlikely moments. During this period, when

Gibran met him, the psychiatrist was beginning to formulate his theory on the unconscious which he argued was far more than a bundle of instincts, unbounded by ego. He saw rather that each person's consciousness emerges like an island from the great sea in which all find their base, with the rim of wet sand encircling each island corresponding to the personal unconscious;[179] yet it was the collective unconscious – that sea – that was the birthplace of all consciousness, and from there the old ideas arise anew, and their connections with contemporary situations are initiated. These ideas were at their peak when Jung talked with Gibran.

Jung was becoming increasingly interested in creation myths, which seemed to parallel his patients' experiences,[180] and he found in Gibran a man steeped in the myths and legends of his own cultural heritage. Gibran, inspired by his meetings with this "master physician of the soul,"[181] published an article about Avicenna (Ibn Sina), the tenth-century Muslim physician who had written *A Compendium on the Soul*: "There is no poem written by the ancient poets nearer my own beliefs and my spiritual inclination than that poem of Avicenna *A Compendium on the Soul*." He believed that Avicenna, "the genius of his age," reached the "mystery of the soul by studying physical matter, thus comprehending the unknown through the known." Gibran may have been thinking of his new friend Jung when he continued to write that Avicenna's work "provides clear proof that knowledge is the life of the mind, and that practical experiments lead to intellectual conclusions, to spiritual feelings and to God."[182]

The article on Avicenna appeared in *al-Funoon*[183] – in a series of essays and imaginative drawings on Islamic philosophers. The articles reflected Gibran's conviction that in the Arab world there was a "precious store of mystical philosophy hitherto untapped by outsiders."[184] He wrote a short piece on the twelfth-century Sufi poet Ibn al-Farid, whose "unquenchable soul drank the divine wine of the spirit, wandering intoxicated through the exotic world where dwells the dreams of poets, lovers and mystics . . . a soul pure as the rays of the sun, a heart aflame, a mind as serene as a mountain lake."[185] And in a piece on al-Ghazali he wrote: "I found in Ghazálí a golden chain linking the mystics of India who preceded him with the deists who followed him. There is something of al-Ghazálí in Buddhism and there is some of Ghazálí's thinking in Spinoza and Blake."[186] As well as writing regularly for *al-Funoon*, Gibran fulfilled his Parisian dream to "capture" Sarah Bernhardt, who was by now dominating the international stage of the day. He reported to Mary:

At last the divine Sarah is caught. The drawing I made of her . . . though it does not show her *real age*, is a great success. But if I am to go through the same process with the rest of the great men and women, I might as well give up art and become a diplomat! She wanted me to sit at a distance so that I may not see the *details* of her face. But I *did* see them. She made me take off some of the wrinkles. She even asked me to change the shape of her huge mouth! Sarah Bernhardt is very hard to please, very hard to understand and very hard to be with. She has a temper. She must be treated as a queen . . . I think I understood her yesterday – and I behaved accordingly, and perhaps that is the reason why she liked me a little, for when I wanted to leave she gave me her left hand to kiss. This honor, I am told, is only given to people she likes![187]

His next study was nowhere near as temperamental, but equally passionate – General Ezio Garibaldi, the grandson of the great Italian military leader and politician Giuseppe Garibaldi, a man in Gibran's words "who goes from one part of the world to another to fight with the people against any form of slavery."[188] A friendship quickly developed between the soldier-adventurer and the artist, and the two men sometimes dreamt "great dreams." Garibaldi's fiery personality appealed to Gibran's own passionate nature and the two men often fantasized about Garibaldi leading a regiment of immigrant Lebanese and Syrians to overthrow the Turks.

IV

In late June 1913 the First Arab Congress was due to take place in Paris to discuss the liberation of Arab lands from Ottoman rule. Gibran was invited to attend and represent the Syrian and Lebanese community of New York. However he refused to go, because those who were to pay his expenses, expected him to express their thoughts, with which he was in disagreement.[189]

The aim of the conference was to make an appeal to the powers of Europe, and, by diplomatic means, obtain home rule. Gibran believed they would not be given home rule by diplomatic means: "Their very asking for it diplomatically obliges them to accept Turkey's consent diplomatically given." He feared that Turkey would consent and make promises, only to renege.

Surprisingly, given his remarks to the Golden Circle just over two years previously, Gibran maintained that only by revolution could home rule be realized. Many of his Syrian compatriots preferred "safety" and "patience," which Gibran called "The Oriental poison." In contrast he called for the oppressed peoples of the Arab world to appeal not to the powers of Europe, but rather "to the *people* of Europe."[190] He called not for reform, which he believed would merely give the Arabs rights within the Ottoman empire, but for outright Arab independence and autonomy.

His trenchant views made him many enemies, and he was met with "storms of abuse." Mary observed that this was a period of "great anguish" for him – "sleepless, unspeakably solitary."[191] Gibran's uncompromising views, however, could not be deflected and he remained determined not to conceal from others "what should be told."[192] A few months previously, he had made his own feelings about the Ottoman empire abundantly clear when he wrote to Mary that he hoped for the *dismemberment* of the Turkish empire.[193]

As it turned out, the congress was "a failure." Gibran believed that by advocating patience over passion the Lebanese and Syrians might rule over themselves, but they would never triumph over tyranny. "Passion," he wrote to Mary, "is the only thing that creates a nation. Without it no form of justice could exist." The oppressed peoples of the Middle East, he continued, would not get any justice without passion, "that burning element in life," for "Passion is God in motion."[194]

However, ten years later in *The Prophet*, the poet's view had developed into passion tempered by reason:

> Your reason and your passion are the rudder and the sails of your seafaring soul. If either your sails or your rudder be broken, you can but toss and drift, or else be held at a standstill in mid-seas. For reason, ruling alone, is a force confining; and passion, unattended, is a flame that burns to its own destruction.[195]

Gibran's revolutionary sympathies caused him to guard closely his Arab ties just as he was making connections with the American literary world. The intense conflict between his calls for revolution and the pacifism of many of his American friends caused him considerable turmoil.[196] Five months after the congress he published "An Open Letter to Islam," entitled by *al-Funoon* "To the Muslims from a Christian Poet," in which he called for an alliance of the religious factions in Ottoman-occupied countries.

Although these divided loyalties upset him deeply,[197] Gibran was able to find some peace and quiet in his new studio. For two months he was "everything . . . from carpenter to a *scrubman*," and felt no longer that he was living in a cage. At last he was able to move about without "touching the walls with my wings!"[198] When Mary visited him at the end of June she helped in his plans to build a partition for his washstand and looked for a Sears Roebuck stove for him to cook on. She felt that the studio would improve his nights, for, being prone to sleepwalking, he was less likely to end up in the corridor outside, as he had so often done in his previous apartment.

That summer Gibran left New York City three times. He visited his sister in Boston, stayed with some friends in Vermont, and spent two recuperative weeks at the Japanese-style estate of the lawyer Alexander Tison in Denning, New York. Mary spent a month alone camping in the mountains, trying to learn Arabic. When they met at the end of August in New York the relationship was strained.

Mary brought up the problem of money again, telling Gibran that their relationship had been maintained only because of money. This comment, borne out of her insecurity about how he truly felt about her, exasperated Gibran. The ensuing explosive scene – nearly destroying the arrangement they had come to earlier in the year – was fueled by Gibran's furious reaction:

> Just tell me what really was your idea in giving me the money, and I shall know where I stand. Tell me simply and so that I shall not make a mistake. Was it a gift? Was it a loan? Was it meant to make a bond between us? Tell me . . . I can't stand the uncertainty. It has been one of the hardest things of my life. You have said opposite things with equal earnestness, and I really do not know which you mean. Months at a time I have suffered terribly from it.[199]

Mary told him that initially the money had been a gift, but, knowing how his pride could not accept this, she now would prefer him to repay her in pictures. She apologized for bringing up the "money relation" again, but two days later they were quarreling again.

The painter Arthur B. Davies had arranged to draw Mary. When she arrived at his studio he unexpectedly asked her to pose nude. She was surprised but not shocked: "it never occurred to me to suggest waiting till we were better acquainted. It seemed wholly impersonal . . . We talked – it was over – we arranged that I should bring Kahlil at three next afternoon, and I went."[200] When she told Gibran that she had posed nude for Davies he burst into a jealous fury. "You are too impersonal," he accused her, "and in some ways you are very ignorant about the world."[201] When they met up with Davies the next day, Gibran hardly said a word. Before they left, however, he proposed that he draw Davies. The American brusquely responded with: "I simply can't think of it." The aloofness of the reply infuriated Gibran:

> Why did that man refuse me *that way*? There was no reason why he should
> – Well, some day I am going to do something for America. And I am going
> to *hit hard*. I can't now, for I have no arms: I have them but they are tied to
> my sides. Some day they will be free. Then I shall strike."[202]

However, money and a rival artist were not the only causes of disagreement, and Gibran's quarrels with Mary intensified. In a moment of weakness Mary told Gibran that when he died she wanted to go to Mount Lebanon with his body – authorized by him. He reacted: "I'm not going to die for a long time. Why do you care about these matters of the body after death? Why?"[203] Mary began to cry. She told Gibran that she felt she deserved to be identified with him publicly. She wanted people to know he loved her, "because it was the greatest honor" she had, and she "wanted credit for it, wanted the fame of his loving" her. Gibran told her he had no desire to conceal their friendship but did not want it to be called "a mistress-and-lover affair." He revealed to Mary how he was painfully aware of other people's preconceptions of him, and how, because he is "passionate," they considered him to be "full of affairs." He had even thought when Mary told him that others considered him to be "kept" by "some older woman," that she herself had felt that she was buying his *friendship* with money.[204] Mary found herself in tears again and Gibran felt drained by the acrimony and series of misunderstandings that overshadowed their few days together.

Mary, later reflecting on these turbulent days, pointedly noted in her journal: "Marriage! The wonder is that we are friends! He has said to me, 'You have hurt me as nobody else ever hurt me,'" but then she philosophically added, "Had he not begun now to speak more of what is in his mind, perhaps I should never have had my eyes opened and might have worn out our friendship by unconscious outrages."[205]

Their last day together was less confrontational and they distracted themselves with the practicalities of finding things for the studio – cushions, curtain rods, rings, cords, brackets, threads, and a couch cover – Gibran telling her that he felt "independent" of the world in his "hermit-home." This growing sense of independence was in part due to the subtle changes that were slowly taking place in his relationship with Mary.

After enduring the strain of misunderstandings over their respective roles, the ambivalence subsided and Mary's role began to change from that of mentor to collaborator. He began to send Mary some lines written in English.[206] Previously they had attempted to translate some of his Arabic writings without much success and Mary contemplated learning Arabic, but soon realized she simply did not have enough time.[207] Although his English was constantly improving he still needed her advice. Throughout their relationship, Mary, in order to sharpen Gibran's linguistic abilities and expand his literary knowledge, would share her own literary discoveries with him. Sometimes she would suggest a book or author that he should read and at other times she would send him books such as John Symonds' translation of Michelangelo's sonnets, which he found moved him "as no other thing does."[208] At other times she would copy down word for word a piece that had inspired her, and one night in April she stayed up until dawn writing out six pages of poems by the mystical poet Thomas Traherne.[209] This devotion to Gibran's betterment was, in a way, her own form of creativity: "I've no impulse to creative expression but to appreciative expression."[210]

By the end of the year, the previous resentments resolved, they were able to talk more frankly and freely than ever about the "suffering of our lesser selves in the money relation."[211] Mary told him that she did not want money to come between them, and Gibran reiterated that his works in Arabic and his paintings were *his* gift to her. Mary also revealed the inner struggle she had endured over whether she should have married him. But by talking about these things with him, she found the conflict easing. She then gave Gibran $120 saying that above everything else she desired that he be independent. He asked her, "Do you grow through it?" and when she told him that indeed she did, he accepted it, imploring her not to give away large sums on the spur of the moment. The evening was choked with intensity, as they tried to understand each other; their meal, which they had sat down to eat at seven, was not started until eleven.[212]

The former repose returned to their relationship when she visited him in New York at the end of the Christmas vacation in January 1914. She recorded in her journal: "Today I was unusually aware of him. – It is my joy of joys that he never hides from me."[213] Before she left she lay by his side on the yellow couch, and in the dim light looked at his profile and "thought again of the day when it will not turn to me. Beautiful face! That this realest being is so beautiful, tells me all is well – always."[214]

V

The winter of 1914 in New York was cold and the newspapers were beginning to admit that a business depression was under way. At the beginning of March processions of unemployed people marched to the city's churches demanding shelter for the night. Their leader, Frank Tannenbaum, was arrested and harshly sentenced to one year in prison. During and after his trial there were further demonstrations on behalf of the unemployed and exploited and a mass rally was held at Rutgers Square. The whole episode disturbed the conservative press, especially when it was learnt that the "extremists" were supported by many intellectuals of the day.[215] Inspired by the revolutionary thought of Nietzsche, Maeterlinck, Bergson,[216] Baudelaire, Marx and Zola – these Young Intellectuals,[217] who had learned a fierce contempt for nineteenth-century bourgeois values were fusing political radicalism with aesthetic revolt.

George Santayana, before leaving his professorship in philosophy at Harvard in 1912 to live in Europe, analyzed the period as an age of transition, the new movements in art and literature being a conscious reaction to nineteenth-century materialism;[218] and Van Wyck Brooks compared early twentieth-century America to "a vast Sargasso Sea – a prodigious welter of unconscious life, swept by ground swells of half conscious-emotion."[219]

As well as knowing many of those engaged in the contemporary literary and artistic revolutions, Mary was a friend of some of the leading socialists of the day, notably William English Walling, who was the brother-in-law of her sister Fredericka Walling.[220] Walling, a social reformer, Russian historian, and a founder of the National Association for the Advancement of Colored People, was deeply respected by Mary, and she called him "a Spirit like the North Star – and honester than day, or the Surgeon's knife."[221] She lent Gibran Walling's book *Larger Aspects of Socialism*, which he enjoyed:

> I, too, have been reading a good deal about Socialism. To me it is the most interesting human movement in modern times. That does not mean that I agree with all of its details. It is a mighty thing and I believe it will go through many changes before it becomes a form of government.[222]

Gibran sensed that 1914 was a year charged with possibilities.[223] His hopes for a New York exhibition were raised when Alexander Morten brought the art dealer William Macbeth to his studio. Although interested by what he saw, Macbeth felt unable to exhibit "so many nude figures to the public!"[224] The decision left the artist depressed, but two weeks later he wrote philosophically to Mary: "I realize now that one cannot possess reality and 'be successful' at the same time – simply because reality is a success in itself . . . I must be patient"; also expressing his determination not to succumb to servility or sycophancy when dealing with art dealers, "to ask a favour from those whose very existence is unnecessary to my *real* life."[225]

He continued to add to a growing series, which he called "Temple of Art," and drew the innovative dancer Ruth Denis. Among his ever-growing circle of acquaintances he was, at last, beginning to be perceived as an artist in his own right. This was nowhere more evident than at the literary dinners of Julia Ellsworth Ford, the wife of the hotel owner Simeon Ford and a longtime admirer of the Pre-Raphaelites.[226] Increasingly at ease in the artistic and literary circles of New York, Gibran relaxed among the convivial and interesting company: "I always feel there that I could say what I wished to say – and I say it."[227] Here he formed a close friendship with Judge Thomas Lynch Raymond, a bibliophile and art-minded scholar who was to become mayor of Newark, New Jersey, and whom Gibran painted. He met W. B. Yeats again, who remembered their talk in Boston three years previously. Over dinner at the Fords' the two men discussed the work of Rabindranath Tagore, whose free verse re-creations of Bengali poems had won him the Nobel prize for literature the previous year.[228] Another face from the past invited to these dinners was Josephine Peabody Marks. She was still active in the world of poetry, had won first prize in an international playwriting competition in Stratford-upon-Avon in 1910, and was now happily married with two small children. To Gibran she appeared "to be of Cambridge and not of the world." The pain and confusion of his youthful love so many years ago had subsided; and writing to Mary he rather dismissively said: "She is simply a little Cambridge woman."[229]

In March Gibran published "The Beginning of Revolution," a blistering attack in Arabic on the Ottoman empire and its policies toward his homeland. In the piece he again promoted the advantages of a Christian–Muslim alliance in Lebanon and Syria to overthrow the oppressors. The piece, he told Mary, created the feeling he "wanted [it] to create." He had kept the two-page letter in his "pocket for two years before publishing it." Aware that the Turkish government had a network of spies in America intent on suppressing dissidents who espoused revolution, some of Gibran's friends were afraid that he had signed his death warrant with his own hand.[230] Later in the year, shortly after the outbreak of World War I, he told Mary that if Turkey joined Germany, a protectorate of Syria would emerge, supported by France and Britain, and after twenty or so years Syria would then govern herself.

Throughout the year Gibran's political involvement often distracted him from his work. Frequently called from his studio to answer the telephone, and spending time going downtown with his countrymen,[231] he told Mary how he longed to be "in Syria now! The longing is terrible. But I must stay here."[232]

The conflict he was enduring between his love of nation and his anger at the oppression she endured, between invocations for peace and calls for revolution, becomes evident in a prose-poem Gibran wrote around this time called "Daughters of the Sea (Banat al-Bahr)." Finding the body of a youth washed up by the sea, the maidens wonder how he died. They find a letter in his pocket from his beloved, written to him when he went to war:

> If duty exiles peace from among nations, and patriotism makes havoc of man's tranquillity, then away with duty and patriotism! . . . No, my darling, heed not my words, but be brave and a lover of your land. Do not hearken to the words of a woman whom love has blinded . . . If love brings you not back to me in this life, then love will join me with you in the life to come.[233]

VI

"Daughters of the Sea," with other prose-poems Gibran had written for *al-Mohajer* and *Mir'at al-Gharb*, was published that summer in *Dam'ah wa Ibtisamah* (*A Tear and a Smile*). As with *The Broken Wings* the poet dedicated the book to M.E.H.: "that noble spirit who loves with the breeze and walks with the tempests."[234] Gibran viewed *A Tear and a Smile*,[235] a retrospective of his youthful work, as "the era of erotic songs, sighs and plaints,"[236] and believed they represented "the unripe grapes of my vineyard."[237]

During the period in which he wrote *A Tear and a Smile* the "tears" of the homesick young poet were more abundant than the "smiles":[238] "I am forsaken and abandoned in the corners of civilization and its seduction."[239] The work reflects the estrangement of Gibran's early years in exile, and the "smiles" are the expression of the precious moments when Lebanon becomes transformed in his imagination into a metaphysical homeland.

Gibran's alienation becomes not only that of an emigrant poet, but with echoes of Avicenna's *A Compendium on the Soul* represents too the vision of a soul descended into a foreign world;[240] his homesickness, the yearning for reunion in the higher world – human life is "a tear," descent and alienation, and a "smile," return and homecoming.

This idea of return and homecoming, so evident in many of the mystical traditions of the world, is represented by Gibran in the analogy of the sea,[241] which becomes common from this point on in his writings. Rain is the weeping of water that falls over hills and fields estranged from the "Mother Sea," while running brooks sound the happy song of homecoming. "Such is the soul,"[242] writes Gibran, "separated from the greater spirit to move in the world of matter, and pass as a cloud over the mountain of sorrow and the plains of joy to meet the breeze of death and return whence it came. To the ocean of Love and Beauty – to God."

In his earlier published works Gibran had directed his frustration and anger at those who had defiled his beautiful homeland, the object of his longing. But now that his homeland had gradually assumed a platonic meaning, his attack was no longer specifically directed towards the corrupting influences within Lebanon; by 1914 it was aimed at those who defile the image of humanity, the emigrant in the world of matter, who, in "the heart of the darkness," "disturbed as the tempest," confused, lost, and astray from the "Forest," embarks on a journey of self-destruction.[243] Like Rousseau before him, Gibran argues that materialism blinds us to the true nature of humanity, which can only be redeemed by awakening to a relationship with the natural world: "This earth with the ever open mouth is the saviour of your spirit from the body's slavery."[244] Human souls, he wrote, have become imprisoned, "bowed down by the weight of gold," in the "battlefield" of the city with its "clank of iron, . . . grinding of wheels, and whistle of steam."[245]

In many of the poems, too, Gibran's concern about environmental degradation reemerge: "The sun rose from behind a mountain and crowned the treetops with gold, the while I asked myself why men pull down what Nature has builded up."[246]

Like Blake[247] Gibran acknowledges the necessity of contraries if progression is to be achieved; even the life of a flower is a "longing" and a "fulfilment," "a tear and a smile."[248] His three states of the soul – descent, alienation, and return – parallel Blake's innocence, experience, and higher innocence. In "The Life of Love (Hayat al-Hubb)" Gibran uses erotic and sensuous imagery to depict the coming of spring: "The dawn of spring has unfolded the garment concealed by the winter night, and the peach tree and the apple wear it, adorned as brides on the Night of Power."[249] Summer is depicted as the time "ripened by the sun" when lovers make the grass their "couch and the heavens [their] coverlet."[250] With echoes of Shelley's opening verses in his "Ode to the West Wind,"[251] Gibran's autumnal mood is melancholic when the winds have scattered the leaves "to make of them a burial shroud for flowers that died grieving at summer's passing."[252] Gibran's winter is a Urizenic figure with a dim complexion, icy breath, and snowy limbs. It is a time to "Make fast door and window," to fight frost with fire and wine, and, in the warm embrace of his woman the poet isolates himself from the lamenting elements.[253]

One of his dominant themes in the collection concerns peaceful coexistence, and in "The Voice of the Poet" (Sawt al-Sha'ir) he writes:

> You are my brother and I love you. I love you when you prostrate yourself in your mosque, and kneel in your church, and pray in your synagogue.
>
> You and I are sons of one faith – the Spirit. And those who are set up as heads over its many branches are as fingers on the hand of a divinity that points to the Spirit's perfection.[254]

This poem echoes the declaration of the great Sufi master Muhi'l-Din ibn 'Arabi:[255]

> My heart is capable of every form:
> A cloister for the monk, a fane for idols,
> A pasture for gazelles, the votary's Ka'ba,
> The tables of the Torah, the Quran.
> Love is the creed I hold; wherever turn
> His camels, Love is still my creed and faith.[256]

Gibran believed that the religion of the spirit has its own practical-political aims, which if applied to the human heart could alleviate many of the problems that faced his people in Lebanon.[257] Ideally he wished to see a spiritual conquest over the hearts of his country's oppressors. The political situation in ancient Syria and Phoenicia, similar in some ways to that of the twentieth century, had given rise to beliefs corresponding in their practical ends to Gibran's own philosophy of reconciliation. The Cypro-Phoenician thinker Zeno[258] projected an ideal state with no national boundaries; the Syrian Neoplatonist Porphyry of Tyre[259] developed a metaphysical basis for the doctrine of universal love; and Gibran expressed his belief that "we are the children of one universal holy spirit."[260]

Although *A Tear and a Smile* thinly veils the poet's own geographical, social, and spiritual alienation, it also reveals his growing acceptance of the ambiguity of good and evil in the world: "As the flower takes its fragrance and life from the soil, so in like measure does the spirit distill from the frailty of matter its erring wisdom and strength,"[261] and his view of the role of the poet as visionary:

Clad in simplicity and fed upon gentility, he sits alone in nature's lap to learn the miracle of creation and remains awake in the stillness of the night awaiting the descent of the spirit. He is the husbandman sowing the seeds of his heart in the fields of feelings so that mankind may feed upon the plentiful yield. This is the poet whom men ignore in this life and only recognize when he forsakes this world for his sublime abode. It is he who asks naught of men but a mere smile and whose breath rises and fills the horizon with beautiful living images; yet he is refused both bread and refuge by his fellow-men.

How long, O man, how long, O universe, will you erect mansions in honour of those who cover the face of the earth with blood, and ignore those who give you peace and joy and the beauty of themselves? How long will you glorify murderers and tyrants who have bent necks with the yoke of slavery, and forget the men who spend the light of their eyes in the darkness of the night to teach you the glory of daylight, those that spend their life a prey to misery so that no pleasure may pass you by? And you, O poets, who are the very essence of life, you have conquered the ages despite the cruelty of the ages; and you have won the laurels of glory plucked out from the thorns of vanity; you have built your kingdom in the hearts, and your kingdom has no end.[262]

As the young poets of Europe and Syria prepared themselves to face the impending cataclysm Gibran warned of the coming "darkness" which would "steal the treasure of the mind," and the "mighty procession" falsely hailed as "free." Yet despite the foreboding, the pain and anger, Gibran's "A Vision" expresses his hope that ultimately all will be well:

When I beheld all these things I cried out in agony: "Is this, then, the earth, daughter of the gods? Is this indeed man?" And she answered in a still wounding voice: "This is the path of the spirit, paved with stones and thorns. This is man's shadow. This is the night, but morning will come." Thereupon she put her hands on my eyes, and when they were lifted I beheld myself and my youth walking slowly. And hope ran before me.[263]

VII

In June 1914 Gibran met the art dealer Alexander Morten again. He had first met Morten in the spring of 1912, but now the dealer brought a shrewd Fifth Avenue gallery owner called N. T. Montross to "the Hermitage." Gibran was interested to learn that Morten had told Montross that Gibran was an artist who "doesn't care whether he sells or not."[264] This perception of him, he later learnt, was common. After Morten left, impressed by what he had seen, Gibran was amused when Montross said: "Of course, I understand that you paint these pictures for the satisfaction of expressing your poetic imagination. But after they have passed out of your vision and you are on other things, I suppose you have no objection to selling them." The artist found the twenty-five percent commission "pretty steep;" but nevertheless replied, "Certainly not." They then discussed prices. Morten asked, "What would you say for this, for instance?" Gibran unflinchingly replied, "Fifteen hundred dollars." Montross responded with "Very good, very good, but we can easily do a little better than that." Montross, knowing that the paintings before him would find a ready market, wisely decided not to push the artist into selling any paintings he wanted to keep, but rather would "feel his way with" Gibran. The two men arranged for the pictures to be shown in December, which gave Gibran enough time to prepare. Montross left the studio with the words: "I guess we'll have something to surprise New York."[265]

When Mary arrived to share Gibran's news with him, he showed her what he considered to be the "biggest thing" he had done – a memory portrait of his mother. Mary saw in the portrait the faces of Kahlil, Marianna, Sultanah, and Boutros, and the story of a hard life etched in Kamileh's face. He said: "That is a portrait of my mother's soul – done without tricks, without artistry. I have done what I wanted to. The soul is there, the simple majesty."[266]

When war broke out in Europe Gibran was working feverishly preparing for his December exhibition. He had also spent three weeks in Boston staying with Marianna, who earlier in the year had been ill with a "terrible vaginal state." Although he enjoyed visiting his sister and was relieved to see her well again, his feelings toward Boston had changed: "I can never be myself there,"[267] he wrote to Mary. After two weeks his uneasiness with the city had even made him question his own sanity:

There must be something the matter with me. I am becoming like my madman. I see people and I *know* they are good souls; and yet whenever I sit beside them, or talk to them, I feel a demonic impatience . . . when they speak, my mind takes frantic flights, beating away like a bird with a cord fastened to its feet.[268]

This "madman" referred to was the subject of a series of writings he had been working on in English with Mary's help since 1913.[269] When Mary returned to New York at the end of August they worked together on the prose-poems, Gibran dictating and Mary writing and advising.

The Madman: His Parables and Poems, which was not published until 1918, expressed the multiple levels of isolation Gibran had experienced in his own life. He had found in his madman "a sort of comfort, a refuge" in times of illness and strain, and he called him, "my only weapon in this strangely armed world."[270] This conflict, exacerbated by the onset of war, reached a climax in September when Gibran wrote to Mary: "There is something struggling in my soul . . . It has never been so terrible before."[271] Mary sensitively tried to ease his angst: "Yes you are convulsed; but you convert it to breath of life for yourself . . . you are changed but not shattered."[272]

The psychological turbulence Gibran was experiencing[273] was eased and counterpoised by his art. Throughout his life, Gibran never renounced or feared his own prodigious welter of unconscious life but rather aimed through his endeavors to transform his "mystic pain" into art and poetry: "The flames within us must take beautiful shapes otherwise they burn us."[274]

Despite his passionate artistic temperament Gibran had always been intensely practical;[275] and although his constitution was not robust, he was blessed with a strong pair of hands,[276] and made small delicate woodcarvings. Although some may have thought him a mystical dreamer, an unworldly artist lost in the ethereal realms of the "poetic imagination,"[277] Gibran's practical approach to work was ever-present: "True Art should be made practical . . . I said *practical* because anything that adds to our world of vision is practical."[278]

The next three months were spent preparing for the exhibition at the Montross gallery on Fifth Avenue. Amidst all the practicalities he astounded Mary by finishing three drawings and four paintings as well as adding to the portrait series by drawing Marjorie Morten. He told her that during this period he was worn out by "the confusion of too much" – *The Madman*, Lebanon, the "visions crowding in" on him, and the forthcoming exhibition.[279]

The weeks leading up to the exhibition were frenetic, and Gibran was again incapacitated with the grippe: "I am already half dead. The thousand and one details that swim around my tired head are apt to drive one to the Mad House! Art is one thing and exhibiting another."[280]

The tension of this time is palpable in the patron and painter's correspondence as the big day approached. Mary told him how his dream of four years ago of "conquering New York" was finally becoming a reality. Gibran replied, telling her that the paintings were "only a means. My whole being is directed towards a fresh start. This exhibition is the end of a chapter."[281]

7

The Madman

(1914–1920)

I

Gibran's exhibition, which opened at the Montross gallery on Monday, December 14, 1914, received mixed reviews. By far the most encouraging was an article in the *American*:

> It is a world of original creation that unfolds itself; a world visibly composed of mountains, scanty vegetation and sky; with feelings of solitariness, sometimes of desolation, and always, even in contracted space, with suggestion of a margin of immensity. But it needs only a little familiarity with the things seen to realize that there is symboled here a world of the spirit. The impression of this world is elemental; as of vast forces, still inchoate, stirring in the womb of infinity in preparation for the struggle of birth. It is the symbol of the world of the spirit, as it may seem to an individual human soul awakening to the loneliness of self-consciousness in the presence of the mystery of the rhythmic oneness of life and death.[1]

Other reviews were not as kind. The anonymous critic of the *New York Times* spoke of "Cloudy visions of striving and unhappy humanity";[2] the *Evening Post* reviewer thought the pictures produced "a feeling of irritation";[3] and Henry McBride, the art critic for the *Sun*, denounced the pessimism of the artist, "the crushed mortal striving for he doesn't know what."[4] The *Evening Sun* however, was intrigued by the personal views of the artist on romance and marriage, and featured an interview on the women's page. Gibran was reported as saying:

> Romance! The world is stuffed with romance. In my opinion little can be hoped of marriage based on the sentimental idea of love . . . A [successful] marriage has its foundation on comradeship not romance . . . it is the attraction of complement and supplement, invariably the coming together

of two great natures for whom there is no other choice but marriage, from which eternal recreating is the only result.[5]

Gibran was thrilled to learn that the sales of his paintings amounted to $6,400,[6] and delighted when he heard that the painter Albert Pinkham Ryder had visited the exhibition. The critic Henry McBride had inadvertently found the reclusive sixty-seven-year-old artist standing alone gazing at Gibran's paintings. McBride introduced himself. Ryder made his vague apologies for having broken off a previous engagement and continued to gaze at the paintings. The critic, in a desperate attempt to engage the reticent artist in conversation asked, "How do you like these? He seems to be after something mysterious. All of them are the same," to which Ryder replied, "He seems to mean it at any rate. That's the main thing."[7]

In April of the previous year Gibran had expressed a desire to meet Ryder and draw him.[8] On hearing that Ryder had visited his exhibition Gibran decided to write him a prose-poem as a tribute and as a gesture of thanks for taking the time to see his work. He sent the poem to Mary to read and correct, saying if she liked it he would publish it separately on Japanese paper and send it to Ryder to "warm his old and weary heart."[9] Mary liked the poem and began her criticism gently before launching into seven pages of notes and suggestions.[10] The poem was privately printed by the Fifth Avenue firm of Cosmus & Washburn, and was Gibran's first published English work. The theme of the poem was that although the artist followed a solitary path he was not alone, for his was "the Giant-World of super-realities . . . of primal truth and unveiled visions."[11]

Ryder had lived most of his life as a recluse in New York. When Gibran finally tracked him down he found him living in one of the poorest houses on Sixteenth Street, unkempt and sleeping on three chairs with clothes on them, living "the life of Diogenes."[12]

Gibran read Ryder the poem and the old man had tears in his eyes when he said that he was not worthy of such a "great poem."[13] Ryder was surprised to hear that Gibran was a poet as well as a painter and thrilled to learn that he had been born on Mount Lebanon – the place, said Ryder, where "every poet and painter should be born," adding that he should have known that Gibran came from Lebanon after seeing his pictures.[14] The two men struck up a friendship and by the middle of March Gibran had made two drawings of him, spending some of the most creative hours of his life with Ryder,[15] who because he could not use his hands any more painted "pictures in his mind."[16]

Getting a sitting with Albert Pinkham Ryder was not an easy task. Gibran avoided making an appointment with him because he knew it would only make the old man anxious. One afternoon, however, he was fortunate to see Ryder shuffling along near Sixteenth Street. When he went into a restaurant and slowly ate his corned beef and cabbage, Gibran waited outside. When he finally emerged the two men walked a few steps before Ryder went into a saloon for a drink. Before they reached Ryder's studio he had visited another two bars, Gibran concluding that he was probably in need of a "stimulant." When he had finally finished his drawing the elder artist looked at the picture carefully. Gibran recalled: "It was a great revelation to me – such looking – as if he were looking – as he was – to see what life was in it."[17] He then turned to Gibran and said: "Wonderful work. You've drawn what's inside me – the bones and the brain."[18]

Ryder, in spite of his self-imposed isolation, had become well known in his lifetime. His pictures reflected a rich inner life constantly seeking and expressing the wonder of existence. He had once said:

Have you ever seen an inch worm crawl up a leaf or a twig, and then clinging to the very end, revolve in the air, feeling for something to reach something? That's like me, I am trying to find something out there beyond the place on which I have a footing.[19]

In his work he had expressed the mysteriousness of life through boldly simplified forms and eerie lighting. Gibran was greatly taken with his paintings, feeling they exhibited "a magic that was unique," and entranced by Ryder's personality, his magnetism and delicacy.[20]

Although bedraggled and living in squalor, Ryder had once been the best-dressed artist in New York, and a conspicuous figure on Fifth Avenue. But he had fallen in love with a married woman whose husband treated her badly. Ryder had to go on a trip, and when he returned she had mysteriously gone. The heartbroken artist was never himself again, and, said Gibran, "Probably he hasn't bathed since."[21] In August 1915 Ryder was admitted to hospital, and Gibran frequently visited him until his death two years later.

Their association, borne out of a common artistic search for the ineffable, gave Gibran much comfort. Ryder had understood Gibran's art as soon as he had seen it at the Montross gallery: "Your pictures have imagination," he had told the younger artist, "and imagination is art."[22] Gibran found in Ryder an artist who had refused to compromise his imaginative powers, whose alienation from society somehow mirrored his own feelings of being an outsider.

In March Gibran's tribute to Ryder was read out in church by Dr. Percy Grant, a liberal vicar who worked at the nearby West Tenth Street Church of the Ascension. It was the second time Grant had spoken from the pulpit about Gibran's work, earlier in the year telling his parishioners about the "remarkable" exhibition at the Montross gallery.[23]

That month two of Gibran's as yet unpublished pieces from *The Madman* were read at the Poetry Society of America. In the discussion that followed the response was mixed. While some thought the parables wonderful, Corinne Robinson, the sister of former president Theodore Roosevelt, called them "destructive and diabolical stuff . . . contrary to all our forms of morality and true beauty," exclaiming, "We must not encourage such a spirit in literature."[24] His paintings also received a rebuff in April when his letter to the Boston Art Club, requesting an exhibition there, was answered with a terse telegram: "Regret unable to have your exhibition, will explain by letter." But no letter arrived, suggesting that the Bostonians had lost interest in their once favorite son of Lebanon.

A younger Gibran would have been devastated by such rejections, but now he merely thought that if his work was worthwhile then it must also be worthwhile for him to wait.[25] Mary, unaware of this philosophical response, thought she must buoy him up by immediately arranging for another exhibition venue in Boston. She began to make hasty plans but Gibran told her that she need not worry, for the rejection was a "bodily relief" to him. He then chided her: "Do you think for a minute that I am yet a child who must have a new doll once so often?" His work, he told her, was a matter of a life-time and not merely a "passing mood."[26]

A new sense of certainty was emerging in Gibran's character, and his raw sensitiveness was fading, although he still "strangely" felt "saddened by praise," which only reminded him of "things not yet done."[27] Ryder's influence on Gibran is detectable in a letter he wrote to Mary in April: "As I grow older, Mary, the hermit in me becomes more determined. Life is a vision full of infinite, sweet possibilities and fulfillments. But people are so thin, Mary; their souls are thin, and their speech is thin." To bridge the gulf between himself and others in the superficial social swirls meant "twisting his soul and becoming contorted," and he asked, "Is it worthwhile for an artist to be an acrobat?"[28]

This tension between "essence" and "form," between the "elemental" and "highly civilized," was to find fuller expression in artistic terms in his longest Arabic poem, *al-Mawakib* (*The Procession*) published four years later.

Gibran's growing independence was in part due to the realization that after the sales of his paintings – and for the first time in his life – he had no serious financial worries.[29] But more importantly his acquaintance with Ryder taught him that in the uncompromising search for self-expression his ultimate task was to direct his creative impulses into the service of his being: "I don't want to be just a painter of pictures, or a writer of poems. I want to be more."[30] True artists, he told Mary later, are not those who merely create art or poetry but those "whose hearts are full of the spirit of life."[31]

Like Ryder he too began to withdraw from the world, confident that creativity was sufficient unto itself, and poetic vision was "the most practical thing on earth."[32] Ever since childhood Gibran had always yearned for solitude and believed that even when embroiled in the most intimate of relationships, the human condition was always ultimately marked by "aloneness" – detachment, self-abnegation: that state that cannot be achieved by any other agency except by struggle with self. For Gibran the state of "aloneness" fired his creative urge, a state captured by W. B. Yeats in the lines, "We make out of the quarrel with others, rhetoric, but of the quarrel with ourselves, poetry."[33] Loneliness however, was another matter: "Loneliness is the great suffering upon the earth, the desire to be loved, to be understood, to have some other heart to be near to."[34]

With the coming of spring Gibran spent his days sketching or writing in Central Park, returning home at dusk "avoiding the faces of the people as much as possible."[35] He sensed a growing gulf between himself and others: "Sometimes I say to myself, 'This gulf is caused by something wrong in me. When that wrong is made right I shall be very much nearer to all people and shall perhaps love them with a new love.'"[36]

Spring, which usually revived him, failed to improve his poor health. When Mary visited him he looked pale and ill and complained of pains around his heart,[37] caused by a punishing work routine and irregular sleeping and eating habits. On visiting Boston in June he deliberately avoided the distractions of Oliver Place and booked in at lodgings in Newbury Street, alternating his visits between Marianna and Mary. Mary observed that he looked burnt out, "as if he were to die young,"[38] and his face was *white*. "All that suffering is underneath his face and every now and then it comes through like a searing iron, and withers skin and features."[39]

The headmistress had recently been worrying over difficulties of her own at school, where her innovative methods often clashed with the conservative governing body. A poem which Gibran had recently finished, "The Perfect World," brilliantly captured her prevailing mood:

> I dwell in the midst of a perfect race, I
>   the most imperfect . . .
> I move amongst finished worlds
>   – peoples of complete laws and pure order,
>   whose dreams are arranged,
>   and whose visions are enrolled and registered.[40]

The poem was the first work Gibran had written directly in English and not translated from Arabic: "this writing in English is *very hard* for me," he said. "I've been finding out that English is a very wonderful language if I can learn how to use it."[41] Mary read through some other English works which were later to be published in *The Madman*[42] and *The Earth Gods*.[43] Their serious collaboration had begun.

Gibran, who wrote in white heat, was primarily concerned with the "essence" of his creation. Mary, however, provided the discipline of "form" and gently guided him in paying attention to matters of punctuation, rules of grammar, and tense sequences. However she never presumed to touch the flame-like revelations of his poetic genius. On his return to New York he wrote to her: "The poet seeks nothing . . . His one desire is to become a flute or an arrow or a cup. As by becoming one of them he suddenly finds himself standing in the presence of God. He becomes one of the discoverers of this world."[44]

On her annual summer vacation Mary, as always, wrote Gibran long detailed letters about her experiences and feelings. She would dearly have loved to share these holidays with Kahlil[45] but instead took comfort in imagining his presence.[46] This summer her thoughts in particular turned to the last five turbulent years together: "Never in all these years have I let you be yourself, save as by one of these hopes, whose shattering meant more pain . . . I said I wanted you to be free with me. But if ever you were free, I hit you."[47] Gibran replied that although the years were filled with pain they were "extremely creative," and had helped him see that his work was a powerful means of expressing his soul.[48]

That summer he went on holiday with Marianna. It was the first vacation brother and sister had taken together. They stayed at Cohasset, a seaside village twenty-five miles south of Boston. The countryside around the village, the deep woods, the clear sea air, and the refreshing silences briefly bolstered Gibran's health and within days he felt better than he had for years.[49] His idyll was, however, broken three weeks later when he was called away to attend to the "Syrian affair."[50]

The entrance of the Ottomans into World War I ushered in an agonizing period of Lebanese history. Intent on monopolizing the country's resources – natural and human – the Turks ruled by terror. Military conscription was imposed; suspected dissidents – Muslims and Christians – were imprisoned, banished, or condemned to death; on May 16, 1916 fourteen people were hanged on suspicion of treason in Beirut and seven in Damascus.[51] Monasteries were converted into castles. The Maronite bishop of Beirut was exiled; people were forced to hand their animals over to the troops; trees were felled by the thousands to fuel the military machine. By 1916 inflation was rampant and for the first time in the history of the country depreciated Turkish paper money was introduced.

With the economic situation rapidly deteriorating, by 1916 the people of Lebanon faced famine. An army of beggars appeared in Beirut, and the sight of emaciated men, women, and children ransacking garbage cans or eating the dead carcasses of animals became commonplace. Others too weak to continue the struggle died in the streets.

Meanwhile the entire land became plagued by disease. House flies spread typhoid, body-lice typhus, rats bubonic plague, mosquitoes malaria, and swarms of locusts veiled the sun. During this terrible period some 100,000 people, out of a population of 450,000, died.[52]

For the Lebanese community in America these were intense and agonizing days. Concerns about their villages, families, and friends provoked many young men to fight while others, like Gibran, raised much-needed money for the huge refugee camps that were appearing across the once abundant land.[53]

The tensions of being back in New York destroyed any peace Gibran had found with Marianna in Cohasset. He was besieged by blinding headaches. During these painful weeks, as before in his life, his only solace came in the form of his correspondence with Mary. Each cherished the other's letters, and Gibran said they made him feel like "a plant growing in light, able to forget his own shadows."[54] Mary, after relating her wonder at being able to talk "by wireless," told him of the importance of their letters for her: "We express *through* words, not *with* them when we write from our hearts' desires. That's why letters are written I suppose – it's why this one is written anyhow – and the next one is yet in the lap of Allah."[55]

Gibran, like Mary, was enthralled by being able to talk long distance by wireless. He thought that such technological advances expressed the "Mind of the world," and opened up a "new window" on the world. He felt that people had always talked by wireless without knowing it, "a different wireless which transferred all the *real* messages from one part of the earth to another." The human subconscious, according to Gibran, always intuitively perceived these messages: "A world-deed that happened in India became known to the soul of the Egyptians. And what the soul knows is often unknown to the man who has a soul. We are infinitely *more* than we think. And all we can do is simply to find how much we are."[56] Gibran's correspondence with Mary about the marvels of modern science continued throughout the year. Keen to feed his interest, she sent him some second-hand books on astronomy. Astronomy, Gibran thought, was "the proper study of man," who was often too prone to terrestrial parochialism: "When human consciousness becomes like that of God – a desire for *more* – then all human strife will come to an end, and the strife for the beyond will start, a strife for more space, more life, more consciousness."[57] Gibran thought this sense, this "*wandering largeness*" evoked by astronomy, could be found in early Arabic poetry and in the art of the Chaldeans, which vibrated with a "consciousness of the stars."

Mary sent Gibran a tiny meteorite which she sensed was "crowded with Infinities, and as *grim* and as heavy as Birth and Loneliness."[58] It came from the Diablo Canyon in Arizona, having fallen to earth in a massive stellar shower when the earth was struck by a huge meteor. Gibran said of his gift – which arrived by registered post – that it was the "most wonderful thing" anyone had ever given him.[59]

These discussions and gifts inspired the poet to write a piece called "The Astronomer" in which he expresses his view that blindness compensated by insight is "real" sight:

In the shadow of the temple my friend and I saw a man sitting alone. And
    my friend said,
"Behold the wisest man of our land."
Then I left my friend and approached the blind man and greeted him.
And we conversed.
After a while I said, "Forgive my question; but since when hast thou been
    blind?"
"From my birth," he answered.
Said I, "And what path of wisdom followest thou?"
Said he, "I am an astronomer."
Then he placed his hand upon his breast saying, "I watch all these suns
    and moons and stars."[60]

As the bitter New York winter approached Mary sent her increasingly confident protégé a woollen scarf and a robe to keep him warm. Unlike the money that Gibran had received from Mary, gifts such as the scarf and the meteorite caused him no confusion or consternation. Throughout the years Mary bestowed on him small tokens of her love – fur slippers, books, clothes, bottles of lotion, a Russian lacquer bowl, ties, a watch, tiny Hawaiian wooden salt bowls, cushion covers, Japanese straw-and-strap slippers, a Chinese brass spoon, and, every year, a laurel from the Sierras. Gibran would repay her with delicate designs of a laurel leaf, a shield or a ring, all of which Mary would cast in bronze or silver and present as awards to her girls for scholastic achievement. These small charms were unsigned and no one knew of their source except Mary, who was slowly filling her school with secret reminders of him. "Demonstrations of love are small," said Gibran, "compared with the great thing that is [at the] back of them."[61] He told her:

> We have become one, Mary. You have entered my being – and you can't cut off either of us without destroying the other. But we couldn't shake loose from each other. This relation belongs to our greater selves. I can no more think and imagine and create and work without you than without myself. And a relation must be strong to endure as ours has – and to stand such a shock as that period of pain we went through. But without that period of pain I think it wouldn't have become so beautiful.[62]

Mary's days, busy as they were, were filled with thoughts of Kahlil. She told him: "You are so different from all the rest of the World . . . With their well-Know-ness I am always so ill at ease, deep within, and with your un-Know-ness always so at home."[63]

Mary knew that her relationship was changing her. The confident social graces, the ease with which she had mixed with people from all walks of life had seemingly deserted her. She felt "ignorant, uncertain" when in company, uninterested in the superficialities of socializing: "their talking interrupts my seeking . . . solitariness no longer seems questionable."[64] She felt liberated, and told Gibran that his recent prose-poem "My Friend" reflected her feelings:

> My Friend, I am not what I seem. Seeming is but a garment I wear – a care-woven garment that protects me from thy questionings and thee from my negligence. The "I" in me, my friend, dwells in the house of silence, and therein it shall remain for ever more, unperceived, unapproachable . . .

Thou canst not understand my seafaring thoughts, nor would I have thee understand. I would be at sea alone.[65]

The poet himself was spending much of the winter alone, deliberately seeing as few people as possible.[66] Increasingly "tortured" by others he wrote to Mary: "I'm continually tortured by people's talking; I can't stop listening to what they say. A stream of words, words, words – just the workings of an active mind and a bubbling heart said without realization in the saying, gives me actual pain."[67] Gibran's thoughts turned to metaphysical questions: "God desires man and earth to become like Him, and a part of Him. God is growing through His desire, and man and earth, and all there is upon the earth, rise towards God by the power of desire. And desire is the inherent power that changes all things. It is the law of all matter and all life."[68] On the soul: "The soul is a newly developed element in Nature – and like other elements it has its own inherent properties. Consciousness, desire for more of itself, hunger for that which is beyond itself; these, and others, are the properties of the soul, the highest form of matter . . . And the soul never loses its path, anymore than water runs upward."[69] And on death, he wrote: "Death does not change us. It only frees that which is real in us – our consciousness."[70]

Twelve months later he told Mary that these philosophical speculations over the winter of 1916 had been captured in his prose-poem "God."[71] He said that this poem was "the Key" to all his thoughts and feelings, and expressed as best as he was able what he had been going through.[72] In the poem the narrator makes three attempts to speak with God, without receiving a response. On the fourth occasion, climbing the sacred mountain, he addresses God no longer as an entity separate from him, but as an integral part of the divine order of things:

"My God, my aim and my fulfilment; I am thy yesterday and thou art my tomorrow. I am thy root in the earth and thou art my flower in the sky, and together we grow before the face of the sun."

Then God leaned over me, and in my ears whispered words of sweetness, and even as the sea that enfoldeth a brook that runneth down to her, he enfolded me.

And when I descended to the valleys and the plains God was there also.[73]

Despite Gibran's desire for solitude he allowed some visitors into "the Hermitage" that winter. John Masefield, the English poet and author of *Salt-Water Ballads*, spent an afternoon with him. Gibran liked the man, describing him as "good . . . and kind" and made a drawing of him for his "Temple of Art series."[74] In February several Arab-American writers and editors descended on his studio, and as a tribute to Gibran presented him with a ruby ring, which he began to wear on his index finger.[75]

By May he found himself being drawn into soliciting funds for his increasingly beleaguered country and was made secretary of The Syrian–Mount Lebanon Relief Committee. Gibran believed that the famine in Lebanon and Syria had been planned by the Turkish government: "80,000 have already died. Thousands are dying every day."[76] He was convinced that the same iniquities that had befallen the Christian population in Armenia – when over a million people had been massacred by Turkish troops – were now occurring in the predominantly Christian area of Mount Lebanon.[77]

By June he realized that his political commitments meant that any hopes he may have had for solitude were dashed. The committee soon concurred with Gibran that the Turkish government had deliberately provoked this human tragedy because many Syrian leaders were supporting the Allies in the war. The only real hope, they believed, lay in the American government using its good offices to alleviate the famine which was beginning to take on biblical proportions. Gibran made contact with the State Department in Washington. However, in his heart he held out little hope, knowing that the Americans, in the dark year of 1916, had little time for his homeland.[78]

Mary, on hearing of the genocide in Lebanon, sent $400. Gibran, thinking the amount too extravagant, wrote back: "I want the Syrians here to feel that they must unite and help themselves before others can help them."[79] On June 29, he told her that he had given, in her name, the sum of $150 to the Relief Committee: "It is the largest contribution from an American so far."[80]

By July his energies were being completely absorbed by his relief work.[81] The work was not without conflicts, for, although the suffering in Lebanon was terrible,[82] many Syrians in America displayed an apathy that infuriated Gibran:

> As for the Syrians, they are even *stranger* than they used to be. The bosses are getting bossier, and the gossips more gossipy. All these things make me hate life . . . and if it had not been for the cries of the starving which fill my heart, I would not have stayed in this office for one second . . . and had I been given the choice of death in Lebanon or life among these creatures I would have chosen death.[83]

With events deteriorating in Lebanon by the hour, and the Turks flagrantly violating human rights, Gibran's life would undoubtedly have been in grave danger had he returned. Christians and Muslims were being publicly hanged as a warning to any would-be Syrian nationalists, and under this reign of terror religious leaders and dissidents were deported, while others were tortured and put to death. One of Gibran's friends from college, Dr. Ayub Tabet, an organizer of the First Arab Congress in Paris, had been charged with treason and sentenced to death *in absentia*. Tabet, in exile in New York, and in almost daily contact with Gibran, tried to rally the emigrants around a pro-French position. However, even in America there were dangers. Turkish spies were watching everything, including the committee's activities in New York: "If *any* Syrian in America displeases Turkey, his relatives are killed," wrote Gibran: "That is why the U.S. Syrians are so infinitely cautious and watchful."[84]

In October his poem "Dead Are My People," subtitled "Written in exile during the famine in Syria," was published in the recently revived *al-Funoon*. The poignant piece begins with an elegy dedicated to the victims of the recent genocide, then moves into a self-condemnatory mood before concluding with an appeal to the poet's fellow exiles to support the relief effort.[85]

Gibran finally managed to escape the incessant commitments to Syria for two weeks when he went on holiday with Marianna to Cohasset. However, illness struck and he spent much of his time in bed, convalescing. Stress and overwork had taken their toll, bringing a cold dull ache down the left side of his body – always vulnerable since his fall as a child.

His spirits were lifted a little when, on his return to New York, a friend, James Oppenheim, whom he had met earlier in the year, asked him to join the advisory board of a new magazine, *Seven Arts*. In the first issue the magazine called on American writers to carry on in the spirit of Walt Whitman, who had written, in *Democratic Vistas*, that American regeneration could be brought about by literature. Oppenheim, the editor of *Seven Arts*, accepted this mission, sending out a spirited challenge to young American writers:

It is our faith and the faith of many that we are living in the first days of a renascent period, a time which means for America the coming of that national self-consciousness which is the beginning of greatness. In all such epochs the arts cease to be private matters; they become not only the expression of the national life but a means to its enhancement . . . What we ask of the writer is simply self-expression without regard to current magazine standards. We should prefer that portion of his work which is done through a joyous necessity of the writer himself.[86]

Gibran's passionate literary expression and his social idealism were immensely appealing to Oppenheim and the man from Lebanon joined a staff and contributors whose names were a roster of the innovative of the day. Oppenheim, the editor, was a free-verse poet from the Midwest, but his chief assistants were typical young intellectuals from the East coast. Waldo Frank, the second in command, was a Yale graduate just beginning a literary career. Van Wyck Brooks, a major spokesman of the day, was the most prolific contributor; Paul Rosenfeld covered the arts; and Alfred Kuttner wrote on the newly emerging obsession among wealthy Americans: psychoanalysis. The names of the staff members and contributors included a host of radical thinkers, ranging from Theodore Dreiser and Amy Lowell to Robert Frost, D. H. Lawrence, and the dramatist Eugene O'Neill, who had recently associated himself with the experimental theater group, the Provincetown Players.[87] Mary was delighted when she heard that Gibran's work was being included in such a prestigious publication and implored him to contribute to every issue.[88]

His own greatest pleasure came, however, when he heard that the Relief Committee had been granted a steamer in co-operation with the Red Cross and the American navy. The steamer, called the *Caesar*, was to be packed with $750,000 worth of foodstuffs, medicine, and other necessities. Although this meant a tremendous amount of work – and for the first time in his life Gibran had to acquire a telephone – he felt the work was, by far, the best he had done in his life.[89]

After a hectic few weeks the committee's dreams were realized when the *Caesar* sailed for Syria on Sunday, December 17, 1916.[90]

II

Gibran, relieved that the committee's efforts had achieved practical results, turned his attention to preparations for another major exhibition. This time the exhibition was to be held at the prestigious Knoedler galleries of New York. It had been instigated by Mrs. Albert Sterner, a gallery employee, who, after visiting Gibran's Greenwich Village studio, had recommended his work. Gibran chose forty wash drawings, which were more vibrant in color than many of his earlier paintings and built around the motifs of dancers, centaurs, and mothers and children – paintings he had done in Cohasset in 1915.

The exhibition, which opened on Monday, January 29, 1917, marked a new breakthrough in his artistic career, and recognition at last appeared. His work was beginning to be appreciated by some of the most perceptive minds in New York. Alice Raphael Eckstein, a leading art critic and scholar of Goethe, wrote:

> An illuminating beauty informs his work; to him the idea becomes beautiful if it is true; the emotion becomes truth if it is real. He possesses a singular power of dividing what is essential from what is extraneous in the presentation of beauty and truth. And he keeps to a simplicity of manner in the portrayal of an idea which is closely akin to the spirit of the Primitives, albeit the art of the centuries has gone into the moulding of his powers; but in his statements he is simple, almost instinctively simple. In fact, he may be described as an intuitive artist – as that type of artist whose feeling is like the divining rod which leads down to shafts of golden values and who does not obfuscate his mind with intellectual conceptions of what or how he should create. And having followed his instinctive flair for truth he now applies his conscious powers to perfect his finding and to create his embryonic expressions into paintings of beauty and value.[91]

Similar perceptions of art were reflected in the views of contemporary writers, such as P. D. Ouspensky, whose work *Tertium Organum* (translated into English by one of Gibran's friends and admirers, Claude Bragdon) deeply impressed Gibran:[92]

> Art is a powerful instrument of knowledge of the noumenal world: mysterious depths, each one more amazing than the last, open to the vision of man when he holds in his hands this magical key. But let him *only think* that this mystery is not for knowledge but for pleasure in it, and all the charm disappears at once. Just as soon as art begins to take delight in that beauty which is already *found*, instead of *the search for new beauty* an arrestment occurs and art becomes a superfluous aestheticism, encompassing man's vision like a wall. The aim of art is *the search for beauty*, just as the aim of religion is the search for God and truth. And exactly as art stops, so religion stops also as soon as it ceases to search for God and truth, thinking it has found them. This idea is expressed in the precept: *Seek . . . the kingdom of God and his righteousness . . .* It does not say, find; but merely, seek![93]

Mary, unannounced, went to the exhibition and eavesdropped on some Syrian visitors whom she heard saying that Gibran was the "greatest thing we have here," that he "had the divine in him."[94] The success of the Knoedler show sparked off another offer for an exhibition at the Doll and

Richards gallery in Boston due to open on April 6. However, Gibran's thoughts, like those of everyone in the spring of 1917, were turned toward the awful global events unfolding before his eyes.

Ten days before the exhibition opened, Congress declared war on Germany. Gibran wrote to Mary: "The world is moving so swiftly, and the elements of the world are giving birth to so many new things that you and I cannot but stand in awe before the whole drama."[95] Earlier in the year President Wilson had made a strong demand for a peace of conciliation and was hailed by pacifists as their champion. Indeed, America had done well by remaining neutral. Its overseas trading surplus had increased from $690 million in 1913 to $3 billion in 1916. The first three years of the war had also seen the emergence of no fewer than eight thousand new American millionaires. The basis of this remarkable prosperity had been the dependence of the Allied war economies on massive imports from the United States and the booming arms trade.

By March, however, German submarines had sunk American merchant ships with heavy loss of life. Also, an ideological barrier was removed from the Allied cause by the Russian revolution; as Wilson explained, the Russian people, always "democratic at heart," had moved "in all their naive majesty and might."[96] Finally, Germany was discovered to be plotting combined action with Mexico and Japan in case of war with America. Yet Wilson still hesitated while ships sank and passions mounted. By the time he had called a special session of Congress at the beginning of April, the emotions of the most respectable citizens had reached a dangerous pitch, and even the clergy were condemning pacifists from the pulpit. In Baltimore, the day before Wilson's announcement, rioters broke up a meeting addressed by pacifists. The *New York Times*, ardently interventionist, noticed that the mob was led by "men socially prominent," including "college professors, students, bankers and lawyers."[97] Despite his deep pacifist inclinations Wilson was forced to concede to his "distressing and oppressive duty . . . to lead this great peaceful people into war."[98] Gibran wrote: "The spirit of tomorrow is righteousness and the voice of tomorrow is righteousness . . . nothing happens to the human race which does not happen first to the individual human being . . . all the Czars and all the Kaisers of the world cannot make time walk backward."[99]

When World War I had broken out in 1914, Gibran had written to Mary: "We are living this great war; you and I. All those who live the collective life of this world – are struggling, like you and me, with the nations of Europe."[100]

On April 16, the Doll and Richards gallery in Boston[101] showed Gibran's paintings. Mary went to the exhibition and reported back to him on people's impressions. Her sister Louise Daly had been most appreciative, saying they were "most wonderful as presenting Man as work of Earth's, an earth-product . . . The forms were . . . most delightful – and so full of imagination and feeling." Charles Peabody, whose daughters attended Mary's school, did not care for the form but thought the "colour glorious," reminding him of the finest old Pompeiian.[102]

The Boston *Sunday Herald*, in its review, related something of Gibran's earlier Boston connections, calling him an "assistant" at the Harcourt studio of Fred Holland Day. In the article, entitled "Syrian Suggestions," the writer F. W. Coburn said Gibran's "vague" and "mystical" expression was the "beau ideal" of advanced Bostonians in the days when "wealthy ladies scrubbed church steps." Today, he continued, "the Philistine titters. A student of race psychology, on the contrary, feels sure that here is an expression of the same kind of mentality that produced the delightful 'Automatics' of Saracen art (the Arabic art of Spain) or the exquisite Persian miniatures." The review concluded: "Art conceived in a sublimated ether this of Gibran's surely is."[103]

However, opinions from the critics of Boston were of secondary importance to Gibran. Since the Americans had joined the war, many Syrian and Lebanese exiles had decided to join the French army, which was on the verge of entering Syria. With others in the Syrian community Gibran began to organize a Syria–Mount Lebanon Volunteer Committee. The editors of several Arabic newspapers were on the executive committee,[104] including Dr. Ayub Tabet, who was president, Ameen Rihani, who was vice-president, and Gibran, secretary of English correspondence. The committee used as its slogan the words of President Wilson: "No People must be forced under sovereignty under which it does not wish to live."[105] Gibran wrote to Mary that never before in human history had there been such a "consciousness of State righteousness," and that such nationalism was a necessary step to global consciousness.[106]

Gibran's renewed commitment to the Syrian cause, however, conflicted with his role on the Board of *Seven Arts*,[107] which, by the summer of 1917 was leading with editorials condemning the war. The dilemma that faced Gibran was one being replayed in the lives of many other Americans that summer. Pacifists such as Mary's friend William English Walling and Gibran's colleague James Oppenheim had similar sentiments to those of the poet William Carlos Williams who wrote: "Everything I wanted to see live and thrive was being deliberately murdered in the name of church and state."[108] Friendships were strained – often to breaking point – as people felt compelled to choose either pacifism or patriotism. Charlotte Teller chose pacifism while Mary Haskell was busy collecting money to send to Syria, France, and Belgium. Charlotte stingingly wrote to her old friend: "And you I fear, like Aunt Rose, glory in Red Cross, service badges, thrift – and the whole subtle armament which war begets for the enthusiasts."[109]

By October Gibran's dilemma over his involvement with *Seven Arts* was solved for him, when the magazine, in severe financial straits, had to close. His intense involvement with the Liberation League, however, continued well into the winter. Mary recognized the tremendous strains he was under in trying to reconcile his artistic temperament with heavy political involvement, acknowledging that these pressures were bound to affect his creative output.[110]

When she saw him in Boston just after Christmas he seemed restless, gaunt, and ill at ease. He spent his days quietly recuperating with Marianna, who had recently moved to new accommodation on 76 Tyler Street,[111] and his evenings with Mary. She found him disoriented and obsessed with the war, disclosing that he had recently been sent a death threat, as had Dr. Tabet: it had read "Turkey is not dead – and she has a long arm – if you do not stop what you are doing."[112] He said, the war "robs one's soul of its silence"[113] and showed Mary the scar on his arm that the "shot in Paris" had given him.[114] However, despite his preoccupations he was able to find some solace in her company as she gently encouraged him to write and draw.

By the beginning of January 1918, thanks to Marianna's homely comforts and Mary's encouragement, the scars of the previous year were beginning to heal. On his birthday, January 6, which Gibran believed was the same day that Jesus was born, he told Mary:

> Christ changed the human mind and men found a new path . . . A supreme spirit is born with a vision. He thinks that all other people have the same vision. It takes him years, usually, to find that no one else has it. Perhaps eighty times out of a hundred, the discovery makes him bitter and cynical. Another one of these lovely spirits will simply be supremely lonely. His inner self becomes a hermit. He learns the language of the others and speaks it. He throws a little of his real self into what he says and does, but there are a few – perhaps five percent – who just live their inner life all the time, despite the world about them.[115]

On January 12, his composure and self-confidence returning, he left for New York. Mary was worried about his cold and draughty studio and hoped that he would find enough coal for the winter. Gibran told her that the deprivations of the war years were helping him to appreciate life's necessities.[116] His return to New York brought with it growing demands for his presence at literary gatherings. During the next few weeks he addressed the Poetry Society of America on two separate occasions – receiving such an enthusiastic reception that he was invited back in June to speak on "Walt Whitman and his Influence"[117] – read at some literary gatherings, and turned down two invitations to read his work in Chicago and Pittsburgh. This new-found interest in his work by the American literati convinced Gibran that the horror of war was changing people's attitudes to life and art, creating a thirst for beauty and truth.[118]

This was no more evident than in the attitude of Corinne Roosevelt Robinson. The previous spring she had called for Gibran's "diabolical" work to be discouraged, but now she openly received him at her elite gatherings.

In April Gibran was invited to stay at the writer Marie Tudor Garland's rambling estate at Buzzard's Bay, Massachusetts. He had a "glorious time," wandering by the sea and in the pine forest, watching the herds of Welsh ponies and sheep, talking and playing with the innumerable children who roamed free in the idyllic community. The gentle impressions of woods, streams, and children did him much good, and on his return to Boston Mary observed that he looked "marvellously well – solid, browned, bright-eyed and unnervous, unworn."[119]

During his stay Gibran told her he had been working on "One *Large* thought," which had been filling his mind and heart.[120] The work had been "brooding" in him for eighteen months or more. He and Mary called it "The Counsels" and by June 1919 it had evolved into its final form: *The Prophet.* He had periodically worked on the book since 1912, when he "got the first motif, for his Island God" whose "Prometheus exile shall be an Island one."[121]

This was the beginning of his preoccupation with a work that was to become his *magnum opus,* published in 1923 under the title *The Prophet.* He wrote to Mary:

A voice is shaping itself in my soul and I am waiting for the words. The perception is the largest and most creative I have ever known . . . My one desire now is to find the right form, the right garment, that will cling to the human ear. The World is hungry, Mary, and I have seen and heard the hunger of the World; and if this thing is bread it will find a place in the heart of the world, and if it is not bread it will at least make the hunger of the world deeper and higher.[122]

Gibran still maintained that English was a foreign language to him, but Mary recorded in her journal that his English was the finest she knew: "It is creative and marvellously simple."[123] Gibran, whose understanding of English under Mary's guiding hand was improving all the time, expressed a love for his adopted language: "I have a sense of English and I know many words, for I've an ear for words. It is the shaping of my English expression that comes slowly to me. English is a fine language."[124]

A new era meanwhile was arriving for Mary. She had been asked to become headmistress at the Cambridge School, which eventually became Radcliffe College. Over the years she had grown increasingly disillusioned that her alternative educational approaches had not been fully appreciated by the governors, and she gratefully accepted a new challenge at a school with a pioneering reputation. In her last night at her school, she wrote to Gibran reminiscing over the times they had spent together at 314 Marlborough Place.[125]

However, Mary's hopes that her new school would more readily accept her progressive philosophy were soon to be dashed when a parent refused to send her daughter there because Gibran's painting *The Crucified* was hanging on the wall. The incident, an issue of nudity, deeply upset Mary, who believed Gibran's pictures taught her girls that there was nothing shameful in nakedness. She was outraged that her detractors foolishly thought that "the pictures might make *girls* feel uncomfortable and that girls cannot feel 'the spiritual' quality of the drawings." The artist replied immediately:

> The wisest and the kindest thing to do is to take down from the walls all the pictures that offend the girls and their mothers. The thought that a drawing of mine is making someone uncomfortable, in body or in spirit, is a source of pain and unhappiness to me. We cannot teach the chastity of the nude. People must find it for themselves. We cannot lead people to the hearts of life. They must go by themselves, and each one must go alone.[126]

III

Gibran himself was only too aware of the often intransigent Bostonian mind, and after his seven years in New York, he viewed the petrified traditions of Boston with some distaste:

> This city was called in the past the city of science and art, but today it is the city of traditions. The souls of its inhabitants are petrified; even their thoughts are old and worn out. The strange thing about this city . . . is that the petrified is always proud and boastful, and the worn-out and old holds its chin high.[127]

In contrast, he had come to love New York:

> Such a wonderful city. It is always changing . . . It is like a flower always opening wider . . . Whenever I come back to New York after being away, I feel that here is a life always opening and lifting, up and out, with a freedom and a willingness, and eternal newness, that makes it the most joyous city on the earth.[128]

Still looking for an American publisher Gibran was fortunate when his friend Witter Bynner, onetime editor of *McClure's Magazine*, arranged a dinner in Greenwich Village with a young publisher called Alfred Knopf, whose acquaintance with Gibran would eventually propel them both onto the world stage. Knopf, who in 1915 had announced a new venture, the firm of Alfred A. Knopf,[129] was a graduate of Columbia who had studied comparative literature and had been inspired to enter publishing after seeing the work of the publisher William Heinemann on a visit to England. By 1917 he had published books by Carl Van Vechten, Ezra Pound, Joseph Hergesheimer, and Henry L. Mencken, winning himself a reputation as an innovative publisher.[130] Bynner intuitively sensed that the twenty-four-year-old publisher would be interested in the work of his Syrian friend, and was proved right when Knopf agreed to publish Gibran's *The Madman* in October.

Gibran wrote a poem, "Defeat, my Defeat," for a pamphlet advocating self-determination for the fragmented countries of Eastern Europe, a piece later published in *The Madman* (under the title "Defeat"). Although the poem's message that defeat is dearer "than a thousand victories" was explicitly political, its underlying theme reflected Gibran's more personal feelings:

167

Defeat, my Defeat, my shining sword and shield,
In your eyes I have read
That to be enthroned is to be enslaved,
And to be understood is to be levelled down,
And to be grasped is but to reach one's fulness
And like a ripe fruit to fall and be consumed.[131]

Along with the other prose-poems in *The Madman*, this piece expressed the multiple levels of isolation that Gibran had experienced during his thirty-five years: a Christian from a predominantly Muslim region; the offspring of a broken marriage; a Lebanese *émigré* in America; and an artist living in a materialist society. Often he found himself a stranger, not only among the native population of America, but also among his own kin and countrymen in exile. To be an emigrant is undoubtedly to be an alien, but to be an emigrant mystical poet is in many ways to be thrice alienated. To the geographical alienation is added the estrangement from both conventional society and the world of spatio-temporal existence. Often Gibran was gripped with a triple longing; a longing for his homeland; for a more just and tolerant society; and for a higher world of spiritual union – a triple longing which fired his creativity.[132] Now, in 1918, Gibran found that the Western world was prepared to listen to him.

In *The Madman* Gibran offers a self-commentary on the condition of being an artist. In his solitude he finds "freedom and safety" in his "madness" – his creativity.[133] Gibran once wrote to a friend about "madness":

> So you are on the brink of madness. This is a good bit of news, majestic in its fearfulness, fearful in its majesty and beauty. I say that madness is the first step towards unselfishness . . . Be mad and tell us what is behind the veil of "sanity." The purpose of life is to bring us closer to those secrets, and madness is the only means. Be mad, and remain a mad brother to your mad brother.[134]

On the publication of *The Madman* Gibran recounted to Mary a story of a man he had once seen sitting on the same rock day after day, high up in the Lebanese mountains. When he asked someone about this strange behavior he was told: "'Oh, he is a little off *here*' (touching his forehead)." Gibran said: "People called 'touched' are very significant to me." He then recounted to Mary how he had approached this man, asking him: "What do you do?"

"I look upon the fields," the hermit replied, "Isn't that enough?" meaning, "Wouldn't one thousandth part of all that wonder and glow, more than fill you up?"[135]

Gibran, well versed in the parables of the Sufi tradition in which "the madman," by uttering the most outrageous and unexpected things, provides the Sufi teacher with a method of attracting attention to something in order to make a point, had always been interested in the theme of "madness."[136] The twelfth-century Persian poet Fariduddin Attar of Nishapur, who wrote the classic text *Parliament of the Birds*, was particularly fond of the image of "the madman," and his tales include "The Madman and the Muezzin," "The Madman and the Wrestler," "The Perception of the Madman," and "The Heart," all of which portray the "madman" as a man of insight:

> Someone went up to a madman who was weeping in the bitterest possible way. He said: "Why do you cry?" The madman answered: "I am crying to attract the pity of His heart." The other told him: "Your words are nonsense, for He has no physical heart." The madman answered: "It is you who are wrong, for He is the owner of all the hearts which exist. Through the heart you can make your connection with God."[137]

Other stories concerning the wisdom of "the madman" are to be found in the subtleties of Mulla Nasrudin, a classical figure in Sufi literature resembling the "Shakespearean fool," who bridges the gap between the mundane life and the transmutation of consciousness through his humorous stories. Through the framework of such tales the reader is led from the familiar to the unknown, from the seen to the unseen. In a classic Sufi text, *Revelation of the Veiled*, Shibli, a disciple of the Sufi Master Abu'l Qasim el-Juniad, is mocked as "a madman" because of his cryptic talk. Shibli's reply to his detractors reveals the true significance of "the madman":

> To your mind, I am mad.
> To my mind, you are all sane.
> So I pray to increase my madness
> And to increase your sanity.
> My "madness" is from the power of Love;
> Your sanity is from the strength of unawareness.[138]

As well as employing Sufi notions of "the madman" as an inspired poet-seer whose madness is a mark of special wisdom, Gibran built on a tradition explored by Shakespeare and Blake, stretching back to Plato[139] who perceived that madness can be akin to a state of illumination; while Jacob Boehme, one of Blake's spiritual masters, enthusiastically testifies to this the most powerful and universal folk tradition:

> It is true the world will be apt enough to censure thee for a madman in walking contrary to it: And thou art not to be surprised if the children thereof laugh at thee, calling thee silly fool. For the way to the love of God is folly to the world, but is wisdom to the children of God. Hence, whenever the world perceiveth this holy fire of love in God's children, it concludeth immediately that they are turned fools, and are besides themselves. But to the children of God, that which is despised of the world is the greatest treasure.[140]

In *King Lear*, as well as investing the king with motley, the tragedy is also the crowning and apotheosis of the fool, and in *A Midsummer Night's Dream* the lunatic is ascribed as a man of vision:

> The lunatic, the lover, and the poet
> Are of imagination all compact.[141]

In the same vein, Blake wrote:

> "Madman" I have been call'd: "Fool" they call thee,
> I wonder which they Envy, Thee or Me?[142]

The thirty-five prose-poems and Sufi-style parables of *The Madman* present a considerable change in the tone of Gibran's writing. Published within weeks of the end of World War I it represents the pessimism of a man who has just experienced one of the darkest periods in human history. The dominant note is that of mordant irony, unlike the confident affirmations expressed in his previous work, *A Tear and a Smile*.

Each parable in *The Madman* contains a moral, with some subjects foreshadowing those dealt with in some of Gibran's later works. Themes such as malevolence, hypocrisy, injustice, conformity, ambition, blindness, and puritanism are explored with poignancy, and, although expressed lyrically, the sardonic note ultimately prevails. The influence of Nietzsche is detectable in the parables – a perception of man and woman as yet *unrealized*, still shackled by slavery and conditioned morality.

Gibran explores the Sufi idea that humankind has no fixed nature, no unity; yet behind the conditioned masks of personality lies an unmistakable "essence." This essence can only grow at the expense of personality,[143] "the masks" which must be torn from him. In the opening to *The Madman* Gibran encapsulates this idea, describing the narrator's epiphany when he becomes a madman:

> You ask me how I became a madman. It happened thus: One day, long before many gods were born, I woke from a deep sleep and found all my masks were stolen, – the seven masks I have fashioned and worn in seven lives, – I ran maskless through the crowded streets shouting, "Thieves, thieves, the cursèd thieves."
>
> Men and women laughed at me and some ran to their houses in fear of me.
>
> And when I reached the market place, a youth standing on a house-top cried, "He is a madman." I looked up to behold him; the sun kissed my own naked face for the first time. For the first time the sun kissed my own naked face and my soul was inflamed with love for the sun, and I wanted my masks no more. And as if in a trance I cried, "Blessed, blessed are the thieves who stole my masks."
>
> Thus I became a madman.
>
> And I have found both freedom and safety in my madness: the freedom of loneliness and the safety from being understood, for those who understand us enslave something in us.
>
> But let me not be too proud of my safety. Even a Thief in a jail is safe from another thief.[144]

The theme of "masks" reappears in other parables. In "Faces" the Madman has seen "a face with a thousand countenances," but with his newfound perceptiveness, he is able to "behold the reality beneath."[145] In "My Friend," which captured Mary Haskell's recent ambivalent mood toward conventionality, the narrator maintains that people's appearances differ from their reality and "mask" their true selves in a futile attempt to cross "the unbridgeable gulf" to others.[146]

Gibran goes on to attack social values by revealing the motives that contradict their overt expressions. In "The Sleep-Walkers" he illustrates the subconscious emotions behind everyday civility.[147] In "The Two Hermits" the demand for legal justice, for correct weight and measure, is another "mask" that really hides a secret desire to fight for the sake of fighting.[148]

The parables also attack conventional values by portraying them in their most extreme and extravagant forms. In "The Blessed City," everyone blindly adheres to scripture, yet by following the letter as distinct from the spirit of the law, everyone has a single eye and only one hand – for it is more profitable for one member to perish than for the whole body to "be cast into hell." The only healthy people are those too young to read scripture and understand its commandments.[149] In "The Other Language" an infant talks to older people in the language of the other world from which he came, but they do not understand him. He continually objects to the lies they tell him, but as he grows older and more crystallized in his thinking, and identified with his masks, he forgets "the language of that other world," and as a result loses contact with his essential self.[150]

Other parables deal ironically with the laws, customs, and conventional norms of society. In "The Two Cages," a caged sparrow addresses a caged lion as his "brother prisoner" – imprisonment having tamed the lion and brought him down to an equal status. The cage, a symbol of oppression, keeps the strong and brave at the same base level as the weak,[151] echoing Blake's maxim: "One Law for the Lion and Ox is oppression."[152] This general trend of thought permeates *The Madman*, finding its most powerful expression in "The Perfect World" where in the "civilized" world "virtues, O God, are measured . . . sins are weighed, and even the countless things that pass in the dim twilight of neither sin nor virtue are recorded and catalogued."[153]

The other key theme of *The Madman* is concerned with the liberation of the greater self from the lesser selves that manifest themselves in humankind's multiplicity. In the parable "The Seven Selves" Gibran explores the legions of selves which incessantly struggle with each other for supremacy. Again Sufi thought is evident here: "Man thinks many things. He thinks he is One. He is usually several. Until he becomes One he cannot have a fair idea of what he is at all."[154] Gibran names seven of these selves: the negative self, full of emotions that "renew his pain by day and recreate his sorrow by night"; the joyous self; the passionate self; the "tempest-like self" locked in hatred and loathing; the pitiful laboring self; and the thinking self – all of which rebel against "this restless madman."[155] The seventh self, however, is able to observe the clamour of the other selves.[156]

In "The Grave-Digger" the theme of liberation is also explored. Inner freedom can only be attained if individuals can let go of their "dead selves," those aspects of false personality that, being the ultimate cause of suffering, must be sacrificed.

The themes of sacrifice and loss are continued in such pieces as "When my Sorrow was born" and "And When my Joy was Born." In "Crucified," the madman asks men to crucify him. On the cross he smiles, and asks only that men remember that he smiled. He does not consider his action to be an atonement, a sacrifice or a means of obtaining glory, nor has he anything to forgive. He only "thirsted," beseeching men to "give me my blood to drink," for he was imprisoned and "sought a door into larger days and nights." As he dies he says: "And now I go – as others already crucified have gone. And think not we are weary of crucifixion. For we must be crucified by larger and yet larger men, between greater earths and greater heavens"[157] – death becoming the burial of an old self and the acquisition of a new and a greater self.

"The Greater Sea" is the parable alluding to this, the sea representing the great spirit or greater self.[158] In this piece Gibran distinguishes between the "Great Sea" and the "great sea." The shores of the latter are littered by different "types" or personalities: the "pessimist," the "optimist," the "philanthropist," the "mystic," the "idealist," the "realist," and the "puritan," who is the "most deadly" of all. The madman seeks "a hidden and lonely place" where he can bathe unjudged and naked in the "Great Sea." He discovers that he will only find such a place to disclose his "sacred nakedness" when he leaves the shore of the "great sea."[159] The sense of the limited existence of humankind is symbolized by the shore, and reflects Gibran's lifelong distrust of arid intellectuals caught up in a one-dimensional view of reality. They remain by the "great sea" clothed in the garments of convention and trapped in a mundane, self-absorbed, and meaningless existence; the scientific materialist, obsessed with subjecting natural forces, even turns his back on the "Great sea . . . the whole he cannot grasp," and merely "busies himself with a fragment."[160]

In the "Scarecrow," Gibran presents the philosopher or empty intellectual as a man of straw. His sterility and one-dimensional view of reality leads him into an ugly pessimism, symbolized by two crows who have built a nest under his hat. The crows' nest is also intended to illustrate that the scarecrow, or philosopher, is useless and incapable of doing the only work he was meant to do, scaring the crows and thus allowing the seeds to grow.[161]

Gibran's first English work in 1918 contains parables that elicit inner meaning far removed from a literal level of meaning. In some of the parables Gibran subtly attacks literal interpretation as in "The Blessed City,"[162] his parables succeeding in lifting the reader's natural level of comprehension to another level of meaning, to "the language of that other world."[163] The parables explore the nature of the distances between individual egos and suggest the means whereby these distances may be spanned: "Know you not that there is no distance save that which the soul does not span in fancy? And when the soul shall span the distance, it becomes a rhythm in the soul."[164] It is precisely this rhythm that Gibran's parables attempt to reveal.

One of the first critics to penetrate the depths of Gibran's parables was Annie Salem Otto, who wrote:

Gibran's parables delineate repeatedly the possibility that man's dreams or fancy, which are man's ability to perceive the ideal or universal character of experience, can, rather than separate man from man, create a communion or a sharing in the existent spiritual essence of man. In this possibility lies man's only hope of resolving the recurrent, useless conflicts in himself and consequently in earthly experiences, which collectively is called civilization. Gibran's parables portray first an awareness of existing relations, of the possibility that these relations can be changed, and finally, of the motivations and behaviour necessary for change.[165]

Newspaper reviewers of the day, however, only vaguely detected the higher meanings that the poet aimed to convey. Howard Willard Cook, who was acquainted with Gibran, rather non-committedly called him "a new psalmist . . . who gives to us in the Western world a note too seldom found in the writings of our own poets."[166] A critic in *The Dial* thought that in his parables Gibran "curiously seems to express what Rodin did with marble and clay";[167] and the *Evening Post* wrote that the poet employed his parable "with great skill"; the pieces "might have been taken directly out of Jung's revealing 'Wandlungen und Symbole der Libido.'"[168] Mary's response came from the heart: "In *The Madman's* presence . . . many veils dissolve between my soul and me. That is why I love it."[169]

In March 1919 the *Evening Post* compared Gibran with Rabindranath Tagore[170] in terms of his use of the parable and his Eastern origins; "But," wrote Joseph Gollomb, "there resemblance ends and differences appear":

Tagore . . . is a figure from some canvas Sir Frederic Leighton might have painted of a religious mystic. Gibran is Broadway or Copley square or The Strand or Avenue de L'Opera – a correctly dressed cosmopolitan of the Western world.

His dark brows and moustache and somewhat curly hair above a good forehead; the clear brown eyes, thoughtful but never abstracted in expression; the sensibly tailored clothes, smart but not conspicuous – there seemed to me a chameleon-like ease of adaptiveness about him. In his studio in West Tenth Street he looked a sensible denizen of Greenwich Village – for such there be. But had I seen him at a congress of economists, or in a Viennese cafe, or in his native Syria, I feel he would look equally in the picture in each instance.

Gollomb concluded by saying that Gibran "has come to stay, if one is to judge by the impression created by his first work . . . He is emerging into the citizenship of the whole new world. Is it Kahlil Gibran, the individual, who is thus emerging? Or is it the voice and genius of the Arabic people?"[171]

Marguerite Wilkinson, in an anthology of contemporary poetry, *New Voices*, felt that *The Madman* expressed "the best parables that can be found in contemporary poetry."[172] Some reviewers, however, doubted the lasting appeal of his work. *The Nation*'s reviewer found the work "repellent in its exotic perversity," unlikely to bridge the chasm between East and West.[173] Another reviewer challenged the popular notion, reinforced by the flyer for *The Madman*, that Rodin had called Gibran "the William Blake of the Twentieth Century." The *Poetry* editor Harriet Monroe, who had met Rodin, recalled that the Frenchman was prone to "serene amiability towards all fellow artists" and in any case if by chance he had said this of Gibran, it was his art and not his poetry that he was referring to.[174]

Gibran sent some of his reviews to May Ziadah in Cairo, including the one from *The Dial*:

> Rodin compared Gibran to William Blake. But the parables collected in *The Madman* are more reminiscent of Zarathustra's maskings and unmaskings, of the long rising rhythms of Tagore. The English language never seems a fit medium for work of this nature. It is too angular, too resisting to hold the meanings which Oriental literature crowds as thickly and dazzling as jewels on an encrusted sword-hilt.[175]

May Ziadah too had reservations about the work, and in a letter back to Gibran told him that she perceived in *The Madman* elements of "cruelty" and "dark caverns." Gibran replied:

> The reason those Westerners are so happy with the madman and his dreams is that they are bored with their own dreams and have an innate weakness for the strange and the exotic, especially if it be dressed in Oriental garb . . . What am I to say about the caverns of my soul? Those caverns

that frighten you so – I take refuge there when I grow weary of the ways of men, of their rankly blossoming fields and overgrown forests. I retreat into the caverns of my soul when I can find no other place to rest my head; and if some of those whom I love possessed the courage to enter into these caverns they would find nothing but a man on his knees saying his prayers.[176]

A year later, reviewing his relationship with the Madman, Gibran wrote to May:

The madman is not wholly myself, the thoughts and inclinations I tried to express are by no means a complete picture of my own thoughts and inclinations; indeed the tone I chose to suit the character of the madman is not the tone I chose to adopt when sitting talking to a friend whom I love and respect. However, if you must define my reality through what I have written, what stops you from identifying me with the young man of the forest in *The Processions* instead of with the madman? My soul, May, is far more akin to the young man of the forest and to the tune of his flute than it is to the madman and his cries.[177]

IV

The "young man of the forest" alluded to by Gibran in this letter appeared in *al-Mawakib* (*The Procession*), which was published in the beginning of March 1919 by *Mir'at al-Gharb*. Gibran had been inspired to write most of this work, which contained ten drawings, during his summer vacations in the forests around Cohasset. The fact that the poem is the only major one he wrote in the traditional style (*qasidah*) confers upon it a certain significance. The work is also significant on a number of other counts. *The Procession*, in its theme and style, weaves together elements of both the Sufi and Romantic traditions, inaugurates an original form of Arabic poetry, and represents the very essence of *mahjari* (Arab immigrant) verse.

The Procession is written in the form of a dialogue between a youth, who sings of freedom and joy and love of nature, and a sage, who laments the futility of the world. The sage, who would be more appropriately translated as the "Old Man," expresses Gibran's boredom with the world, its paradoxes, its miseries, and its pain. In the style of a Sufi poem, *The Procession* relies heavily on symbol and metaphor. The enduring metaphor of the poem is that of the "forest" out of which the youth has emerged and on the edge of which the conversation takes place – the "forest," where all dichotomy vanishes and fragmentation disappears:

In the forest dwells no freeman,
Nor is there a humble slave.
Honors are but false delusions,
Like the froth upon the wave.

Should the almond spray its blossoms
On the turf around its feet,
Never will it claim a lordship,
Nor disdain the grass to greet.[178]

The forest thus represents the wholeness that the world has lost through mistaken perceptions of duality. To the poet living in the world of the imagination, this duality is but a chimera; for the essential truth of all things rejects fragmentation, and in its perfect condition humanity does not suffer from opposing forces pulling its internal pendulum in opposite directions.

Gibran challenges too established religions, which, emphasizing the externalities of form and ritual, have separated themselves from their original spirit, sentiments echoed by William Blake in *The Marriage of Heaven and Hell*.[179] In *The Procession*, Gibran makes an energetic attempt to reject duality, level by level:

In the forest no distinction
Of soul or body is instilled.
Air is water aerated
And the dew – water distilled.[180]

In challenging duality, death is conquered in the forest, which becomes a symbol of immortality:

There is not a death in nature,
Nor a grave is set apart;
Should the month of April vanish
"Gifts of joy" do not depart.[181]

In addition to representing unity of being, the forest symbolizes the world of nature as worshiped by Rousseau, Wordsworth, Blake, and the Romantics. Nasib Aradiah, who wrote the introduction to *The Procession*, describes it not as a call for a return to nature, as made by the thinkers of eighteenth-century Europe, but rather a call to simplicity. "Nature," as

Gibran understood it, could be found in the city. However, the distinction is not a strong one, for if the city were to become completely free of corruption and confusion, it would consequently return to nature. In fact, the entire philosophy behind this attitude toward nature is really a protest against the confusion, corruption, and deception that city life has created, against which poets such as Shelley had protested.[182]

It is perhaps the seeming impossibility of returning to an ancient time that prompts Gibran to celebrate the natural world around him. His youth sings of the delights that are possible in the forest:

> Have you taken to the forest,
> Shunned the palace for abode?
> Followed brooklets in their courses,
> Climbed the rocks along the road?
>
> Have you ever bathed in fragrance,
> Dried yourself in sheets of light?
> Ever quaff the wine of dawning,
> From ethereal goblets bright?[183]

The images of nature that the poet allows his youth to convey – winter and spring, shepherd boy and singing reed, birds, trees, flowers, air, and blades of grass – all symbolize the freedom and tranquillity that only nature can bestow upon those who are its children.

The refrain of the youth throughout the poem is "Give to me the reed and sing thou!" and in some sense it is this melodious reed that even surpasses the main metaphor of the poem, for in its music, true unity between body and soul is achieved and within its scope all requirements of justice, knowledge, and love are fulfilled. It is the melodious reed with its music that can bridge the gap, bringing about unity and perfection.

The rhythmic *Procession* could be described as a philosophical poem, and in fact it represents an original form of Arabic poetry partially for this reason: before Gibran, such a long reflective poem of a philosophical nature had not been written in Arabic. It is also significant for being the single most influential work in the *mahjari* poetic tradition. The forest as a metaphor came to permeate the imagination of immigrant poets such as Rashid Ayoub, Nasib Aradiah, and Nadra Haddad. For such poets, nature becomes a measure of perfection, humanity's teacher and guide. In this, the *mahjari* poets concur with Wordsworth:

One impulse from a vernal wood
May teach you more of man,
Of moral evil and of good,
Than all the sages can.[184]

The Procession, expressing as it does Gibran's faith in nature, is written in the great Romantic tradition conveying an almost Wordsworthian faith in the sanctity of nature and in the innate excellence of humanity itself. *The Procession* cries out for the statement of innocence passionately expressed in Blake's *Songs of Experience*:

Hear the voice of the Bard!
Who Present, Past, & Future, sees;
Whose ears have heard
The Holy Word
That walk'd among the ancient trees,
Calling the lapsed Soul.[185]

In its original Arabic, *The Procession* is 200 lines long and takes the form of rhyming quatrains, each quatrain possessing its own *qafiyeh*, or rhyming scheme. The quatrains are followed by couplets which form the refrain sung by the youth. The meter of the lines spoken by the youth is lively, light, while the meter of the sage's lines is heavier and carries the tone of sermonizing and oratory.

Between four and seven quatrains comprise the sage's sections. The poem ends with a rhyming triplet which is completely independent of the structure of the rest of the poem. Gibran selects certain themes out of the many diverse forms of duality, in one place speaking about justice, will, and knowledge, and in another about gentleness and kindness. A thematic pattern emerges as the discussion moves from love to happiness, to the soul, the body, and then death.

The demands of the *qafiyeh* impose certain constraints on Gibran's ability to carry out consistently the thematic pattern of the poem. For example, he begins one quatrain by referring to *adl* (justice), but the requirements of the *qafiyeh* prevent him from ending the quatrain with the word for injustice (*thulm*), so instead he uses *al-'iqab* (punishment).

The poem ends on a note of despair, with "The Capitulation of the Sage":

Had I the days in hand to string,
Only in forest they'd be strewn,
But circumstances drive us on
In narrow paths by Kismet hewn.

For Fate has ways we cannot change,
While weakness preys upon our Will;
We bolster with excuse the self,
And help that Fate ourselves to kill.[186]

This discordant note contrasts with the optimism of *The Prophet*, yet in some sense by expressing the voice of doubt through the sage, Gibran is better able to convince us of the truth of the passion and belief expressed throughout by the youth. There is an endearing quality about Gibran's recognition of human weaknesses and failures. The moral of the poem is in no way diminished by the question and the doubt. Although "Fate has ways we cannot change," the earlier passages in which the human spirit is celebrated and sung prompts a further question: Even if fate dissipates our hopes and ambitions, might not our strong spirits create triumph out of failure and defeat, in some other way?

The Procession is about life, about the procession of those who have gone astray in their search for happiness, freedom, and immortality. It is the image of a humanity that has lost its way, lost the forest, and grown deaf to the awakening tune of the melodious reed. Conforming to the great traditions of both Romantic and Sufi poetry, and reflecting the themes of *mahjari* poetry, the forest almost becomes a utopia, signifying immortality. Singing represents perfection, for the forest does not recognize a religion or will, or justice other than the truth, whereas singing is the most exalted form of religion, of will and of justice. It is love, it is fire, it is light, both body and soul united.

The delicate tones and lyrical charms of *The Procession* meant that it soon became a popular poem to be recited or sung. Gibran attended one of these occasions,[187] and one year after its publication the poem was sung by choirs in Cairo.[188]

May Ziadah's spirited review[189] of *al-Mawakib* ignored the poem's irregularities in syntax and grammar, dismissing these as merely expressing the poet's rebellious voice. The review instead concentrated on emphasizing those salient features of the poet's message – the mystical elements of his vision, the innovative style, imagery, and symbolism – uncommon in the current literature of the day. In the eyes of the traditionalists Gibran was an iconoclastic and a corrupter of the purity of the Arabic language. Twenty years after the publication of *al-Mawakib*, Omar Farroukh's[190] scathing criticism of the style and grammatical structure of the poem still represented, in its ferocity, the intense emotional opposition of the traditionalists against all forms of innovation and creativity introduced by *al-mahjar* poets into modern Arabic literature. Gibran, however, was aware that the major poets before him in the history of Arabic literature had defied, like him, the rules of syntax and grammar in their brilliant innovative experimentation with poetic technique.

As a classical poem *al-Mawakib* was a complete failure, but as an experiment in the creation of new imagery and rhythm as well as the employment of symbolism as a powerful poetic tool, it will remain as the most original and influential poem of the school of Romanticism in Arabic literature.

Gibran's thoughts turned to Cairo in 1919 when he renewed his correspondence with May Ziadah. In the summer of 1919 he told her that his growing reputation meant he was being inundated with invitations, visitors, and people who "devoured" his precious time. He wanted to "escape to the East," away from his growing renown which seemed like responsibility foisted on him by others, causing him to become aware of his own weaknesses.[191]

Although invited to speak about his work to the literati, he most enjoyed himself when he visited Mary Haskell's new school – "the sweetest audience" he had ever had.[192] Soon afterwards he made some designs for the school shield and school ring.[193]

Gibran's social life was full, particularly in the company of Rose O'Neill's distinguished and flamboyant coterie at her Washington Square studio, yet he still took on other responsibilities: his publisher in Egypt, Emile Zaydan of *al-Hilal*, was pressing him for an anthology of prose-poems and he was contributing to a local magazine *Fatat-Boston* (*Young Women of Boston*).

Most of his days and evenings taken up, Gibran wrote late into the night[194] and, despite his fatigue, felt excited by the post-war atmosphere:

Everything is different. Everybody is different. The faces on the streets and in shops and on cars and trains are different. There is a new look in people's eyes and a new ring in their voices. And it is not just the victory of one part of the world over the other that brought this heavenly change. It is the victory of the Spirit over that which is less spirit.[195]

Despite his relief that the war had ended he was still deeply concerned about the fate of Syria, and his involvement with Syrian affairs continued: "Our good friends the missionaries are working hard for Turkey," he sarcastically explained to Mary: "They would have us be where we were in 1914 . . . and some of them have the ear of President Wilson. We are indeed busy protesting."[196]

Wilson meanwhile had visited Europe expecting to build a new world on the ruins of the old with a League of Nations to uphold the law. Although Gibran felt "the gracious spirit with which the mighty ones of the earth meet at Paris," he asked, "But how can they help it [the world]? The new day is upon them and Life is whispering in their ears. Life at heart is a well of sweet justice." Gibran's belief in justice was one not held by the world leaders, who, in their demands for reparation from Germany, were unwittingly to sow the seeds of an even greater apocalypse twenty years later.[197] Gibran wrote to Mary that it was only "our extreme youth that makes us doubt Life," and that had justice tempered by forgiveness been done, people would in time have realized the "sacredness of the war to all the nations of the earth."[198]

By February the fate of smaller nations such as Lebanon in the great scheme of things was still unclear: there appeared to be a disagreement among the nations of Europe about the Near East – particularly about Lebanon and Syria. Gibran believed that whatever the nations agreed upon the people themselves must make or unmake the future of Lebanon and Syria. The destiny of small nations, he believed, lay within themselves and he felt he could play his part:

No matter what happens in Paris I, among many Syrians, shall go on fighting for my country. Perhaps the best form of fighting is in painting pictures and writing poetry – that means I have to fight my own countrymen. It is worthwhile – anything that burns and makes others burn is worthwhile.[199]

His thoughts at this time turned to the East and to May Ziadah. In July he wrote to her:

I have recently established a bond, abstract, delicate, firm, strange and unlike all other bonds in its nature and characteristics, a bond which cannot be compared to the natural familial bonds, a bond which, indeed, is far more steadfast, firm and permanent even than moral bonds. Not a single one of the threads which form this bond was woven by the days and nights which measure time and interspace the distance that separates the cradle from the grave. Not a single one of those threads was woven by past interests or future aspirations – for this bond has existed between two people who were brought together by neither the past nor the present, and who may not be united by the future either.[200]

V

In the autumn of 1919 a book of his drawings[201] was published. Alice Raphael Eckstein, in her Introduction to *Twenty Drawings*, declared Gibran to be a worthy representative of the genius of the Arab world to which the Western world owed such a debt. She informed her predominantly American audience that Gibran's art contained a clue to the "entrancing mystery of the harmonies and dissonances" that exist between the East and the West. His work, she felt, constituted the moving current of life in all nations and throughout all ages, and his poetry was a blend of "ancient imagery coupled with the poignant irony of modern introspection."[202]

Raphael[203] in her essay attempted to contextualize Gibran's place in the history and development of art. His paintings, she wrote, transformed traditional Western conceptions of oriental art. In spite of his filial allegiance to the Middle East she perceived him to be a citizen of the world. Though Westerners have at times acknowledged their debt in literature and science to the Arab world, Raphael believed that it was part of Gibran's task to introduce to Western art the vast poetical conceptions which constitute a part of the heritage of the Arabian mind. She perceived that he was also engaged in the struggles between the classic and the Romantic tendencies in art, and in the reconstruction of a new era which aimed to adjust the imperishable legacy of the old world with the ever-evolving, fluctuating tendencies which constitute the essence of true Romanticism.

The recent global cataclysms which had shattered philosophies, dogmas, and artistic beliefs undoubtedly demanded that civilization reevaluate its ethical and spiritual foundations, its "standards in the life of the soul, of which art is the most profound manifestation." If humanity, argued Raphael, was to redeem itself from the pit, it must turn to more vital forms of self-expression. Religion in the traditional meaning, therefore, would not and could not lift humankind out of its rut of suffering. Only in another form of expression which portrayed the realities of the soul, either in terms of science, art, or social creeds, would the human race effect a transition between the death agony of the old world and the travail of the new. During these opening moments of transition in 1919, Raphael detected certain germinating influences whereby the art of the future would not be evaluated in terms of self-expression alone, but would be measured by its relation to the organic process of which it is an integral part. It is at this point, she stated, that "symbolism in its truest applications reveals itself," whereby artists again must become concerned with the life of the inner world.

Raphael felt that Gibran's work was at the dividing-line of East and West, the symbolist and the ideationist, and had absorbed both traditions of forms and the inner meaning of the idea. The qualities of East and West were thus blended in him with a "singular felicity of expression," and as such, Raphael asserted, he transcended the conflict of schools. The deep, unifying nature of his work ensured that no conflict arose in his creations over whether the idea shall prevail over the emotion, or whether the emotion shall sway the thought: "They co-exist in harmony and the result is an expression of sheer beauty in which thought and feeling are equally blended."[204] Raphael detected in the instinctive simplicity of his paintings the art of the sculptor who does not obfuscate his mind with intellectual conceptions and so cannot deal with anything other than the essential idea and the beauty of form. As such, she wrote, Gibran's art is symbolic in the deepest sense of the word because its roots spring from those basic truths which are fundamental for all ages and experiences:[205]

For amidst the deluge which has overwhelmed our world of art, when Cubists collide with Vorticists and both are submerged by the onrushing of the Orphicists – when school and type arise and as swiftly decline in the quest of the new and the age is seeking a picture of its soul in barbaric imitation of genuine barbarism, it is of inestimable value to come upon an artist who is fulfilling himself in his work apart from any claptrap of modern devices. Gibran has not gone to strange lands to study the new but he has walked the silent path of the meditative creator and he has brought out of his own depths these eternal verities of the history of man's inner life. He has recreated the symbolic incarnation of the All-Mother[206] – he has divined the flying wish of humanity and he has laid bare and retold the story of the Passion.

In the poetic revelation of these psychologic conceptions of humanity he exhibits a world of consummate beauty to the younger artists of America whose life he has chosen to share. He is expressing the vast, the infinite forms of the ever fluid past and is showing us how these imperishable memories can stimulate the art of the future . . .

> For Gibran belongs to that group of artists whose message always heralds a period of transition and whose voice challenges the present to a recapitulation of its standards.[207]

In a letter to May Ziadah shortly after the publication of *Twenty Drawings*, Gibran spoke of those creative souls he considered to herald such a period of transition.[208] It is interesting that along with the sculptor Rodin and painter Carrière, Gibran names a composer, Debussy. Although he played no musical instrument, he had loved music from an early age, and over the years had learned something of its principles and structures. He was equally fond of Western and oriental music and hardly a week went by without him visiting some musical event. "Of all European music I prefer those pieces known as symphonies, sonatas and cantatas . . . opera lacks the artistic simplicity which suits my nature and is tuned to my likes and dislikes."[209] Two of his favorite composers were Beethoven, whose symphonies he thought were "one of the pillars of the temple of Art," and Debussy, whom he had met in Paris.[210]

For Gibran music represents the possible reconciliation between the ideal world and the real world in which we live.[211] How can we transcend the threshold of the world and enter the ideal world in which all earthly divisions disappear? It is music that par excellence has the efficacy to achieve this – a spiritual power that Gibran's beloved Beethoven realized in his music and words:

> Music is indeed the mediator between the spiritual and sensual life. Do not the spiritual contents of a poem become sensual feeling through melody? . . . There, the spirit extends itself to unbounded universality, where, all in all forms itself into a bed for the stream of feelings, which take their rise in the simple musical thought, and which else would die unperceived away . . . One must have rhythm in the mind, to comprehend music in its essential being: music gives presentiment, inspiration of heavenly knowledge, and that which the spirit feels sensual in it, is the embodying of spiritual knowledge.[212]

Twenty Drawings received a perspicacious review in *The Nation*,[213] and when Gibran saw Mary in November she told him that his paintings were, in her opinion, becoming "more infinitely expressive." Gibran told her of his plans to publish another book of poems and parables, *The Forerunner*[214] before publishing *The Prophet* – the work he had been living with for most of his life: "I have the Arabic original of it, in elementary form, that I did when I was sixteen years old. It is full of the sacredness of my inner life. It's been always in me; but I couldn't hurry it. I couldn't do it earlier."[215]

The day after meeting Mary, and exactly a year after World War I ended, Gibran wrote to May in Cairo, revealing that he believed *The Prophet* to be the most important work of his life:

> *The Prophet* . . . is my rebirth and my first baptism, the only thought in me that will make me worthy to stand in the light of the sun. For this prophet had already "written" me before I attempted to "write" him, had created me before I created him, and had silently set me on a course to follow him for seven thousand leagues before he appeared in front of me to dictate his wishes and inclinations.[216]

During the winter months Gibran's commitments continued to grow. Knoedler & Co. exhibited some of his paintings at their Fifth Avenue galleries alongside the work of Bonnard, Carrière, Cezanne, Pissaro, and others,[217] and the prestigious Macdowell Club of New York invited him to read from his work.[218]

As the first winter snows fell on New York, Gibran's thoughts once again turned to Lebanon:

> It is an awe-inspiring scene, gloriously pure and untarnished, taking my thoughts back to the north of Lebanon, to the days of my childhood when I used to make shapes and figures from the snow, which melted as soon as the sun came up. I love these showers of snow just as I love storms.[219]

When winter turned to spring Mary visited him in New York. He greeted her with the news that the twelve artists in 51 West Tenth Street, on hearing that their rent was to be increased by 300 percent, had decided to buy the building themselves. He had recently given five readings – "three of them I was paid for, but I gave the money back for one – my reading in the Public Library – for them to buy more Arabic books with." He told Mary he had also read in a theater to a predominantly Jewish audience: "perhaps the most thrilling audience I have ever had . . . such fine young men and women. So full of flame! So ardent! And so keen! They just devour you with their minds. You feel that they not only love what you read, but they understand it – they know what you mean. A remarkable people!"[220] Mary also learnt that he had nearly completed *The Forerunner*. Unlike their previous collaborations she found that he now "rarely misspells a word, though he still uses the dictionary as aide, and rarely misses an idiom."[221] He showed her the five pictures he had done for the forthcoming book[222] and showed her three large unfinished paintings: one called *Three Women*; one of "A face – a woman's – a mother's, and within her breast two babies," of which Gibran said, "This is the face I've been trying for twenty years – and I've drawn it at last"; and another face, "terrible, with prisoned flames, and a look as if drenched with flowing tears – though never weeping." Gibran said to Mary: "That's a face I saw in the subway; she was between two women who were taking her, I suppose, to a sanitorium. It was so full of things and all bottled up tight!"[223] These faces often took Gibran four or five days to finish.[224] He told Mary: "When I paint a picture, I try to give the picture a presence. It is the coming together of certain elements in a certain way, as if they made a sort of path along which God can come through to our consciousness."[225]

He spoke again of his mother to Mary, and remembered that when he was sixteen she had said to him that his writing abilities would reach fruition when he was thirty-five. "People will always love what you write. And I like those things, too. You've found yourself. But you'll have to live a great deal before you find that other man. And you'll have to write what he has to say . . . When you're thirty-five."[226]

8

A Literary Movement is Born
(1920)

I

"This country needs hundreds of soul-doctors . . . They must have a universal consciousness and be able to help people look in a different direction,"[1] Gibran declared to Mary when she visited him in New York in April 1920. He was by now working toward unifying the Arabic literary world by establishing an official mouthpiece for the work of Arab immigrant poets (*Shu'ara' al-Mahjar*).

Seven months earlier, he had written to fellow Lebanese writer Mikhail Naimy, who had reviewed some of Gibran's earlier works,[2] asking him to come to New York to "revive" *al-Funoon*:

> If you wish to revive the magazine, you should come to New York and be the trigger behind every move . . . If your return to New York means a sacrifice on your part, that sacrifice must be considered as placing that which is dear, and offering the important upon the altar of that which is more important. To me the dearest thing in your life is the realization of your dreams, and the most important thing is the reaping of the fruit of your talents.[3]

Gibran, by now tired of the reactionaries of Arabic literature, nurtured an ambition to shake them out of their complacency. He felt that Naimy was the man who could help him achieve this.

Born in Baskinta in northern Lebanon in October 1889, Naimy had at the age of thirteen won a scholarship to the Russian Teachers' Institute at Nazareth in Palestine, and in 1906 found himself the recipient of another scholarship. This time he studied in czarist Russia, where for five years he proved himself to be a brilliant student at the theological seminary in

Poltava in the Ukraine. He immersed himself in Russian literature, being particularly drawn to Lermontov, Tolstoy, Dostoevsky, and Chekhov. The many evils of Russian society at that time reminded him of conditions back home – class distinction, feudalism, enormous prosperity for a corrupt and idle aristocracy, biting poverty for a labor-crushed working class and peasantry, a religious despotism that allied itself with the ruling authorities to crush in the name of God any liberal movement and to silence any voice crying for social justice – intensifying Naimy's disgust with the corruption of civilization. After reading Tolstoy he thanked Leo Nikolaevich in his diary: "I fell upon a light that would guide me in every step I take . . . Yes, for in this respect and without you knowing it, you have become my guide and teacher."[4]

When he entered the University of Washington in November 1911 to read literature and law, Naimy had thrown himself into studying Western literature, Transcendentalism, theosophy, Blake, Wordsworth, and others. Awestruck by what he found and alarmed by the sterility of Arabic literature at home, Naimy began his literary career in 1913 as a critic. His first article in Arabic, "Fajr-al-'Amal Ba'da Layl al-Ya's" ("A Dawn of Hope after a Night of Despair"), in which he included an analysis of Gibran's influence on Arabic literature, was published in *al-Funoon* in 1913. By 1916 he had written *al-Aba' wa al-Banun* (*Fathers and Sons*), a four-act play which appeared in serial form in *al-Funoon*, and in 1917 he wrote the greater part of his major contemplative fictional work, *Mudhakkarat al-'Arqash* (*Memoirs of a Vagrant Soul*) which was published in serial form, again in *al-Funoon*.

From June 1918 to July 1919 he was a private soldier in the American army, spending time on the front lines in northern France. The horrifying experiences of trench warfare left a deep impression on him, and strengthened his already formulated conviction that modern civilization was based on violence and slavery. The diary he kept in France bears witness to a troubled soul, torn between his love for the godly in man and his hatred of man's basic self: "O night, O Stars, bear witness with me. Man is baser than animal. He who takes pride in his reason becomes in war, without reason . . . Why? Why? Why? How long is this madness to continue?"[5] These concerns he most certainly shared with Kahlil Gibran.

The letter Naimy received from Gibran on his return to Washington after the war convinced him to join his compatriot in New York. When he arrived he found that *al-Funoon* was in severe financial difficulty, with any ideas of revival impossible. Gibran, Naimy, and other *émigré* writers decided instead to organize the progressive literary-minded family of *al-Funoon* into a unified effective bond. Their aim was to function as the mouthpiece for a new literary movement to lift existing Arabic literature from its medieval state, in which substance had been sacrificed to form, to modern standards; to transport their "literature from stagnation to life, from imitation to creation." Naimy believed that the tendency to keep Arabic literature within the bounds of aping the ancients both in form and substance was a pernicious tendency. He also envisioned that this bond, to be called *ar-Rabitatu'l Qalamyiah*, meaning the "Pen Bond" (Arrabitah), would not break away completely from the ancients:

> For there be some among them who will remain to us and to those who follow a source of inspiration for many ages to come. To revere them is a great honour. To imitate them is a deadly shame. For our life, our needs, our circumstances are far different from theirs. We must be true to ourselves if we would be true to our ancestors.[6]

On the evening of April 20, 1920, Mikhail Naimy reported on a historic gathering at the home of Abdul Massih Haddad, the editor of *as-Say'eh*:

> The discussion arose as to what the Syrian writers in New York could do to lift Arabic literature from the quagmire of stagnation and imitation, and to infuse a new life into its veins so as to make of it an active force in the building up of the Arab nations. It was suggested that an organization be created to band the writers together and to unify their efforts in the service of the Arabic language and its literature. The suggestion was met with warm approval by all the poets and the writers present; viz., Gibran K. Gibran, Nasseeb Arida, William Catzeflis, Rasheed Ayoub, Abdul-Masseeh Haddad, Nadra Haddad, Mikhail Naimy. The time not permitting to work out details and by-laws, Gibran invited the company to spend the evening of April 28 at his studio.
>
> On the evening of the 28th, eight men, Abdul Haddad, Nadra Haddad, Elias Atallah, Naseeb Arida, Raschid Ayoub, Kahlil Gibran, William Catzeflis and Mikhail Naimy, came to 51 West Tenth Street:
>
> After a thorough discussion the following points were unanimously agreed upon:
>
> 1. The organization to be called in Arabic AR-RABITATUL QALAMYIAT (meaning the Pen-Bond), and in English, ARRABITAH.
> 2. It is to have three officers: A president who shall be called "Chieftain", a secretary who shall be called "Counsellor" and a treasurer.

3. The members shall be of three categories: Active, who shall be known as "Workers", supporters who shall be known as "Partisans", and correspondents.

4. Arrabitah to publish the works of its own members and other Arab writers it may consider worthy, as well as to encourage the translation of world literature masterpieces.

5. Arrabitah to foster new talent by offering prizes for the best in poetry and prose.

The worker Mikhail Naimy was charged with the final drafting of the by-laws. The present then unanimously elected G. K. Gibran for Chieftain, Mikhail Naimy for Counsellor, and William Catzeflis for treasurer . . . I drafted the by-laws with a preamble from which I quote the following extracts showing the aims and tendencies of the new organization:

". . . Not everything that parades as literature is literature; nor is every rimester a poet. The literature we esteem as worthy of the name is that only which draws its nourishment from Life's soil and light and air . . . And the man of letters is he who is endowed with more than the average mortal's share of sensitiveness and taste, and the power of estimation and penetration together with the talent of expressing clearly and beautifully whatever imprints Life's constant waves leave upon his soul."[7]

Gibran drew an emblem for Arrabitah, a circle surrounding an open book with a quotation from the *Hadith*[8] written across the open pages: "How wonderful the treasures beneath God's throne which only poets' tongues can unlock!"[9] Soon after it was launched, with active membership limited to a maximum of ten,[10] the literary contributions by members of Arrabitah began to appear in *as-Say'eh* with the name of each always followed by the words "a worker in Arrabitah."

Naimy, as Gibran had anticipated in his letter, was the main trigger behind the movement. He introduced the first annual collection of Arrabitah, produced in 1921, and wrote extensively on literary criticism. In this respect he acted as the theoretician and literary expert. Arrabitah, with its well-defined aims, quickly and forcibly struck the Arab world as an independent literary school, an "academy of Arab letters" in New York. Newspapers and magazines in the Arab world, especially *al-Hilal* in Egypt, excited by the novelty and revolutionary spirit of Arrabitah literature, began to reproduce it at home.[11] The movement started to symbolize a new literary era for an Arab world already on the move. Its influence on modern Arabic literature was to be profound,[12] and observers of this new movement called it a source "of illumination to an Arab life beginning to awake";[13] "the strongest school that modern Arabic literature has known";[14] and "an accomplished school in action."[15]

William Catzeflis, himself a founding member, wrote: "Purism was the god of the writers and poets. Steeped in traditionalism of the narrower sort, there were hundreds of versifiers but few poets. They sacrificed substance to form and no one dared to deviate from the trodden path."[16] Arrabitah provided the catalyst whereby poets felt liberated from the clutches of standardized neo-classicism. Mikhail Naimy wrote of their breathtaking success:

> The name of *Arrabitah* spread wide and far becoming tantamount to renaissance, to rejuvenation in the minds of the younger generations, and to iconoclasm and hot-headed rebellion in the eyes of the older and more conservative ones. The lines of battle were clearly drawn: the issue was never in doubt. So quickly was the tide turned in favor of *Arrabitah* that those who hailed it were no less puzzled than those who opposed it . . . no one knows the "secret" save that hidden power which brought the members of *Arrabitah* together at a certain spot, in a certain time, and for a certain purpose entirely irrespective of their conscious planning, endowing each with a flame that may be more, or less brilliant than that of another, but all coming from the selfsame fireplace.[17]

Gibran's pervasive influence on his colleagues in Arrabitah made them reassess their own work, and his Romanticism answered a latent need in them to liberate their own Romantic expression. This yearning sprung not only from expatriation, although exile undoubtedly helped them release its dynamism, for in truth they had always carried its seeds from home.[18]

Arrabitah has been the focus of much debate and conjecture since its formal inauguration in 1920. Ameen Rihani, whose membership status of Arrabitah was never clear, remained outside its activities after 1920. However, he used to sign his name as a member of Arrabitah as early as 1916, as did other members contributing at the time to *al-Funoon*. Prior to 1916 many thought Arrabitah to be a political organization, and the true nature of its aims and activities only became clear after the publication of its manifesto which in fact was the preamble to the by-laws drafted by Mikhail Naimy.

As Gibran was elected 'Ameed ("doyen" or president or chairman) of Arrabitah, the organization and its aims became identified with the personality of its chief figure. The question that is still asked is whether Arrabitah was a political organization under the guise of an academy of letters and whether Gibran was a political activist with a specific political agenda. Naimy many years later spoke of these days:[19] "Gibran joined Arrabitah in the hope of participating in the process of education and enlightening the immigrants to achieve the liberation of Syria . . . This was a sufficient impulse for Gibran to join Arrabitah . . . He never had any political affiliations."[20] Arrabitah's political stance, according to Naimy, was first and foremost to bring about, and as soon as possible, the independence and autonomy of Syria and the Arab world. Arrabitah found it expedient to enhance the French role in the area to the degree that it might help to achieve total liberation. This was a position adopted by Gibran as well. Although many observers at the time referred to the "Syrian writers" of Arrabitah, Gibran and Naimy were committed Lebanese nationalists:

> We were convinced that the liberation of "Syria" would lead to the liberation of Lebanon. We were not ready to single out Lebanon as the only defender of liberty in this struggle of independence, considering its small size and limited resources . . . this would have unleashed the full wrath of the occupying forces against one single country.[21]

Naimy and Gibran were of one mind as to how the struggle should take place; their aim above all was to serve their country and only follow the dictates of conscience. The two countries, Syria and Lebanon, would remain separate entities, but united in the cause; thus preventing factionalism and disunity. No member of Arrabitah could at that time foresee how the Arab world would develop, although many Syrians, both Christian and Muslim, felt betrayed by the West which after the fall of the Ottoman empire in 1918 had given repeated assurances of Arab independence as a reward for Arab assistance in defeating the Ottoman armies.

There were, however, some members of Arrabitah or close associates who were politically active and who had certain political influence in Western circles. Both Ayub Tabet and Ameen Rihani, according to Naimy, were men of this ilk.[22] Tabet had a "foothold" in Paris and strong French connections, while it was no secret that Rihani profoundly believed in American democracy and its role in the region. Rihani's experiences of the democratic system as he came to know it firsthand in the United States led him to believe that America would guarantee the independence of all

193

nations; and so he supported an American mandate over Syria and Lebanon.[23] Naimy remembers the choices before Arrabitah:

> Our strategy was clear. First get rid of Turkish occupation, and then afterwards – get rid of foreign mandates. Gibran and I joined Arrabitah in this spirit – the intricate political manoeuvering did not interest us in the least. What we wanted was independence and liberation . . . Gibran and I had no allegiance except to literature and no love except the love of country. Some people have interpreted this as though we were employed by some foreign power, or we were even carrying on espionage activities.[24]

When President Woodrow Wilson declared his fourteen principles of self-determination, Naimy, Gibran, and their colleagues at Arrabitah felt they were seeing the "beginning of the end" of foreign rule. They decided to nurture friendly relations with President Wilson, and in 1921 Gibran, Naseeb Arida, Abdul Massih Haddad, and Naimy took a gift to the president on behalf of the Syrian community in Brazil.[25] Naimy remembered the incident and captured Gibran's mood:

> Gibran's eyes *embraced* the entire map of the Arab World. His pen expressed the agony and suffering of a persecuted society. He worked for the liberation of Syria which meant the liberation of Lebanon. And nothing else! Gibran was not so much concerned with the sands of the desert, as much as he was concerned with the soil of the cedars, the Valley of Qadisha and the mountain of Sunnin.

On the question of Arab unity, it is too simplistic to say that Gibran was against the idea of Arab unification. He knew that unity without an acceptance of diversity would fail, and he was intent on maintaining Lebanese independence, believing in "separateness in togetherness," and rejecting any policies that might precipitate the disappearance of Lebanon into an Arab environment without a trace of its identity.[26]

In expressing the aggressions inflicted by the outside world and the fetters imposed within the Arab world, Gibran was one of the first true rebels in Arabic literature. As early as 1906, when he had published his *'Ara'is al-Muruj* (*Nymphs of the Valley*), he was putting forward challenging ideas about freedom and unity – new ideas that were infectious and stimulating to a whole generation of succeeding writers. His innovative prose contained a strong poetic style, and after Gibran Arab writers were able to experiment on any level and in any sphere of literature because he had liberated the creative spirit.

Gibran's Christian background enabled him too to express themes hitherto hardly explored. His belief in universal love and his fascination with the personality of Christ reoccurs in many of his writings. His loose flow of biblical style, the devotional and incantational tone, the emotional repetitiveness of certain phrases, are reminiscent of the Bible. The rhythm of his prose style was dictated by his Romanticism, with its undulating sweep and breath of rhythm so smooth yet energetic – a fine roll and flurry in the rhythm adequately appealing to modern sensibilities.[27]

II

That summer Gibran often worked right through the night, galvanized only by strong coffee and cigarettes.[28] He met William Butler Yeats again at the Society of Arts and Sciences, and spent an evening talking to the poet and his wife.[29] He finished the drawings for *The Forerunner*, continued to work on the "Counsels," completed some short narratives and poems in Arabic which had appeared in *Mir'at al-Gharb* and *al-Funoon* between 1912 and 1918, and, in the summer of 1920, finally published them in *al-'Awasif* (*The Tempests*), which exhibited the unmistakable influence of Nietzsche's blistering polemic.[30]

In Boston on August 31, 1920, as Gibran told Mary the news of his latest publication, a "big storm broke, with torrents of rain and with thunder." He was elated: "Mary, a storm does something for me that nothing else on earth does. In a storm like this one I rode on a white horse at a run, galloped fifteen or sixteen miles. The horse was probably a little bit maddened. I was exceedingly happy . . . My latest book is named *Storms* (*The Tempests*)." As Gibran recounted his story, there came another great thunder roll.[31]

The hero in Gibran's title-piece, the thirty-year-old hermit Youssof al-Fakhry, alone in his cottage among the forbidding mountains, is an enigma to the people of the valley. Only to Gibran, the narrator, seeking refuge one stormy evening, does he reveal the secret of his four-year seclusion. Winning his confidence the narrator learns that Youssof has renounced the "old and corrupt tree of corruption" with its greed and evil and fruits of "misery and fear". He has left it "to avoid the people and their laws, their teachings, and their traditions, their ideas and their clamour and their wailing," seeking solace in nature, turning away from "civilization – that symmetrical monstrosity erected upon the perpetual misery of human kinds."[32]

Alone in the wild majestic mountains he yearns "to learn the secrets of the Universe" and approach the "throne of God," comparing society to a sick man who, after rather foolishly killing his physician, closes his eyes and

195

says, "He was a great physician." He views the trappings, inventions, and amusements of the world as nothing but vain fabrications. The faith with which Youssof al-Fakhry clings to life is not a faith in the future of humanity trapped in "phantoms of tragic deception," but a conviction that there is only one thing, "dazzling and alone," that the spirit longs for:

> It is an awakening in the spirit; it is an awakening in the inner depths of the heart; it is an overwhelming and magnificent power that descends suddenly upon man's conscience and opens his eyes, whereupon he sees Life amid a dizzying shower of brilliant music, surrounded by a circle of great light, with man standing as a pillar of beauty between the earth and the firmament.[33]

The narrator, however, unlike the hermit, still believes that there must be something in civilization that might improve the plight of humanity, and expresses a Sufi-like belief in the possibility of conscious evolution forged by intense participation in life:

> Is not civilization, in all its tragic forms, a supreme motive for spiritual awakening? Then how can we deny existing matter, while its very existence is unwavering proof of its conformability into the intended fitness? The present civilization may possess a vanishing purpose, but the eternal law has offered to that purpose a ladder whose steps can lead to a free substance.[34]

This dialogue in *The Tempests* perfectly encapsulates Gibran's own internal conflict: the hermit-poet and outsider alone in his Greenwich Village studio but also the man who knows that engagement with life can, consciously undertaken, lead to transformation. This dichotomy intensifies during this period, reflecting Gibran's own oscillating aspirations between 1912 and the end of the war. The general impression of this collection is of a writer whose work, although not entirely distinct from his more optimistic moods in *A Tear and a Smile*, is again driven by the impulse of despair. In "Satan" ("al-Shaytan") he condemns corrupted civilization as an entity created in the name of Satan: "In every city under the sun my name was the axis of the educational circle of religion, arts, and philosophy. Had it not been for me, no temples would have been built, no towers or palaces would have been erected. I am the courage that creates resolution in man."[35] The concept of evil and its personification in a fallen god is, argues Gibran, a fabrication, a "tremendous myth," a malign invention by Babylonian dualists. Consequently the church has been built on a foundation of fear and on an ancient unsubstantiated conflict that enables it cunningly to remove the "gold and silver from the faithful's pocket" and deposit it "forever into the pouch of the preacher and missionary."[36]

This denunciatory attitude toward institutionalized religion is tempered in the story entitled "Slavery," in which Gibran concedes that ignorance and corruption are conditioned: "In truth, she is an everlasting ailment bequeathed by each generation unto its successor." Physical and psychological slavery, manifesting as economic, ecclesiastical, sexual, geo-political and cultural slavery are universal, possessing "the vicious powers of continuation and contagion." The narrator portrays Liberty as a cadaverous specter, defeated and on her knees gazing at the moon. He asks her, "Where are your children?" Liberty, weakly, gasps, "One died crucified, another died mad, and the third one is not yet born"[37] – echoing Gibran's earlier portrayals of Liberty, once a beautiful maiden, but now a specter, "frailed by aloneness and withered by solitude."[38]

The theme of humanity's hypnotic slavery is continued in "The Grave-Digger" ("Haffar al-Qubur"). The narrator, walking in the "Valley of the Phantoms of Death" comes across a "giant ghost" whose ghastliness fascinates him. In the ensuing dialogue this "Mad God" advocates the destruction of all conventional morality:

> You cling with terror to the small circle of gifts from your ancestors, and your affliction is caused by your parents' bequest, and you will remain a slave of death until you become one of the dead.
>
> Your vocations are wasteful and deserted, and your lives are hollow. Real life has never visited you, nor will it; neither will your deceitful self realize your living death.[39]

With diabolical sarcasm he mocks the poet's craft and denounces "empty words" such as "God" and "Religion" as having been "placed on human lips by past ages and not by knowledge."[40] He would not have the "truly living man" accept any of these, but would have him acknowledge that he worships nothing but ego. Religion and morality are thus both traced to egoistic motives. The mad god laughs as he thinks of men worshiping their own selves which are nothing but "earthly carcasses." He urges the poet to give up writing and become a grave-digger so that he may relieve the living of "the corpses." The poet asks why he has never seen these corpses, to which the mad god replies: "Your illusioned eyes see the people quivering before the tempest of life and you believe them to be alive, while in truth they have been dead since they were born."[41]

This brooding nihilism was in part caused by Gibran's despair at the obscene abomination of World War I, and in "The Giants" ("al-Jababirah") he writes: "The world has returned to savagery. What science and education have created is being destroyed by the new primitives. We are now like the pre-historic cave dwellers. Nothing distinguishes us from them save our machines of destruction and improved techniques of slaughter." The indignation, pity, and compassion that the poet felt about war could not moderate his grim analysis. Those power-possessing beings who live between the "wolf lair and the pig-sty" under one convenient rubric or another became "intoxicated" with the "tears of widows and orphans." Failing a radical spiritual regeneration nothing could be done.[42]

In "Narcotics and Dissecting Knives" ("al-Mukhadarat wa al-Mabadi' ") the poet turns his anger specifically toward those in the East who had attacked his writings as being "heretical":

> Numerous are the social healers of the Orient, and many are their patients who remain uncured but appear eased of their ills because they are under the effects of social narcotics. But these tranquilizers merely mask the symptoms . . .
> The people of the Orient demand that the writer be a bee always making honey . . . [and] seek to make their past a justification and a bed of ease . . .
> Thus the Orient lies upon its soft bed. The sleeper wakes up for an instant when stung by a flea, and then resumes his narcotic slumber.[43]

In "My Countrymen" ("Ya Bani Ummi") Gibran asks:

> What is it you would have me do,
> My countrymen? Shall I purr like
> The kitten to satisfy you, or roar
> Like the lion to please myself? I
> Have sung for you, but you did not
> Dance; I have wept before you, but
> You did not cry . . . [44]

In "Decayed Teeth" ("al-Adrass al-Mussuissah") Gibran continues his assault on the status quo, his wrath now specifically directed at corrupt politicians:

> In the mouth of the Syrian nation are many rotten, black, and dirty teeth that fester and stink. The doctors have attempted cures with gold fillings instead of extraction. And the disease remains. A nation with rotten teeth is doomed to have a sick stomach. Many are the nations afflicted with such indigestion.[45]

A recurring theme in the collection is his perception that "the storm" is both a symbol of destruction and regeneration. Youssof al-Fakhry has taught the narrator to love the storm, the mad god to walk with it, while the narrator of *The Tempest* directs it against the corrupt tree of civilization.[46]

In "The Crucified" ("Yasu' al-Maslub"), Jesus is described as "a strengthening torrent," which "carries into oblivion the dry branches of the trees, and sweeps away with determination all things not fastened to strength." For centuries humanity, "like a child standing in glee before a wounded beast," has been worshiping "weakness in the person of the saviour." But Gibran implores: "Jesus was not a bird with broken wings. He was a raging tempest who broke all crooked wings" – a tempest that did not arise to build mighty churches but came to "make the human heart a temple, and the soul an altar and the mind a priest."[47]

The depiction of Jesus as "the tempest" continues in "Eventide of the Feast" ("Massa' al-'Eid"). While the people are celebrating Easter the narrator meets a dignified stranger in the public garden. To his amazement he sees the marks of nails on the palms of the strange "madman's" hands and hears him cry in anguish:

> The people are celebrating in My honour, pursuing the tradition woven by the ages around My name, but as to Myself, I am a stranger wandering from East to West upon this earth, and no one knows of Me. The foxes have their holes, and the birds of the skies their nests, but the Son of Man has no place to rest His head.[48]

III

On September 7, 1920, Gibran brought Mary a draft of *The Prophet*. She wrote down as much as she could recall, some of which was very close to the final version: "Almustafa, the chosen and beloved, he who was a dawn unto his own day, had waited twelve years in the city of Orphalese, for the ship of purple sails to return and bear him back again to the isle of his birth."[49]

199

Back in New York Gibran's work schedule continued to intensify. When a reading tour in various North American cities was canceled, he expressed relief: "Somehow the idea of reading that *Prophet* from city to city, under advertisement was sacrilege to me. It is my religion, my most sacred life."[50] Gibran preferred to read to small groups, usually in his studio – his aspirations now lying not in lecture tours and public acclamation: "I am trying my best not to be a *talker* about things;"[51] he told Mary:

> My life has a great deal of seeing people in it, just individuals, one by one, and groups as well. And I want it to be so more and more. I want to *live* reality. Better than to write ever so truly about fire, is to *be* one little live coal. I want some day simply to live what I would say, and talk to people. I want to be a teacher. Because I have been so lonely, I want to talk to those who are lonely.[52]

The poet at this period was increasingly aware of the defects of his own personality:

> I've moved very slowly. I ought to have been ten years ago where I am now. But there are certain streaks in me that held me back – a certain inheritance. In my father's people is much temper, and restlessness, and vainness. And I have all these and they held me back for long: The caring for fame and what people said and thought. But they will not hold me back longer. For I know them now. Therefore, I shall be free of them.[53]

The narcissistic impulses of his youthful years withering, he found himself standing at the threshold of a new era, Mikhail Naimy observing that he was "on the verge of a new dawn":

> The violent storms which Nietzsche had unleashed in his soul, and which almost uprooted him from his eastern soil and left him suspended between earth and sky, were beginning to subside. Slowly his old faith in the wisdom and justice of Life and his resignation to her eternal will were returning to him, imbued with a new meaning and new force.[54]

Struggling to balance passion and reason, Gibran turned his attention to his own inner life:

> In my work I am as solid as a rock, but my real work is neither in painting nor in writing. Deep inside me, May, there is another dynamic intelligence which has nothing to do with words, lines or colors. The work I have been born to do has nothing to do with brush or pen.[55]

The intensity and dynamism of the last few years, when Gibran had fired, melted, and recast his "madness," his creative passion, was maturing into a desire to develop his own spiritual understanding. On September 10, 1920, he told Mary: "To think about oneself is terrifying. But it is the only *honest* thing: to think about myself as I am, my ugly features, my beautiful features, and wonder at them. What other *solid* beginning can I have, what to make progress from except myself?"[56] Three weeks later, *The Forerunner: His Parables and Poems*, was published. The underlying theme in this collection, the need to awaken, accurately reflected Gibran's own aspirations of this time. For Gibran the notion of "sleep" was not merely a poetic device, but described the human condition; the parables in *The Forerunner* define his social concepts and illustrate his belief that the individual must first understand himself or herself before any social or personal transformation can take place, a transformation that can only be accomplished by observing how one's actions affect others.[57]

Gibran utilizes Sufi-like figures – "God's Fool," "the King-Hermit," "the Slave," and "the Saint" – to intensify his search for that part of himself that "though ruled in flesh rules in spirit."[58] *The Forerunner* opens with the words:

> You are your own forerunner, and the towers you have builded are but the foundation of your giant-self. And that self too shall be a foundation.
> And I too am my own forerunner, for the long shadow stretching before me at sunrise shall gather under my feet at the noon hour. Yet another sunrise shall lay another shadow before me, and that also shall be gathered at another noon.[59]

In "The King-Hermit" the narrator hears of a powerful and rich ruler who has renounced his kingdom and gone to live in the forest as a hermit. Hoping to learn the secrets of the hermit's heart,[60] he leaves the city and goes to the forest. In this story Gibran encapsulates the Sufi idea of journeying and "yearning" (*shawq*), whereby a person longs for the divine state he or she has previously known.[61] The narrator learns that the king-hermit no longer wants to rule over those who "assume his vices and attribute to him their virtues." Thus, as in *The Procession* and *The Tempests*, Gibran explores the dualist mind-set, symbolized by "the City": good and evil, sovereignty and slavery, weakness and strength. The king-hermit asks: "Seek you a lost self in the green shadows, or is it a home-coming in your twilight?"[62] The seeker replies that he longs to know what made the king leave his kingdom for a forest. The king-hermit explains:

> There are those who renounce the kingdom of dreams so that they may not seem distant from the dreamless. And those who renounce the kingdom of nakedness and cover their souls that others may not be ashamed in beholding truth uncovered and beauty unveiled. And greater yet than all of these is he who renounces the kingdom of sorrow that he may not seem proud and vainglorious.[63]

Gibran's yearning is expressed by the king-hermit who tells the narrator to return to the "great city" and sit at its gate and observe the multiple selves entering and leaving: "And see that you find him who, though born a king, is without kingdom; and him who though ruled in flesh rules in spirit – though neither he nor his subjects know this; and him also who but seems to rule yet is in truth slave of his own slaves."[64] The man obeys, observing that "from that day to this numberless are the kings whose shadows have passed over me and few are the subjects over whom my shadow has passed."[65]

This theme of self-observation continues in "The Greater Self" when a king's "naked self" steps out of a mirror made by magicians. The symbol of the mirror employed by Gibran in this parable is one of the most immediate symbols of spiritual contemplation and indeed of knowledge (*gnosis*) in general, for it portrays the union of subject and object. The naked self admonishes the king: "If you were mightier yet, you would not be king." Only when the king awakens to his own wrong psychic functions and liberates the "slave of his own slaves" will he be fit to govern.[66]

The symbolism of the mirror is a powerful one in mystical traditions for in a profound sense the mirror is the symbol of the symbol.[67] In this sense St. Paul wrote: "For now we see through a glass, darkly; but then face to face: now I know in part; but then shall I know even as also I am known."[68] In Sufi thought when the heart becomes a pure mirror, the world is reflected in it as it really is:

> For a being's knowledge of himself in himself is not the same as knowledge of himself by means of something other that acts for him like a mirror. Such a mirror shows him to himself in the form corresponding to the "plane of reflection" and the reflection resulting from it.[69]

And in Christian thought Meister Eckhart perceived that:

The soul contemplates itself in the mirror of Divinity. God Himself is the mirror, which He conceals from whom He will, and uncovers to whom He will. The more the soul is able to transcend all words, the more it approaches the mirror. In this mirror union occurs as pure undivided likeness.[70]

Gibran concludes his parable with the crowning glory of this union: "And the naked man, gazing lovingly upon the king, entered into the mirror. And the king roused, and straightaway he looked into the mirror. And he saw there but himself crowned."[71]

In "God's Fool" the poet underlines the vision of a man whose heart has become like a pure mirror.[72] A dreamer imbued with purity of vision gazes in awe at all around him – the temples, towers, and palaces, perceived with the clarity of a child, and even though his oblique activities get him arrested he remains full of wonderment at all he surveys.[73]

"The saint" is identified as another forerunner whose vision is undistorted by illusion and whose mind has transcended worldly dualities. He consoles a murderous brigand and claims that he, "the saint," has also committed countless heinous crimes himself. The perplexed narrator questions the saint:[74]

"Wherefore did you accuse yourself of uncommitted crimes? See you not that this man went away no longer believing in you?"

And the saint answered: "It is true he no longer believes in me. But he went away much comforted."

At that moment we heard the brigand singing in the distance, and the echo of his song filled the valley with gladness.[75]

In the story entitled "Repentance," a man steals a melon from his neighbor's garden and afterward feels remorse; however, the thief does not feel remorse until *after* he has sliced open the melon and found that it was not ripe.[76] His remorse, because it does not arise from his conscience, is therefore an empty form of "repentance," unrepresentative of the awareness of the king-hermit, God's fool, and the saint.

The argument that the far-sighted person trusts to the deeper power of the soul is illustrated in the story of a bird[77] that flies from the forerunner's heart:

Out of my deeper heart a bird rose and flew skyward.
Higher and higher did it rise, yet larger and larger did it grow.

203

At first it was but like a swallow, then a lark, then an eagle, then as vast as
a spring cloud, and then it filled the starry heavens.
Out of my heart a bird flew skyward. And it waxed larger as it flew. Yet it
left not my heart.[78]

The bird, symbolizing the power of spirit and its expansion as far as the
heavens, recalls the mysticism of the Hindu *Upanishads* as well as the
sayings of the Sufi masters:

A bird I am: this body was my cage
But I have flown leaving it as a token.[79]

In "Beyond my Solitude" Gibran, as he so often did in *The Madman*,
expresses his views that it is the existence of each person's multiple selves,
our "burdened selves," that prevent liberation: "And how shall I become my
freer self unless I slay my burdened selves, or unless all men become free?
How shall my leaves fly singing upon the wind unless my roots shall wither
in the dark?"[80]

Gibran's belief in reincarnation reappears in "Dynasties." As a king
anxiously awaits the birth of his firstborn he is told of the death of his chief
enemy, another monarch. Soon afterward a son is born to the king and the
"true prophet" reveals that the new heir to the throne is none other than the
soul of his recently deceased enemy. The king is enraged and kills the
prophet.[81] Hence the wisest who sees furthest is punished by the less gifted,
a moral that is repeated under various guises in many of the parables.

Representative of this category is the story of the three frogs, each of
whom has an explanation for the movement of the log upon which they are
floating downstream. One frog says the log itself is moving; a second says it
is being borne along by the river; and a third says the sensation of
movement is purely subjective. When a fourth asserts that all of them are
right, the others become angry and push him into the river.

Such discussions in *The Forerunner* illustrate Gibran's belief that the
limited notions of truth entertained by the literal mind are only fragments
of unlimited reality. Thus in "Other Seas" a fish is ridiculed because he
suggests that "above this sea of ours there is another sea."[82]

In "The Plutocrat" these limiting conceptions are shown to have been
exacerbated by the likes of the rapacious capitalist, who defiles, destroys,
and divides. Depicted as an all-consuming beast who eats well beyond its
fill, this "man-headed, iron-hoofed monster" is itself a personification of

duality and division. In a note of pessimism Gibran writes, "I am afraid that tomorrow there will be no more earth to eat and no more sea to drink"[83] – highlighting his awareness of the dangers of environmental degradation – a foreboding that in the America of the 1920s was well ahead of its time.

In contrast, in "Love" Gibran expresses the idea of the unity and interconnectedness of nature:

> They say the jackal and the mole
> Drink from the self-same stream
> Where the lion comes to drink.[84]

This theme continues in "The Dying Man and the Vulture," in which Gibran uses the symbol of the bird to express the soul's yearning for unity.[85]

In contrast Gibran turns his attention to the divisive policies of Western governments. In "War and the Small Nations" he depicts them as squabbling eagles fighting over a smaller nation, symbolized by a lamb who prays that God will make peace between its "winged brothers."[86] In "Poets" Gibran chides those, who, lost in their own dreamy world of empty words and with "unlyrical hatred in their eyes," condemn the poet as rebel;[87] and in "Critics" he asks why people judge someone who condemns evil, rather than the evil-doers themselves?[88] – an obvious reference to his own critics in the Arab world.

The last parable in the collection, a parable of lamentation and awakening,[89] deals with the reception afforded *The Forerunner*. Gibran told Mary Haskell that in this piece was a "promise," and, as "*The Madman* ends with the bitterest thing in it; *The Forerunner* [ends] with the sweetest."[90]

> The thing in *The Madman* and *The Forerunner* which is nearest to people is the Last Watch. Everyone has experienced that truth: that love, like a running brook, is disregarded, taken for granted; but when the brook freezes over, then people begin to remember how it was when it ran, and they want it to run again . . . One of the saddest things is the irony of life. You express something and you are misunderstood. You try another way, and you are misunderstood far worse.[91]

In "The Last Watch" the forerunner, "he who calls himself echo to a voice yet unheard,"[92] prepares the way for an even mightier love: "Night is over, and we children of night must die when dawn comes leaping upon the hills; and out of our ashes a mightier love shall rise. And it shall laugh in the sun and it shall be deathless."[93]

With the Last Watch closing and the darkness of war retreating, Gibran was shaking off Nietzsche's influence and transforming the nihilistic energy of the German philosopher into a positive, creative power of healing and of hope: "Out of the dark mist a new world is born . . . The air is crowded with the sound of rushing waters and the beating of Mighty Wings. The voice of God is in the wind."[94]

9

A Strange Little Book
(1921–1923)

By 1921 Kahlil Gibran's name was becoming increasingly known in the worlds of Arabic and English letters. *The Madman* (1918) and *The Forerunner* (1920) had established his standing as a writer in English of great promise; on the other hand, his latest poem in Arabic, "The Political Farewell," was receiving unprecedented attention in the Middle East after being published in *al-Hilal* in Egypt.

The censors had banned its publication in Syrian papers and all papers going into Syria from New York, South America, and Cairo. Courageously the editorial board of *al-Hilal*, under Emile Zaydan, did not cut, from the contents page, Gibran's name or the new title "You have your Lebanon and I have my Lebanon" ("Lakum Lubnankum wa Lya Lubnani"), prompting the author to say: "So now everybody knows the piece was there, and they are determined to get it, and will do more than if the government had let it alone."[1] In the poem Gibran compared "his Lebanon," a vision of a harmonious people, with "your Lebanon" (the pronoun directly referring to the supporters of the social, ecclesiastical, and political status quo), a "snarled political knot," a "chess game" between church and state and an "international problem" to a largely indifferent world[2] in which "Scepticism is its captain, and its port is a cave of goblins; for is not every capital in Europe a goblin cave?"[3] In a letter to Emile Zaydan, the rebellious poet expressed surprise that censorship in Syria had become "so bad" and said that those who had extracted his article out of *al-Hilal* had inadvertently praised him.[4] The censors were by now acutely aware of Gibran's soaring reputation, particularly in the Arab world, where he was being hailed as the authentic voice of *al-Mahjar*. For many in the East, however, his message was not a comfortable one:

The Near East has a disease – a disease of imitation, of the cheaper things of the West – especially of America – but not of your railroads, and your fine sanitation, and your educational system – but of your dress and your guns. They have taken to heart that if the greatest philosopher in the world and the smallest gun in the world are pitted against each other, the philosopher has no chance . . . The Near East has been conquered from time to time . . . and so they were turned to a more contemplative life. And they developed a consciousness of life, and of self, and of God – that the West has not yet developed. I would rather have them still conquered, still subject, and developing that consciousness, than have them free, with that consciousness becoming less.[5]

Censorship was not a new experience for the poet. The previous year he had discovered that some employees in the censor's office in Cairo were quite openly reading all his mail from the East. Brazenly, on some of his letters they had even added their own footnotes, greetings, and personal observations on politics, culture, and literature; some even went so far as to request money from him and, stranger still, one of the censors had written a long panegyric poem to him.[6]

Despite these intrusions the correspondence between Gibran and May Ziadah in Egypt increased. The relationship that was flowering was very different from the one he was experiencing with Mary. In Mary he had found an intellectual companion and a loving and nurturing soul; yet even in his most emotional outbursts to her, the underlying impression is that of a grateful protégé trying to find a way to repay the kindness and support she had abundantly bestowed on him. Gibran's relationship with May Ziadah differed in many respects. It is impossible to define such a love, though it included spiritual and platonic elements. Gibran and May, who were destined never to meet face to face, were becoming spiritually united and striving towards the "God Self," the "Blue Flame," "that transcendent element" which "glows immutable," and "transforms but is not to be transformed."[7]

The symbol used by Gibran to express the essential divinity of man was now becoming too the symbol of his eternal love for May – the two loves joined in a spiritual procession toward the "Blue Flame," the eternal flame of reality. In his correspondence with May, Gibran's use of the word "longing" reflects a spiritual yearning, a love that needed no words to express itself because it was a serene hymn heard through the silence of the night:

I am mist, May, I am mist that cloaks things but never unites them. I am mist unchanged into rain water. I am mist, and mist is my loneliness and my being alone, and in this is my hunger and my thirst. My misfortune, however, is that this mist is my reality, and that it longs to meet with another mist in the sky, longs to hear the words: "You are not alone, there are two of us, I know who you are." Tell me, tell me, my friend, is there anyone in this world who would be able or willing to say to me: "I am another mist, O mist, so let us cloak the mountains and the valleys, let us wander among and over the trees, let us cover the high rocks, let us together penetrate the heart and the pores of all creation, and let us roam through those faraway places, impregnable and undiscovered"?[8]

Gibran's friendship with Mikhail Naimy was also deepening. "Mischa," as Gibran affectionately called him, was a man he could trust, a respected friend who burned with the same spiritual longing as himself and one who understood the language and layers of meaning in his work. Naimy had soon discovered that he and Gibran had an "astonishing affinity" in their thinking on life and death and in their disposition regarding literature and its appropriate message.[9]

These two writers, alongside Ameen Rihani, had created the most renovating and revolutionary movement that Arabic literature had known in modern times. In an epoch when a global consciousness was growing, the three Arabs harmonized the knowledge of the West with the wisdom of the East. As foreigners in New York they were driven by their very alienation and the worldly nature of the city to ground themselves in their own mystic heritage. Always they remained true to their own tradition despite living and working in America. As Americans, on the other hand, having lived sufficiently long in the West to comprehend it, they spoke with a confidence and an authority that did not sound alien.

By virtue of the literary movement they created and the spiritual stance they unashamedly adopted, focusing on the essence and not the form, their three magisterial English works – Rihani's *The Book of Khalid*, Gibran's *The Prophet*, and Naimy's *The Book of Mirdad*[10]– were invariably prophetic in tone and messianic in approach.[11]

As a friend of Gibran, Mikhail Naimy found in his compatriot a man who struggled to make his soul "as beautiful as the beauty he glimpsed with his imagination and so generously spread in his books and paintings."[12] On a professional level his admiration for Gibran's work was unbounded:

Who shall inscribe the name of the present generation in the scrolls of Time, who they are and where they are? I do not find them among the many "nightingales of the Nile and the warblers of Syria and Lebanon," but among the few whose lips and hearts have been touched by a new fire. Of those some are still within the womb of Creative Silence; some are breathing the air we breathe, and treading the ground we tread. Of the latter –, nay, leading the latter – is the poet of Night and Solitude, the poet of Loneliness and Melancholy, the poet of Longing and Spiritual Awakening, the poet of the sea and the Tempest – Gibran Kahlil Gibran.[13]

The America in which the two friends from northern Lebanon found themselves – Naimy the mystic-philosopher, and Gibran the poet, in his long dervish robe stained with ink and paint – was the land of Henry Ford and Alphonse Capone; of jazz, electrification, the fox-trot, Gershwin's *Rhapsody in Blue*, psychoanalysis, and Prohibition.[14] Gibran bought whiskey from "a smuggler" for $35, and drank it with Naimy, despite the fact that it was "a diabolical concoction whose component parts are known to only those who concocted it." As they drank, Naimy recalled Gibran saying:

> This is a land of hypocrites and Pharisees. They have prohibited intoxicants in the belief that God will not admit into His heaven anyone not cut after their pattern – clean on the outside, but full of impurities within. Their Prohibition turned out to be a marvellous net for hauling tremendous profits.[15]

Gibran felt that alcoholic drinks were "bracing and beneficial to the heart" and in the remaining years of his life was increasingly to use alcohol as a stimulant.[16] Warned by doctors that his excessive intake of strong coffee was unhealthy and perhaps the cause of his heart palpitations, Gibran was sure that alcohol medicinally used could, to a certain extent, alleviate such symptoms.

The revitalizing force of spring, which in younger days had helped improve his health, failed to penetrate his frail constitution, and the early months of 1921 found him suffering from chronic fatigue. He told May that his body lacked "order, balance and rhythm."[17]

Over the years, visitors permitting, he had pursued a punishing work regime, painting as long as there was daylight and writing long into the night. When invited out to dine he would eat very little, and satisfy his hunger with continual cups of coffee. Returning home, often after midnight, he would breathlessly climb his stairs, rouse himself with a cold shower and more coffee, and spend the rest of the night working. Since his accident as a child of ten he had not been blessed with a constitution robust enough to remain unaffected by such demands.[18] Despite recurring illness Gibran continued to smoke heavily. As far as he was concerned smoking was a "pleasure rather than an irresistible need," and although he often smoked over twenty cigarettes a day, sometimes a whole day would pass when he did not smoke at all.[19]

When Mary visited him in February she was shocked by his appearance. "The flesh seemed to have dropped away from his body, and his legs seemed limp. His clothes hung upon him." He told her: "There seems nothing left in me . . . I'm tired, played out."[20] He told her that his life had become a battle-ground, fending off female admirers, fighting the men who are "all critics," struggling to cope with the life he "must lead as a Syrian . . . The Syrians come whether I'm sick or well. Every little Syrian town represented there wants to send its own delegation, to be kind to me, or to ask something."[21]

During this period he painted *Towards the Infinite*, a stunning picture of his mother, whose presence he still felt: "To me she was and still is a mother of spirit. I feel her nearness, her influence and her succour more than I ever did before she passed away, and in a way which is quite unparalleled." He said of this painting that it portrayed Kamileh "at the last moment of her life here and the first moment of her life over there."[22]

In the early summer he went on a ten-day vacation with Naseeb Arida, Abdul Massih Haddad, and Mikhail Naimy to Cahoonzie in the Catskills, some hundred miles from New York. They stayed in a farmhouse amid the heavy scents and abundant growths of nature's bounty, surrounded by a huge forest with lakes, waterfalls, and running streams. Here the four friends spent their days hiking, drinking arak, singing Lebanese folk songs, and composing extemporaneous verse. One afternoon as they were sauntering back from a beautiful waterfall Gibran suddenly stopped. Striking the road with his cane, he exclaimed, "Mischa! I'm a false alarm."[23]

Naimy, later pondering on this statement, concluded that Gibran's expression was that of a man who thought himself "overestimated" by his friends and admirers.

Gibran's awareness of his personal weaknesses – juxtaposed with the public persona of an inspirational figure – created a tension between the outer and inner man. This searing conflict was beginning to tear Gibran apart, a tension perhaps exacerbated by his awareness of the Sufi ideal that "the Sufi is he whose language . . . is the reality of his state."[24] In one of his aphorisms Gibran wrote: "Every thought I have imprisoned in expression, I must free by my deeds,"[25] an expression of his wish to unify his art with his life. However, first and foremost he was a consummate artist and if he failed to express his ideals in his life he had to learn to live within the bounds of this creative tension.

Several times when working with Mary on *The Prophet* he said to her: "This is not I, but the Prophet,"[26] and just before it was published Naimy confirmed that Gibran never once intended to "parade before men in a prophetic mantle."[27] Gibran told Mary: "The difference between a prophet and a poet is that the prophet lives what he teaches – and the poet does not. He may write wonderfully of love, and yet not be loving."[28]

He also told May Ziadah that people, against his will, were beginning to attribute non-existent qualities to him:

> They have gone to extremes in expressing their opinions, thinking me a camel rather than a rabbit. And God knows, my dear friend, that I have not read any such eulogy of myself without its etching itself painfully on my heart. Approbation is a form of responsibility foisted on us by others, causing us to become aware of our own weakness. However . . . we must draw strength from our weakness . . . Some say I am a "visionary," but I do not know what they mean by this word. I do know, however, that I am not so much of a "visionary" that I would lie to my Self. Even if I were to do so, my Self would not believe me.[29]

Struggling to overcome such paradoxes, Gibran's personal longing for integration between his life and his work intensified. His growing awareness of an underlying unity within the phenomenal and noumenal worlds was not mere intellectual assent, but a passionate conviction, a certainty that he now aimed to weave into the fabric of his being: "I know now that I am a part of the whole."[30]

II

This fervent yearning for wholeness was encapsulated in his last major Arabic work, *Iram Dhat al-'Imad* (*Iram, City of Lofty Pillars*), which was published in 1921.[31] The work, a play which tends to lack dramatic interest, is enlivened by the profound message that permeates every scene, and was to be a fitting precursor to *The Prophet*. Set in a forest in the year of Gibran's birth, the play has three characters: Zain al-'Abedeen, a Persian dervish, known as al-Sufi, the mystic; Najeeb Rahme, a thirty-year-old Christian man of letters who is Lebanese; and 'Amena, age unknown, a mysterious prophetess-seer known in the vicinity as the "Houri of the Valley," based on the figure of the ninth-century Sufi mystic Rabi'a al-'Adawiyya.[32] They meet in a forest between the Orontes river (Nahr el-'Asi) and a village in North Lebanon called Hermil. The title of the play may have been influenced by an Arabian legend, often cited in the Qur'an, of a fantastic city built on pillars by a tribe known as the 'Add, a people who occupied a great tract of southern Arabia, extending from Umman at the mouth of the Persian Gulf to Hadramaut and Yemen at the southernmost end of the extremity of the Arabian peninsula, an area in which the long twisting lands of *ahqaf* (sands) were irrigated by canals.[33]

Najeeb Rahme, who has heard that the prophetess 'Amena once entered this wondrous city of Iram, visits Zain al-'Abedeen who comes from Nahawand and is apparently in communion with her. Throughout the drama Najeeb Rahme, who incidentally possesses the name of Gibran's maternal grandfather, poses some fundamental questions dear to those who seek truth. He finds 'Amena with the features, gestures, and raiment of a goddess worshiped in past ages rather than an oriental woman of her time. When the three are seated Najeeb asks the prophetess whether she entered Iram the mysterious city of lofty pillars in body or in spirit. Her revelatory words carry an answer asserting how far Gibran had traveled on the path of spiritual consciousness:

All on earth, seen and unseen, is spiritual only. I entered the Golden City with my body, which is merely an earthly manifestation of my greater spirit, and which is, in all persons, a temporary vault for the safe-keeping of the spirit. I entered Iram with my body concealed within my spirit, for both are ever-present while on earth, and he who endeavours to cleave the body from the spirit, or the spirit from the body is directing his heart away from truth. The flower and its fragrance are one . . . Time and place are spiritual states, and all that is seen and heard is spiritual. If you close your eyes you will perceive all things through the depths of your inner self, and you will see the world, physical and ethereal, in its intended entirety, and you will acquaint yourself with its necessary laws and precautions, and you will understand the greatness that it possesses beyond its closeness. Yes . . . if you will close your eyes and open your heart and your inner perception you will discover the beginning and the end of existence . . . that beginning which in its turn becomes an ending, and that ending which must surely become a beginning.[34]

When Najeeb inquires if everyone is capable of seeing the truth, 'Amena replies:

> Man is empowered by God to hope and hope fervently, until that for which he is hoping takes the cloak of oblivion from his eyes, whereupon he will at last view his real self. And he who sees his real self sees the truth of real life for himself, for all humanity, and for all things.[35]

> All things in this creation exist within you, and all things in you exist in creation; there is no border between you and the closest things, and there is no distance between you and the farthest things, and all things, from the lowest to the loftiest, from the smallest to the greatest, are within you as equal things. In one atom are found all the elements of the earth; in one motion of the mind are found the motions of all the laws of existence; in one drop of water are found the secrets of all of the endless oceans; in one aspect of *you* are found all the aspects of *existence*.[36]

The message of *Iram, City of Lofty Pillars*, touched upon earlier by Gibran's "Astronomer" in *The Madman*, powerfully reflects the Sufi concept of the unity of being (*wahdat al-wudjud*);[37] and although Gibran's works should not be viewed as attempts to represent Sufi doctrine faithfully, they do express his interpretation of Sufi concepts as seen through the lens of his own poetic sensibilities. The unity of being, a doctrine that is repeatedly explored and expressed in the play, indicates the simultaneous transcendence and immanence of the absolute being as regards the phenomenal world.[38]

Although concepts similar to *wahdat al-wudjud* (unity of being) existed in other mystical traditions before the rise of Islam, in Sufism the principle was first formulated by the twelfth-century mystic philosopher of Andalusia, Ibn 'Arabi, also known as the greatest master (*al-sheikh al-akbar*). According to Titus Burckhardt's analysis of one of Ibn 'Arabi's principal works, *The Wisdom of the Prophets*, supreme union is "a mutual interpretation of Divinity and man"; God is manifested through Creation and "the Divine nature (al-Lahut) becomes the content of human nature (al-Nasut)" while at the same time "man is absorbed and, as it were, enveloped by Divine Reality."[39] The absolute, according to Ibn 'Arabi, is manifested in the phenomenal world through the divine names, or archetypes. "In truth, there is but one single essential Reality (*haqiqa*),"[40] which is that of God, the perfection, the infinity. Creation is the manifestation or realization of this unconditioned absolute in the world of infinite conditioned forms. "The world is then the shadow of God."[41] It is the result of God's yearning to be known.[42]

Intermediate between the plane of the absolute being (*wudjud mutlaq*) and the phenomenal world (*wudjud muqayyad*) is the plane of *at-tadjalli* which is God's revelation of the divine names.

The relation between God and the world has been metaphorically expressed by comparing God,[43] or the absolute being, to a boundless ocean – a metaphor Gibran was to use in *The Prophet* – and the concrete things and individual beings to numberless waves differing from the ocean in their definiteness and particularity, yet not diverging from it in their substance and reality.[44] "The Divine essence is the immanent cause of all being; it is eternal and at the same time perpetually manifesting itself in an unfathomable number of creatures."[45] In contrast to the naturalistic pantheism that dissolves God in nature, its maxim being "God is All," the Sufi concept of unity of being dissolves nature in God, insisting on the principle "All is God."[46] In the *wahdat al-wudjud* system, human nature synthesizes all the forms of divine revelation. If, on the cosmic level, the unity of being means "All is God," on the phenomenal level the unity of the absolute means "All is Man." Humanity is the intermediate link between God and the phenomenal world, thus ensuring the unity of cosmic and phenomenal being.[47]

In *Iram* Gibran's prophetess reveals that she entered the Golden City after enduring "pangs of hunger and the madness of thirst,"[48] Sufi metaphors for "yearning" (*shawq*) and journeying to God:

> Therefore, in simplicity, were it not for the hunger and thirst within me I would not have obtained food and water from my environs; and were it not for the longing and affection within me, I would not have found the subject of my longing and affection about me in the Golden City.[49]

'Amena tells the young Christian that sectarianism is a curse and unity a blessing:

> There is no God but *Allah* . . . there is nothing but *Allah*. You may speak these words and remain a Christian, for a God Who is good knows of no segregations amongst words or names, and were a God to deny His blessing to those who pursue a different path to eternity, then there is no human who should offer worship.[50]

She then reveals that, between the spiritual world and the physical world of substance, there is a way:

A path upon which we walk in a swoon of slumber. It reaches us and we are unaware of its strength, and when we return to ourselves we find that we are carrying with our real hands the seeds to be planted carefully in the good earth of our daily lives . . . Truly I say unto you, and the outcome of time will prove it, that there are ties between the upper world and the lower world as surely as there is a binding tie between a mother and her child. We are surrounded with an intuitive atmosphere that attracts our inner consciousness, and a knowledge that cautions our judgement, and a power that strengthens our own power. I say unto you that our doubt does not disprove or fortify our surrender to that which we doubt, and the fact of busying ourselves in self-gratification will not divert us from the accomplishment by the spirits of their purpose; and blinding ourselves to the reality of our spiritual being will not conceal our spiritual being from the eyes of the universe . . . The believer acquaints himself with the sacred realities through deep senses different from those used by others. A believer looks upon his senses as a great wall surrounding him, and when he walks upon the path he says, "This city has no exit, but it is perfect within." The believer lives for all the days and the nights, and the unfaithful live but a few hours.

How small is the life of the person who places his hands between his face and the world, seeing naught but the narrow lines of his hands!

How unjust to themselves are those who turn their backs to the sun, and see naught except the shadows of their physical selves upon the earth![51]

III

Through July, August, and September 1921, Gibran stayed with Marianna in Boston and frequently visited Mary in Cambridge. He spent much of his time working on "The Farewell" from *The Prophet*, copying it all down as Mary dictated it to him from the manuscript. Again he was keen to allay any misconceptions that he was in any way synonymous with the prophet, telling Mary: "This is not I, but the Prophet."[52]

On August 8 Mary filled two of her notebooks with their conversations, in particular about Gibran's interest in P. D. Ouspensky's recently published *Tertium Organum*.[53] In his introduction to *Tertium Organum*, Claude Bragdon hints at why Ouspensky's book, which built a bridge between Western rationalism and Eastern mysticism, would have appealed to Gibran's temperament:

To persons of an artistic or devotional bent the book will be as water in the desert . . . [they] will find in Ouspensky a champion whose weapon is mathematical certitude, the very thing by which the practical-minded swear . . . But most of all Ouspensky will be loved by all true lovers, for his chapter on the subject of love. We have had Schopenhauer on love, and Freud on love, but what dusty answers do they give to the soul of a lover! Edward Carpenter comes much nearer the mark, but Ouspensky penetrates to its very center.[54]

Gibran continued to complete his own work on love, specifically Almustafa's "Farewell" to the people of Orphalese:

But sweeter still than laughter and greater than longing came to me.
It was the boundless in you;
The vast man[55] in whom you are all but cells and sinews;
He in whose chant all your singing is but a soundless throbbing.
It is in the vast man that you are vast,
And in beholding him that I beheld you and loved you.[56]

To complete *The Prophet*, "the only thought that will make me worthy to stand in the light of the sun,"[57] Gibran returned to Boston, to Marianna's tenement in Tyler Street. Here he was able to cloister himself away from his growing commitments in New York, leaving the neighborhood only to meet Mary in Cambridge. It was fitting that the book that was to be his *magnum opus* should be completed in such humble surroundings and in the company of two women who had been so close to his heart.

It was fitting too, that on September 9, as Mary's journal faithfully recorded, when "He copied the closing paragraphs of *The Prophet*,"[58] this entry marked the end of their face-to-face collaboration. Unbeknown to them "The Farewell" of *The Prophet* was to herald another parting of the ways. In November Mary's oldest cousin, "Aunt Loulie," Louise Gilmer Minis, died. When Mary next saw Gibran she told him that the widower, Jacob Florance Minis, had asked her to come to live with him as companion and hostess. Formerly president of the Southwestern Railroad and the Savannah Cotton Exchange, Minis enjoyed a luxurious lifestyle. Mary, now forty-eight and somewhat worn by the constraints of a reactionary educational system, was seriously debating going to live with him. However she couldn't decide whether to give up her vocation. Knowing of Mary's dedication to teaching, Gibran's initial response was: "Wait, you will know presently."[59]

Earlier in the year he had said to her: "We ought to come to our work as we come to a beautiful child, with reverence and love."[60] For Mary teaching was a creative vocation – as she had expressed to Gibran in 1912:

> Aren't children – isn't the begetting of children – the Larger Being's resource with us when we are ourselves unfinished instruments of expression? We become links then in the development of finished instruments . . . Great works *must* initiate new human varieties, just as new human varieties *may* initiate great works. It is another kind of procreation and breeding from seed and fecundity surely not less potent than that generally recognized.[61]

During her career, wishing to nurture her pupils' aesthetic sensibilities, Mary had ensured that Gibran's pictures adorned her school walls, her journal faithfully attesting to each individual hanging: *Spirits of Night, The Fountain of Pain, Mary, The Dance of the Thoughts, Micheline, The Three Women, Fredericka, Mother of Heaven, The Lamb Prayed in his Heart, Consolation, The Beholder,* and *The Crucified,* which had recently caused such controversy in Cambridge. Her happiest days had been spent at her school in Marlborough Street where even the tensions and strain of work itself

> seems but part of what goes to create a beautiful something that I am aware of . . . With a certain pitch of life there comes a look, a bearing, almost like an exaltation, in teachers and girls. Almost a slender being, like a *youth* made of light, seems to float about the mid-air of school. The others make him, and I see him. His presence is our success – work turned to ecstasy, to life.[62]

Gibran had responded:

> What you told me about "Haskell" is beautiful and wonderful. The Spirit, that half visible Being that speaks in silences, is the greatest reality in a school or in a house or in a nation or in the world. Living up to that super-being is the only living worthwhile. A House-God is the living, growing godly desires of those who dwell in the house. The "Haskell" "youth made of light" is really the light of your larger self and the larger selves of your teachers and girls.[63]

Gibran had learnt a great deal about the art of teaching from Mary's inspired classes: "It is the *being* that teaches, not the ideas, and not the organizations we create . . . Plato organized nothing – yet he lives, and lives among people who actually know none of his ideas."[64]

As Gibran approached the school at their next meeting in Boston in April 1922, Mary observed that he walked slowly and "was dark and thin, his face full of shadows." He told her that he had been seeing a specialist for cardiac pains and nervous debility. By now he was worried about the state of his health and wanted to escape from New York and live in the country.[65]

He had recently been expressing similar sentiments to Mikhail Naimy, as the two men reminisced about the beautiful gorge of Qadisha, the serenity of the Mar Sarkis monastery, and the grandeur of the Holy Mountain of the Cedars. Like so many times before in his life, Gibran's longing for Lebanon was intense. When Naimy had recently gone to stay in the mountains in northern Lebanon, Gibran wrote to him saying that he often dreamt of going to live in a hermitage, and one day hoped to live on the edge of a Lebanese valley.[66]

In the past Gibran had been a good sleeper, but over the war years his nights had become restless, exacerbated by piercing pains in his chest. Mary gave him some thyroid medicine[67] and made arrangements for him to see a specialist in Boston. The specialist, Dr. William H. Smith, "the most talkative person" Gibran had ever met, found no enlargement of the heart or valvular trouble, and rather vaguely diagnosed that Gibran had "a nervous heart." He gave the patient "a little dissertation" on the artistic temperament, saying how he might be paying now for irregular eating and sleeping habits, but could not specify the exact nature of the illness. Gibran said: "I don't know myself why I am. What I do know is that I've got to stop working and learn how to live."[68]

At the beginning of May his attempts to complete the phrasing of *The Prophet* were interrupted by more hospital visits as doctors struggled to reach a firm diagnosis of his mysterious illness. He underwent breathing tests but again the doctors found that there was nothing wrong with his heart or lungs. Gibran was perplexed that the doctors failed to notice the pain in and around his heart. He did not have a great deal of faith in Western medicine – perhaps a reaction to the sudden and devastating losses, years before, of his mother, Boutros, and Sultanah. More interested in studying "effects," without paying the "slightest heed" to "causes,"[69] doctors, according to Gibran, lacked a holistic conception of health, treating "this part or that, not knowing that the illness of any part is the illness of the whole," its cause not always "physical":[70]

My greatest pain is not physical . . . There's something big in me and I can't get it out. It's a silent greater self, sitting and watching a smaller me do all sorts of things. All the things I do seem false to me; they are not what I want to say. I am always conscious of a birth that is to be. It's just as if for years a child wanted to be born and couldn't be born. You are always waiting, and you are always in birth pain. Yet there is no birth.[71]

These were anxious and challenging times for Gibran, yet he retained a stoical determination to continue his work at all costs. He told Mary: "Pain can be creative . . . Some people reach the big thing in life through joy – and some through neither pain nor joy. They just live into it. And a great number never reach it at all."[72]

As he paced the floor one night early in May, Mary noticed that his face was dark as he spoke of doubts about whether *The Prophet* expressed all the miracles of his living soul: "All that I can say and do say is foreign to the real thing that I would say and cannot. Only this one book, *The Prophet*, has as it were a shadow of that thing – a bit every now and then."[73] Mary, aware of his ability to transform his negative emotions through his work, watched him as he put the finishing touches to *The Prophet*:

Nearness with him is different from nearness with anyone else. It is not an emotion – not a forgetting or a mood – not a regard one for the other nor a turning of thought or eye one upon the other. It is a living one's own life as one does when one is alone – but leaving the door open, or opening it, to the other. There is no bidding you in; rather, you are shown about in there only incidentally, if it so comes about – and nothing is changed or arranged for your benefit. In silence he says, "Be at home," though he may be busily talking at the moment. Never was there so utter a genuineness, such absence of plan for effect, such willingness for your eye to see just what is.[74]

Throughout the early summer Mary wrestled with the choices in her life. Gibran told her to follow her heart, for "your heart is the right guide in everything big . . . What you *want* to do is determined by that divine element that is in each of us."[75] Sometimes Mary's journal unwittingly reveals a sense that if Kahlil had uttered one word of caution, one indication that he himself needed her, she would have jettisoned all plans of moving. When he boarded the train for New York on June 16, she observed that his shoulders "looked forty years old, for the first time," and she was overcome with "an unutterable pain and sadness."[76]

That summer Mary went on holiday with Jacob Florance Minis to Europe, an unusual trip for an unmarried woman of her class and time. Gibran meanwhile spent the summer with Marianna in Scituate, south of Boston. At last he was able to relax, spending his time painting watercolors by the ocean and befriending the local children: "When they saw I was working they would go away quietly. But when a kite flew, that was the signal – and then they all came . . . There are ninety-seven children on that hill."

Over the next few weeks Gibran began making a selection of beautiful Syrian kites for the children: "I must have made sixty or seventy."[77] The children had never seen such kites before and soon, along with their parents, they were making their own. The youngsters asked Gibran to be a judge at their parade, and, obliging, he presented his own, "the signal kite," as the first prize to a big fat boy, one of twelve children: "Those three months," he later told Mary, "were the best I've ever had in my life . . . Everything came easy and its still coming easily."[78] Gibran found a sense of joy and freedom in the company of children, their innocence and purity of heart enriching his own awareness, which he expressed later in a whole sermon in *The Prophet*.

When Gibran and Mary met again in September they exchanged their summer stories. Mary, having basked in luxury for the first time in her life, had enjoyed her trip to Europe. She told Gibran that she had finally decided to go and live with Jacob Florance Minis. He reassured her that his own relationship with her was the most wonderful thing that he had known.[79] When she said that Florance was always asking her whether she loved him better than anyone else in the world, Gibran said:

Every love is the best in the world, and the dearest. Love isn't like a pie that we can cut pieces of, large or small. It's all one: It's all love. Of course you can say he's the dearest thing in the world to you. – Anyone we love and everyone we love, is the dearest person in the world to us.[80]

As always, after a vacation, she had returned laden with gifts for him: overcoats, ties, suits, a cigarette case and an opal chain and pendant. In turn he showed her the twenty-six watercolors he had been doing over the summer, saying she could have the originals. Mary exclaimed: "These pictures can stand by the finest hitherto painted in the world, and be honored with them."[81] He had painted some of them specifically for *The Prophet* while others he planned to save for poems yet unwritten.[82]

On what was to be Gibran's last visit to Cambridge, he and Mary looked at the final choice of illustrations for the book. Absorbed in attending to the final arrangements and refreshed from his stay by the sea Gibran found he was more reconciled with himself than ever before: "If one will accept himself he hinders himself no longer . . . Let me rejoice in Kahlil Gibran just as he is, and then I'll be something for people to love who can love what I am. Nobody can love me if I'm *not* myself."[83] On December 31, 1922 they read from *The Prophet* to see if anywhere it proselytized or "sounded preachy," a concern probably prompted by a recent review of *The Forerunner*.[84] It did not.[85] Suddenly, as they read, a bell rang and a whistle blew and Gibran said, "The New Year is in."[86]

Two days into 1923 came their last meeting before Mary went south. He disclosed he had another book in mind – "He is on his island with his seven disciples – and he talks of the largest aspect of things. And it is of the simplest things he speaks – a drop of dew, the light from a star."[87] He also revealed that while working on *The Prophet* he was always conscious of writing in a language that was not his mother tongue, and he told Mary that for a long time he had had a fear about his English: "Is my English, modern English, Mary, or is it the English of the past? For English is still to me a foreign language. I still think in Arabic only. And I know English only from Shakespeare and the Bible and you." "I told him the simple truth," Mary answered, "that like his Arabic, his English too is creative. It is not of any one period. It is his own."[88]

That winter they kept in touch, and in March he sent her the galley proofs of *The Prophet*.[89] Gibran was thrilled to see that a collection of his works had been published under the title *al-Badayi' wa'l Tarayif* (*Beautiful and Rare Sayings*).[90] Published by Maktabti-al-'Arab in Cairo, *al-Badayi' wa'l Tarayi'f* was an anthology of some of his Arabic works published in periodicals over recent years. The pieces were selected by the publishers, who also gave the collection its title, and included Gibran's articles on Ibn Sina,[91] al-Ghazali,[92] and Ibn al-Farid;[93] *Iram, City of Lofty Pillars*; "The Political Farewell"; a collection of aphorisms;[94] and prose-poems,[95] many imbued with Sufi yearning:

> O Soul! if I had not been baptized with tears and my eyes had not been
>   mascaraed by the ghosts of sickness, I would have seen life as through
>   a veil, darkly.
> O Soul! life is a darkness which ends as in the sunburst of day.
> The yearning of my heart tells me there is peace in the grave.

O Soul! if some fool tells you the soul perishes like the body and that which dies never returns, tell him the flower perishes but the seed remains and lies before us as the secret of life everlasting.[96]

IV

At the end of September a small black book, neat but unassuming, and costing $2.25, made its appearance on the overcrowded New York book market.[97] Mary, on receiving a copy, was the first to recognize that its appeal would be universal. On October 2, 1923 she wrote:

> Beloved Kahlil, *The Prophet* came today, and it did more than realize my hopes. For it seemed in its compacted form to open yet further new doors of desire and imagination in me, and to create about itself the universe in nimbus, so that I read it as the centre of things. The format is excellent, and lets the ideas and the verse flow quite unhampered. The pictures make my heart jump when I see them. They are beautifully done. I like the book altogether in style.
>
> And the text is more beautiful, nearer, more revealing, more marvellous in conveying reality and in sweetening consciousness – than ever . . . The English, the style, the wording, the music – is exquisite, Kahlil – just sheerly beautiful . . . This book will be held as one of the treasures of English literature. And in our darkness we will open it to find ourselves again and the heaven and earth within ourselves. Generations will not exhaust it, but instead, generation after generation will find in the book what they would fain be – and it will be better loved as men grow riper and riper.
>
> It is the most loving book ever written.[98]

Soon after it was published Mikhail Naimy visited Gibran in "his Hermitage":

> Although severely furnished, as a hermitage ought to be, it spoke not so much of prayer as it did of work. It contained a cot that served Gibran as a bed at night and a lounge in the daytime, three upholstered chairs and a small bed-table on which stood a telephone. The whole studio was cluttered with folios of drawings, books, and papers and the tools of creative effort – brushes, paint tubes, pencils, pens and inkwells.
>
> I had scarcely arrived when Gibran handed me a letter and said, with a twinkle of deep satisfaction in his eyes, "Read this, Mischa." The letter was from the president of Colorado College and asked permission to engrave a verse from *The Prophet* on the master bell of the chimes of the college

memorial chapel. The verse was, "Yesterday is But Today's Memory, and Tomorrow Is Today's Dream."

As I handed it back with warm, congratulatory words, Gibran looked at me with eyes half moist and said in a grave voice, "It's a strange little book, Mischa."[99]

Barely 20,000 words long, philosophical in nature and mystical in tone, *The Prophet* was hardly a book one would expect to capture the attention of the reading public. Yet eventually it did. Its author began to be "overwhelmed" with letters of praise,[100] and he gave a reading of it at the Poets' Club. The actor Butler Davenport read from *The Prophet* at St. Mark's-in-the-Bouwerie in New York. Gibran commented: "To my regret he read the whole book . . . but his spirit was ever so good . . . I had wanted it first read in a church."[101] Slowly word spread that a strange little book was on the streets of New York. How far that reputation spread Gibran did not know until the day he received a letter from a friend relaying to him the unbounded admiration of the queen of Romania to whom someone had given a copy.[102] Gibran wrote to her of his gratitude that the "Queen of a race" had put her "Royal Seal" upon his work.[103]

Naimy sensed the passionate heart of his friend pulsating through every page of the book: "an impassioned, high-strung and over-sensitive soul that had known the full range of human experiences, from extreme dejection to the highest exaltation . . . It is the gates of a heart flung open to the world that it may see what miracles the magic hand of suffering had wrought in it."[104] He wrote that the message of *The Prophet* was that "man's end was nothing short of omniscience, omnipotence, omnipresence and immortality" and in that light compassion, gentleness, forgiveness, and kindred virtues become necessities for right living. To deviate from them is to inflict pain upon oneself. Pain is subsequently, in the words of Almustafa, an "eye opener," it is "the bitter potion by which the physician within you heals your sick self."[105]

Naimy perceived too that there was an intensely personal side to "Gibran's masterpiece,"[106] thinly veiled by names such as "Almustafa," "Orphalese," "Almitra." Gibran can be identified as Almustafa; the city of New York as Orphalese; Mary Haskell as Almitra; Lebanon as Almustafa's isle of birth; and the twelve years in Orphalese as the twelve years Gibran spent in New York prior to the publication of the book.

Within a month all 1,300 copies of the first edition had been sold, setting in motion a trend that was to continue steadily up to the present day, and may perhaps be maintained for years to come. By the end of December 1937, the book had sold 129,233 copies, and during the darkness of World War II, demand for the life-affirming work sharpened.[107] By 1957 it had sold its millionth copy, been translated into twenty languages, and become one of the most widely distributed books of the century.[108] Its immediate success represented a just reward and vindication for Alfred Knopf. Gibran had a deep respect for the publisher who had followed his wishes to the letter, the final text concurring with Gibran's manuscripts and the typescripts that are available to us.[109]

The Irish writer George Russell (AE)[110] thought on reading *The Prophet* that the East had not spoken with so beautiful a voice since the *Gitanjali* of Rabindranath Tagore:

> I have not seen for years a book more beautiful in its thought, and when reading it I understand better than ever before what Socrates meant in the *Banquet* when he spoke of the beauty of thought, which exercises a deeper enchantment than the beauty of form. To the mother he cries:
>
> Your children are not your children,
> They are the sons and daughters of Life's longing for itself.
> You may give them your love but not your thoughts,
> For they have their own thoughts.
> You may house their bodies but not their souls.
> Their souls dwell in the house of to-morrow, which you cannot visit, not
>   even in your dreams.
>
> He asks of the dweller in the house, has he beauty there –
>
> Or have you only comfort, that stealthy thing that enters the house a
>   guest, and then becomes a host then a master?
>
> I could quote from every page, and from every page I could find some beautiful and liberating thought. How profound is that irony of Gibran's about the lovers of freedom "who wear their freedom as a yoke and a handcuff." Have we not seen here souls more chained to their idea of freedom than a prisoner is limited in his cell? The most terrible chains are those that gnaw at the soul.[111]

Sarwat Okasha, former minister of culture in Egypt and himself a translator of Gibran, heard in *The Prophet* an echo of Gibran's own aphorism, "How shall my heart be unsealed unless it be broken":[112]

It is a book dipped in blood. It is a book like a cry bursting from a wounded heart. Great pain can crush its victims; it can overcome him who suffers it, but when it encounters a spirit like that of Gibran, it becomes a power, fertile and productive.[113]

Almustafa preaches twenty-six poetic sermons on a wide range of subjects before his final departure from the land of Orphalese. It is Almitra, the seeress, who although aware of his "longing for the land of [his] memories and the dwelling place of [his] greatest desires,"[114] begs him to "give us of your truth."[115] Almustafa's departure for "the isle of his birth" symbolizes his return to the unborn state from which, as he promises at the end, he will again be reincarnated: "A little while, a moment of rest upon the wind, and another woman shall bear me."[116]

Gibran's prophet, like Krishna in the *Bhagavadgita*, reincarnates not only out of the need for continued self-realization, but also to provide an example for the spiritually uninitiated. However, he is solitary and has experienced long "nights of aloneness." He asks: "Who can depart from his pain and his aloneness without regret?"[117] But, as Almustafa later explains in his sermon on joy and sorrow, such suffering is a prerequisite for true happiness and indeed, in its deepest reality, is indistinguishable from it.[118] At the close, Almustafa explains too why he has spent so much time alone:

And some of you have called me aloof, and drunk with my own
    aloneness . . .
How could I have seen you save from a great height or a great distance?
How can one be indeed near unless he be far?[119]

Almustafa speaks first on love, perhaps the most beautiful of all his sermons, and used so many times over the years in countless marriage ceremonies that the words must be read again with fresh eyes:

Love has no other desire but to fulfil itself.
But if you love and must needs have desires, let these be your desires:
To melt and be like a running brook that sings its melody to the night.
To know the pain of too much tenderness.
To be wounded by your own understanding of love;
And to bleed willingly and joyfully.
To wake at dawn with a winged heart and give thanks for another day of
    loving;
To rest at the noon hour and meditate love's ecstasy;

To return home at eventide with gratitude;
And then to sleep with a prayer for the beloved in your heart and a song
    of praise upon your lips.[120]

The concept of love as wounding and painful, even while it can lift to ecstasy, is found in the writings of both the Sufis of the East and the Christian mystics of the West. Almustafa's insistence on the essential identity of love, joy, pain, and sorrow is a major feature of *The Prophet*, and evidently contained very real personal significance for Gibran. It is also a part of the work's rejection of the limiting dualism of the material world and its recognition that truth never *is*, but is always in the process of *becoming*, always spontaneous.[121] Hence Almustafa's refusal to admit absolute good and bad, and his defense of the guilty as being members of the whole like everyone else: "The righteous is not innocent of the deeds of the wicked," and "You cannot separate the just from the unjust and the good from the wicked."[122] These statements seem at first to contradict the recorded words of Jesus. Gibran probably saw them as corrective of the crudely dualistic interpretations of Christian righteousness that resulted in separation between people. The point is made without recourse to didacticism, and indeed the gentle tone of *The Prophet* is remarkable for the absence of the controversial element present in his early Arabic works and of the sardonic irony of *The Madman*. What Gibran had done, in fact, was to distil and express with greater profundity the beliefs of his earlier writings. In the sermon on prayer, for example, the condemnation of religious hypocrisy is subtle and implicit: "You pray in your distress and in your need; would that you might pray also in the fullness of your joy and in your days of abundance."[123]

The note of compassion is expressed again in his view of humanity, seen to be in need of self-realization, to bridge the gap between the "pigmy" in us and our "god-self."[124] Self-knowledge comes through listening in silence to the heart's knowledge. This, however, is always harmed by the attempt to form it in words. Nonetheless, the power of universal love is to be felt in all: "Who among you does not feel that his power to love is boundless?"[125] Compared with this power, evil does not exist; as in Dante's view, evil is a misdirection of the desire for good, or rather it is merely a limitation of that desire. Gibran echoed Walt Whitman's transcendental affirmation in *Song of Myself* that "What is called good is perfect, and what is called sin is just as perfect."[126] Gibran would also have agreed with Emerson that even a fallen person is moving toward the greater good:

You are good when you walk to your goal firmly and with bold steps.
Yet you are not evil when you go thither limping.
Even those who limp go not backward.[127]

Beside this transcendentalism is an avowal of immanent divinity that recalls both the Psalms and William Blake:

And look into space; you shall see Him walking in the cloud,
    outstretching His arms in the lightning and descending in rain.
You shall see Him smiling in flowers, then rising and waving His hands in
    trees.[128]

Among the major significant influences evident in *The Prophet* is that of Friedrich Nietzsche's *Thus Spake Zarathustra*. The early title of Gibran's masterpiece "The Counsels" owed its origins to the form and structure of *Thus Spake Zarathustra*. Both works exhibit lofty biblical language, aphoristic, parenthetic sentences, and a strong epigrammatical style. Gibran was fascinated with Nietzsche's towering figure of Zarathustra – a prophet who left society to discover his "spirit and his solitude"[129] amidst the mountains before descending with his wisdom to the people below.

Although Nietzsche's prophet had been demythologized by his creator, Gibran still perceived that Zarathustra was a prophet with considerable spiritual presence and power. This prophetic element – the literary fiction of speaking with authority – became the strongest single leitmotiv of Nietzsche in Gibran.[130] When he wrote *The Prophet* Gibran imitated the scenario of *Thus Spake Zarathustra* without in any way subscribing to Nietzsche's nihilistic philosophy.

In *The Prophet* East and West meet in a mystic union unparalleled in modern literature. Inspired by the vision of Blake, the Bible, Buddhism, Hinduism, the Romantics, popular American schools of thought, Ralph Waldo Emerson, Walt Whitman, Friedrich Nietzsche, Ameen Rihani, and Christian and Sufi mysticism, *The Prophet* provoked the critic Claude Bragdon to write of its "extraordinary dramatic power, deep erudition, lightning-like intuition, lyrical lift and metrical mastery with which [the] message is presented, and the beauty, beauty, beauty, which permeates the entire pattern, with which everything he touches seems fairly to drip, as it were."[131] Gibran's own testimony indicates that he found the inspiration for the work's spellbinding language and cadences in nature:

Poets ought to listen to the rhythm of the sea. That's the rhythm in Job –
and in all the magnificent parts of the Old Testament. You hear it in that
double way of saying a thing, that the Hebrews used. – It is said – then said
right off again – a little differently. And that's like the waves of the sea. You
know how a big wave rolls in – whish! – and carries the big pebbles with it
in a crashing noise. Then some of the pebbles roll back again, with a smaller
noise, a sort of undercurrent of sound – and then a second wave will roll up,
smaller than the first – whish! – And then there's a pause. – And soon
another big wave will come – and the same thing happens all over again.
That's the music to learn from – and the music of the wind – and the rustle
of leaves.[132]

Bragdon felt that Gibran aimed to discover some workable way of feeling,
thinking, living which shall lead toward *mastery* – "how to serve the forces
which enslave us until they are by us enslaved."[133] He sensed that Gibran's
power came from "some great reservoir of spiritual life else it could not have
been so universal and so potent"; yet "the majesty and beauty of the
language with which he clothed it were all his own."[134]

This reservoir lay in Gibran's background: his identity as an Arab
immigrant in America; his birthplace, "a nursery of prophets, one of those
places where the sacred flame has never been permitted to snuff out,"[135]
which, perhaps more than any other, had been a melting-pot of religions,
cultures, and ideas; his Maronite Christian upbringing; and his Arabic
culture which was influenced not only by his own religion but also by Islam,
especially by the mysticism of the Sufis.

Since early childhood he had been moved by the teachings of the gospels
and in particular by the figure of Christ, eventually producing his own
unique and powerful portrait, *Jesus, the Son of Man*.[136] Christ is also one of
the models for Almustafa in *The Prophet*, and the form of the latter's
teachings bears some comparison to the Sermon on the Mount in its
eloquent guidance for humanity. In 1921, Mary's journal records Gibran
as describing Christ as "the most powerful personality in history," who
"first perceived the Kingdom of Heaven in man's own heart, a world of
beauty, of goodness, of reality, of truth."[137] Similarly Gibran's depiction of
the essence of Christ's teaching, again as recorded by Mary, is close to
the central message of *The Prophet*: "If the Kingdom of Heaven is
within you, if you have that calm in yourself, that quiet in your centre, if
you are in love with life, you love your enemy because you love
everybody."[138]

One of the most striking features about *The Prophet* is its biblical language, which Gibran saw as the ideal medium for conveying profound teachings capable of being understood and digested:[139] "The Bible is Syriac literature in English words. It is the child of a sort of marriage. There's nothing in any other tongue to correspond to the English Bible. And the Chaldo-Syriac is the most beautiful language that man has made – though it is no longer used."[140] There is virtually no part of *The Prophet* in which the language of the King James Bible does not reverberate:

> At night the watchmen of the city say, "Beauty shall rise with the dawn from the east."
> And at noontide the toilers and the wayfarers say, "We have seen her leaning over the earth from the windows of the sunset."
> In winter say the snow-bound, "She shall come with the spring leaping upon the hills."
> And in the summer heat the reapers say, "We have seen her dancing with the autumn leaves, and we saw a drift of snow in her hair."[141]

The passage calls to mind the incantational Song of Solomon:

> My beloved spake, and said unto me, "Rise up, my love, my fair one, and come away.
> For lo, the winter is past, the rain is over and gone;
> The flowers appear on the earth, the time of the singing of birds is come, and the voice of the turtle is heard in our land, . . .
> The watchmen that go about the city found me: to whom I said, Saw ye him whom my soul loveth?[142]

Gibran's use of rhetoric is exemplified by the following passage from the sermon on houses:

> Would that I could gather your houses into my hand, and like a sower scatter them in forest and meadow.
> Would the valleys were your streets, and the green paths your alleys, that you might seek one another through vineyards, and come with the fragrance of the earth in your garments.
> But these things are not yet to be.[143]

Here the influence of Christ's lamentation over Jerusalem may be inferred: "O Jerusalem, Jerusalem, thou that killest the prophets, and stoneth them which are sent unto thee, how often would I have gathered thy children together, even as a hen gathereth her chickens under her wings, and ye would not!"[144]

In the sermon on prayer, however, Almustafa says: "God listens not to your words save when He Himself utters them through your lips."[145] This is more reminiscent of one of the sayings of the Prophet Muhammad recorded in the *Hadith*: "A servant draws near to me in prayer when I become the eyes with which he sees and the ears with which he hears."[146]

The same sermon contains a passage which is close to Sufi doctrine:

And if you but listen in the stillness of the night you shall hear them
    saying in silence,
"Our God, who art our winged self, it is thy will in us that willeth.
It is thy desire in us that desireth.
It is thy urge in us that would turn our nights, which are thine, into days
    which are thine also.
We cannot ask thee for aught, for thou knowest our needs before they are
    born in us:
Thou art our need; and in giving us more of thyself thou givest us all."[147]

Gibran's attachment to Sufi philosophy found its clearest manifestation in *al-'Awasif* (*The Tempest*), which contains his short essays on three of the greatest figures in Sufi literature.[148] He could almost have been describing his own Almustafa in these essays, which were written many years before *The Prophet* was published.

The teachings of *The Prophet* correspond closely to the first level of Sufi teachings, which concern personal behavior and the eternal and fundamental subjects central to life. And while the language and sentiment of *The Prophet* puts one constantly in mind of the Bible and the English Romantics, the spirit and message is Sufi to its very core. The book is the sum of Gibran's Sufi thought and his social creed. It contains, in one form or another, all the major Sufi ideas: the universal self, unity of life and death, unity of body and soul, unity of good and evil, unity of time and place, unity of religion, unity of humankind and collective responsibility, the divine in the human soul, and the relationship between essence and form. Both in this and in many of his other writings, Gibran makes reference to the Sufi ideal of the "Greater Self," that is God. Above all, Almustafa is Christ and Muhammad merged into one, the embodiment of *al-insan al-kamil*, the "Perfect Man" of Sufi tradition:

The Perfect Man is a miniature of Reality, he is the microcosm, in whom
are reflected all the perfect attributes of the macrocosm. Just as the Reality
of Mohammed was the *creative principle* of the Universe, so the Perfect Man
was the *cause* of the Universe, being the epiphany of God's desire to be
known; for only the Perfect Man knows God, loves God, and is loved by
God.[149]

Hence Almustafa's words to the people of Orphalese: "If aught I have said
is truth, that truth shall reveal itself in a clearer voice, and in words more
kin to your thoughts" and "I only speak to you in words of that which you
yourselves know in thought."[150] This Eastern concept of the perfect man is
paralleled in the West by that of the universal man and its variants, which
include Emerson's Oversoul and perhaps even Nietzsche's Superman.
Although derived from Jewish mysticism, the idea of the universal man –
the universe as a single giant man composed of four elements – is clearly
expressed in the works of Swedenborg and, more especially, William
Blake.[151] The following, which could almost have been written by a Sufi, is
from Blake's poem *The Four Zoas*:

> Four Mighty Ones are in every Man; a perfect Unity
> Cannot Exist but from the Universal Brotherhood of Eden,
> The Universal Man, to Whom be Glory Evermore. Amen.[152]

Every man and woman then, according to Gibran, is a longing for the
divine, destined for Godhead; like the seed, each bears within a longing, the
fulfillment of which is God, who is also the road leading to this fulfillment.
He has utter faith in the capacity of each individual, as a self-perfecting
organism, to become divine by realization; that is, by making real the divine
in the human life. The keynote of *The Prophet*, as in much work of the
Romantic poets, is pantheism. Its central article of belief is that God is
latent within everyone as a greater self, and that this is attained through
aspiration, or "yearning," which is comparable to prayer in religion, and
also through successive reincarnations. Life is a journey, and God is both
starting-point and destination. "Like a procession you walk together
towards your god-self," says Almustafa in the sermon on good and evil,[153]
while the Qur'an (v: 18) tells us that "Allah's is the Sovereignty of the
heavens and the earth and all that is between them, and unto him is the
journeying.[154] The journey thus represents the condition of full awareness
when the soul has embarked on the path leading to its desired union with
God. The enlightened wayfarer (Almustafa is one of the names given to the

Prophet Muhammad)[155] offers directions for anyone who would undertake such a journey:

> Almustafa can . . . symbolize the man who . . . has become his freer self, who has realized the passage in himself from the human to the divine, and is therefore ripe for emancipation and reunion with life absolute . . . the people of Orphalese . . . stand for human society at large in which men, exiled in their spatio-temporal existence from their true selves, that is from God, are in need in their Godward journey of the guiding prophetic hand that would lead them from what is human in them to what is divine. Having made that journey himself, Almustafa poses in his sermons throughout the book as that guide.[156]

The idea of "journeying" was developed by the great Sufi poet-philosopher Ibn 'Arabi into the theory that understanding of oneself and knowledge of the cosmos is attained by traveling through it.[157] For him all creation was symbolized by a gigantic circle: the individual begins from any point on the circumference and faces an abundant choice of paths and radii toward the center, where he or she merges with the divine presence or the absolute. The principal way is through self-purification by heeding God's solemn covenant and following the example of the perfect man or "prophet." This concept, although purely Sufi in origin, no doubt greatly appealed to Gibran on account of its universality:

> Implicit in Ibn al-'Arabi's theory of journeying is the unity of religions. To him revelation is universal and every prophet has transmitted an aspect of God's Will to mankind. Therefore, if we examine the inner contents of all religions by journeying inwardly from the external forms toward the inner one we will find a transcendent unity: they all emanate from the same supreme Center.[158]

The essence within the diversity of forms is the love of God, as Almustafa teaches. And the journey is an inner one, a spiritual one, in contrast to the travels of the majority of twentieth-century men and women.[159] Hence the timelessness of *The Prophet's* message. The spiritual journey is analogous, as Mikhail Naimy points out, to Gibran's own career up to the publication of his finest work in 1923:

> *The Prophet* represents the peak in his literary career. Viewed in the light of Reincarnation, a doctrine which he embraced and made the cornerstone of

his philosophy of human destiny, Gibran's life from his own birth to the birth of *The Prophet* may be seen as a steady ascent to that peak.[160]

If *The Prophet* represented the peak of Gibran's literary career it also marked the pinnacle of his artistic endeavors. Arguably none of his earlier illustrations surpass the twelve to be found in *The Prophet*,[161] particularly the frontispiece depicting the face of Almustafa. In June 1923 he described to Mary how this face had come about:

> I was reading one night in bed late and I stopped, weary, and closed my eyes for a moment. When I closed my eyes, I saw quite plainly That Face. I saw it for one or two minutes, perfectly clearly – and then it disappeared . . . Sometimes I have been sitting at a dinner table in a company – and all of a sudden this drawing would be before me and I would see just the shade, just the line, to put here or there – and I would think, I wish to God I could go back right now to the studio and put that in. And sometimes in the night I would wake up, knowing a new thing to do – and I would rise and do it.[162]

This drawing, and the last illustration in the book, the *Creative Hand*, were originally done in black and white, the other ten being wash drawings. Mikhail Naimy wrote an apt and penetrating description of the frontispiece:

> The large, dreamy eyes seem to look away beyond the present moment and the immediate circumstance. Sorrowful and penetrating, they speak eloquently of a most sympathetic heart and a soul suffused with loving understanding. The mouth, though thick-lipped and passionate, is rich in sensitiveness, patience, forgiveness and delicacy of taste. It is the mouth of one who has tasted the pleasures of the world and found them bitter, and would no longer soil his lips with a drop from that fountain. The effect of that delicate veil of sadness drawn all over the face is broken by the barely suggested circle of hair forming a halo of light. Framed within that halo are eternities of painful struggle against all the things that keep man chained to the earth and make of his life a tug of war between good and evil, birth and death. Though the struggle be yet going on, and the wounds it caused be yet bleeding, the issue is not in doubt.[163]

The illustrator's art is in many ways analogous to that of the piano accompanist, whose task is neither to outshine nor be submerged, but to complement the soloist. Gibran's illustrative work generally harmonizes so well with his poetry that it is difficult to conceive of the one without the other. Indeed his art may be approached in the same manner as his parables, for his art is parabolic in that it describes events in human life or in nature by which some great spiritual truth is illustrated or enforced.[164]

Gibran's drawings portray movement – outward movement suggesting the struggle of men's and women's inner worlds. His drawings are simple, and aimed directly at the revelation of the spiritual lesson embodied in the natural processes of life. Alice Raphael set forth the province of an artist such as Gibran:

> Life in its elemental functioning is but a transformation of the processes of birth, love, and death. The hunger of the appetites and the fear of the unknown; to love and be loved; out of these essential simplicities, man has erected the vast complexities of life and to these essential simplicities the artist must return who seeks new means of expression amidst the clutter of religions, arts and moralities.[165]

Gibran said of his drawings and paintings: "Art is a step from nature toward the Infinite . . . a mist carved into an image,"[166] believing that art must reveal the essence of the natural symbols, "by means of other, more suggestive symbols."[167]

Gibran was particularly attracted to Chaldean symbols which stirred "distant and mysterious memories" within him, and loved Chaldean culture, its myths, poetry, geometry, music, arts, and craft, even the "minutest relics"; he thought that this great civilization brought man "out of the darkness and into the light."[168] He felt that the art of the modern day ultimately owed its best elements to the Arabs who kept and cherished the spirit of Chaldean art, as well as Phoenician and Egyptian art, which all possessed that "Third Eye;" and thought that Greek art, so often vaunted in the West, borrowed ideas from these other civilizations and did not embody the vision, insight, and that "peculiar consciousness of what is deeper than depth and higher than height."[169]

He felt that the artist, in trying to express beauty and truth, *actually approaches* "a step nearer to Beauty" and becomes one with truth;[170] yet an artist can only claim to be truly creative when he makes over the impression that comes to him into something of his own, giving it a being of its own.[171] He had told Mikhail Naimy:

> Some think the business of art to be a mere imitation of nature. But Nature is far too great and too subtle to be successfully imitated. No artist can ever

reproduce even the least of Nature's surpassing creations and miracles. Besides, what profit is there in imitating Nature when she is so open and so accessible to all who see and hear? The business of art is rather to understand Nature and to reveal her meanings to those unable to understand. It is to convey the *soul* of a tree rather than to produce a fruitful likeness of the tree. It is to reveal the *conscience* of the sea, not to portray so many foaming waves or so much blue water. The mission of art is to bring out the unfamiliar from the most familiar.[172]

In his work Gibran aimed to make direct communication between the artist and the beholder. Referring to his picture *The Soul's Return to God* he once said to Mary that after seeing this face with the eye, the next step is to see it with the imagination. He pointed to a shaft of light rising from the bottom of the picture and told Mary that now she should have no difficulty in seeing in it a soul returning to God after death.[173]

Both the beautiful molds of his art and the visionary clarity of the words in *The Prophet* clearly evolved over a number of years, perhaps even for as long as two decades, between Gibran's adolescence and maturity. He was not prepared to finalize the work until he felt sure it would be nothing less than perfect. Gibran was awaiting his moment.

The moment came, perhaps not surprisingly, in the wake of World War I, a shattering experience even for those not directly involved. Gibran finally began to piece together the fragments of inspiration that had come to him, adding to them, developing and molding them into the final form of *The Prophet*. He was now ready to make his definitive statement.

Gibran as a mystic saw the eternal happiness of heaven beating its wings against the misery of a recusant world which declined to listen.[174] Like Blake before him, he believed that all the world's troubles begin in the human heart. In a century often characterized as the "Age of Anxiety," *The Prophet* is among the most consoling and least cynical literary works to attain universal acclaim. The poet, by flinging open his own heart to the world and being willing to have it "break" to express his truths,[175] manifested a rapture of the soul that struck a chord with the deepest yearnings of modern humankind. It was this impassioned sincerity that spoke to the urgent needs of a desperate age, "all in pieces, all coherence gone,"[176] in which "the development of man's capacity for feeling is the most urgent of all needs."[177]

The utterances of the heart – unlike those of the discriminating intellect – always relate to the whole. The heartstrings sing like an Aeolian harp only to the breath of a premonitory mood, which does not drown the song but listens. What the heart hears are the great things that span our whole lives.[178]

For Gibran the basis of the fragmentation and tyranny of his own time – the raging chaos of World War I; the seething slums and desecration of the environment in East Coast America; the poverty, pestilence, and persecution of his own people during that terrible period of reciprocal destruction; the violation of human rights in East and West – was psychological. In his writings he struck at the root of the "old corrupt tree of civilization,"[179] maintaining his conviction that humankind in its wondrous diversity is a manifestation of one spirit. The oppression he saw about him, the struggle of the poor and weak for justice, had its counterpart and its source in the human heart – a shadow cast on the outer world by humanity's distressed inner world. In *The Prophet* Gibran aims to ignite the inner light, and show that humanity "awakened" can burst through the bondage of sleep.

The work represents an appeal for a return to, and a reconciliation with, nature, emphasizing the relationship that binds individuals to their environment and fellow creatures. All become denizens of one world bound together by life and death. Those who err are not alone, and those who reach the sublime heights share it with all; our destiny lies in the way we act toward one another, and the salvation of the individual is the salvation of society. Thus Almustafa sets out his own version of the golden rule common to all great religions: that we must do as we would be done by. What he voices is not some unattainable ideal but practical wisdom laced with a strong sense of Sufi destiny: for everything there is a time, as in sunrise and sunset, ebb and flow.

The Prophet occupies a unique place in world literature, which makes assessment of its true value a difficult task for the critic. Often unjustly branded as a romanticized version of universal, philosophical, and religious teachings, it has in some ways been a victim of its own astonishing success. The reality is that it is a work of remarkable compassion, insight, hope, and inspiration, with a timeless message that combines the dignity of the Christian Bible and the wisdom of the Sufis of Islam, phrased with a simplicity and rhythmical quality that renders it accessible to a wide readership. The secret of *The Prophet's* appeal probably rests, then, in its positive approach and its choice of words of praise rather than of criticism, raising the heart of the reader rather than putting it down. To this must be added an acknowledgment of the work's unique mixture of poetry and insight, humanitarianism and inspiration. Like all great poets, Gibran endeavors to show how opposites can be reconciled: good and evil are inseparable; joy and sorrow are one because each feeds on the other, as do body and soul; life and death are a source of each other; and we have neither past nor future, only the eternal now. The poet himself is representative of this reconciliation at all levels. In him the East and the West, the pagan and the Christian, the ancient and the modern, the past and the present, came together to reaffirm his faith in the "Unity of Being"; and the image of the eternal rebirth of beauty and passion in the secular figure of Adonis joined forces with the message of Christ.

The Prophet proved to be the quintessence of Gibran's message, purifying and enshrining all he had desired to say until then. With the exception, perhaps, of one other work – *Jesus, the Son of Man*, which was written with a slightly different intention – Gibran would not reach the same heights again. Yet for Gibran himself the book represented "only a small part of what I have seen and of what I see every day, a small part only of the many things yearning for expression in the silent hearts of men and in their souls."[180]

In revealing himself to himself Gibran reveals us to ourselves. Mikhail Naimy reflected that "such books and such men are surety that Humanity, despite the fearful dissipation of its incalculable energies and resources, is not yet bankrupt."[181] Gibran himself told Mary: "The whole Prophet is saying just one thing: 'You are far far greater than you know – and All is well.'"[182] In the words of Ibn 'Arabi:

How do you deem yourself but a meagre planet
When locked within you is the whole universe?

At the beginning of December 1923, two months after its publication, Gibran wrote to May Ziadah from New York:

The Prophet, May, is only the first letter of a single word. In the past I was under the impression that this word was mine, in me and derived from me; for that reason I was unable to pronounce the first letter of that word. My inability to do so was the cause of my illness, indeed the cause of my soul's pain and suffering. After that God willed that my eyes be opened so that I could see the light, and God willed that my ears be opened so that I could hear other people pronounce this first letter, and God willed that I should open my lips and repeat that letter. I repeat it with joy and delight because for the first time I recognized that other people are everything and that I with my separate self am nothing.[183]

10

The Master Poet

(1923–1928)

I

After completing *The Prophet*, Gibran had barely more than seven years to live. The exhilaration of unburdening himself had, however, for a short while thrown his illness into the shadows, and he wrote to May Ziadah that his ailment had "forsaken" him and he was in good spirits despite the grey streaks traced on his hair.[1]

By 1924 he was becoming something of a celebrity in Greenwich Village, and his reputation continued to soar in the Arabic-speaking world as new editions of his works were produced and his English works translated. The poet expressed ambivalent feelings toward fame when he wrote in *Sand and Foam*, his next published work: "Fame is the shadow of passion standing in the light."[2]

Although there was a part of him that was "the most social human being in the world," he found the intensity of his social life "a real problem."[3] This need for "aloneness" reemerged in his life and was to reveal itself in his next major work, *Jesus, the Son of Man.* He told May: "I am a very industrious man . . . But I am also a stranger among men, entirely on my own . . . despite possessing seventy thousand friends of both sexes."[4]

The dinners, some given in his honor, the lunches and parties, inevitably led to interesting new acquaintances, but also meant more visitors to entertain in his Hermitage. Demand for his presence at literary gatherings increased too and therefore he found little time for his painting or writing. Although some came to meet the author of *The Prophet*, others came in search of wise counsel:

And there is one side of it all that is really part of my work. A woman, or a man . . . will call me up and say, "Can I come round to the studio and talk

239

with you?" And the voice shows something is the matter. And he or she comes and tells me the story of unhappiness. Some strange thing in me makes them use me as a confessor. Sometimes they ask just to *come* here – to *sit* – or to talk – because as soon as they get in this room they seem to find peace. It makes me feel so sad for them – and so hopelessly grateful, *so* grateful – because it means such trust they give.[5]

Whether it was the need to "confess," or the desire to be comforted, or simply curiosity that brought the steady stream of visitors to the studio, all who met Gibran were struck by his presence. Mary had felt for a number of years that the "Hermit poet" of *The Prophet* was a masterful and accurate description of Gibran himself – "the relation of the people of the City to him . . . a description to the very heart of the way people are toward himself."[6] A young poet, Robert Hillyer, vividly recalled his own meeting with Gibran:

Young and easily embarrassed, I had let fall an evasive and perhaps frivolous remark in response to a characterization of me as a young poet. It was trifling; I have forgotten it. But I have not forgotten how Gibran looked at me long and intently as if searching out my real nature, and at last made some observation on the sacredness of poetry and the high calling of its votaries, which disposed of any possibilities of touching the subject lightly. "Ah," he concluded, "but you must not talk that way, you must not do the usual things that other men do, for a poet is holy." A lifetime passion was behind the quiet rebuke.[7]

Another of his friends, Claude Bragdon, recorded for posterity the first encounter he had had with Gibran at one of those cultural tea parties that Gibran attended more out of duty to his admirers than for any personal satisfaction:

Physically [Gibran] is compact, strong, swarthy; all his movements are powerful and graceful; he seems charged with the dark fire of a *maleness* mitigated by the sweetness of his smile, the gentleness of his glance. His face is sensitive; one would say that it was a face of suffering were it not even more a face of peace. Buttoned underneath his coat is an ever-burning lantern; he does not mean that we should see it, but somehow we know that it is there. Only by some such preposterous metaphor am I able to suggest the sense of inner happiness, harmony, unity, which his presence projects . . . for though the most modest and unpretentious of men he has certain traits of the commander and the conqueror . . . the captain of his soul and the master of his fate.[8]

Konrad Bercovici, a Romanian-born writer who met Gibran, described a self-possessed "oriental" living harmoniously above the hectic street life of New York:

> Faultlessly attired, Kahlil Gibran looks more like a cultured Frenchman than a Syrian. But at home, in his large studio on Tenth Street, discussing with me the Orient, he instinctively bends his knees under him as he sits down on the divan to sip the thick coffee, the preparation of which is his particular pride, when he makes his guests feel at home. Everything Occidental is forgotten on entering his room and facing him. Instantly all feeling of hurry is banished. The day seems to be longer; the hours seem to be slower; even the rumbling below, in the street, the noise coming through the heavily shuttered windows, seems to be more distant than it actually is.[9]

Traces of Gibran's youthful inclination to shroud details of his background re-emerged as journalists, sycophants, and acquaintances put pressure on him to reveal something of himself. Many of his visitors fell prey to his self-created myth – Gibran, who had once said that those who understand us enslave us, was content to feed it. Despite a friendship over many years, Claude Bragdon was still writing: "His was what is called in the East a 'fortunate birth,' for he was brought up in an atmosphere of love, beauty and abundance."[10] Witter Bynner, who had known Gibran for over ten years, was even greeted with an evasive response when he requested information from his friend:

> It is very hard for me . . . to tell you what my position is in the Arabic world. The Eastern peoples like to say that I have founded a new school of literature. If I had, I certainly was not conscious of doing so. Writers and critics like to repeat two words: The first is "a Gibranite" meaning a *new* or a *different* person; the other is "Gibranism" meaning *freedom in all things* . . . There have been many fights about me in the East – and always between the old and the young. I think I still live because the young were not conquered.[11]

The "legend of Gibran," undoubtedly tended by the man himself, was augmented by the mysterious, almost monastic quality of life in his Hermitage. His studio – smelling of incense and furnished with sacred images, symbolic paintings, and a church table on which candles always stood[12] – gave the impression that its occupier was more than a poet and painter: "He was a hermit."[13] Lean, intense, and dressed in black, he was thought by some visitors to be "like an anchorite," his life spent before an altar, "a long-chained censer in his hand, burning incense before his God."[14] This, however, was by no means the only mask that Gibran wore in 1924 as he continued to entrance his many admirers.

By now a respected figure, Gibran moved in the highest echelons of American society, his friendship with the Roosevelts deepening as he visited them annually at their summer house in Herkimer, New York: "I think that the genius of the Roosevelt family is in its simple and wholesome *family* life. They are very clannish and strangely devoted to one another. And they know so much, and they are interested in so many things."[15]

He also met with some of the most popular writers and artists of the day, including John Galsworthy, G. K. Chesterton, the Irish dramatist and associate of Yeats, Edward Dunsany,[16] and the dominant force in modern South American art, the Mexican painter José Clemente Orozco.[17]

Gibran struck up a close friendship with the revolutionary painter, whose stunning murals reflected his concern over human rights violations and aimed to awaken the masses to the horror and futility of war. The exuberant Mexican felt a deep affinity with his Arab friend, and the two artists found they had much in common. They were exactly the same age; both were immigrants living in Manhattan, Gibran in his "Hermitage," Orozco in his "Ashram"; both had been sponsored by American women – in Orozco's case by Alma Reed, a journalist, archaeologist, and prime mover in the Delphic Group;[18] and both had spent their lives championing the causes of their oppressed peoples, in Central America and the Middle East respectively.

Their relationship, however, was not without its tensions, particularly over the men's divergent views on art, and there existed "a well-controlled but active antagonism between the two artists." These differences, however, did not prevent them from enjoying each other's company at their frequent meetings. Gibran's ethereal art, with its deeply moving tempera of striving figures, and Orozco's "violent art of Mexico" were in stark contrast – and once Gibran asked Alma Reed, who lived with the Mexican, how she could endure "living in the Ashram when Orozco's scenes of horror and tragic death covered the walls."[19]

Gibran's growing circle of friends included a number of beautiful models, many of whom he painted nude. One such young woman was Mariita Lawson, an aspiring artist who had been trying to capture something of Gibran in her photographs. Gibran viewed his relationship to Mariita, who was in her twenties, as that of an older relative. Although he loved children the only time he expressed any desire to be a father was in a letter to May three years previously: "A man's life will stay like a desert – empty except of sand – until God endows him with a daughter . . . he who does not have a daughter should adopt one, because the secret and meaning of time are hidden in the hearts of young girls."[20] His correspondence with Mariita suggests that he "adopted" her as a member of his family, signing his letters "always your loving uncle"[21] and addressing her as "Princess":[22]

> A princess can be disguised, and very cleverly disguised, but her uncle always knows who she is and what and where she is. Uncles, like mothers, are capable of knowing much more than you think they do . . . We want you to rise and grow and be a wonderful person – because we believe that you can do it. And I am so glad your sweet mother agrees with me on some things . . . You must be very proud and happy in having such a mother. Here I am preaching again! I think it is in my blood![23]

Although he told Mary Haskell that he was looking forward "to being alone in old age,"[24] the sociable side to his personality was enthralled by the many different types of people he was meeting: "I love people . . . entirely without discrimination or preference. I love them as one unit, I love them because they are of God's spirit . . . Are the galaxies more awe-inspiring and beautiful than what moves within the heart of man?"[25] Aside from his hectic social life in 1924, another factor prevented Gibran from pursuing his creative quest. Although his royalties had been steadily increasing since the war, the "roaring twenties" was a period of rampant inflation. By now aware of his worsening illness, and increasingly concerned about Marianna's long-term security, he decided to invest his money in real estate. In partnership with a friend, Faris Malouf, he bought a large building in Boston, at 409–411 Marlborough Street.

In the heady days of intense speculation their outlay of $24,000 for prime real estate on one of the city's busiest corners seemed like a sound investment. Before the two entrepreneurs were able to see a profit margin, however, they needed to borrow between $10,000 and $15,000 to renovate the seven stories of the twin brownstones. The venture began to fail when they discovered that they were unable to raise the money. Gibran, swallowing his pride, wrote to Mary for help, but although she responded with personal cheques to cover the most outstanding demands, it was to no avail. By October he was forced to admit that his project had failed: "I have made a mistake, a grave mistake in trying to move in a world so different from my own . . . It is the error of small people trying to do big things. It is the error of the greedy . . . the stupid. I have been both, and I am very sorry."[26] After he had paid back all his debts he was left with $3,000, which he put in a savings bank in Marianna's name.

The affair was a staggering blow to Gibran, and Mikhail Naimy sensed that the disastrous episode had "scattered" his friend's thoughts, "shut the avenues" of his inspiration, and "quickened the march of the disease in his body."[27] In the midst of this turbulence Gibran had written to Naimy from Boston: "God knows that never in my past life have I spent a month so full of difficulties, trials, misfortunes and problems . . . Had it not been for my sister, I would leave everything and go back to my hermitage shaking the dust of the world off my feet."[28] The unfortunate events, painful as they were, served to motivate him to put everything else behind him and begin his real work anew. He was reminded of his own words from *The Prophet*: "Yet you cannot lay remorse upon the innocent nor lift it from the heart of the guilty. Unbidden shall it call in the night, that men may wake and gaze upon themselves."[29]

In the aftermath of this living "hell of worldly problems,"[30] and obliged to "simplify" his business affairs, he began to concentrate again on his writing and painting. A letter he wrote to Mary on a visit to the country illustrates that the impressions of the natural world soon reoriented him after the worldly calamities:

> I have heard of men who, after leaving prison, find themselves so lost in the world that they go back and ask to be imprisoned again. I shall not go back . . . I shall try to find my way above the ground . . . In the morning about 6 o'clock I looked out of my window. The trees were budding, the birds were singing – the grass was wet – the whole earth was shining. And suddenly I *was* the trees and the flowers and the birds and the grass – and there was no I at all.[31]

With Mary's marriage to Jacob Florance Minis imminent, Gibran was in need of another source of secretarial support, and fortuitously he was approached at this time by a woman called Henrietta Boughton, née Breckenridge, a forty-six-year-old writer who had been intrigued by the man from Lebanon after hearing Butler Davenport read from *The Prophet* at St. Mark's-in-the-Bouwerie in 1923.[32] In March 1925, when she discovered that Gibran was living and working in Greenwich Village, she requested an audience with him, and by the autumn her ambition to acquaint herself with Gibran was realized when he asked her to become his secretary.

Over the next three years Henrietta, herself an aspiring writer, wrote a book of verse entitled *The Keys of Heaven* under the pseudonym of Barbara Young. She was captivated by the personality and brilliance of Gibran and became one of his greatest champions, arranging a public reading of his poetry at the Brevoort hotel and organizing other events such as a reading at the prestigious Fifth Avenue Bookstores Association.[33] Their relationship was one built on Henrietta's utter devotion to the poet and artist. She became a self-appointed devotee and her own hagiographic account of his life, *This Man from Lebanon*, which was published in 1945,[34] reflected her feelings of awe toward him.

Over the remaining years of his life his correspondence with Mary became practically non-existent, as did her references to Gibran in her journal; both were now aware that their remarkably intense and creative relationship – which had reached its zenith in their collaboration over *The Prophet* – had fulfilled its purpose. However, their dwindling letters did not reflect any loss of a deep kinship. In what were to be some of his last letters to Mary he wrote: "You are the only one in the world who could advise me about 'me' . . . I always think of you as one to whom life owes more than life can give; simply because you have given so much – so much."[35]

His correspondence with May Ziadah meanwhile continued, but not without some difficulties. May was somewhat diffident over a relationship that was now based on an open admission of love on both sides. She was evidently constrained by an oriental sense of propriety: "I even blame myself for writing to you, for in writing I find myself taking too much freedom."[36] Gibran, however, continued to send her invitation cards and a variety of postcards bought in the museums he had visited, and to share unrestrained expressions of his longings for the East.

By 1925 the ever-growing success of *The Prophet* meant that Gibran found himself an international figure. The prestigious New Orient Society in New York asked him to become an officer and to contribute to its quarterly journal. The man from Lebanon was honored to find himself on the same board as Mahatma Gandhi, "one of the greatest men living,"[37] and other leading thinkers including Annie Besant, Ananda Coomaraswamy, George Russell (AE), John Dewey, Bertrand Russell, Alma Reed, Claude Bragdon, and H. G. Wells. In his editorial for *The New Orient* the Indian editor Syud Hussein expressed the society's respect for its newest member:

"There is no more sincere and authentic or more highly gifted representative of the East functioning today in the West than Kahlil Gibran."[38]

For a writer who did not wish to be forgotten by the public in his own lifetime,[39] pressure for a sequel to *The Prophet* intensified: "One must keep abreast. Else one is likely to be soon forgotten. We must remind the readers of ourselves from time to time," he told Mikhail Naimy.[40] Nearly three years had passed, and, as yet, a new book had not appeared under his name – a long pause for a writer in America.

Gibran had originally intended *The Prophet* to be the first book of a trilogy, to be followed by *The Garden of the Prophet*, dealing with humanity's relationship with nature, and *The Death of the Prophet*, concerned with humankind's relation to God. However, these ambitions were not to be realized – although he did begin work on *The Garden of The Prophet*, which finally appeared in a posthumous publication of the same title, having been completed by Barbara Young. He also wrote two plays in English, *Lazarus and his Beloved* and *The Blind*,[41] although neither was published in his lifetime.

In May, after her marriage, Mary visited Gibran in New York. He showed her a collection of aphorisms he had written over the years which were soon to be published by Knopf as *Sand and Foam*. Gibran enjoyed overseeing the design of the book, reminding his editor to print it in the same manner as the manuscript, "that is in regard to the number of aphorisms on *one* page and the number of pages it should contain."[42]

This dedication to detail was in part a consequence of Gibran's belief that certain numbers, particularly three and seven, are imbued with sacred qualities.[43] The significance of the number seven in all spiritual traditions[44] was not lost on the poet,[45] and several times in *Sand and Foam* he makes reference to this number: "Behold every closed door is a mystery sealed with seven seals";[46] "We shall never understand one another until we reduce the language to seven words";[47] and "Seven centuries ago seven white doves rose from a deep valley flying to the snow-white summit of the mountain."[48] He also wrote a piece entitled "Seven Times Have I Despised my Soul,"[49] perhaps echoing Sufi teaching that the seeker has to pass through seven stages of preparation in the transmutation of consciousness before individuality is ready for its true function.[50]

Although he described it as a "stop-gap" work,[51] *Sand and Foam* contained a number of memorable sayings:

Trees are poems that the earth writes upon the sky. We fell them down and turn them into paper that we may record our emptiness.[52]

Strange, the desire for certain pleasures is a part of my pain.[53]

The significance of man is not in what he attains, but rather in what he longs to attain.[54]

A sense of humor is a sense of proportion.[55]

The real in us is silent; the acquired is talkative.[56]

Genius is but a robin's song at the beginning of a slow spring.[57]

Friendship is always a sweet responsibility, never an opportunity.[58]

You see but your shadow when you turn your back to the sun.[59]

You cannot laugh and be unkind at the same time.[60]

Some of the aphorisms were translated from Arabic and had already received publication in that language.[61] To Almustafa's sermon on love could be added, "Love which is not always springing is always dying", and a variation on the same theme, "Love that does not renew itself every day becomes a habit and in turn a slavery."[62] The sermon on giving in *The Prophet* is almost surpassed by two aphorisms in *Sand and Foam*:

Generosity is not in giving me that which I need more than you do, but it is in giving me that which you need more than I do[63]

and

Generosity is giving more than you can, and pride is taking less than you need.[64]

Many of the themes in *Sand and Foam* are those explored by Gibran in *The Prophet*, and some undoubtedly reflect the poet's own personal experiences: "Be grateful that you do not have to live down the renown of a father";[65] "When you reach the heart of life you will find yourself not higher than the felon, and not lower than the prophet";[66] "What we long for and cannot attain is dearer than what we have already attained."[67]

Seemingly on cue, the critics of Boston – a city Gibran now described as a "city of dead silences"[68] – castigated his work. A review in the Boston *Transcript* dismissed *Sand and Foam* as "a mixture of pungent observations, absurdities and meaningless mysticism."[69] Gibran, as always, paid little heed: "The creator gives no heed to the critic unless he becomes a barren inventor."[70] He wrote to May Ziadah about his own perceptions of the mystery of language: "What a strange effect certain words have on us sometimes – and how similar the sound of that word is to the peal of church-bells at sunset. It is the transmutation of that invisible inner self from mere utterance to silence, from mere action to worship."[71] He also revealed to May some premonitions of death, and how he felt that his work was still, as yet, unfulfilled:

> Whenever I think of the Departure which the people call Death, I find pleasure in such thinking and great longing for such departure. But then I return to myself and remember that there is one word I must say before I depart. I become perplexed between my disability and my obligation and I give up hope. No, I have not said my word yet, and nothing but smoke has come out from this light . . . if I don't depart before I spell and pronounce my word, I will return to say the word which is now hanging like a cloud in the sky of my heart.[72]

Although Gibran's references to reincarnation usually lacked conceptual depth, the emotional force of the poet's lifelong conviction bursts through in both his correspondence and in his works. Influenced by the Sufi notion of the unity of being, he believed that after successive lives the individual soul ultimately merges into the greater self, or absolute, where the limitations of space, time, and materiality are overcome and when the yearning for the divine is fulfilled. In this state death becomes glad tidings – giving him every reason to develop a philosophy of hope against despair – in which humankind triumphs over history and becomes part of the great order of the divine, a vision Gibran aimed to express through his writings and encapsulate in his art.

However, as always with his writings he struggled with the tension of not having yet expressed all he yearned to say. Even the torturous knowledge that his broken-down body was ailing fast could not deflect him from his belief that there was always the next book to be written. Toward the end of *Sand and Foam* the subject of this new book becomes clear: "There are three miracles of our Brother Jesus not yet recorded in the Book: the first that He was a man like you and me; the second that He had a sense of humor; and the third that He knew He was a conqueror though conquered."[73]

II

To write on the life of Jesus had long been an ambition of Gibran. As far back as 1909 he had written to Mary from Paris that his work could "find no better resting place than the personality of Jesus."[74] From a very young age he had been fascinated and enchanted by the charismatic figure of the Nazarene. A story is told of how, as a tiny boy, he had gone missing one Good Friday after being told the story of the Passion. His distressed parents were relieved to find Kahlil sitting in the village graveyard, clutching a bouquet of flowers, apparently wanting, in some childlike way, to share in the suffering of the Messiah.[75]

Throughout his life he had experienced the most stunning dreams of Jesus, as early as 1908 describing one such visionary dream to Mary:

> O if I could only describe Him to you: if I could only tell you of the sad joy in His eyes, the bitter sweetness of His lips, the beauty of His large hands, the rough woolen garment, and the bare feet so delicately veiled with white dust. And it was all so natural and clear.[76]

In 1923 he described his latest dream to her:

> And He came – just the same face – with the wonderful dark eyes and the clear, outdoor skin, and the abundant chestnut hair, and the strong frame . . . He came from the west – and the light was behind him and made his outline glow – for the sun was declining.[77]

As a young man he had read everything about Christ he could lay his hands on, being particularly impressed with Ernest Renan's *Life of Jesus*,[78] which influenced his perceptions of Jesus as: "the greatest of poets . . . .To call him God makes so light of him. Because as God's his wonderful sayings would be small but as man's they are most perfect poetry."[79]

Over the years Mary Haskell's journal records the poet's enduring fascination with Christ:

> His courage in not seeking to escape death . . . must have been reached after great struggle within himself. He died, that the Kingdom of Heaven might be preached, that man might attain that consciousness of beauty and goodness and reality within himself. Jesus was the most powerful personality in history . . . Christ's death, as well as his life, had a wonderful effect on his followers. The day will come when we shall think but just of the Flame – of the fullness of Life that burned in him. Socrates and his followers' relation was more mental, but Christ's followers felt him more than they felt any of his ideas. And look what he did to them. See John –

what a poet he became. Paul was a splendid advertising agent and his work worked against as well as for the real Christ . . . Christ changed the human mind . . . and found a new path.[80]

They also reveal the deep affinity Gibran felt toward Jesus, a kinship that once provoked Mary, after Gibran had visited her in Marlborough Street, to exclaim: "Christ had been sitting in that place as well as Kahlil – the two friends."[81] Again, after a huge thunderstorm she recorded Gibran saying, "That went through me like Christ speaking to me,"[82] and she noted his belief that Jesus would have been called a "Socialist" had he lived today.[83]

Witter Bynner later remembered how others noticed Gibran's affinity with the man from Nazareth:

> One night at dinner the maids failed to bring on one of the courses, and after a considerable wait and several bell ringings, Mrs. Ford rose and went to the pantry. There, behind a screen, stood two maids. When reprimanded, one of them explained, "But, Mrs. Ford, how can we go about our business when Mr. Gibran is talking? He sounds like Jesus." And he did. Odd as it was in many respects, the core of it was Christ-like.[84]

Mary's journal also reveals the distinction Gibran often made between true Christianity, as represented by the life and teachings of Jesus, and the diluted form of Christianity of the church:[85]

> Christianity has been very far from the teaching of Christ. In the second or third century, people were not vigorous enough to take the strong food that Christ gave; they ate only the weak food in the Gospels, or what they thought they found there and in the teaching of the men that came after Christ. They could not face the gigantic self that Christ taught . . . The greatest teaching of Christ was the Kingdom of Heaven, and that is within you.[86]

At the end of World War I Gibran had joyously exclaimed: "Out of the dark mist a new world is born. It is indeed a holy day. The most holy since the birth of Jesus"[87] – an expression of his lifelong belief that Jesus' entrance onto the world stage was the most important event in human history, representing the descent of the spirit "from the centre of the circle of divine light." For the poet, the entry of the infant Jesus into the firmament marked the moment when the spiritual might of Ba'al, Jupiter, Apollo, Venus, Minerva, and Pan – the ancient gods – was transmitted and transmuted into the human realm, to "the brokenhearted beggar by the wayside," through the unifying presence of Christ.[88]

Gibran's portrait, captured in *Jesus, the Son of Man*, evolved in his many writings over the years.[89] It is significant and moving that he decided to complete his testament while his own life was beginning to ebb away. The idea of the book had been nourished for over twenty years, drawing its power from Gibran's readings and contemplations, and his childhood memories, when the language of the Bible and the electrifying figure of the Nazarene filled the consciousness of the Maronite boy from the mountain.

The semi-autobiographical heroes of his early Arabic period, Khalil the heretic and Yuhanna the madman, are insistent that Jesus' mission never consisted in establishing hierarchical institutions with structures and sanctions, but rather in awakening humanity to its own cosmic potentiality.[90] Christ as revolutionary inspires Gibran's fearless heroes in their struggles against the violators of his spirit, particularly the power-possessing priest.[91] In these early works, and in a later one entitled "The Crucified," Gibran was intent on portraying Christ's "tremendous personal power":[92]

> The Nazarene was not weak! He was strong and is strong! But the people refuse to heed the true meaning of strength . . . He lived as a leader: He was crucified as a crusader; He died with a heroism that frightened His killers and tormentors. Jesus was not a bird with broken wings; He was a raging tempest who broke all crooked wings.[93]

He also depicts the Nazarene in his prose-poem "Eventide of the Feast" as "the Son of Man" who is "a stranger wandering from East to West," an outsider who has "no place to rest His head."[94]

Gibran's passion was also expressed in many of his paintings, and when he gave Mary *The Crucified* in 1920 she exclaimed: "It is so terrible in its pain that talking about it seems like talking about a soul in torture. It's the most beautiful, the most appealing, the most rebuking, wonderful, and dearest thing I ever had. It is the Heart unveiled."[95] Gibran had said of his picture *Christ's Head* that it was nearer to his heart than any other picture he had ever drawn.[96]

He now turned to what was to be his most ambitious work in English.[97] With an advance of $2,000 from Knopf, he settled down, on November 12, 1926,[98] to write *Jesus, the Son of Man*. As he began his book he told Mikhail Naimy that he was "sick and tired" of those who portrayed Jesus as a "sweet lady with a beard," and weary of "scholars" arguing about "the historicity of his personality." For Gibran, Jesus was the most "real personality" in human history, "a man of might and will, a man of charity and pity. He was far from being lowly and meek. Lowliness is something I detest; while meekness to me is but a phase of weakness."[99]

Any author's portrait, like that of an artist, is dependent upon the existence of a model. For Gibran, the inspiration and template for his unique portrait of Christ was provided by the indelible impression left on him by 'Abdu'l-Bahá[100] in 1912, which moved Gibran to exclaim: "For the first time I saw form noble enough to be a receptacle for the Holy Spirit."[101] Bahá'u'lláh, the founder of the Bahá'í faith, had pronounced his eldest son 'Abdu'l-Bahá to be the perfect exemplar of his teachings, the infallible interpreter of his word, and his successor as head of the faith. Born in 1844, in Tehran, 'Abdu'l-Bahá had, as a child, recognized his father's great station, but on becoming head of the faith was the victim of much jealousy and opposition. A prisoner for forty years in the fortress city of Akka in the Holy Land, he was finally liberated when the Young Turk Revolution of 1908 deposed sultan Abdu'l-Hamid and set free all those in the Ottoman empire who had been imprisoned for their religious beliefs. Widely respected by religious leaders and politicians worldwide, 'Abdu'l-Bahá was later knighted by the British for the part he played in alleviating the famine in the Holy Land during World War I. He began to carry the teachings of Bahá'u'lláh to the West, and between 1911 and 1913 he visited Britain, France, Germany, Austria-Hungary, the United States, and Canada. Central to his message to the people of America – a message echoed by Gibran himself – was the realization of unity in diversity:

> The sun is one but the dawning-points of the sun are numerous and changing. The ocean is one body of water but different parts of it have particular designation, Atlantic, Pacific, Mediterranean, Antarctic, etc. If we consider the names, there is differentiation, but the water, the ocean itself is one reality. Likewise the divine religions of the holy manifestations of God are in reality one, though in names and nomenclature they differ.[102]

During his nine-month visit to the United States and Canada – a strenuous tour that saw him traveling constantly up and down the Eastern seaboard into the Chicago heartland and traversing the continent via Montreal, Minneapolis, St. Paul, and Denver to the West Coast before returning to

New York – he expounded the fundamental principles of the revelation and teachings of Bahá'u'lláh. He spoke of the equality between men and women, the harmony of science and religion, the need for universal education and a universal language, the independent investigation of truth, the oneness of God, the oneness and continuity of the prophets of God, the oneness of the human race and the elimination of all forms of prejudice and discrimination. The American press gave his tour extensive coverage and his speeches were widely circulated in the daily press. Gibran avidly followed the news of one whom he ardently desired to draw.

'Abdu'l-Bahá's visit to the United States took place just before the outbreak of a war that was to claim ten million lives and maim millions more. He foresaw the cataclysm ahead: "Just now Europe is a battlefield of ammunition, ready for a spark and one spark will set aflame the whole world," and he called for America to raise "the standard of international peace," maintaining that no other country had "greater capacity for such an initial step."[103]

After being drawn by Gibran on April 19, 1912, 'Abdu'l-Bahá delivered two speeches at Columbia University and at the Bowery mission in New York where he proclaimed his message of unity:

> All the divine Manifestations have proclaimed the oneness of God and the unity of mankind . . . The fundamental truth of the Manifestations is peace. This underlies all religion, all justice . . . Read the Gospel and the other Holy Books. You will find their fundamentals are one and the same. Therefore, unity is the essential truth of religion and, when so understood, embraces all the virtues of the human world.[104]

Speaking at churches, universities, sanatoriums, literary societies, and synagogues, and addressing Christians, Bahá'ís, Jews, Esperantists, suffragettes, theosophists, students, the sick, and the poor, he often made references to Christ. Gibran, who heard him address an audience at the Astor hotel in New York, found his own reflections on Jesus being in accord with the views being expressed by this great spiritual teacher from the East:

> His sword was to be a sword of iron . . . He did not conquer by the physical power of an iron rod; He conquered the East and the West by the sword of His utterance . . . he conquered and subdued the East and West. His conquest was effected through the breaths of the Holy Spirit, which eliminated all boundaries and shone from all horizons.[105]

Such ideas resonated with Gibran, particularly 'Abdu'l-Bahá's teachings on the equality of men and women, a theme Gibran was to address in *Jesus, the Son of Man*. 'Abdu'l-Bahá asserted that men and women must be treated as equals if humanity is to progress:

> The world of humanity is possessed of two wings: the male and the female. So long as these two wings are not equivalent in strength, the bird will not fly. Until womankind reaches the same degree as man, until she enjoys the same arena of activity, extraordinary attainment for humanity will not be realized; humanity cannot wing its way to heights of real attainment. When the two wings or parts become equivalent in strength, enjoying the same prerogatives, the flight of man will be exceedingly lofty and extraordinary. Therefore, woman must receive the same education as man and all inequality be adjusted. Thus, imbued with the same virtues as man, rising through all the degrees of human attainment, women will become the peers of men, and until this equality is established, true progress and attainment for the human race will not be facilitated.[106]

He also spoke about terrible conflicts that had erupted between Christians and Muslims, and in a speech in Brooklyn[107] expressed his belief in the essential oneness of religion.[108]

Gibran's own condemnation of fanaticism, forged in the crucible of his own country's bloody history, was in accord with 'Abdu'l-Bahá's belief. Quoting Bahá'u'lláh, 'Abdu'l-Bahá spoke of the horrors of religious prejudice and sectarian hatred:

> It is not becoming in man to curse another; it is not befitting that man should attribute darkness to another . . . all mankind are the servants of one God . . . There are no people of Satan; all belong to the Merciful. There is no darkness; all is light. All are the servants of God, and man must love humanity from his heart. He must, verily, behold humanity as submerged in the divine mercy.[109]

Gibran was captivated by 'Abdu'l-Bahá calling him "complete. There are worlds in his soul";[110] and he was enthralled and electrified by his life-affirming message:

> The station of man is great, very great. God has created man after His own image and likeness. He has endowed him with a mighty power which is capable of discovering the mysteries of phenomena. Through its use man is

able to arrive at ideal conclusions instead of being restricted to the mere plane of sense impressions. As he possesses sense endowment in common with the animals, it is evident that he is distinguished above them by his conscious power of penetrating abstract realities. He acquires divine wisdom; he searches out the mysteries of creation; he witnesses the radiance of omnipotence; he attains the second birth.[111]

III

Gibran wrote most of *Jesus, the Son of Man* in Boston – away from the pressures of New York – staying with Marianna. Although he was overjoyed to be absorbed again in a project so close to his heart, his creative endeavors continued to be punctuated by periods of ill health;[112] his new amanuensis, Barbara Young, noted the turbulence the poet had to endure while writing the book – as though he "had come through a mighty and terrible struggle."[113]

When he finally completed his first manuscript it was his longest work. Employing an original scheme – which has been likened to Robert Browning's method in *The Ring and the Book*[114] – Gibran presents seventy-eight different impressions of Jesus imaginatively attributed to his contemporaries, both real and fictitious; "His words and deeds as told and recorded by those who knew Him."

His vision of Christ, as it emerges through these imaginary accounts, is poetical and highly unorthodox, with no pretensions to historical accuracy.[115] His Jesus is not born of a virgin, he does not die for our salvation, nor is he resurrected. His miracles are the result of natural phenomena, and he teaches the doctrine of reincarnation, Gibran placing him in the context of other avatars who have walked the earth:

> Many times the Christ has come to the world, and He has walked many lands. And always He has been deemed a stranger and a madman.
> . . . Have you not heard of Him at the cross-roads of India? And in the land of the Magi, and upon the sands of Egypt?[116]

In *Jesus, the Son of Man* Gibran synthezises a number of ingredients that are also apparent in his idea of the prophet: recalling Krishna's words when he tells Arjuna he has been born many times; implying acceptance of the depiction of Christ found in the opening chapter of St. John; reaffirming the notion of the prophet as an outsider and a "madman"; asserting the prophet as the eternal awakener of the heart; naming him as the exemplar of compassion: "And were it not for sorrow in all of you I would not have stayed to weep."[117]

Gibran's imaginative reconstruction was undertaken with the aim of challenging the one-dimensional view of Christ that had prevailed among western theologians[118] – and rather than dealing with his divine nature alone, Gibran attempts to explore aspects of Christ's human nature. Often he describes the Nazarene as having ambivalent emotions – compassion toward the dispossessed and disadvantaged, raging anger against the complacent and conceited – and as such creates a personality who, though deeply involved in man's emotional life, is masterfully unidentified with it too.

By plunging his Jesus deep into the turbulence of earthly existence Gibran had no wish to negate the master's divinity, but aimed instead to replace a somewhat distant conception of a figure, conjured by the church, with a more approachable personality. His title[119] for a book he had waited over twenty years to write expressed his own beliefs.

The self-designated title of Jesus, "Son of Man," which appears sixty-nine times in the first three gospels, was the same meaning as the assertion that Jesus is the "image of God." It is the only title Jesus actually applied to himself and as an idea embraces his total work as does no other. By designating himself in this striking and mysterious way, Jesus established direct contact with a particular view current in certain circles among his people. The concept itself was not exclusively Judaic, the idea of a divine "original man," the ideal prototype, being evident in Chaldean, Egyptian, Persian, and gnostic thought.[120] Jesus used the title both in his eschatological work and in his earthly task, the eschatological application representing a profound statement of cosmic power corresponding to the Jewish view as expressed in the visionary writings of Daniel:

> I saw in the night visions, and, behold, one like the Son of man came with the clouds of heaven, and came to the Ancient of days, and they brought him near before him. And there was given him dominion, and glory, and a kingdom, that all people, nations, and languages, should serve him: his dominion is an everlasting dominion, which shall not pass away, and his kingdom that which shall not be destroyed.[121]

By calling himself "Son of Man," Jesus thus embraced the highest imaginable role in the eschatological drama, confirming this role in his own words: "When the Son of man shall come in his glory, and all the holy

angels with him, then shall he sit upon the throne of his glory."[122] The
primary eschatological role of the Son of Man is that of judgment: "And
before Him shall be gathered all nations: and he shall separate them one
from another, as a shepherd divideth his sheep from the goats."[123] Jesus
however, profoundly transforms this idea of judgment. By becoming both
the future "Man" who is the judge, and the incarnate man who is the
representative Suffering Servant of God, he plunges himself into the earthly
drama of human existence. The Son of Man is thus incarnate in man, in the
ordinary matrix of human life, a man among men. Jesus' unification of the
title Son of Man with the suffering of the Servant of God, and his
designation of Jesus of Nazareth as this Son of Man, becomes also a
declaration of his humility: "For even the Son of Man came not to be
ministered unto, but to minister."[124] He explains his human life and death
in terms of the work that the Servant of God has to fulfill: "The Son of Man
must suffer many things, and be rejected . . . and be killed."[125]

In Gibran's treatment, the poet acknowledges the messianic nature of
Christ, both in his choice of title and in the words of John, the son of
Zebedee, who expresses Gibran's own belief in the divine nature of his
subject:

He is the first Word . . . Jesus the Nazarene was born and reared like
ourselves; His mother and father were like our parents, and He was a man.
But the Christ, the Word, who was in the beginning, the Spirit who would
have us live our fuller life, came unto Jesus and was with Him. And the
Spirit was the versèd hand of the Lord, and Jesus was the harp.[126]

Gibran's attitude toward Christ begins to reveal itself in the artist's finely
sketched frontispiece to the book – a powerful head with steep forehead,
heavy eyebrows, a full mouth and strong chin, and a neck that might
withstand a guillotine – all quite different from the traditional image.
Mikhail Naimy, who himself was later to write a book on Christ,[127]
described this face thus:

A beautiful and noble face delicately veiled with something expressive of
pity gripping the heart, rather than of sorrow crouching in the soul. In the
sensitive mouth is a firmness too gentle to wound, and a self-respect too
proud to be meek . . . a face suggestive of many meanings, the most
pronounced of them being a will that has not yet conquered, but is
determined to conquer.[128]

This stunning image prepares the reader for Gibran's portrayal of Jesus in words.

> I am sickened and the bowels within me stir and rise when I hear the faint-hearted call Jesus humble and meek, that they may justify their own faint-heartedness; and when the downtrodden, for comfort and companionship, speak of Jesus as a worm shining by their side.
> Yea, my heart is sickened by such men. It is the mighty hunter I would preach, and the mountainous spirit unconquerable.[129]

The effectiveness of *Jesus, the Son of Man* lies in Gibran's examination of Christ from the viewpoints of many well-known characters from the gospels, thus giving a fresh angle on a number of familiar stories. Alongside the disciples, the Virgin Mary and Mary Magdalene, there are also the views of "anti-heroes" such as Caiaphas, Pontius Pilate, and Barabbas who makes the rueful remark that "his crucifixion endured but for an hour. But I shall be crucified unto the end of my years."[130]

In the first testament in the book, James the son of Zebedee recalls Jesus looking down from the summit of Mount Hermon, his face shining "like molten gold," and saying: "In truth the earth is fair and all that is upon her is fair. But there is a Kingdom beyond all that you behold, and therein I shall rule."[131] Jesus is perceived to be a lord of the landscape about him, a man from the "North Country" whose attributes are, as in Nathaniel's description, often evoked by lofty natural images.

> Shall a man bold enough to say these things to those who ruled Judea be deemed meek and humble?
> Nay. The eagle builds not his nest in the weeping willow. And the lion seeks not his den among the ferns.[132]

Jesus is seen by one contributor – "a philosopher" – as a visionary who continually experienced the truth of the created world with the depth and intensity of an awakened one:

> His senses were all continually made new, and the world to Him was always a new world.
> To Him the lisping of a babe was not less than the cry of all mankind, while to us it is only lisping.

To Him the root of a buttercup was a longing towards God, while to us it
is naught but a root.[133]

Nicodemus the poet also expresses the truth of Jesus in natural terms:

But Jesus was not claiming more than the month of May claims in her
high tide.
Was He not to tell the shining truth because it was so shining?[134]

To Mary Magdalene, Jesus had beauty, strength, gentleness:

His mouth was like the heart of a pomegranate, and the shadows in His eyes
were deep.
And He was gentle, like a man mindful of his own strength.
In my dreams I beheld the Kings of the earth standing in awe in His
presence.[135]

More abrasive is the opinion of Mannus the Pompeiian, who writes to a
Greek:

And Jesus, the man who revealed God as a being of joy, they tortured
Him, and then put Him to death.
These people would not be happy with a happy god. They know only the
gods of their pain.[136]

Gibran's striking portrait is not chronologically based and its subsequent
unpredictability can often surprise the reader. Beginning with James the son
of Zebedee's reflections, his account moves to Jesus' grandmother, Anna,
lovingly describing a free-spirited and "hard to govern"[137] boy, reminiscent
of the young Gibran. Similar sentiments are later expressed by Susannah of
Nazareth, a neighbor of Mary, who describes a boy "full of laughter and
little wanderings . . . venturous and over-daring";[138] a young man whose
"eyes were like honey and full of the surprise of day," and whose beauty
entranced "the maidens of Nazareth."[139]

The captivating beauty of Gibran's Jesus is a recurring theme. Salome
tells a friend: "Whenever He passed by, my heart ached for his loveliness";[140]
Mary Magdalene is moved to say: "He was beautiful. His body was single
and each part seemed to love every other part";[141] and John at Patmos saw
in his face "a night where candles burn in space, a dream beyond our
reaching."[142]

Like Almustafa, Gibran's Jesus possesses the quality of "aloneness." Rachael, a disciple, recalled: "He was among us yet not one with us";[143] Joseph surnamed Justus describes him as "a stranger, a wayfarer on His way to a shrine";[144] and Pontius Pilate remarks of him: "The lonely man is the strongest man."[145] This theme of inner force permeates Gibran's portrait: "Jesus despised and scorned the hypocrites, and His wrath was like a tempest that scourged them. His voice was thunder in their ears and He cowed them."[146] The hypocrites, "vultures" preying on the "guileless",[147] are more often than not revealed to be the priests, and through the mouthpieces of Caiaphas, Annas, and an anonymous young priest from Capernaum, Gibran vividly captures the brooding animosity that must have stalked the land as these enemies of Christ plotted his demise. In their fear of him they call him "a brigand, a mountebank, and a self-trumpeter";[148] the "enemy within";[149] "a defiler and a corrupter";[150] "a conjuror and a deceiver";[151] a "magician, warp and woof, and a sorcerer,"[152] who "spoke the bastard language of the low-born and the vulgar."[153]

Joseph surnamed Justus, in contrast, maintains that although Jesus' enemies portrayed him as a man uncouth and violent, "the Man despised sounded a challenge and the sound thereof shall never cease."[154] The Nazarene enthralled and captivated Joseph and Phumiah the high priestess of Sidon, Benjamin the scribe, and a disciple called Rachael. To them he was the "dauntless Man . . . the fearless Hunter on the hill . . . The sky-hearted and the ocean-handed Man . . . The valiant Youth who conquered the mountain cities . . . the first Golden Hawk";[155] "an awakening";[156] and "the Great Event . . . Himself a miracle wrought in Judea."[157] As well as dealing with the mystic dimension of Jesus, by whom "the elements of our bodies and our dreams came together according to law,"[158] Gibran creates a rounded description of his human qualities too: "He would make merry with His listeners; He would tell jests and play upon words and laugh with all the fullness of his heart, even when there were distances in His eyes and sadness in His voice."[159] Others tell of his great ability to tell stories and parables the likes of which "had never been heard in Syria"[160] before, or of his skills as a carpenter which prompted a rich Levi who had two doors made by Jesus to say of them: "They in their stability mock at all else in my house."[161] For others it was his gentleness that is remembered – movingly expressed by "one of the Marys," who likened his smile to "the dust of stars falling upon the eyelids of children";[162] yet he possessed too "the sadness of the wingèd who will not soar above his comrade."[163]

Jesus' awesome power, a recurrent theme in the book, is described by an unnamed man from the desert: "Men and women fled from before His face, and He moved amongst them as the whirling wind moves on the sand-hills."[164] Others portray him as a man who could be patient as "a mountain in the wind," yet also impatient of "men of cunning", a man who "would not be governed."[165]

Those who heard him speak remembered the beauty and passion of his oratory. Assaph, himself an orator from Tyre, perceived that "when you heard Him your heart would leave you and go wandering into regions not yet visited."[166] At her wedding in Cana, Rafca the bride remembered that "His voice enchanted us so that we gazed upon Him as if seeing visions,"[167] and a character named Cleopas of Bethroune says, "His voice was like cool water in a land of drought."[168]

Susannah of Nazareth describes Mary, mother of Jesus, as she awaits her son's imminent death on Good Friday: "At dawn she was still standing among us, like a lone banner in the wilderness wherein there are no hosts."[169] Gibran constantly expresses his wonder at the beauty and mystery of womanhood: "Woman shall be forever the womb and the cradle but never the tomb."[170] His reverence toward woman, a theme that permeates many of his works, reaches its profoundest and most moving expression in *Jesus, the Son of Man*, reflecting Gibran's love for the many women in his own life. He had once said to Mary: "Woman has deeper mind that is hers only. We call it intuition. And man uses woman's intuition . . . Women are better than men. They are kinder, more sensitive, more stable, and have a finer sense about much of life."[171] These views bear a striking resemblance to the teachings of 'Abdu'l-Bahá, who called women "more tender-hearted, more receptive," possessing "intuition more intense" than men.[172]

Jesus is depicted as having many female friends, knowing them as they should be known "in sweet comradeship."[173] In particular Gibran's portrayal of Jesus' relationship with Mary Magdalene is arguably the most moving and vivid account in literature, before the discovery of the remarkable Nag Hammadi texts of 1945.[174] Other attributes were recognized by 'Abdu'l-Bahá in a talk to a suffragette meeting: "It is certain from the evidence of the Gospels that the one who comforted and re-established [the disciples'] faith was Mary Magdalene."[175] Gibran portrays Jesus' love toward Mary as transformational: "The sunset of His eyes slew the dragon in me, and I became a woman."[176]

Mary Magdalene appears in three separate vignettes in the book, and describes her first meeting with the Son of Man thus:

He was sitting in the shadow of the cypress trees across my garden, and He was as still as if He had been carved out of stone, like the statues in Antioch and other cities of the North Country . . . And I gazed at Him, and my soul quivered within me, for He was beautiful.[177]

Mary, attired in scented garments and golden sandals given to her by a Roman captain, approaches Jesus, who says:

You have many lovers, and yet I alone love you. Other men love themselves in your nearness. I love you in your self. Other men see a beauty in you that shall fade away sooner than their own years. But I see in you a beauty that shall not fade away, and in the autumn of your days that beauty shall not be afraid to gaze at itself in the mirror, and it shall not be offended.

I alone love the unseen in you.[178]

As he walked away Mary felt that "no other man ever walked the way He walked. Was it a breath born in my garden that moved to the east? Or was it a storm that would shake all things to their foundations?"[179]

In some of his earlier writings, Gibran expressed his concern about the cruel treatment of the prostitute,[180] and his contempt for the hypocrisy of those who label her. Andrew's portrayal of a forgiving and compassionate Christ recalls the time when the Pharisees brought a prostitute to him; Jesus turned to the men who had brought her there, looked long and hard at them, and wrote on the earth, "the name of every man, and beside the name He wrote the sin that every man had committed. As He wrote they escaped in shame into the streets." He then looked into the woman's eyes, telling her: "You have loved overmuch. They who brought you here loved but little."[181]

Perhaps the most moving testimony of the book is given by Cyborea, the mother of Judas, whose love for her son reflects Gibran's own experience of the mother–son relationship:

When he took his first step, I too took my first step. For women travel not save when led by their children . . . I loved him and I shall love him forevermore. If love were in the flesh I would burn it out with hot irons and be at peace. But it is in the soul, unreachable. And now I would speak no more. Go question another woman more honored than the mother of Judas. Go to the mother of Jesus. The sword is in her heart also; she will tell you of me, and you will understand.[182]

The poet, who had witnessed the inhumane subjugation of women in the East and in the West, summed up his views in the last chapter of the book entitled "A Man from Lebanon Nineteen Centuries Afterwards":

> Your mother is with us;
> I have beheld the sheen of her face in the countenance of all mothers . . .
> Master, Master Lover,
> The Princess awaits your coming in her fragrant chamber,
> And the married unmarried woman in her cage;
> The harlot who seeks bread in the streets of her shame,
> And the nun in her cloister who has no husband;
> The childless woman too at her window,
> Where frost designs the forest on the pane,
> She finds you in that symmetry,
> And she would mother you, and be comforted.[183]

This reverence for the feminine aspect influenced his own conception of God as "both the father and mother in one," the God–Father reached through intellect and the God–Mother reached through the heart – "only through love."[184]

Echoing his own lifelong belief that Jesus was "the Master Poet," Gibran describes Jesus thus: "Aye, He was a poet whose heart dwelt in a bower beyond the heights . . . the sovereign of all poets,"[185] and in the last essay writes: "Master, Master Poet, Master of our silent desires, The heart of the world quivers with the throbbing of your heart. But it burns not with your song."[186] In what is often an unconventional portrayal, Jesus is depicted as having traveled to lands both in the East and the West: Philemon, a Greek apothecary, depicts him as "the Master Physician" who visited India where "the priests revealed to Him the knowledge of all that is hidden in the recesses of our flesh." Again the influence of 'Abdu'l-Bahá, who called Jesus "the real Physician," is evident – a "physician" who came to heal the world.[187] Reflecting Gibran's own holistic views on medicine, Philemon witnesses in Jesus a supreme spiritual healer, to whom the sacred secrets of another age have been revealed:

> To this man also certain sealed doors were opened. He entered the temple of the soul, which is the body; and He beheld the evil spirits that conspire against our sinews, and also the good spirits that spin the threads thereof.

Methinks it was by the power of opposition and resistance that He healed the sick, but in a manner unknown to our philosophers. He astonished fever with His snowlike touch and it retreated; and He surprised the hardened limbs with His own calm and they yielded to Him and were at peace.[188]

Gibran also refashions some of the words of the gospels, as for instance in St. Matthew's remembrance of the Sermon on the Mount: "Blessed are the serene in spirit. Blessed are they who are not held by possessions, for they shall be free. Blessed are they who remember their pain, and in their pain await their joy";[189] and attributes some new sayings to Jesus: "Your neighbour is your unknown self made visible,"[190] and "Would that you seek the Father as the brook seeks the sea."[191]

In the gospel according to Gibran[192] Jesus is portrayed as consciously going to his death, a view he expressed to Mary Haskell as early as 1914: "Jesus wanted to die, wanted to be crucified – as an *expression* – the only expression that would satisfy him."[193] Zacchaeus is reported as saying: "He could indeed have escaped had He chosen, but He did not seek safety . . . He knew that to build the temple invisible He must needs lay Himself the corner-stone."[194] His death is perceived as a victory: "The whole world stood to honor Him upon that hill."[195]

When he is delivered to Pontius Pilate the governor is struck by Jesus' dignity and bearing: "I cannot fathom what came over me . . . but it was suddenly my desire, though not my will, to rise and go down from the dais and fall before Him."[196] After Jesus' death Pilate, now returned to Rome, observes that his wife has become "a woman of sorrow" who "talks much of Jesus to other women of Rome," leaving Pilate to question his decision in Jerusalem: "Can it be that the Syrian is conquering us in the quiet hours of the night?"[197] And in a later vignette Pilate's wife herself tells another Roman woman that after seeing Jesus she knew she had "passed by a god," and that ever since, "His voice governs the stillness of my nights and I am held fast forevermore."[198]

Perhaps the most powerful account of the dignity with which Jesus faces his death is that of Claudius, a Roman soldier who guarded him the night before the crucifixion:

I had fought in Gallia and in Spain, and with my men I had faced death. Yet never had I been in fear, nor been a coward. But when I stood before that man and He looked at me I lost heart . . . a man facing death with the sap of life upon His lips, and with compassion for His slayers in His eyes. And now I am old. I have lived the years fully. And I think truly that neither Pompey nor Caesar was so great a commander as that Man of Galilee.[199]

It is left to Barabbas to record the last words of Jesus: "Now it is finished, but only upon this hill"; and to a woman of Byblos to sing a heart-rending lament:

> Weep with me, ye daughters of Ashtarte, and all ye lovers of Tamouz
> [Tammuz].
> Bid your heart melt and rise and run blood-tears,
> For He who was made of gold and ivory is no more . . .
> Now He lies stained with the leaves of yesteryear,
> And no longer shall His footsteps wake the seeds that sleep in the bosom
> of spring.
> His voice will not come with the dawn to my window,
> And I shall be forever alone.[200]

The identification of Jesus with Tammuz reminds one of Shelley's poem in which he identifies Keats with Adonais,[201] who is Tammuz under another name, and, according to some scholars,[202] one of the gods whose cults were absorbed into Christianity at a very early stage.

Again, as so many times before, Gibran's work bears the hallmark of Blake, and there is a striking resemblance in the two poets' conceptions of Jesus[203] who is a far cry from the "Creeping Jesus"[204] so often depicted by the church: "The Modern Church Crucified Christ with the Head Downwards"[205] wrote Blake; and Gibran named those who corrupt Christ's teachings as "monstrous" beings with "a hyena's teeth, and viper's fangs."[206] For Blake and Gibran Jesus is a revolutionary and visionary figure who "came your King & God to seize"; a "Scourge" who "traced diseases to their source: He curs'd the Scribe & Pharisee"; a spiritual warrior "Trampling down Hypocrisy: Where'er his Chariot took its way"; a conqueror who "with wrath" subdued;[207] and a supreme artist: "I know of no other Christianity and of no other Gospel than the liberty both of body & mind to exercise the Divine Arts and Imagination,"[208] wrote Blake. "The Spirit of Jesus is continual forgiveness of Sin";[209] "Can I see another's woe, and not be in sorrow too?";[210] "Jesus was all virtue and acted from impulse, not from rules";[211] "Upon his heart with Iron pen, He wrote, 'Ye must be borne again.'"[212] By virtue of the imagination, the universal cosmic knowledge is available to whoever raises their heart and mind into those regions: "Henceforth every man may converse with God and be a King & Priest in his own house."[213] In their magisterial works, *Jesus, the Son of Man* and *Jerusalem*, both poets challenged orthodox doctrine – in Gibran's case by breathing new life into a story perhaps grown stale through age and constant repetition.[214] As well as refocusing attention on the joyous side of the gospels, Gibran effectively conveys an inexorable and revivifying natural power operating through Jesus, giving the book its visionary force and making its inspirational intensity perhaps exceed even that of *The Prophet*.

Was Gibran a Christian? There is no doubt that he had accepted the Christian revelation, taking Jesus as an exemplar and the Bible as a treasury of revealed spiritual and moral truth. However, true to the followers of the Sufi path, he could not accept Christianity as exclusive.[215] His was a firm belief in the unity of religion and the unity of being which directed his enthusiastic attention to universal ecumenicalism. His creed involved a diversity of strands of belief: the *Upanishads*; Syrian Neoplatonism; Judeo-Christian mysticism; Islamic Sufism; and the Bahá'í teachings on universal love and the unity of religion as he heard them from 'Abdu'l-Bahá. To these influences can be added those spiritual elements he gleaned from his reading of Ibn Sina, Ibn Rushd, Ibn al-Farid, and al-Ghazali. He forged his own personal spiritual philosophy in which he would connect all the traditions and join William Blake in declaring that "all religions are one."

III

Although it was to be his last successful work, *Jesus, the Son of Man* is not the anguished cry of a failing man but a magnificent testament of a poet whose soaring prose continued to rail against the dying of the light. In the months running up to its publication in October 1928, he had been suffering from what he called "summer rheumatism." He told Mariita Lawson that all the joints in his body ached, and that sometimes he could "hardly walk." He also ominously revealed to her that the medics, in their desperation, were trying the excruciating – yet at the time scientifically acceptable – method of "electric" treatment on him.[216] Constantly racked with pain, Gibran was drinking heavily again and despite Prohibition was able to find alcohol with the help of his cousin Assaf George.[217] As his health deteriorated concerns about Marianna's security provoked Gibran to invest in some real estate. Burnt by his last venture into business, he viewed his options carefully this time around – finally purchasing two houses at 180–182 Broadway, near Tyler Street in Boston.

He also commissioned Assaf George to investigate the possibility of buying the Mar Sarkis monastery near Bisharri, a location full of happy childhood memories for the poet. By now, increasingly aware of the seriousness of his condition, an intense longing for his homeland returned.

He wrote to May Ziadah: "My longing for my country almost melts my heart."[218] For some time now, Gibran had been contemplating a permanent return to this small deserted monastery, and according to Mikhail Naimy had planned to spend his declining years at Mar Sarkis in "fruitful work and peaceful meditation."[219]

Unexpectedly, toward the end of 1928 he received an invitation to return to Lebanon to take up political office.[220] The gesture by the newly formed Republic of Lebanon was probably due to the influence of his friend Dr. Ayub Tabet, who for a short period had served as minister of the interior and health. However, Gibran himself had never seriously nursed political ambitions and, by now physically incapacitated, felt he should stay in America to pursue his work: "I can do better in this strange, old room than anywhere else."[221] In the past it had been either force of work or fear for his own safety that had prevented the poet's triumphant return to Lebanon. By his forty-sixth birthday, however, it was a realization that his rapidly deteriorating health made any ideas of a homecoming impossible, for as well as his visceral disorders he was developing severe swelling of the feet and legs. His appetite, never large, had dwindled to almost nothing, and his formerly trim physique was beginning to show signs of bloating.[222]

As the cruel winter winds blasted their way onto the eastern seaboard, Gibran, alone in "the Hermitage," struggled to come to terms with the reality of his condition. Meanwhile in the outside world his latest book was receiving universal acclaim. A front-page article in the 1928 Christmas edition of the *New York Times Book Review* called it "brilliant in phrase and accurate in perception";[223] and in the *Manchester Guardian* a reviewer wrote:

> It is a great delight to the jaded reader, wandering about in the endless forest of books which has sprung up around the Four Gospels, to come suddenly upon one that has great beauty and distinction peculiarly its own. Such a book I have found in *Jesus, the Son of Man*. This is a book for those who can read with understanding.[224]

In the *Herald Tribune* Claude Bragdon wrote a feature article on the artist:

> [To Gibran] "nothing is higher than the human" – the only supernatural he recognizes is man's own supernature, and he has utter faith in man's power to become divine by *realization*; that is, by *making real* the divine, in the human life. Of this process and its results he chooses Jesus as the great exemplar and he is so eager that his readers should both see and understand Him, that he adopts the device of *straining* Jesus, so to speak, through the

consciousness of His immediate contemporaries, enemies and friends alike
– each one a cloth of finer or coarser texture, in which some trait or aspect
is netted, or on which it leaves an azure or crimson stain.[225]

John Haynes Holmes, the former minister of the Community Church in
New York, wrote in his review that Gibran had "attempted a unique and
daring experiment . . . It is as though a contemporary (of Jesus) sat down at
a belated hour, to write another and different gospel . . . It has a simplicity
which is disarming and yet a majesty which at times is overwhelming,"
calling Gibran a poet with "austere purity of thought . . . amplitude and
beauty of phrase . . . wisdom, serenity and lofty vision . . . If any man were
fitted to attempt this adventurous task, it is Mr. Gibran."[226] A reviewer in
the *Springfield Union* wrote that *Jesus, the Son of Man* "attains a degree of
perfection that might well serve as an inspiration for other writers to whom
English is their native tongue."[227]

Gibran wrote to Mary telling her that by such praise he "was *made* shy,"
and again revealed his longing for home.[228] The growing adulation, for
which he had once hungered, meant little to him now as he acknowledged
to Naimy that his disease was terminal: "The ailment has settled in a place
deeper than muscle and bones."[229]

Although increasingly crippled by his illness and "unable to move
about,"[230] Gibran refused to abandon his work: "It seems to me that there
is nothing worth while but work. All else is nothing but a slow death."[231]
Although Knopf was waiting for him to complete *The Garden of the
Prophet*, the poet told Naimy that he felt it "wise to get away from the
publishers at present."[232]

Claude Bragdon recalled Gibran during this time:

> Gibran lived in an old, elevatorless apartment house in lower New York,
> with high ceilings, rambling corridors, and winding stairways, the climbing
> of which to his high perched studio doubtless shortened his life, though he
> could not be persuaded to move. Shortly before his death we planned to
> write a book together on the subject of architecture, in which he was greatly
> interested. We used to meet at the penthouse apartment of Madame
> Henriette Sava-Goiu, a golden-haired and golden-hearted Rumanian of
> extraordinary vitality and charm. There, the centre of an entranced circle,
> Gibran would make free translations of Sufi poetry, and tell folk-tales of his
> native land. It was there, indeed, that I saw him last, only a short time
> before his tragic death from cancer, after two years of secret suffering.[233]

Despite his illness, Gibran's creative imagination was still envisioning new projects, and he wrote to Naimy: "What do you think of a book composed of four stories on the lives of Michelangelo, Shakespeare, Spinoza and Beethoven? What would you say if I showed their achievements to be the unavoidable outcome of pain, ambition, 'expatriation' and hope moving in the human heart?"[234] The three identical tensions of Gibran's own life were now taking their toll. Seven years earlier in 1921 he had written: "Never mind, Meesha, whatever is destined shall be. But I feel that I shall not leave the slope of this mountain before daybreak. And dawn shall throw a veil of light and gleam on everything."[235]

As the first winter dawn of 1929 rose, shedding its ghostly light through the windows of "the Hermitage," the man from Lebanon knew that his descent from the mountain had begun.

11

The Return of the Wanderer

(1929–1931)

I

On January 6, 1929 Gibran dramatically broke down at a party given to celebrate his forty-sixth birthday. The occasion, at José Orozco's "Ashram," began with readings from Gibran's early works before the poet himself was called to recite extracts from *The Forerunner* and *The Madman*. On finishing he was pressed by the enthusiastic audience for more.[1] As he began reading from his parables his voice began to betray deep emotion and suddenly, asking to be excused, he rushed into the dining room and began to cry.

Alma Reed, the hostess for the evening, attempted to comfort Gibran. He told her that there was nothing in the much-publicized books of his maturity to equal these spontaneous works of his youth and that the wellspring of his creativity had dried up.[2]

Although desperately ill and depressed, he put on a brave front and maintained his public appearances. The evening before his birthday party he had been guest of honor at a large banquet arranged by Arrabitah at the McAlpin hotel in New York. The honor was of the highest form, almost as if the Arab world was crowning him as the "poet laureate" of Arabic literature. The keynote speaker, Philip K. Hitti, the most distinguished professor of Arabic history at the time and one of eighteen people to address the audience that evening, spoke of Gibran's achievements:

You can hardly nowadays pick up an Arabic paper printed in Beirut, Cairo, Baghdad, São Paulo or Buenos Aires without finding somebody consciously trying to write Gibran-like. Of course, the esoteric, figurative, imaginative style . . . is not a new thing in Arabic literature . . . But our hero of tonight,

270

through his unmatched mastery of this art . . . be it in Arabic or in English – has become the father of a new school of thought all of his own.[3]

In a letter to May shortly after this event the poet revealed that despite the praise being lavished on him he was worried because his creative abilities had deserted him: "I am, May, a small volcano whose opening has been closed. If I were able to write something great and beautiful, I would be completely cured. If I could cry out, I would gain back my health."[4]

Overawed by demands for his presence and besieged by visitors to "the Hermitage," he left New York and made for his refuge in Tyler Street. Any peace he found there, however, was quickly shattered when at the end of January x-rays revealed a life-threatening enlargement of the liver.

A short while after receiving this devastating news those closest to Gibran gathered around him before he was due to undergo a major operation. Suddenly, unexpectedly, he announced that he had decided not to undergo the operation. Concerns over Marianna's distress – fueled by an immigrant's fear of the impersonal environs of New York's awesome hospital system – had convinced Gibran to reject any further medical intervention.[5]

In the spring, despite his personal agonies, he announced in the *Syrian World* that *The Garden of The Prophet* was to be published that autumn; however, he was never to finish this work[6] as he could "no longer see *The Garden of the Prophet* with the same clear eye with which he had seen it before."[7]

In a letter to Mary he continued the masquerade of a sick man capable of recovery: "I do not feel well. I think it is nothing more than nervous 'tiredness.' The Autumn and Winter were hard."[8] He turned instead to a work the seeds of which he had sown in February 1911:

> The earth-God has gone mad, and destroyed all life save one man and one woman. The earth is in the form and likeness of a skull – its hollows dry, riverbeds gray – its surface cinders-gray. The man and woman are to water it with their tears, make it fruitful again and repeople the earth.[9]

Over the years the one earth-god had become three, and by 1915 represented the "three moods" or the three "primal elements" in man: "the desire for power, the desire to rule a greater world, and Love, a greater desire for Now."[10]   The epic scale of the final version of the work, which was finally published three weeks before Gibran's death, is reminiscent, in its opening lines and atmosphere, of Keats's last poem, *Hyperion*,[11] which begins with a description of the gods towering above the earth:

Sat gray-haired Saturn, quiet as a stone,
Still as the silence round about his lair;
Forest on forest hung about his head
Like cloud on cloud.[12]

In *The Earth Gods* Gibran writes:

The three earth-born gods, the Master Titans of life,
Appeared upon the mountains.
Rivers ran about their feet;
The mist floated across their breasts.[13]

In Keats's unfinished work, which he had called "a Fragment" written in a "Grecian manner," he presented two gods – the failing Hyperion, Titan of the sun, and the young Olympian, Apollo, who is "dying of life" down on earth.[14] Gibran, however, in his own piece, by deliberately introducing a third god, expresses his belief in the profound distinction between Greek and Arabic thought.[15] Unlike many Romantic poets Gibran did not utilize his considerable knowledge of Greek mythology.[16] Although he loved Greek culture he felt that it did not "possess the third Eye" of Chaldean, Phoenician, and Egyptian art: "She brought from Byblos and Nieth the jug and the cup, but not the wine."[17] As such he could only find in Greek art the visual and not the visionary:[18] "I cannot find in these the living God. I see only a shadow of His shadow."[19]

Like many *mahjar* poets, he sought his inspiration not from Greece but from the Arabs, believing that apart from being the nursery of "three great births: the Chaldeans and Assyrians, the Hebrews, and Islam," they possessed "that unconquered ripeness of life as simple as it were ages ago – as direct – between earth and the stars."[20] For Gibran it was the rich mythology of the Chaldeans that particularly struck an answering chord in expressing humanity's cosmological significance: "that eternal thought which plunges deep down to the bottom of the sea only to rise up to the Milky Way."[21]

In *The Earth Gods* a debate takes place between the first god and the second god. The former is pessimistic, tired of the unending cycle of life and death:

Weary is my spirit of all there is.
I would not move a hand to create a world
Nor to erase one.

I would not live could I but die,
For the weight of æons is upon me,
And the ceaseless moan of the seas exhausts my sleep.[22]

The second god, on the other hand, believes that the life they see below them contains within it the seeds of transcendence:

We are the beyond and we are the Most High,
And between us and boundless eternity
Is naught save our unshaped passion
And the motive thereof.

You invoke the unknown,
And the unknown clad with moving mist
Dwells in your own soul.
Yea, in your own soul your Redeemer lies asleep,
And in sleep sees what your waking eye does not see.[23]

This is the voice of Almustafa, encouraging spiritual quest. But there is a Third God, the youngest of the three,[24] who moderates the debate, and counsels acceptance of their predicament:

Love triumphs.
The white and green of love beside a lake,
And the proud majesty of love in tower or balcony;
Love in a garden or in the desert untrodden,
Love is our lord and master.
It is not a wanton decay of the flesh,
Nor the crumbling of desire
When desire and self are wrestling;
Nor is it flesh that takes arms against the spirit.
Love rebels not.[25]

Here is the voice of one who has come to realize that humankind, so often preoccupied with philosophical speculation, has forgotten how to live life to the full. It is the voice of a man who, knowing that his long alienation is nearly over, turns his thoughts in the evening of his life to his youth. It is the voice too of the artist trying to explicate humanity's relation to the divine[26] – a soul still raging against those who see people as little more than creatures "bred on hunger and made food for hungry gods."[27] Above all it is the voice of the mystic-poet:

Love is a distant laughter in the spirit.
It is a wild assault that hushes you to your awakening.
It is a new dawn upon the earth,
A day not yet achieved in your eyes or mine,
But already achieved in its own greater heart.

Brothers, my brothers,
The bride comes from the heart of dawn,
And the bridegroom from the sunset.
There is a wedding in the valley.
A day too vast for recording.[28]

The other Titans awaken to

Behold a brighter world
And creatures more starry supple to my mind.[29]

The three gods personify the denying, affirming, and reconciling forces that permeate all things, and although Gibran affirms in his piece that ultimately primordial substance is one, he also develops the idea, common to many spiritual traditions, that "one is three."[30] The oscillations between these forces in the human psychic life and the conflicts caused by their non-correspondence – tensions that Gibran was only too familiar with – provided him with the inspiration for a book he described as being written "out of [a] poet's hell."[31]

Although *The Earth Gods* is concerned with the all-embracing power of love, the prevailing mood is somber. The spiritual turbulence of youth and the high aspirations of early manhood have given way to the mellow resignation of a dying man, sometimes causing the work to come across like a didactic piece dressed in literary finery.[32]

Despite its flaws, the epic backdrop of the work is at times awesome, especially in its representation of humanity conceived on a cosmic scale – the cosmic dimension of Gibran's writings not mere metaphysical enlargement but a conception of humanity that is literally universal.[33] He echoes Blake, who wrote: "Thou art a Man, God is no more,"[34] when he writes in *The Earth Gods*: "Man is god in slow arising."[35]

Although Gibran had a certain "tenderness"[36] toward the book it was not to be the work that fulfilled him. For many years now he had been haunted by a fear that he would never succeed in expressing himself completely.[37] The poet was sure that his illness was a manifestation of malfunction on a deeper level, and convinced himself that his ailments were caused by his inability to produce a sequel to *The Prophet*: "I am unable to shout, and this is my very ailment; it's a spiritual ailment whose symptoms have appeared in the body." He wrote to May: "I was born to say . . . one living and winged word . . . I was unable to do this because I was a prattler. It's a shame, and I am filled with regret because I remained a chatterbox until my jabbering weakened my strength."[38]

As he completed *The Earth Gods* he stayed with Marianna in Boston for most of 1929. As always she nursed him, prepared his favorite Lebanese foods, pleaded with him to take strolls, and entertained the streams of neighbors and friends who visited her brother. Unable to awaken his creative energies he turned instead to some parables collected over the years.[39]

Returning to New York in the autumn he finally admitted to Mary the extent of his illness, calling it "a general breakdown."[40] Determined to distract himself from the gathering shadows he had the Hermitage repainted, organized his drawings and writings so that he could put his "hand on anything without going through the torture of finding it," and disentangled himself from Middle Eastern political affairs. He told Mary that he just wanted to write,[41] and in March, after finalizing his last will and testament, he wrote to May:

> We have already reached the summit, and the plains and the valleys and the forests have appeared before us. Let us rest, May, and talk a while. We cannot remain here long, for I see a higher peak from a distance, and we must reach it before sunset.[42]

Having rejected the ministerings of the medical profession, Gibran's chief source of pain relief came from alcohol. Although he tried to conceal the extent of what had by now become an addiction, his resort to desperate measures to ease his "tempest of pain"[43] was becoming increasingly obvious to those who visited him. Early in 1930 the Chilean poet Gabriela Mistral, a great admirer of Gibran's work, noticed that during the course of their evening together Gibran excused himself for a moment and stepped behind an oriental screen to "take a swig out of a bottle which, in the unfortunately arranged mirror, didn't look like a medicine bottle!"[44]

In June he handed the manuscript of *The Earth Gods* over to Mary for final editing. Although they now had little contact, mainly because of Florance Minis's continuing insecurities about his wife's relationship with

Gibran, Mary continued to work on Gibran's manuscripts, usually concealing the fact with a series of coded entries in her journal.[45]

While Mary carefully balanced her time between her husband and her secret editing in Georgia, Kahlil and Marianna rented a house by the sea for the summer. Despite the disease which was "tightening its grip on his heart,"[46] brother and sister were intent on trying to recapture the joy of summers past.

Like so many times before in his life the proximity of the sea brought the poet some repose. A descendant of those wandering Phoenician seafarers of three thousand years ago, the sea was in Gibran's soul and, perhaps as he stood by the great seaboard and listened to the waters, he remembered his own joyous "Song of the Wave" written so many years before:

> I and the shore are lovers:
> The wind unites and separates us.
> I come from beyond the twilight
> to merge the silver of my foam with the gold of its sand;
> And I cool its burning heart with my moisture.
> At dawn's coming I read passion's law to my beloved,
> And he draws me to his breast.
> At evening I chant the prayer of longing,
> And he embraces me.[47]

Over the summer he began painting what were to be his last works. The pictures from this time mirror his own struggles which he had so exquisitely expressed seven years before in *The Prophet*: "Your pain is the breaking of the shell that encloses your understanding."[48] They also suggest the realms of peace and silence, the sacred spaces of the earth.[49]

In *Fountain of Pain* the desperate writhing figures express the utter loneliness of pain – isolated individuals imprisoned in the agony of their own private suffering. In *Wrack of Man*, bodies are thrown carelessly and indiscriminately onto the shore of life – humanity's wretched existence appearing hopelessly insignificant before the monumental indifference of an awesome cosmos. *Man's Servitude* reflects Gibran's despair and sorrow at those who blindly follow tradition and negate the mysteries of life.[50]

In some of the drawings Gibran's life-affirming belief in the unity of being reemerges, as for instance in *The Blessed Forge* where the final benediction is bestowed on all those who awaken to their divinity, thus becoming united with the mother-of-all, whose benevolence consoles and envelopes them. Again in *Mother Earth* the artist portrays men and women, rooted to the earth and at the same time endowed with the transformational and unifying power of fire, expressed in *The Earth Gods* thus:

Behold, man and woman,
Flame to flame,
In white ecstasy.
Roots that suck at the breast of purple earth,
Flame flowers at the breasts of the sky.
And we are the purple breast,
And we are the enduring sky.
Our soul, even the soul of life, your soul and mine,
Dwells this night in a throat enflamed,
And garments the body of a girl with beating waves.
Your sceptre cannot sway this destiny,
Your weariness is but ambition.
This and all is wiped away.
In the passion of a man and a maid.[51]

II

Gibran knew that by now his body was incapable of absorbing nature's healing qualities and that the end was not far off. In a letter to May he explained that the long months of the summer retreat had merely "prolonged" the distance between his body and spirit.[52] When Kahlil and Marianna finally had to go from the house by the sea, aware that their days together were numbered, they left with heavy hearts.

Returning to Boston Gibran immediately turned his attention to Marianna's long-term welfare, a problem that had been worrying him for some time. He spent hours trying to convince her that the quality of her life would improve if she moved from the gloomy South End, where she had lived for over thirty years. Although the prospect was daunting for her, Marianna knew that Kahlil's peace of mind was dependent on her compliance and she finally agreed. With the help of their cousin Zakia Gibran Diab they found a pleasantly situated apartment for her opposite Franklin Park,[53] still within easy reach of her family.

Relieved that he had managed to see his sister settled in a secure and healthy neighborhood, Gibran left the city for the last time and returned to New York. His condition deteriorating, and losing weight,[54] he did not want Marianna to see him in this dreadful condition and pleaded that it was pressure of work that prevented him from spending Christmas with his family in Boston.

When the Great Depression of the thirties began, Gibran's growing fame and fortune must have appeared enviable to many in New York. As his books were going through new editions and his English works were being translated, his royalties grew.[55] A lecture bureau offered to take him on a reading tour, and rarely a day went by when the mail, telegraph, or telephone did not bring fresh testimonies of appreciation.[56] Publishers, no doubt aware of the cataclysmic days ahead, pressed their authors for new work and Gibran began to put the finishing touches to the parables of *The Wanderer* – a man with "a veil of pain upon his face"[57] – the work he had begun in Boston in 1929.[58]

Returning to the irony of *The Forerunner* and *The Madman* there is at times a pungency in many of these new tales which bespeaks a soul tired of the world's absurdities.[59] In this last work, despite a weariness with the world, the poet still manages to evoke the life-affirming spirit of a man who believed that ultimately "All is well."[60]

The narrator tells of a story-teller who has just left him and his family: "And when he left us after three days we did not feel that a guest had departed but rather that one of us was still out in the garden and had not yet come in."[61]

> Once on a time I met another man of the roads. He too was a little mad, and thus he spoke to me: "I am a wanderer. Oftentimes it seems that I walk the earth among pygmies . . .
>
> But in truth I walk not among men but above them, and all they can see of me is my footprints in their open fields.
>
> And often have I heard them discuss and disagree over the shape and size of my footprints . . .
>
> But you, my friend, you know full well that they are naught save the footprints of a wanderer.[62]

It is striking that in Gibran's last work, one of his seers reappears – the Madman – who has the clarity of vision to see beyond the chimera of a fleeting world. Gibran's interior relationship with this figure had evolved ever since the outbreak of war in 1914 which made him tortured and "possessed," telling Mary that he sometimes experienced a state akin to madness – "a demoniac impatience."[63] He perceived that his madman represented one aspect of his personality which included "Grave-Diggers,

Giants . . . Oh! I'm in a world of them . . . we are like nuts, we have to be cracked open . . . The gentle touch does not wake people."[64] Many times during his life it was to his madman that he turned, "my only weapon in this strangely armed world,"[65] and now as he faced death, the madman reappears.

In *The Wanderer* he reveals himself as "a youth with a pale face . . . lovely and full of wonder." Although his wandering days are now spent in an asylum, he is still as intensely aware of "those who live in the madhouse on the other side of the wall."[66] It transpires that the young madman is incarcerated because he had been cast out of a society determined to have him "but a reflection of [their] own face[s] in the mirror."[67] As for the madman there is a freedom in madness,[68] a sense that by truly *being* there and accepting one's predicament, one can escape from the world of illusionary "freedom." The youth, "the thrice alienated"[69] artist, the young outsider from the South End who could only find freedom through his work, his "love made visible,"[70] is Gibran.

As in Gibran's previous collections the fabular ingredient in *The Wanderer* is utilized to telling effect in the condemnation of the Christian who teaches there is salvation only for baptized Christians, and who, eventually, is himself consumed by fire;[71] the philosopher incapable of empathy, who "cannot enfold [his] feet with the shoes of another man;"[72] and the politicians who in the East and West "fill the air with noisy and rhymeless sound."[73] His contempt for these figures is matched by his loathing for a civilization that binds men and women to a multitude of useless laws and shackles them in a "thousand prisons,"[74] chains that even move a dog to exclaim: "For God's sake, run for your lives. Civilization is after us."[75]

In contrast, Gibran reaffirms his peaceful message in "Peace Contagious," with inimitable simple imagery, describing a dialogue he envisages between two branches that discover their affinity: "And if the upper air makes peace it seems to me that those who dwell in the lower might make peace also. Will you not wave in the wind a little nearer to me?"[76] and in "The Two Hunters" he reaffirms his reverence for nature when joy and sorrow are united in their praise for "the beauty which is upon the earth, and of the daily wonder of life in the forest and among the hills, and of the songs heard at dawn and eventide."[77]

Crystallizing Gibran's message of unity is the parable called "The River," a piece strongly reminiscent of Longfellow's *Hiawatha*. The river becomes a symbol of impermanence, renewal, and heavenly mercy, a source of luminosity and rapture[78] and, as in Buddhism and Hinduism, the confluence of river into sea symbolizes the unification of individuality into the absolute: the self returning to its source. Thus the wanderer's lifelong alienation is finished and his memories in his twilight days turn to the shimmering rivulets of the Qadisha valley, a place where a small child many years before had first sensed the unity of being.

> In the valley of Kadisha [Qadisha] where the mighty river flows, two little streams met and spoke to one another.
>
> One stream said, "How came you, my friend, and how was your path?" And the other answered, "My path was most encumbered. The wheel of the mill was broken, and the master farmer who used to conduct me from my channel to his plants, is dead. I struggled down oozing with the filth of those who do naught but sit and bake their laziness in the sun. But how was your path, my brother?"
>
> And the other stream answered and said: "Mine was a different path. I came down the hills among fragrant flowers and shy willows; men and women drank of me with silvery cups, and little children paddled their rosy feet at my edges, and there was laughter all about me, and there were sweet songs. What a pity that your path was not so happy."
>
> At that moment the river spoke with a loud voice and said: "Come in, come in, we are going to the sea. Come in, come in, speak no more. Be with me now. We are going to the sea. Come in, come in, for in me you shall forget your wanderings, sad or gay. Come in, come in. And you and I will forget all our ways when we reach the heart of our mother the sea".[79]

Gibran's use of "the River" as a symbol for the course of human life is an eloquent testimony of his love for his homeland. It sums up his view of life in an open, straightforward manner, and the imagery is so simple that it could have come from a children's story. Effortless, but deeply felt, Gibran's perspicuous prose is the fruit of a lifetime's dedication to perfecting an instrument whereby he could communicate to others, in the most effective and beautiful manner possible, the unseen order he believed to be at the heart of everything on earth.

Yet, there is still a poignancy in the tales. The wanderer has not yet found his soul-mate. "The Love Song" expresses the contradictions of Gibran's own life when he depicts a poet's exquisite verse as attracting a young woman who perceives that it is written to her alone.

The poet, however, declares that his love poem is a hymn to universal love: "a song of love out of a poet's heart, sung by every man to every woman." The girl, feeling that she's been cheated by the beauty of his verse, calls the poet a "Hypocrite and liar in words."[80]

Less abrasive, although no less poignant, is the story "The Hermit and the Beasts," in which the beasts, after listening to the hermit speaking of love, ask him in exasperation, "Where is your mate?" and then proceed to gossip among themselves: "How can he tell us of loving and mating when he himself knows naught thereof?" The hermit-poet concludes the piece with the tragic picture of a man, alone and despairing in his hermitage: "That night the hermit lay upon his mat with his face earthward, and he wept bitterly and beat his hands upon his breast."[81]

Although spending more and more time in his Hermitage, Gibran had many female admirers; yet, despite what was at times an adoring audience, he experienced a loneliness more intense than he had ever felt before.[82] In the past his solitude and "aloneness" had been so dear to him that he would let no woman disturb it for long,[83] but now, desolate and overpowered by his illness, he longed for a close female companion.[84] Despite his wariness that passionate love could be a "quenchless thirst," he succumbed to his desires and let a young woman called Gertrude Stein into his life.

Although she was by no means a soulmate, the presence of a partner brought the ailing poet some succor.[85] In her late twenties and an office worker in the garment business, "his last amour"[86] had a keen interest in literature. Like so many others, after reading *The Prophet* she desperately wanted to meet the poet. Gertrude was fortunate in knowing Isaac Horowitz,[87] an acquaintance of Gibran who arranged for her to visit "the Hermitage." The dying man was attracted to the intelligence and vivacity of the young woman and an intense relationship developed, continuing right up until his death. "He was a great soul encased in a small body," Gertrude was to later recall: "That his personality could not always keep up with the greatness of his inner beauty is nobody's business."[88]

III

As 1930 came to a close Gibran wrote to his friend the author Felix Farris:

Pain, my brother, is an unseen and powerful hand that breaks the skin of the stone in order to extract the pulp . . . I must go back to Lebanon, and I must withdraw myself from this civilization that runs on wheels. However, I deem it wise not to leave this country before I break the strings and chains that tie me down; and numerous are those strings and those chains! I wish to go back to Lebanon and remain there forever.[89]

Ten years previously he had made known his thoughts about dying to Mary:

> I sometimes imagine myself, my bodily part, after death, lying in the earth and returning to the elements of earth: the great loosening, the change everywhere, the opening into simpler things, the widening out into those things from which anything may be built up again, the great Return, such deep quietness and a passing into the substance of things.[90]

When Naimy went to visit Gibran early in 1931 he found him in bed with his face showing signs of "fatigue and pallor" such as he had "never seen before."[91] Although Gibran told him that it was nothing serious, Naimy tried to encourage him to get more help. However, the sick man reassured him that Anna Johansen, the janitor's wife, kept an eye on him. From his bed Gibran asked Naimy to read aloud from the manuscript of *The Earth Gods*:

> We shall pass into the twilight;
> Perchance to wake to the dawn of another world.
> But love shall stay,
> And his finger-marks shall not be erased . . .
>
> Better it is for us, and wiser,
> To seek a shadowed nook and sleep in our earth divinity,
> And let love, human and frail, command the coming day.[92]

Deeply moved, Naimy was overcome when he saw the accompanying paintings, with their "masculinity," "vigor," and "depth and ease."[93]

For the last three weeks of his life Gibran continued to finalize the manuscript of *The Wanderer*, and in his last letter to Mary he spoke of little else but his work.[94] The little boy who had so carefully sketched his figures on the mountain snows, the ardent student who had pored over Avicenna and Nietzsche by candlelight, and the man who had gone on to change the literary sensibility of the age[95] had spent an entire lifetime faithful to his tools, charging all things he fashioned with his own spirit: "When you work you fulfil a part of earth's furthest dream, assigned to you when that dream was born, And in keeping yourself with labour you are in truth loving life. And to love life through labour is to be intimate with life's inmost secret."[96]

On the first Thursday after Easter, on April 10, 1931, Anna Johansen walked up the four flights of stairs carrying Gibran's breakfast. When she opened the door Gibran's condition so alarmed her that she telephoned

Mrs. Leonobel Jacobs, an ex-resident of the studio and friend of Gibran. The doctor whom Mrs. Jacobs brought insisted that they leave at once for the hospital.

Gibran, however, refused to be admitted, saying he wished to remain in the Hermitage. Early that afternoon Barbara Young arrived and remained all day as Gibran talked of his current projects, still bothered that his work was unfinished.[97] At about 8:30 that evening Mrs. Jacobs returned with the doctor who again tried to convince Gibran to be admitted to hospital. Once again he refused, determined to remain in his studio through the night.

The next morning at 10:30 as he slipped in and out of consciousness he was carried into St. Vincent's Hospital on Seventh Avenue. Marianna received a telegram, but when she arrived at the hospital from Boston Kahlil had already fallen into a coma at about two o'clock in the afternoon and could no longer recognize anyone.

Around five o'clock Barbara Young telephoned the office of the *Syrian World*, to advise his Syrian friends of the serious and worsening condition of Gibran. At dusk the doctors confirmed Marianna's worst fears and advised her that her brother's death was imminent.

Mikhail Naimy arrived at the hospital, and was greeted at the third-floor ward by Barbara Young, who informed him that nothing could be done. "Did he wish to confess and to commune?" asked Naimy. Barbara Young told him that one of the sisters of the hospital had asked, "Are you a Catholic?" and that Gibran had answered a gruff "No." When he fell into a coma, however, Chor-Bishop Francis Wakim, pastor of St. Joseph's Maronite Church in New York, arrived and tried to rouse the dying man, but Gibran never answered.[98]

Yet perhaps behind closed eyelids, images floated in slow procession: the towering cedars; the dreaming ruins of the temple of Astarte; the whispering pond in Qadisha valley; horsemen bearing a summons to his father; his first sight of Leonardo's *St. Anna*; a steamboat at Ellis Island; the seething streets of Chinatown; Boutros's store; Sultanah's almond eyes; Kamileh's back bent double by heavy packs; the swirling cloaks and whirling cameras of Fred Holland Day; Micheline, Josephine; afternoons with Dr. Jung; the madman, Zarathustra, the grave-digger, and the war; Rodin's studio; *Spirits Rebellious*; Yeats, Ryder, Garibaldi; Mary's meteorite; the *Caesar* setting sail for Syria; 'Abdu'l-Bahá, *The Prophet*, *Jesus, the Son of Man*, Marianna and Mary and May.

Gibran died at 10:50 in the evening, April 10, 1931, the first Friday after Easter. According to Naimy, an autopsy revealed that the cause of death was "cirrhosis of the liver and incipient tuberculosis in one of the lungs."[99]

Marianna sent a telegram to Mary Haskell who immediately left the convention for the arts she was hosting. Within two hours the woman who had helped a young artist from Chinatown realize many of his dreams and who had inspired his Almitra was on the northbound train to Boston.

Gibran's body, banked with lilies and orchids, was taken to the Universal Funeral Parlor on Lexington Avenue, where on Saturday and Sunday hundreds of people from all walks of life silently filed by in a continual stream.[100]

On Monday, accompanied by members of Arrabitah, the coffin was taken to Boston. As the 5:00 train pulled in that afternoon to South Station it was met by Gibran's close friend Chor-Bishop Stephen El-Douaihy, the priest of the Church of Our Lady of the Cedars. Covered with the Lebanese flag, the casket was moved to the Syrian Ladies Aid Society at 44 West Newton Street.

Mary arrived in Boston at 8:00 P.M. and went immediately to support the brokenhearted Marianna who was wearing her mother's black lace scarf. An observer recalled that while others wept, Mary was composed – "aware of Gibran's inner struggles over the years and of his efforts to draw closer to his unnamed Spirit – the sacred spirit who is a vital part of everything he has [or had] written."[101] That night she joined Marianna, Gertrude Stein, Naseeb Arida, Najeeb Diab, Barbara Young, and others for a light meal where they broke bread for Gibran and sipped coffee, calling it a "Last Supper."

On the following day hundreds of mourners followed the cortege to the Church of Our Lady of the Cedars. As it passed through the Boston streets many dropped to their knees while traffic officers saluted the flag-draped casket.[102] In the candlelit church the service was conducted in Syriac while outside on the sidewalk a silent crowd paid their respects to the "Man from Lebanon." From the church, the congregation moved to the vault on the hilltop cemetery of St. Benedict where the casket was temporarily placed.

At a memorial meeting held at Roerich Hall, New York, on April 29, 1931, Mikhail Naimy read from his poem *The Mystic Pact*, and forty days after Gibran's death, delivered an address to the Syrian-Lebanese community in Brooklyn:

> Gibran Kahlil Gibran's was one of those souls that experienced moments of utter clarity in which Truth delights to be mirrored. In that was Gibran's glory. In that was his pain . . . In revealing himself to himself Gibran reveals

us to ourselves . . . It would seem that the all-seeing eye perceived our spiritual drought and sent us this rain-bearing cloud to drizzle some relief to our parching souls.[103]

On the morning of July 23, as a light summer rain fell,[104] the body was moved from Boston to Providence. Several hundred Lebanese from New York and Boston gathered at the pier and as Barbara Young read from Gibran's poems the coffin was lowered onto the Fabre liner *Sinara*. A wreath from seven hundred Lebanese living in Providence was placed at the base of the casket. Wind instruments played the funeral march from *Tannhäuser*, "Asa's Death" from the *Peer Gynt Suite*, and "Nearer, My God, to Thee."

The ship left its moorings and sailed eastwards at 2:00 P.M. Four weeks later, on the morning of Friday, August 21, Gibran's body finally returned to Lebanon. An official delegation boarded, and before a guard of honor the casket was taken onto a government launch. On the shore the coffin was opened and the minister of education solemnly pinned the decoration of fine arts on the poet's breast. In the procession representatives of the high commissariat, the minister of the interior, the French admiralty, and the army of occupation moved in respectful silence to the cathedral. Following them were Shi'ite and Sunni Muslims, Greek and Syrian Catholics and Orthodox, Maronites, Jews, Jesuits, Protestants, Druzes, Armenians and crowds of children. In the magnificent cathedral of St. George, Archbishop Ignatius Mobarek blessed the body of the poet who had spent his entire life challenging the status quo.

That evening Charles Dabbas, president of the Republic, officiated at a governmental reception where among others Gibran's one-time mentor, the Sufi poet Ameen Rihani, spoke movingly of his friend. After the service the procession started to Bisharri fifty miles away by way of Tripoli, winding up and through the mountains.

Along the route people lined the roads and at every village the procession, now more akin to a triumphal procession than a funeral, stopped while village leaders read their eulogies.[105] Following the cortege, men chanted songs while women wailed and beat their breasts. Near the ancient city of Byblos ceremonies evoking traditional rites to the local goddess were enacted as young men in native dress brandished swords, and dancing women scattered flowers before the hearse.

By the time the procession had reached Albahsas, which marks the parting of the ways between the coastal and the higher roads, Bedouin horsemen had appeared from the mountains to pay their respects.

For two days after Gibran returned to Bisharri ancient rituals went on long into the night. He was finally laid to rest in the grotto of the little monastery of Mar Sarkis, hewn into the living rock, in the shade of the sacred cedars, and not far from the house where he was born, for finally:

The stream has reached the sea, and once more
the great mother holds her son against her breast.[106]

Epilogue

One of the major difficulties in any scholarly attempt to study the life and works of Kahlil Gibran is the irreconcilable attitudes of those who have deified him and those who have dismissed him as a mere populist poet on the other. Added to all this is the fact that critical opinions of his works swing violently from the eulogistic to the condemnatory.

Gibran, however, defied every critical apparatus. His work has remained an inspiration to millions throughout the world, young and old alike, and the recent resurgence of interest in his life and works testifies to the permanence of his thought and the continuity of its influence throughout the English-speaking world and beyond.

The history of Gibran studies, both in Arabic and English, has been a gradual process of reluctant recognition coming first from officialdom and then, at last, from academia. His popularity and reputation, however, in the consciousness of the millions who have been moved and inspired by his universal vision and spiritual awareness, have always remained intact. What is irrefutable is that *The Prophet* is among the most widely read books of the century and that Gibran's worldwide reputation is in the ascendancy as never before. Nevertheless *The Prophet* does indeed hold an ambiguous position in English and American literature, a position that has so far debarred it from serious critical attention in the West. It is neither pure literature nor pure philosophy, and as an Arab work written in English it belongs exclusively to no particular tradition.

During his lifetime, apart from reviews in the Arabic and English press, and brief references to him by George Russell (AE), Claude Bragdon, and Robert Hillyer, the field of Gibran studies was non-existent, any acknowledgment being a personal reaction to his inspirational writings rather than a valid critical assessment of his work.

One of the major obstacles to critical analysis has been the absence of a comprehensive bibliography and the unavailability of reliable and authentic records such as original manuscripts and other materials related to Gibran's life or work. The earliest pioneering attempts were the bibliographic compendiums of Yousef Sarkis published in several volumes between 1920 and 1926,[1] his index published between 1928 and 1929,[2] and Ass'ad Daghir's sources for literary studies published in 1956.[3] An enormous anthology by Habib Mas'oud of primary and secondary source material on Gibran, describing some of the events of his life and work, was published in São Paulo, Brazil, in 1932, under the title of *Jubran Hiyan wa Mayetan* (*Gibran in his Life and Death*). Habib Mas'oud's anthology was followed a year later (1933) by Ameen Khalid's critical study aptly entitled *Muhawalat fi Darsi Jubran*[4] (*Attempts in the Study of Gibran*). All other studies that followed, especially Shukrallah al-Jurr's *Nabi Orphalese*[5] (*The Prophet of Orphalese*) in 1939 and Jameel Jabr's *Jubran: Siratuhu, Adabuhu, Falsafatuhu, Rasmuhu*[6] (*Gibran: His Life, Writings, Philosophy and Art*) in 1958, relied entirely on the existing information available so far.

In 1934, three years after Gibran's death, Mikhail Naimy, Gibran's friend and colleague, published his Arabic biography *Jubran Kahlil Jubran: Hayatuhu, Mawtuhu, Adabuhu, Fannuhu*,[7] which was translated into English in 1950 under the title *Kahlil Gibran: His Life and His Works*: this was never meant to be a definitive and objective biography, least of all by Naimy himself.[8] The first introduction to Gibran in English was written in 1945 by Barbara Young, Gibran's amanuensis in his later years – a somewhat panegyric work entitled *This Man from Lebanon: A Study of Kahlil Gibran*. Here was an unashamed devotee who left the reader in no doubt that she was presenting an apotheostic account of Gibran – her book remaining the only study in English for the next twenty years.

In 1963 the first attempt in English at a serious critical analysis of Gibran was made by Kahlil S. Hawi, whose Cambridge University doctoral dissertation was published as *Khalil Gibran: His Background, Character and Works*.[9] Hawi's bibliography contained both Arabic and English sources and despite the fact that he was deprived of the rich fund of letters that later came to light, he raised a number of issues pertinent to a critical assessment of Gibran's work and its influence on modern Arabic literature. Hawi, however, refrained from commenting on Gibran's contribution to American/English literature or more accurately to that literature that has recently been described as "literature in English"; for it is as literature in English that Gibran's work gains validity in the same way as East and West African and Commonwealth literature has become an integral part of academic study in English-speaking universities in Britain and the United

States. Hawi's book, nevertheless, emphasized a crucial point in studying Gibran, namely that in the absence of a complete bibliography representing primary and secondary sources it is impossible to produce a definitive critical biography.

In 1970 there was a turning-point in Gibran studies. Under the patronage of the president of Lebanon, the First Gibran International Festival was held at the American University of Beirut. The event produced an anthology of Gibran's writings in both English and Arabic and was the first attempt at presenting Gibran's works in a bilingual and bicultural context[10] together with as comprehensive a bibliography as was possible to construct at that time. Although certain additions and corrections have subsequently been made, no bibliography has superseded it to date except the updated bilingual single volume produced by Suheil Bushrui, *Kahlil Gibran: A Bibliography,* in 1983.[11] Equally important, the event initiated the first academic program in Gibran studies at the department of English at the American University of Beirut. The program entitled "Kahlil Gibran and his Contemporaries" illustrated and defined the distinctive characteristics of Arab-American literature during the late nineteenth and early twentieth centuries, and centered on the English works of Kahlil Gibran, Mikhail Naimy, and Ameen Rihani. The studies in this context also dealt with the relationship between the creative work of these authors and the social, political, and intellectual movements in the Arab world, Europe, and America.[12]

A new development was to occur in 1972 with the publication of the correspondence between Kahlil Gibran and his American benefactress and patroness Mary Haskell: *Beloved Prophet: The Love Letters of Kahlil Gibran and Mary Haskell and her Private Journal.* The letters furnished scholars and those interested in Gibran's life with an invaluable mine of information provided by the poet himself and secondly by the meticulously detailed recordings of an impeccable and reliable observer.

This was soon followed by another, although not as extensive, volume of unknown and unpublished letters: *The Love Letters of Kahlil Gibran to May Ziadah,* first published in Arabic in 1979 and appearing in an English translation in 1983 entitled *Blue Flame: The Love Letters of Kahlil Gibran to May Ziadah,* and reprinted as *Gibran: Love Letters* in 1987.[13]

The work of Jean and Kahlil Gibran[17] published in 1974 under the title *Kahlil Gibran: His Life and World* represented the most up-to-date biography and included much hitherto unpublished material, especially the diaries of Josephine Preston Peabody, documents on Gibran's Boston years, and new information on Gibran's American experience. The work of this tireless team of husband and wife must be recognized as a worthy attempt toward the construction of a definitive biography. Relying on a fund of original material and primary sources, letters, and manuscript material, *Kahlil Gibran: His Life and World* is an outstanding contribution to Gibran studies and represents the best survey of Gibran's life in America.

In 1975, the year that saw the opening of the Gibran Museum in Bisharri, the village of Gibran's birth, came the publication of *Gibran of Lebanon: New Papers* which applied a new critical apparatus to Gibran's work.[14] In 1977 Salma Khadra Jayyusi published her seminal work on modern and contemporary Arabic literature, *Trends and Movements in Modern Arabic Poetry,* which provided a ground-breaking analysis of the importance of Gibran's work in the Arab world, honoring him as "the greatest literary figure in Arab letters during the first three decades of the century."[15] This outstanding work, which is the most significant critical survey of modern Arabic literature ever published, included a critical assessment of Gibran's Arabic works which has not yet been superseded.

Between 1974 and 1980 some manuscript material began to see the light of day including fragments of Gibran's English works such as *The Madman, The Prophet, The Earth Gods,* and *The Forerunner.* These manuscripts were edited by William S. Shehadi and published by the American University of Beirut in 1991.[16]

During the seventies and early eighties the leadership provided by the late Professor Emile Geagea, chairman of the Gibran National Committee in Lebanon, resulted in a well-studied strategy to achieve some ambitious aims: promoting Gibran studies throughout the world, retrieving as many Gibran manuscripts as possible whether in Lebanon or in the USA; the restoration of all the paintings housed in the Old Gibran Museum in Bisharri; and finally the transformation of the area surrounding Gibran's resting place into a modern museum fully equipped to house paintings and manuscripts guaranteeing their preservation for posterity. It is difficult to overemphasize the importance of the work accomplished by the Gibran National Committee between 1972 and 1983 in the climate of national uncertainty and civil conflict in Lebanon. The real credit, however, must go to the vision, refined taste, and expertise of the author and art critic Farid Salman who was invited by Professor Geagea to be consultant and advisor to the Gibran National Committee. Farid Salman's contribution can never be overestimated and only future generations will fully appreciate the debt we owe him. Not only did he labor to preserve the Gibran heritage and help create the new museum, but he succeeded in doing all this with great artistic integrity and refined sensibility. The appointment of a competent curator greatly enhanced the long-term policies related to the museum. Wahib Kayrouz, himself a Gibran scholar, was appointed to the post and has since contributed two major publications based on hitherto unpublished papers: '*Alam Jubran al-Rassam*[18] (*The World of Gibran the Painter*) and the two-volume '*Alam Jubran al-Fikri (The Thoughts of Gibran).*[19]

The fiftieth anniversary of Gibran's death, in 1981, was officially commemorated by the Gibran National Committee and the ministry of education with a series of activities organized by the American University of Beirut which also published *Fi Thikra Jubran: Abhath al-Mu'tamar al-'Awal Li al-Dirasat al-Jubraniyah (In Memory of Kahlil Gibran: The First Colloquium on Gibran Studies).*[20] These activities were to be followed two years later by the celebrations of the hundredth anniversary of Gibran's birth: a Kahlil Gibran Centenary International Commemoration was scheduled to take place in Beirut, Washington, New York, London, and Oxford.

Under the patronage of Sheikh Amine El-Gemayel, the president of Lebanon, who declared 1983 a "Gibran International Year," a presidential commission was established consisting of Issam Khoury, minister of education; Ibrahim Halawi, minister of tourism; Sheikh Habib Kayrouz, chairman, National Council for Tourism; Dr. Omar Messayikey, secretary to the Council of Ministers; Professor Emile Geagea, Gibran National Committee; and Professor Suheil Bushrui, professor of English literature and Gibran studies at the American University of Beirut. The international activities in connection with the preparations to celebrate the Gibran centenary drew worldwide attention to the life and work of Kahlil Gibran. On this historic occasion events scheduled included the inauguration of the Gibran Memorial Museum in Bisharri; the issuing of a commemorative stamp; the founding of Gibran archives; education programs and conferences; radio and television coverage and various publications. Tragically, however, the bitter and bloody conflict in Lebanon deprived it of the opportunity of honoring its most illustrious son, and these events, with a few exceptions, did not take place.

The centennial celebrations in the United States and Britain, however, went ahead and were marked by the publication of *The Blue Flame: The Love Letters of Kahlil Gibran to May Ziadah*, and in an exhibition assembled by Suheil Bushrui and entitled *The World of Kahlil Gibran.*[21] This exhibition, the first documentary of its kind, was organized at Oxford and Washington, the Oxford event having been co-sponsored by the Poetry Society as well as the Literary Society of the University of Oxford. In support of these activities the Library of Congress in Washington organized a conference on Arab-American Literature, "The Vision of Gibran", which acknowledged Gibran's unique place in modern literature and was attended by leading international scholars.

Perhaps the most significant recognition to be accorded Kahlil Gibran during this centennial year was the announcement on March 5, 1983 by the president of the American University of Beirut, the late Malcolm Kerr, that the university had decided to create a Kahlil Gibran chair in the department of English.[22] However, this historic project was stillborn due to the untimely death of President Kerr and the disruption of university life caused by the then-raging conflict.

What was fated not to take place in Lebanon was destined, however, to reach fruition in Gibran's adopted country, the United States. In 1986 the University of Maryland at College Park declared its intention to establish an endowed Kahlil Gibran chair on values and peace – the first academic program in Gibran studies. The chair, designed to address moral and social determinants of public justice with scholars working on matters of cultural pluralism, human rights, the role of the arts, poetry, and literature in promoting international communication and cooperation, was the first major acknowledgment by a prestigious academic establishment in the United States of the validity in academic terms of creating a center for Gibran studies. Under the auspices of the prospective chair, studies were initiated emphasizing the enduring human values Gibran advocated in his writings and which are essential to the creation of a world vision based on the principles of "unity in diversity." The Kahlil Gibran Research and Studies Project was created to fulfill the functions of the chair and is now an established entity within the Center for International Development and Conflict Management. Under the auspices of the Kahlil Gibran Research and Studies Project an energetic program of research and publication has been developed, the most important aspect of which is the present volume.

Concomitant with these activities were other non-academic initiatives between 1974 and 1983 fired by those inspired by the life and work of the poet – artists such as the internationally acclaimed Irish actor Richard Harris reading *The Prophet* (1974) on record[23] and the distinguished English sculptor Neil Lawson Baker creating a unique series of exceptionally beautiful bronzes depicting themes from *The Prophet*.[24] In addition to this a Kahlil Gibran Park was created in 1977 at Copley Square in Boston and the mayor of the city of Boston designated January 1983 the "Kahlil Gibran Month" during which centennial celebrations included an exhibition of forty of Gibran's paintings at the Boston Public Library.

In 1991 the Kahlil Gibran Centennial Foundation Memorial Garden Dedication Weekend took place at Embassy Row in Washington. The privately funded meditation garden was inaugurated by President George Bush after the Congress of the United States passed legislation providing the land for the memorial with three American presidents signing the legislation, among them former president Jimmy Carter, who chaired the honorary committee of the Foundation, and who described the event on May 23–27 as "a joyous and memorable occasion."[25] The initiatives for passing the legislation were taken as early as 1983 through the dedicated and indefatigable efforts of Shiryl Amin, founder of the Gibran Centennial Foundation; the full realization of the project was achieved under the Foundation chairman William Baroody.

Sixty years after his death, then, Gibran's contribution to American literature was immortalized in the heart of Washington. For a poet who was only beginning to be recognized by the academic world this was a remarkable achievement.

In truth, however, the continuing popularity of the works of Kahlil Gibran is a clear enough indication of his standing among the peoples of the world and no matter what is said, Kahlil Gibran has become an integral part of the literary legacy of both the East and the West. In his work he became not only Gibran of Lebanon, but Gibran of America, indeed Gibran the voice of global consciousness.

Kahlil Gibran's popularity continues unabated, and is reflected in the growing interest in his work in Japan, Korea, the Philippines, Australia and New Zealand, Russia, India, and beyond; the translations of his work into a host of different languages; and the publication of new editions of his work – the most important of these being the recently annotated edition of *The Prophet*.[26] Worthy of note in this respect is the keen interest and rising popularity of Gibran in Italy, France, and China.

In Italy the prestigious publishing house Bibloteca Universale Rizzoli published an annotated edition of *The Prophet* in parallel text,[27] thus giving Gibran a permanent place among the leading writers in world literature in the Italian library.

In France Camille Abousouan's pioneering work and his excellent rendition of *The Prophet* in the 1960s (reprinted with a translation of *The Garden of the Prophet* in 1992) opened France to the influence of Kahlil

Gibran, an influence that has culminated in the publication in 1997 of *Les oeuvres complètes de Kahlil Gibran*[28] *(The Complete Arabic and English Works of Kahlil Gibran)*. The first serious attempt in French at writing a full and comprehensive biography of Kahlil Gibran is Jean Pierre Dahdah's *Kahlil Gibran, une biographie: L'expérience interieur* published in Paris by Albin Michel in 1994. Jean Pierre Dahdah's energy and dedication, evident in his well-researched biography, has also spurred him to produce an anthology entitled *L'oeil du Prophet* (1991) and to translate *The Prophet* (1995).

Dun Mao was the first to translate Gibran into Chinese in 1923. This translation of *The Forerunner* was soon to be followed in 1931 by Bing Xin's translation of *The Prophet*. The leading Chinese Arabist Yi Hong, president of the Association of Research and Study in Arabic Literature, is today the foremost Gibran scholar in China. He has written extensively on Gibran and Arabic literature and has published in Chinese *The Complete Works of Kahlil Gibran* (in three volumes, Kanso Publications, 1994). According to Yi Hong the Chinese consider Gibran among the greatest foreign poets, and as far as Chinese scholars are concerned Gibran is the most popular and respected Arab writer and poet whose works have been translated into the Chinese language.

Although Gibran scholarship still awaits a comprehensive evaluation of his artwork, major exhibitions in prestigious galleries continue to flower, and a resurgence of interest in the man and his work is acknowledged by such influential bodies as U.N.E.S.C.O. which housed an exhibition The World of Kahlil Gibran: A Pictorial Record of His Life and Work at the U.N.E.S.C.O. palace in Paris on March 19–22,1996. In the same year Kahlil Gibran's *The Prophet* was voted by British readers as one of the most popular books of the century,[29] while a year earlier Penguin included extracts of three of Gibran's works – *The Prophet*, *The Madman*, and *The Wanderer* – in a publication program organized to honor the sixtieth anniversary of the publishing house, and which included representative selections from the works of the most famous names in world literature.

Between December 30, 1999 and January 2, 2000 the First International Conference on Kahlil Gibran was held under the auspices of the Kahlil Gibran Research and Studies Project at the University of Maryland, and had the theme "Kahlil Gibran and the Immigrant Traditions". This seminal event, designed to establish a Gibran canon worthy of his exceptional accomplishments, attracted experts and laypeople alike from all parts of the world, and brought together for the first time most of those in the field of Gibran studies in English and other languages.

Notes

INTRODUCTION

1. Eliot, *The Use of Poetry* quoted in Ackroyd, *T. S. Eliot*, 26.
2. Jayyusi, *Trends and Movements*, vol. 1, 99.
3. Rudyard Kipling, "The Ballad of East and West," in *Sixty Poems*, 97.
4. Malarkey, "Vision and Message."
5. Martin L. Wolf, preface to *Secrets of the Heart* (1965), v; Bushrui and al-Kuzbari (eds.), *Gibran: Love Letters*, 16.
6. *The Books of the Century*, Waterstones in association with Channel 4, Sept. 1996.
7. W. B. Yeats to his father, quoted in Murphy, *Prodigal Father*, 501.
8. Mary Haskell, miscellaneous folder, visit on May 5 1908, recorded on May 10, 1908. Chapel Hill papers, quoted in J. and K. Gibran, "The Symbolic Quest of Kahlil Gibran: The Arab as Artist in America," in Hooglund (ed.), *Crossing the Waters*, 162.
9. Josephine Preston Peabody, Dec. 8, 1898, Peabody papers, in Hooglund (ed.), *Crossing the Waters*.
10. Hilu (ed.), *Beloved Prophet* (hereafter referred to as *B.P.*), 89.
11. *The Procession*, p.11. *The Procession* was one of Gibran's Arabic works (*al-Mawakib*), which translates as "The Processions." In his translation George Kheirallah translated it as "The Procession," and we likewise refer to this work as *The Procession* hereafter.
12. *B.P.*, 259.
13. Ibid., 20.
14. Ibid., 258.
15. The phrase was first used by Louise Guiney in a letter to Louise Chandler Moulton, Sept. 10, 1894, and explored in Parrish, "Currents of the Nineties."
16. Review of Woods, "The Poor in Great Cities," 391.
17. *Twentieth Annual Report of the Associated Charities of Boston* (1899), 2.
18. Kahlil Gibran to Ameen Guraieb, March 28, 1908, in *A Self-Portrait* (1972), 21.
19. *B.P.*, 111.
20. Jessie Fremont Beale to Fred Holland Day, Nov. 25, 1896. Quoted in J. and K. Gibran, *Life and World*, 37–38.
21. Kahlil Gibran to Mariita Lawson, May 19, 1920, in Hunayn, *Rasa'il Jubran*, 142.
22. *B.P.*, 125.
23. Kahlil Gibran to Ameen Guraieb, Feb. 12, 1908, in *A Self-Portrait* (1972), 9.
24. K. G. to M. H., May 1, 1911, Chapel Hill papers.
25. Nietzsche, *Thus Spake Zarathustra*, 67.
26. Naimy, *Kahlil Gibran. A Biography*, 89.
27. *Sand and Foam* (1926), 20.
28. *The Prophet*, 130.
29. M. H. to K. G., June 2, 1914, Chapel Hill papers.

30. Letter from the Syria–Mount Lebanon League of Liberation to Theodore Roosevelt, April 5, 1918. For a full account of Gibran's political views, see chap. 7 of this book, which includes material from a series of interviews conducted by Suheil Bushrui with Mikhail Naimy, Gibran's closest friend, from January to May 1978 while Suheil Bushrui was conducting research for a documentary exhibition illustrating the life and work of Naimy. Hereafter these conversations will be cited as Mikhail Naimy Interviews, 1978.

31. Hawi, *Kahlil Gibran*, 222–23.

32. Quoted in Raine, "Poet as Prophet," 67. AE was the nom de plume of George Russell (1867–1935), a contraction of the word "aeon," which the distinguished Irish Renaissance author, artist, and poet once used as a signature.

33. 'Abdul-Hai, *Tradition*, 111.

34. Quoted in Hawi, *Kahlil Gibran*, 158.

35. Sometimes Gibran and his contemporaries use "Syria" – the name by which present-day Syria, Lebanon, Palestine, and Jordan were collectively referred to under Ottoman rule. (See Mikhail Naimy Interviews, 1978 in chap. 8 of this book for a fuller explanation of the term "Syria.")

36. *B.P.*, 47.

37. *Al-Halaqat al-Dhahabiyah*, unpublished speech, quoted in Hawi, *Kahlil Gibran*, 156.

38. "A Poet's Voice," in *A Tear and a Smile*, 194–95.

39. *Spiritual Sayings*, 39.

40. *B.P.*, 183.

41. Kahlil Gibran to Yusuf Huwayik, in *A Self-Portrait* (1972), 26.

42. *B.P.*, 306.

43. Ibid., 41.

44. K. G. to M. H., March 4, 1915, Chapel Hill papers.

45. *B.P.*, 422.

46. Ibid., 390.

47. Bushrui and Haffar al-Kuzbari (eds.), *Gibran: Love Letters*, 59.

48. *B.P.*, 147.

49. June 25, 1913, Chapel Hill papers.

50. *B.P.*, 142.

51. Ibid., 147.

52. *The Madman*, 8.

53. *B.P.*, 217.

54. K. G. to M. H., Nov. 10, 1911, Chapel Hill papers.

55. Nietzsche, *Thus Spake Zarathustra*, 12.

56. K. G. to M. H., March 14, 1915, Chapel Hill papers.

57. Bushrui and al-Kuzbari (eds.), *Gibran: Love Letters*, 16.

58. Mikhail Naimy Interviews, 1978.

59. K. G. to M. H., Nov. 7, 1928, Chapel Hill papers.

60. *The Tempest* in *A Treasury*, 20; and "The Giants" in *Thoughts and Meditations* (1961), 84.

61. *B.P.*, 270.

62. K. G. to M. H., April 29, 1909, Chapel Hill papers.

63. "The Crucified," in *A Treasury*, 154.

64. Honnold (ed.), *Vignettes*, 158.

65. Jayyusi, *Trends and Movements*, vol. 1, 96.

66. Ibid., 91.

67. Ibid., 94, 102.

68. Ibid., 121.

69. Ibid., 122.
70. Arrabitah is unique in the history of modern Arabic literary societies; the experimental groups "Apollo" in Egypt in 1932 and "Shi'r" in Lebanon in 1957 had either to compromise with the forces of convention or publish works they did not always agree with.
71. William Catzeflis, intro. to *The Procession* (1947).
72. Jayyusi, *Trends and Movements*, vol. 1, 122.
73. Ibid., 97.
74. Ibid., 70.
75. Bloom and Tring (eds.), *Romantic Poetry and Prose*, 9.
76. Jayyusi, *Trends and Movements*, vol. 1, 98.
77. Ibid., 95–95.
78. These are Mikhail Naimy's words quoted in Jayyusi, *Trends and Movements*, vol. 1, 115.
79. El-Hage, "William Blake and Kahlil Gibran", *Dahesh Voice*, vol. 2, issue 1, June 1996, 19. The authors wish to acknowledge George El-Hage's work which explores in considerable detail the affinity between Blake and Gibran.
80. Matti Moosa, introduction to Huwayik, *Gibran in Paris*, 20.
81. El-Hage, "William Blake and Kahlil Gibran," 20.
82. Jayyusi, *Trends and Movements*, vol. 1, 97.
83. Ibid., vol. 2, 361.
84. Ibid., 362.
85. Ibid.
86. Gibran, *A Tear and a Smile*, 75.
87. Goblentz, "Gibran's Companion."
88. *Boston Transcript*, December 1926.
89. H. Singer, review of *Secrets of the Heart*, in *Ethics*, 58, 1947, 228–29.
90. *New York Evening Post*, Feb. 1, 1919, 6.
91. Carl Gustav Jung quoted in King, *New Mysticism*, 222.
92. Mikhail Naimy quoting Gibran in *Aramco World*, XV, 6 (1964), 11.
93. *B.P.*, 323.
94. Ibid., 260. George Kheirallah in his introduction to *The Procession* gives Gibran the title "The Bard of Washington Street."
95. Mikhail Naimy in Bushrui and Gotch (eds.), *Gibran of Lebanon: New Papers*, 3.
96. Bushrui and al-Kuzbari (eds.), *Gibran: Love Letters*, 23.
97. Naimy in Bushrui and Gotch (eds.), *Gibran of Lebanon: New Papers*, 4.
98. *B.P.*, 300.
99. Claude Bragdon interview with Gibran in "A Modern Prophet from Lebanon," *Merely Players*.
100. Martin L. Wolf in editor's preface to *A Treasury*, xi.
101. *B.P.*, 423.
102. Ibid., 397.
103. Kahlil Gibran to Mikhail Naimy, 1928, in *A Self-Portrait*, 84.
104. Kahlil Gibran to Mikhail Naimy, August 11, 1923, in ibid., 72.
105. Kahlil Gibran to May Ziadah, 1930, in ibid., 90.
106. *B.P.*, 306.
107. Bercovici, *Around the World*, 40; repr. "The Syrian Quarter," *The Century Magazine*, 86 (July 1924), 354.
108. Kahlil Gibran to Mariita Lawson, September 26, 1921. Published in Hunayn, *Rasa'il Jubran*.

109. Gollomb, "An Arabian Poet," 10.
110. Gail, *Other People, Other Places*, 229.
111. Robert Hillyer, intro. to *A Tear and a Smile*, xi.
112. Bragdon, *More Lives*, 271.
113. *A Self-Portrait*, 15.
114. *Spirits Rebellious*, 103–04.
115. *The Wanderer* (1995), 39.
116. Abdul-Hai, *Tradition*, 110–11.
117. *Mirrors of the Soul*, 46.
118. Mikhail Naimy, *A Biography*, 60.
119. K. G. to M. H., undated, 1904, Chapel Hill papers.
120. *B.P.*, 418.
121. K. G. to M. H., Jan. 31, 1912, Chapel Hill papers.
122. M. H. journal, Dec. 25–29, 1912, Chapel Hill papers.
123. *B.P.*, 103.
124. Alice Raphael in *Twenty Drawings*, xviii.
125. M. H. journal; Jan. 27, 1911, Chapel Hill papers.
126. Ibid., 147.
127. *Spiritual Sayings*, 40.
128. Quoted in J. and K. Gibran, *Life and World*, 261. The authors of *Kahlil Gibran: Man and Poet*, acknowledge their debt to Jean and Kahlil Gibran, whose seminal work particularly sheds lights on Gibran's early years in Boston.
129. Jayyusi, *Trends and Movements*, 101.
130. Ibid., 107.
131. Hawi, *Kahlil Gibran*, 283.
132. *Time*, quoted in Bushrui and Munro (eds.), *Essays and Introductions*, 1.
133. *B.P.*, 137.
134. Wilber, *Holographic Paradigm*, 2.
135. *The Prophet*, 110.
136. Russell, *Living Torch*, 169.
137. Sarwat Okasha, intro. to *The Prophet*, trans. S. Okasha (1959), xxxviii.
138. George Kheirallah, "The Life of Gibran Khalil Gibran," in *The Procession*, 17.
139. Sarwat Okasha, intro. to *The Prophet*, xxx viii.
140. Bragdon, *Merely Players*, 146.
141. *B.P.*, 81.
142. Jayyusi, *Trends and Movements*, 97.
143. Kahlil Gibran, *Iram, City of Lofty Pillars*, in *Secrets of the Heart*, 272.
144. *The Garden of the Prophet* (1954), 6.
145. Ibid., 23, 26.
146. Jayyusi, *Trends and Movements*, 96.
147. *The Garden of the Prophet* (1954), 21.
148. *Sand and Foam*, 22.
149. *Spiritual Sayings*, 11.
150. Capra, *The Tao of Physics*, 335.
151. Jayyusi, *Trends and Movements*, 101.
152. *B.P.*, 400.
153. "The Blind Force," in *A Tear and a Smile*, 113.
154. Hitti, "Gibran's Place and Influence," 31–33.
155. A professor of English at Georgetown University, *Washington Times*, April 11, 1991. Professor Hect's remarks show an astonishing lack of critical acumen.

156. Those who have suggested the adoption of a new critical mechanism have included George Russell (AE) and Robert Hillyer.
157. Ouspensky, *Tertium Organum*, 198.
158. Hawi, *Kahlil Gibran*, 281–82.
159. K. G. to M. H., Aug. 7, 1914, Chapel Hill papers.
160. *B.P.*, 411.
161. Ibid., 287.
162. Ibid., 147.
163. Ibid., 429.
164. Ibid., 401.
165. Ibid., 294.
166. M. H. journal, April 26, 1914, Chapel Hill papers.
167. *The Madman*, 71.
168. *B.P.*, 350.
169. Ibid., 104.
170. Ibid., 113.
171. M. H. journal, Dec. 25, 1912, Chapel Hill papers.
172. *B.P.*, 133.
173. Ibid., 69; Naimy, *A Biography*, 37, 40.
174. *B.P.*, 69.
175. Ibid., 113.
176. Ibid., 136.
177. Ibid., 68.
178. M. H. journal, Dec. 25–29, 1912, Chapel Hill papers.
179. Ibid., 229.
180. Coward, "Renan's Religion."

1. BEGINNINGS

1. Gibran's full name in Arabic was Gibran Khalil Gibran, the middle name being his father's. It is a convention among Arabs to use the father's name after one's first name. He always signed his full name in his Arabic works, but he dropped the first name in his English writings. He did this and changed the correct spelling of "Khalil" to "Kahlil" at the instigation of his English teacher at the Boston school he attended between 1895 and 1897. The family name Gibran is related to the Arabic word *Jabre*, which means to restore to harmony, to bring unequal parts to unity, as in *algebra*.
2. Bushrui and al-Kuzbari (eds.), *Gibran: Love Letters*, 45.
3. Hawi, *Kahlil Gibran* (1963), 82–90. Hawi interviewed many people about the family including Mrs. Hanni Kayruz, Mrs. Shams Tawq, and Gibran's cousins, Mr. Bulus Bitar and Mrs. Jirjis Rahmi, August 1957.
4. *B.P.*, 26. The nature of this tense and turbulent relationship between Gibran and his father was confirmed in Mikhail Naimy Interviews, 1978.
5. *B.P.*, 257.
6. Ibid., 32.
7. Hawi, *Kahlil Gibran*, 83.
8. The name of Kahlil Gibran's sister has been transliterated in various ways, but the most common spelling is "Marianna." This is the spelling used in Naimy, *Life and Work*; *B.P.*; J. and K. Gibran, *Life and World*; and Young, *This Man From Lebanon*.
9. The spelling of Gibran's second sister, "Sultanah," follows the transliteration used in Hawi, *Kahlil Gibran* and in Bushrui, *Kahlil Gibran of Lebanon*.

10. Hawi, *Kahlil Gibran*, 83.
11. *B.P.*, 336.
12. *The Broken Wings* (1972), 92.
13. Bushrui and al-Kuzbari (eds.), *Gibran: Love Letters*, 30.
14. Maronite priests were able to marry. Although Maronite contacts with the West over the centuries must have been tenuous, a deep sense of affinity with Christian Europe grew amongst the Maronites, and this was consciously fed by France from the seventeenth century onwards through the provision of Jesuit teachers and trade. So successful was *la mission civilisatrice*, which reflected French imperial interests as a Mediterranean power, that many Maronites not only assumed French as their first language, but also "conceived a hopeless love of French" civilization: McDowall, *Lebanon*, 7.
15. Nadeem Naimy, *Mikhail Naimy: an Introduction*, 21.
16. Ibid., 20.
17. Hawi, *Kahlil Gibran*, 10.
18. Ibid., 25.
19. Kahlil Gibran, "From a Speech by Khalil the Heretic," in Bushrui, *Introduction* 23, 26.
20. Naimy, *A Biography*, 22–23.
21. Young, *This Man from Lebanon* (1981), 7.
22. *B.P.*, 135.
23. Ibid., 429.
24. Ibid., 135.
25. Although some biographers claim it is difficult to balance this incident with the hardships of Gibran's childhood (*B.P.*, 7), the discovery of Gibran's letters to May Ziadah sheds a new light on Gibran's introduction to Leonardo, with Gibran himself confirming this story to May in 1925 (Bushrui and al-Kuzbari (eds.), *Gibran: Love Letters*, 88).
26. Young, *This Man from Lebanon* (1981), 7.
27. Bushrui and al-Kuzbari (eds.), *Gibran: Love Letters*, 88.
28. *B.P.*, 397. Alice Raphael in her introduction to *Twenty Drawings by Kahil Gibran* thought that in Gibran's work, the influence of Leonardo da Vinci is detectable (Bushrui (ed.), *Introduction*, 97). Likewise Claude Bragdon in "A Modern Prophet From Lebanon" wrote of Gibran's paintings as having a "strikingly Leonardoesque quality" (in *Merely Players*, 143).
29. Giorgio Vasari (*Le Vite de' piu eccellenti architettori, pittori e scultori italiana, Raghianti ed.* (Milan, 1942–50)), quoted in Bramley, *Leonardo*, 5.
30. Bushrui and al-Kuzbari (eds.), *Gibran: Love Letters*, 88.
31. *B.P.*, 371.
32. Ba'al was a central figure of Phoenician beliefs according to Ugaritic accounts. Ba'al was widely worshiped as a warrior-god in Canaan. The son of either Dagon, the corn-god, or of El, chief Ugaritic deity, Ba'al's consort was Ashtoreth (Ishtar), the goddess of battle; his daughters were Mist and Dew (see Hinnells (ed.), *The Penguin Dictionary of Religions*, 59.)
33. Quoted in an introduction to *A Tear and a Smile*, ix.
34. "Dust of the Ages and the Eternal Flame," in *Nymphs of the Valley*, 30. Gibran also wrote "The Poet from Baalbek," a story with the theme of reincarnation (*Thoughts and Meditations*, 1–8). Ameen Rihani in his magisterial work *The Book of Khalid*, which was to later influence Gibran's own writings, refers to Baalbek as being the place where Shakib spent much of his childhood.
35. "Amidst the Ruins," in *A Tear and a Smile*, 35.

36. *B.P.*, 343.
37. *A Treasury* (1991), 26–27.
38. K. G. to M. H., March 1, 1914, Chapel Hill papers.
39. Quotation marks as in Bushrui's "Gibran and the Cedars," in Bushrui and Munro (eds.), *Gibran of Lebanon: New Papers*, 24.
40. *B.P.*, 341.
41. Ibid., 248.
42. Ibid., 333.
43. Alternate spelling of the Lebanese village Bisharri.
44. Nov. 1915, Chapel Hill papers, quoted in J. and K. Gibran, *Life and World*, 15, 85.
45. Naimy, *A Biography*, 23–24.
46. *A Tear and a Smile*, 57.
47. Ibid., 92.
48. Isaiah 35:2.
49. Some of Gibran's dreams are described in *B.P.*
50. *A Self-Portrait* (1960), 14, 15.
51 Ibid., 22.
52. *B.P.*, 21.
53. Kahlil Gibran, "From a Speech by Khalil the Heretic," in Bushrui, *Introduction*, 24, 25.
54. Antonious al-Besh'alani.
55. The family of Joseph 'Arbili from Damascus.
56. Yousof Meziarah, who traveled to Rio via Portugal.

2. THE NEW WORLD

1. Whitman, *Song of Myself*, 114.
2. Spiller et al. (eds.), *Literary History*, 346.
3. Sheldrake, *Rebirth of Nature*, 50.
4. Emerson, *Selected Essays*, 38–39.
5. Thoreau, *The Maine Woods*, 314–15.
6. Bates, *The United States*, 37.
7. Review of Woods, "The Poor in Great Cities," 391, quoted in J. and K. Gibran, *Life and World*, 25–26. The authors acknowledge their debt to J. and K. Gibran's work which sheds considerable light on Gibran's early Boston days.
8. J. and K. Gibran, *Life and World*, 32.
9. Hourani and Shehadi (eds.), *The Lebanese in the World*, 147.
10. July 23, 1916, Chapel Hill papers, quoted in J. and K. Gibran, *Life and World*, 30.
11. "The Perfect World," in *The Madman*, 71.
12. Sept. 19, 1915, Chapel Hill papers, quoted in J. and K. Gibran, *Life and World*, 31.
13. Sept. 3, 1920, Chapel Hill papers, quoted in J. and K. Gibran, *Life and World*, 31.
14. J. and K. Gibran, *Life and World*, 54. The authors again acknowledge Jean and Kahlil Gibran's work in providing insights into the life of Fred Holland Day and his relationship with Gibran.
15. Ibid., 44.
16. From an unpublished article, Eugene Nassar, "Kahlil Gibran after Fifty Years," quoted in El-Hage, "William Blake and Kahlil Gibran," 18. Different scholars have given different opinions about when Gibran was first introduced to Blake. El-Hage concludes that "there is evidence from his letters, and from the letters of those who were in close contact with him during his early years in Boston, that Gibran knew some of Blake's poetry and drawings, along with other major Romantic poets.

However, this knowledge of Blake was neither deep nor complete" (ibid., 28). El-Hage's thesis has been serialized in *Dahesh Voice*, the first instalment published in vol. 2, no. 3 (December 1996).

17. Maeterlinck, *Treasure of the Humble*, 25–26.
18. K. G. to M. H., Nov. 10, 1909, Chapel Hill papers.
19. M. H. journal, Oct. 22, 1912, Chapel Hill papers. In Barbara Young's early biography of Gibran, *This Man from Lebanon* (1945), she records Gibran as saying of Shelley: "He is a world in himself. His soul is that of an excited god, who, being sad, weary and homesick, passed the time singing of other worlds. He is in a way the least English of the English poets, and the most Oriental" (170).
20. K. G. to M. H., Oct. 6, 1915, Chapel Hill papers.
21. Letter from Lilla Perry to Fred Holland Day, undated, quoted in J. and K. Gibran, *Life and World*, 62.
22. This incident is corroborated in *B.P.*, 68 and in Naimy, *Life and Works* (1974), 31–40.
23. This great honor was first brought to light by the research of J. and K. Gibran who were alerted by a Boston book dealer to the multi-colored hard-bound cover of L. C. Page's publication *Omar Khayyám* which was adorned by Gibran's work. See J. and K. Gibran, *Life and World*, 427.
24. The *Rubáiyát of Omar Khayyám* was first translated into English by Edward Fitzgerald in 1859.
25. Aug. 27, 1915, Chapel Hill papers, quoted in J. and K. Gibran, *Life and World*, 63.
26. Ibid.
27. Naimy in *Life and Works* details this episode and reports on Kamileh's concerns: 37–38.

3. RETURNING TO THE ROOTS

1. William Kazan, "Arabian Encounters" (unpublished), 1989.
2. The reminiscences by Father Yusuf Haddad quoted in this chapter have been translated by the authors from the Arabic text quoted in 'Abbud, *Juddud wa Qudama*'.
3. Nicholson, *A Literary History of the Arabs*, 443.
4. al-Bustani, *Udaba' al-'Arab*, 211.
5. Lewis, *The Arabs in History*, 166–67.
6. *Copies of Original Letters*, 237.
7. Gibb, *Modern Trends*, 39 ff.
8. Cheikho, *al-Adab al-Arabiyyah*, 43.
9. The speech *Khutbah* was published the same year in book form, quoted in Naimy, *Mikhail Naimy*, 47–48.
10. Naimy, *Mikhail Naimy*, 52.
11. Ibid., 55.
12. The version of *L'avare*, together with two other plays by al-Naqqash and selections from his poetry, were published posthumously in one volume, with an introduction by Marun's brother, Niqula, under the title *Arazat Lubnan* (*Cedar Tree of Lebanon*), Beirut, 1869.
13. Gibb, "Studies in Contemporary Arabic Literature," 752, quotes *al-Manar XVI* (1331), 875, a Muslim Egyptian paper established 1898, as saying, "Journalism in Egypt before the *Mu'ayyad* (1889) was exclusively dependent on the Syrian Christians."
14. The novel is *Huyam fi Jinan al-Sham*, published piecemeal in *al-Jinan*, 1870.
15. As a student in later years in Paris, a youthful Gibran fell under the spell of Nietzsche's

Thus Spake Zarathustra.

16. This book, *Ibn Rushd wa Falsafatoh*, was originally published piecemeal in Antun's periodical *al-Jami'ah.*
17. Hawi, *Kahlil Gibran*, 61.
18. Marrash, *Ghabat al-Haqq*, 63, quoted in Hawi, *Kahlil Gibran*, 59, 60.
19. Ishaq, *al-Durar*, 51–2.
20. Ishaq, *al-Durar*, 243, quoted in Hawi, *Kahlil Gibran*, 52.
21. Ibid., 51–52, 44–45, 132–34.
22. Hawi, *Kahlil Gibran*, 57.
23. 'Abbud, *Ruwwad al-Nahdah*, 92.
24. Trans. Jamil Nakhlah Mudawwar, Beirut, 1882.
25. Trans. Najib Mikha'il Gharghur, Alexandria, 1888.
26. Hawi, *Kahlil Gibran*, 86.
27. Interview with Yusuf Huwayik, September 1957, quoted in ibid.
28. Ibid., 87.
29. Yusuf al-Huwayik quoted in ibid.
30. April 19, 1911, Chapel Hill papers, quoted in J. and K. Gibran, *Life and World*, 83.
31. Hawi, *Kahlil Gibran*, 87.
32. *B.P.*, 26–27.
33. Hawi, *Kahlil Gibran*, 87.
34. *B.P.*, 336.
35. *A Self-Portrait* (1972), 24.
36. Hawi, *Kahlil Gibran*, 88, interview with Sa'idi al Dahir.
37. Interviews, August 1957, first publ. in Jabr, *Jibran*, 27–28, cited in Hawi, *Kahlil Gibran,* 88.
38. *The Prophet: Introduction and Annotations*, 161.
39. Hawi, *Kahlil Gibran*, 88.
40. Although Gibran was later to tell Mary Haskell that "not one of the experiences in the book has been mine," scholars suggest that *The Broken Wings* was probably semi-autobiographical (Bushrui, *Kahlil Gibran of Lebanon*, 21; J. and K. Gibran, *Life and World*, 85–86; Hawi, *Kahlil Gibran*, 150; Takla, "Woman Characters," 367).
41. *Broken Wings*, 18–19.
42. Ibid., 83.
43. Ibid., 104.
44. Takla, "Women Characters," 35.
45. *Broken Wings*, 105–06.
46. Naimy, "Mind and Thought," 57.

4. OVERCOMING TRAGEDY

1. Handlin, *Boston's Immigrants*, 115.
2. *B.P.*, 177.
3. Hawi states that he was in Beirut (*Kahlil Gibran*, 89), whereas J. and K. Gibran write that no source exists which can "trace the exact route of the youth's return to the United States in 1902" (*Life and World*, 90).
4. *B.P.*, 177.
5. Ibid., 179.
6. Ibid.
7. Ibid.
8. Ibid., 180.

9. Ibid., 180–81: Boutros dies of "congested lungs and exhaustion."
10. Bushrui and al-Kuzbari (eds.), *Gibran: Love Letters*, 30–31.
11. Ibid., 30.
12. *B.P.*, 315.
13. Ibid.
14. Ibid., 33–34.
15. K. G. to M. H., March 15, 1910, Chapel Hill papers.
16. *Virtue's Household Physician*, 372.
17. Hawi, *Kahlil Gibran*, 90.
18. Interview with Halim Rahbani, July 1957, and Mr. Duwayhi, quoted in ibid.
19. Josephine Preston Peabody to Kahlil Gibran, first draft, December 12, 1898, quoted in J. and K. Gibran, *Life and World*, 79.
20. Josephine Preston Peabody to Kahlil Gibran, Dec. 22, 1902, quoted in J. and K. Gibran, *Life and World*, 102.
21. Ibid., Nov. 21, 1902, quoted in J. and K. Gibran, *Life and World*, 100.
22. Published in 1911. Josephine's play *The Piper* won first prize in an international playwriting competition at Stratford-upon-Avon in 1910.
23. This interpretation is given in J. and K. Gibran, *Life and World*, 101.
24. Josephine Peabody, diary, Jan. 19, 1903, quoted in ibid., 106.
25. Josephine Peabody to Mary Mason, March 9, 1903, quoted in ibid., 109.
26. *The Iris* (Wellesley College, Tau Zeta Epsilon Society, 1903), 4–5.
27. Letter from Gertrude Smith to Fred Holland Day, Nov. 3, 1903, quoted in J. and K. Gibran, *Life and World*, 126.
28. *Boston Evening Transcript*, May 3, 1904, 10.
29. Ibid.
30. *B.P.*, 374.
31. Ibid., 22.
32. Josephine Peabody, diary, May 23, 1904, quoted in J. and K. Gibran, *Life and World*, 139.
33. Guraieb, "Jubran Khalil Jubran," 689–704.
34. "A Vision," in *A Tear and a Smile*, 31.
35. *Boston Sunday Globe*, Nov. 13, 1904, 5.
36. Josephine Peabody, diary, Nov. 26, 1904, quoted in J. and K. Gibran, *Life and World*, 144.
37. This correspondence is exceptionally well documented in two overlapping but by no means identical books based on their correspondence and Mary's journal (see *B.P.* and Otto (ed.), *Love Letters*).
38. K. G. to M. H., undated 1904, Chapel Hill papers.
39. *A Tear and a Smile*, 32–33.
40. Ibid., 34.
41. Burckhardt, *Sufi Doctrine*, quoted in Stoddart, *Sufism*, 45.
42. "Before the Throne of Beauty," *A Tear and a Smile*, 56.
43. *Voice of the Master* (1973), 57.
44. Reference to the letters between Kahlil Gibran and Gertrude Barrie are to be found in J. and K. Gibran, *Life and World*, 423–25.
45. Al-Ghurayyib, "Dhikrayat Jubran," 6–10.
46. Hawi, *Kahlil Gibran*, 121.
47. *A Tear and a Smile*, 71.
48. Ibid., 40.
49. "Lament of The Field," in ibid., 71–72.

50. Bushrui, "Poet of Ecology," 38–40.
51. *A Tear and a Smile*, 83–84.
52. Ibid., 192.
53. Ibid., 193.
54. J. and K. Gibran, *Life and World*, 154.
55. *Nymphs of the Valley*, 6.
56. Ibid., 13–14.
57. Ibid., 41.
58. Ibid., 49, 50.
59. The Husainis were an Arab tribe dwelling in tents around Baalbek.
60. Ibid., 24, 25, 31.
61. *B.P.*, 427.
62. "The Poet from Baalbek," *Thoughts and Meditations* (1973), 2, 5–6, 7.
63. Gibran once told Mary: "To me all reality is movement. Repose is the harmony of motion. But Nirvana is motionless" (*B.P.*, 335).
64. M. H. journal, March 27, 1908, Chapel Hill papers.
65. Professor A. J. Arberry, quoted in Shah, *The Sufis*, 116.
66. Rumi, *Mathnawi-i-Ma'nawi*, quoted in *Reincarnation*, 147.
67. Christie-Murray, *Reincarnation*, 69.
68. Mary Haskell (MH) to Sarah Armstrong, August 23, 1906, Chapel Hill papers, quoted in J. and K. Gibran, *Life and World*, 158.
69. Ibid.
70. *The Cage* was published in 1907.
71. *A Tear and a Smile*, 99.
72. Naimy, *A Biography*, 66.
73. M. H. journal, May 5, 1908, Chapel Hill papers.
74. *A Self-Portrait* (1972), 9–10.
75. MEH is Mary Elizabeth Haskell.
76. "The Beauty of Death," in *A Tear and a Smile*, 168.

5. THE CITY OF LIGHT

1. Benjamin, *Paris*.
2. De Vigny, *Paris*, 162.
3. Ibid.
4. Honoré de Balzac, "Paris en 1831," *Oeuvres diverses*, 3, 610–17, quoted in Prendergast, *Paris and the Nineteenth Century*, 6.
5. The 1900 World Fair, official statement by General M. Picard, quoted in Roman, *Paris 1890s*, 79.
6. Predominantly these artists included Paul Cézanne, Alfred Sisley, Claude Monet, Auguste Renoir, Frédéric Bazille, and Camille Pissarro.
7. Leicht, *History of the World's Art*, 298.
8. Gombrich, *The Story of Art*, 406.
9. Osborne (ed.), *Oxford Companion to Art*, 814.
10. Hemmings and Niess (eds.), *Emile Zola*, 148–49.
11. Hartley (ed.), *The Penguin Book of French Verse*, 489.
12. K. G. to M. H., July 13, 1908, Chapel Hill papers.
13. *A Self-Portrait* (1974), 19.
14. *Spirits Rebellious*, 76.
15. Ibid., 103.

16. Ibid., 110.
17. Ibid., 114.
18. Ibid., 122.
19. Ibid., 71.
20. Ibid., 73.
21. Ibid., 98.
22. Ibid., 107.
23. Ibid., 98.
24. Ibid., 26.
25. Ibid., 31–32.
26. Ibid.
27. Ibid., 10.
28. Ibid., 20.
29. The story actually happened in north Lebanon in the latter half of the nineteenth century, and was told to Gibran by a relation of one of the characters in the story (see footnote on *Spirits Rebellious*, 41).
30. Ibid., 45–46.
31. Ibid., 49.
32. Ibid., 50.
33. Ibid.
34. Ibid., 51.
35. Ibid., 11–12.
36. Dec. 26, 1917, Chapel Hill Papers, quoted in J. and K. Gibran, *Life and World*, 306.
37. Kahlil Gibran in a letter to Nakhli Gibran, March 15, 1908, in *A Self-Portrait* (1972), 15–16.
38. Hemmings, *Culture and Society*, 8.
39. Jayyusi, *Trends and Movements*, vol. 2.
40. Only a few hundred copies reached Lebanon and Syria. Some commentators have written that his books were burnt in public in a Beirut marketplace (Daoudi, *The Meaning of Kahlil Gibran*, 78; Waterfield (ed.), *The Voice of Kahlil Gibran*, xiv; Ghougassian, *Wings of Thought*, 38; and Martin L. Wolf in his introduction to *A Treasury*, 1974, xix), but there is no substantial evidence to support this claim.
41. Sept. 3, 1914, Chapel Hill papers, quoted in J. and K. Gibran, *Life and World*, 190.
42. K. G. to M. H., Dec. 20, 1908, Chapel Hill papers.
43. Nov. 20, 1908, Chapel Hill papers, quoted in J. and K. Gibran, *Life and World*, 180.
44. K. G. to M. H. Nov. 8, 1908, Chapel Hill papers.
45. Yusuf Huwayyik in his *Gibran in Paris* memoirs writes: "The noisy atmosphere did not suit [Gibran's] temperament, and he didn't feel he was learning anything from his teacher at the school, Jean Paul-Laureance."
46. Béronneau (1869–1937) exhibited at the "Salons des Artistes Français et Independents," obtaining medals in 1900 and 1913 and a gold medal in 1926, Chevalier de la Légion d'Honneur. His works are to be found in the Museums of Bordeaux, Chaumont, Clermont-Ferrand, and Valence.
47. K. G. to M. H., Jan. 2, 1909, Chapel Hill papers.
48. K. G. to M. H., Feb. 1909, Chapel Hill papers.
49. Naimy, *A Biography*, 88.
50. By the time Gibran came to publish *The Madman* in 1918, his meeting with Rodin and his kinship with Blake had fused into the idea, improbable rather than impossible, that Rodin had himself compared Gibran to Blake. "I know of no one else in whom

drawing and poetry are so linked together as to make him a new Blake," said the sculptor, according to Alice Raphael in her introduction to Gibran's *Twenty Drawings*. Other authors credit Rodin, or in some cases his associate Henri de Beaufort, with describing Gibran simply as "the William Blake of the twentieth century" (for example Anthony Ferris in his preface to *A Self-Portrait*, 1974). Gibran's American publisher Alfred Knopf, not unnaturally, chose the latter phrase to adorn the dust-covers of *The Madman*, no doubt feeling that it mattered little whether either quotation was true. Whether apocryphal or not, they do serve to highlight the genuine affinity between Gibran and Blake.

51. Gibran had been introduced to Blake's work in Boston in the 1890s but his knowledge of Blake was neither deep nor complete (El-Hage, "William Blake and Kahlil Gibran," 28).
52. Naimy, *A Biography*, 89.
53. K. G. to M. H., May 10, 1916, Chapel Hill papers.
54. K. G. to M. H., Oct. 6, 1915, Chapel Hill papers.
55. Naimy, *A Biography*, 91.
56. K. G. to M. H., Feb. 7, 1909, Chapel Hill papers; K. G. to M. H., March 14, 1909, Chapel Hill papers.
57. *A Tear and a Smile*, 143.
58. *Wellesley College News*, May 26, 1909, p. 4: "The characteristic of his treatment of the human form in the color work is truth with the greatest simplicity; it is almost pure outline work and yet the impression is rounded softness."
59. *B.P.*, 17.
60. Ibid., 418.
61. Osborne (ed.), *Oxford Companion to Art*, 209.
62. *B.P.*, 17.
63. K. G. to M. H., May 10, 1910, Chapel Hill papers.
64. K. G. to M. H., Oct. 20, 1909, Chapel Hill papers.
65. Huwayyik, *Gibran in Paris*, 67.
66. *B.P.*, 137.
67. Huwayyik, *Gibran in Paris*, 95–96.
68. K. G. to M. H., June 23, 1909, Chapel Hill papers, quoted in J. and K. Gibran, *Life and World*, 186.
69. Osborne (ed.), *Oxford Companion to Art*, 867.
70. Huwayyik, *Gibran in Paris*, 65–66, 68.
71. *B.P.*, 125.
72. K. G. to M. H., Oct. 20, 1909, Chapel Hill papers.
73. K. G. to M. H., May 10, 1910, Chapel Hill papers.
74. *Les milles nouvelle nouvelles* (Paris, 1910).
75. Huwayyik, *Gibran in Paris*, 142.
76. Alfred de Vigny, *Paris*, 162.
77. K. G. to M. H., May 10, 1910, Chapel Hill papers.
78. Huwayyik, *Gibran in Paris*, 94–95.
79. Sept. 2, 1914, Chapel Hill papers, quoted in J. and K. Gibran, *Life and World*, 189.
80. K. G. to M. H., Oct. 20, 1909, Chapel Hill papers.
81. Huwayyik, *Gibran in Paris*, 61–62.
82. Hawi, *Kahlil Gibran*, 98.
83. Huwayyik, *Gibran in Paris*, 97.
84. Hawi, *Kahlil Gibran*, 167.
85. Grimsley, *The Philosophy of Rousseau*, 75.

86. Ibid., 1062–63.
87. *B.P*, 93.
88. Nietzsche, *Thus Spake Zarathustra*, 16.
89. Schenk, *European Romantics*, 246.
90. Kaufman, *Nietzsche*, 419. Indeed, many of the greatest Arab and European writers of the twentieth century, including Malraux, Mann, Hesse, Rihani, Naimy, Gide, Sarte, Camus, W. B. Yeats, Iqbal, George Bernard Shaw, and T. S. Eliot were inspired by the dynamic power of his philosophy and his dramatically impassioned style. Yeats called Nietzsche "the strange enchanter" (Hane, *Yeats*, 187).
91. P. D. Ouspensky (1878–1947) wrote: "Nietzsche did not or would not understand that his superman was to a considerable extent the product of *Christian* thought" (*New Model*, 127). Ouspensky, Russian philosopher, author, and a contemporary thinker who later became a pupil of George Ivanovitch Gurdjieff, was a writer Gibran recommended to the readership of the Arab world.
92. Naimy, *A Biography*, 119.
93. Huwayyik, *Gibran in Paris*, 133.
94. Evidence suggests that *Thus Spake Zarathustra* was the only one of Nietzsche's works that Gibran ever read (S. Wild, "Nietzsche and Gibran," in Bushrui and Gotch (eds.), *Gibran of Lebanon: New Papers*, 67, 74; Bushrui in *The Prophet*, 42; Bushrui, *Kahlil Gibran of Lebanon*, 60).
95. Letter from Kahlil Gibran to Adele Watson, Naimy, *A Biography*, 124.
96. Hawi, *Kahlil Gibran*, 210.
97. *Spirits Rebellious*, 116.
98. Nietzsche, *Thus Spake Zarathustra*, 81.
99. *The Forerunner* (1974), 1.
100. Nietzsche, *Thus Spake Zarathustra*, 192.
101. *The Madman*, 41.
102. Ibid., 71.
103. Nietzsche, *Thus Spake Zarathustra*, 46.
104. *B.P*, 36.
105. Naimy, *A Biography*, 142.
106. *B.P*, 137.
107. Ameen Rihani (1876–1940).
108. K. G. to M. H., June 5, 1919, Chapel Hill papers.
109. K. G. to M. H., June 5, 1910, Chapel Hill papers.
110. Bushrui, "Arab–American Cultural Relations."
111. *Unpublished Letters*, 9.
112. Naimy, *Lebanese Prophets*, 14.
113. Rihani, *Rasa'il Amin al-Rihani*, 9.
114. Rihani, *Aina Tajid Amin al-Rihani*, 25.
115. Rihani, *Nubza fith-Thawra el-Faransiya*, 1902.
116. Quoted in *A Chant of Mystics*, 23.
117. Ibid., 106.
118. Rihani's *The Book of Khalid* influenced the writer Mikhail Naimy in his eponymous *The Book of Mirdad*, his first English work, published in Beirut in 1948.
119. K. G. to M. H., July 24, 1910, Chapel Hill papers.
120. K. G. to M. H., July 24, 1910, Chapel Hill papers.
121. *Unpublished Letters*, August 23, 1910, quoted in Bushrui and Gotch (eds.), *Gibran of Lebanon: New Papers*, 82.
122. Huwayyik, *Gibran in Paris*, 173–76.

123. K. G. to M. H., Aug. 30, 1910, Chapel Hill papers.
124. K. G. to M. H., Aug. 30, 1910, Chapel Hill papers.
125. *Unpublished Letters*, October 17, 1910, quoted in Bushrui and Gotch (eds.), *Gibran of Lebanon: New Papers*, 83.
126. *B.P.*, 296.
127. Keynes (ed.), *Blake: Complete Writings* (hereafter *Blake*), 210.
128. Ibid.
129. Reminiscences of Samuel Palmer, quoted in Raine, *Blake and the New Age*, 2.
130. Ibid.
131. *Spiritual Sayings*, 34.
132. *A Midsummer Night's Dream*, act V, scene 1.
133. Raine, *Blake and the New Age*, 9.
134. *Blake*, 750.
135. The cornerstone of Christianity as understood by Blake is "the forgiveness of sins" (Raine, *Blake and the New Age*, 198; *Blake*, 621).
136. *Blake*, 755.
137. *Jesus, the Son of Man* (1993), 107.
138. Ibid., 3.
139. Ibid., 35.
140. Ibid., 67.
141. Ibid., 145.
142. Ibid., 146.
143. Ibid., 62.
144. Ibid., 215.
145. *Blake*, 777.
146. *Sand and Foam*, 29–30.
147. Ibid., 61–62.
148. *Blake*, 622.
149. Ibid., 216.
150. Ibid., 210.
151. Ibid.
152. Ibid., 212.
153. Ibid., 215.
154. Ibid., 214.
155. *Broken Wings* (1989), 84.
156. Ibid., 105.
157. Ibid., 84.
158. *Blake*, 533.
159. Ibid.
160. Ibid.
161. *Spiritual Sayings*, 19.
162. Ibid., 13.
163. Ibid., 37.
164. *Sand and Foam*, 40.
165. Blake, *The Marriage of Heaven and Hell*, xxii.
166. *Blake*, 431.
167. Ibid., 675.
168. Ibid., 153.
169. *Sand and Foam*, 45.
170. *B.P.*, 81.

171. Ibid.
172. Blake, 785.
173. Ibid., 717.
174. Ibid., 98.
175. *Spiritual Sayings*, 81.
176. *Blake*, 782.
177. Ibid., 707.
178. Witcutt, *Blake: A Psychological Study*, 17.
179. El-Hage, "William Blake and Kahlil Gibran," 132.
180. *Blake*, 623.
181. *A Tear and a Smile*, 134.
182. *The Prophet*, 140.
183. *Sand and Foam*, 46.
184. *Blake*, 622.
185. *B.P.*, 193.
186. *Spiritual Sayings*, 7.
187. Ibid., 24.
188. *B.P.*, 385.
189. *Ibid.*, 48.
190. Brown, *The Romantic Imagination*, 11.
191. *Spiritual Sayings*, 40.
192. *Blake*, 778.
193. Quoted in Young, *This Man from Lebanon* (1945), 124.
194. *Blake*, 152.
195. K. G. to M. H., July 31, 1909, Chapel Hill papers.
196. *The Prophet*, 113.
197. According to J. and K. Gibran (*Life and World*, 204), Mary Haskell's theory on reincarnation in relation to Blake and Gibran was that Blake died in 1827, Dante Gabriel Rossetti was born in 1828 and died in 1882, and Gibran was born in 1883.
198. *The Prophet*, 154–55.
199. In his Introduction to *A Tear and a Smile* the poet Robert Hillyer succinctly expresses the kinship between Blake and Gibran:

> Many convictions were common to both: a hatred of sham and binding orthodoxy, personified by evil priests; the manumission of physical love from the bonds of convention in order to attain spiritual completeness; the perception of beauty in the moment that seems to be fleeting but is, in truth, everlasting; and the discovery of miracles in seasonal nature and the commonplace things of daily living. Both warred against reason in the name of imagination. Both defied the snares of logic to cut a straight wingpath directly to God.
>
> To both Blake and Gibran these revelations are the gift of the poet. The Poet and the Prophet are one. (*A Tear and a Smile*, xi)

200. *Blake*, 817.
201. *The Prophet*, 93.
202. *Blake*, 424.
203. *B.P.*, 48.
204. Witcutt, *Blake: A Psychological Study*, 19.
205. *The Prophet*, 134.
206. *Blake*, 151.
207. In Gibran's symbolic structure "clothes" represent attachment to obsolete traditions.

208. *The Prophet*, 99.
209. *Blake*, 214. The forest becomes the metaphor on which Gibran's long Arabic poem *al-Mawakib* (*The Procession*, 1919) is built.

6. THE POET-PAINTER IN SEARCH

1. Persis M. Lane, school historian, quoted in *B.P.*, 312.
2. *Wellesley College News*, Nov. 1896, 110, quoted in J. and K. Gibran, *Life and World*, 137.
3. January 27, 1894, Chapel Hill papers, quoted in J. and K. Gibran, *Life and World*, 138.
4. Howells, *Literature and Life*, 282–83.
5. Aristides Evangelus Phoutrides was later to become assistant professor of classical literature at Yale University, but soon after his appointment he was tragically the victim of a drowning accident in August 1923.
6. *B.P.*, 132.
7. Ibid.
8. Ibid., 107.
9. Ibid., 187.
10. Ibid., 287.
11. Ibid., 396.
12. Ibid., 362.
13. Ibid., 358.
14. Ibid., 237.
15. M. H. journal, Dec. 7, 1910, Chapel Hill papers.
16. Gibran considered Swinburne to be the greatest contemporary English poet: K. G. to M. H., April 29, 1909, Chapel Hill papers.
17. *B.P.*, 20. Such traits cannot always be interpreted as intellectual dishonesty but (as in the case of great writers such as Swift and Yeats, who also fabricated and embellished their biographies) may be constructed as manifestations of the poetic mind's desire to create an imaginative and mythological world. The Irish playwright Denis Johnson wrote a brilliant and humorous account of Jonathan Swift's embellishments in "The Dreaming Dust," *Dramatic Works*, 401–04.
18. Similar responses were made by Gibran on August 25, 1915, when he spoke of a Gibran in the thirteenth or fourteenth century who went to Europe to start a new crusade (*B.P.*, 258).
19. *B.P.*, 23.
20. Ibid., 350.
21. Ibid., 67–68.
22. Ibid., 69.
23. Ibid., 113.
24. Ibid., 124.
25. Ibid., 145.
26. Ibid., 133.
27. Bushrui and al-Kuzbari (eds.), *Gibran: Love Letters*, 59.
28. *B.P.*, 141.
29. Ibid., 222.
30. Ibid., 169.
31. Ibid., 185.
32. Ibid., 221.

33. Ibid., 224.
34. Ibid., 194.
35. Ibid., 195.
36. *Jesus, the Son of Man* (1993), 14.
37. Ameen Guraieb was no longer the editor of *al-Mohajer*, as he had left New York for Lebanon, and Gibran began writing for *Mir'at al-Gharb*.
38. *A Treasury*, 87.
39. Ibid.
40. Letter from Charlotte Teller to Mary Haskell, May 15, 1911, quoted in J. and K. Gibran, *Life and World*, 209.
41. *B.P.*, 32.
42. M. H. journal, Jan. 27, 1911, Chapel Hill papers.
43. M. H. journal, Jan. 27, 1911, Chapel Hill papers.
44. M. H. journal, Jan. 27, 1911, Chapel Hill papers.
45. M. H. journal, Jan. 27, 1911, Chapel Hill papers.
46. *B.P.*, 147.
47. J. and K. Gibran, *Life and World*, 204.
48. M. H. journal, April 14, 1911, Chapel Hill papers.
49. M. H. journal, April 15, 1911, Chapel Hill papers.
50. *B.P.*, 239.
51. *A Self-Portrait* (1972), 26.
52. Brooks, *Indian Summer*.
53. J. and K. Gibran, *Life and World*, 427.
54. K. G. to M. H., April 27, 1911, Chapel Hill papers.
55. *B.P.*, 41.
56. Ibid., 234.
57. K. G. to M. H., May 1, 1911, Chapel Hill papers.
58. K. G. to M. H., May 26, 1911, Chapel Hill papers.
59. Max Eastman quoted in Beard and Berlowitz (eds.), *Greenwich Village*, 295.
60. Hippolyte Havel quoted in ibid., ix.
61. Bender, *New York Intellect*, 228–29.
62. K. G. to M. H., May 2, 1911, Chapel Hill papers.
63. K. G. to M. H., May 3, 1911, Chapel Hill papers.
64. *Al-Halaqat al-Dhahabiyah*, speech, p. 3, unpublished, quoted in Hawi, *Kahlil Gibran*, 156.
65. Ibid., 4.
66. K. G. to M. H., May 5, 1911, Chapel Hill papers.
67. M. H. journal, June 1, 1911, Chapel Hill papers.
68. J. and K. Gibran, *Life and World*, 211. This portrait was later called *Isis* by Gibran.
69. Letter from Charlotte Teller to Mary Haskell, Feb. 2, 1912, quoted in ibid., 232.
70. Gibran's will is published in Mikhail Naimy's biography of Gibran, *Kahlil Gibran: His Life and his Works*, 238.
71. He had begun the book in 1906 and it was finally published in 1912.
72. K. G. to M. H., June 28, 1911, Chapel Hill papers.
73. *B.P.*, 133.
74. *A Treasury*, 65.
75. *B.P.*, 88–89.
76. *A Self-Portrait* (1972), 65.
77. Bushrui and al-Kuzbari (eds.), *Gibran: Love Letters*, 12.
78. K. G. to M. H., Sept. 22, 1911, Chapel Hill papers.

79. Beard and Berlowitz (eds.), *Greenwich Village*, 270. Ignacy Paderewski (1866–1941) was a Polish pianist and composer who became the first prime minister of the newly created state of Poland in 1919.
80. M. H. journal, Oct. 18, 1911, Chapel Hill papers.
81. M. H. journal, Oct. 1, 1911, Chapel Hill papers.
82. This meeeting is corroborated in William M. Murphy's biography of W. B. Yeats's father, *Prodigal Father*, 501.
83. M. H. journal, Sept. 28, 1911, Chapel Hill papers.
84. M. H. journal, Oct. 1, 1911, Chapel Hill papers.
85. M. H. journal, Oct. 1, 1911, Chapel Hill papers.
86. Yeats met Madame Blavatsky in 1887; Tagore in 1913 when he wrote the introduction for Tagore's *Gitanjali*; Babu Mohini Chatterjee in 1885; and Shri Purohit Swami, with whom he worked on a translation of the *Upanishads*, in the winter of 1935–36.
87. M. H. journal, Oct. 11, 1911, Chapel Hill papers.
88. M. H. journal, Oct. 18, 1911, Chapel Hill papers.
89. M. H. journal, Oct. 25, 1911, Chapel Hill papers.
90. M. H. journal, Oct. 25, 1911, Chapel Hill papers.
91. K. G. to M. H., Oct, 28, 1911, Chapel Hill papers.
92. K. G. to M. H., Oct. 28, 1911, Chapel Hill papers.
93. M. H. to K. G., Nov. 3, 1911, Chapel Hill papers.
94. K. G. to M. H., Nov. 10, 1911, Chapel Hill papers.
95. K. G. to M. H., Jan. 6, 1912, Chapel Hill papers.
96. K. G. to M. H., Nov. 10, 1911, Chapel Hill papers.
97. K. G. to M. H., Nov. 26, 1911, Chapel Hill papers.
98. *B.P.*, 56.
99. K. G. to M. H., May 16, 1912, Chapel Hill papers.
100. *The Broken Wings* is discussed in chapter 3 of this volume.
101. See chapter 3 above.
102. Kahlil Gibran, dedication in *The Broken Wings* (1959).
103. K. G. to M. H., January 26, 1912, Chapel Hill papers.
104. *B.P.*, 58.
105. Young, *This Man from Lebanon* (1945), 29.
106. *B.P.*, 88.
107. K. G. to M. H., January 31, 1912, Chapel Hill papers.
108. *B.P.*, 87–88.
109. Ibid., 64.
110. Ibid., 66.
111. Thompson, *Diary*, xviii.
112. Bahá'u'lláh (1817–92), the founder of the Bahá'i faith.
113. Gail, *Other People, Other Places*, 229.
114. 'Abdu'l-Bahá (1844–1921), the expounder of the Bahá'i faith.
115. Gail, *Other People, Other Places*, 229.
116. Thompson, *Diary*, 234–35.
117. 'Abdu'l-Bahá spoke at the Bowery mission on April 19 (see 'Abdu'l-Bahá, *Promulgation of Universal Peace*, 32–34).
118. Honnold, *Vignettes*, 158.
119. Thompson, *'Abdu'l-Bahá*, 21–22.
120. K. G. to M. H., April 10, 1912, Chapel Hill papers.
121. M. H. to K. G., April 11, 1912, Chapel Hill papers.
122. K. G. to M. H., April 16, 1912, Chapel Hill papers.

123. K. G. to M. H., April 16, 1912, Chapel Hill papers.
124. K. G. to M. H., April 16, 1912, Chapel Hill papers.
125. *B.P.*, 74.
126. See, e.g., Upshall (ed.), *The Hutchinson Encyclopedia*, 838.
127. *B.P.*, 74.
128. Gail, *Other People, Other Places*, 228.
129. K. G. to M. H., April 19, 1912, Chapel Hill papers.
130. M. H. to K. G., April 24, 1912, Chapel Hill papers.
131. K. G. to M. H., May 3, 1912, Chapel Hill papers.
132. K. G. to M. H., May 6, 1912, Chapel Hill papers.
133. *Al-Funoon* published its ninth issue in 1913 before stopping because of financial difficulties in December 1913; it reappeared in June 1916. Naimy's work was published without interruption in a semi-weekly called *al-Sayih* established in New York in 1912 by 'Abd al-Masih Haddad.
134. Nov. 15, 1914, Chapel Hill papers; Naimy, "Fajr al-'Amal Ba'da Layl al-Ya's."
135. Naimy, *A Biography*, 125.
136. Bushrui and al-Kuzbari (eds.), *Gibran: Love Letters*, xii. May Ziadah has been called "perhaps the most significant woman essayist in the Arabic literature of the first half of the twentieth century" (ibid., xiv).
137. *A Self-Portrait* (1972), 29.
138. *B.P.*, 98.
139. Ibid., 98–99.
140. Chapel Hill papers, original letter inserted in journal before March 10, 1914, quoted in J. and K. Gibran, *Life and World*, 268–69.
141. K. G. to M. H., Oct. 9, 1912, Chapel Hill papers. Micheline's endearing qualities had been noted too by Lamar Hardy, a young attorney who became special counsel to Mayor Mitchell of New York, and in October 1914 the couple married.
142. K. G. to M. H., May 16, 1912, Chapel Hill papers.
143. K. G. to M. H., May 20, 1912, Chapel Hill papers.
144. *Unpublished Letters*, June 12, 1912 quoted in Bushrui and Gotch (eds), *Gibran of Lebanon: New Papers*, 86.
145. K. G. to M. H., May 20, 1912, and May 26, 1912, Chapel Hill papers.
146. *B.P.*, 99.
147. K. G. to M. H., Sept. 29, 1912, Chapel Hill papers.
148. M. H. journal, Sept. 7, 1912, Chapel Hill papers.
149. Aug. 6, 1912, Chapel Hill papers, quoted in J. and K. Gibran, *Life and World*, 243.
150. *B.P.*, 139.
151. Ibid., 99.
152. Sarkis owned a publishing house and a daily Arabic newspaper called *Lisan-Ul-Hal*. He was one of Gibran's closest friends and highly regarded among the intelligentsia of Lebanon.
153. The Arab League of Progress was an organization composed of many literary figures joined together for the purpose of promoting Arab culture and unity.
154. *Thoughts and Meditations* (1973), 1–8. A year later, in May 1913, another event was held in Mutran's honor, this time in Egypt. On this occasion May Ziadah read "The Poet from Baalbek" to the distinguished audience at the Egyptian University in Cairo where the overwhelming response marked the time when May began to champion Gibran's work actively in the Arab world.
155. *B.P.*, 108.
156. Ibid., 102.

157. Ibid., 103.
158. Ibid., 112.
159. Young, *This Man from Lebanon* (1945), 126.
160. *B.P.*, 185.
161. Arthur Bowen Davies (1862–1928), American painter, printmaker, and tapestry designer.
162. K. G. to M. H., Feb. 9, 1913, Chapel Hill papers.
163. K. G. to M. H., Feb. 14, 1913, Chapel Hill papers.
164. *B.P.*, 115.
165. K. G. to M. H., Feb. 18, 1913, Chapel Hill papers. The ten pictures chosen for the nucleus of the collection were *Angel, Rose Sleeves, The Beholder, The Saint, Let us Rise Together, The Silentest Hour, Morning, The First-Born, Medusa,* and *The Heart of the Desert*; and the arrangement made it unnecessary for him to let go of any picture he would rather not sell (*B.P.*, 119).
166. *B.P.*, 117.
167. The International Exhibition of Modern Art (the Armoury Show) took place in New York between February 17 and March 15, 1913.
168. Mabel Dodge to Gertrude Stein, January 24, 1913, in Gallup (ed.), *Flowers of Friendship*, 71.
169. *B.P.*, 125.
170. M. H. to K. G., May 11, 1913, Chapel Hill papers.
171. June 25, 1913, Chapel Hill papers, quoted in J. and K. Gibran, *Life and World*, 253.
172. *B.P.*, 120.
173. Ibid.
174. El-Hage, "William Blake and Kahlil Gibran," 131.
175. Quoted in Van der Post, *Jung*, 146.
176. *B.P.*, 93.
177. Ibid., 134.
178. Jung, *Memories, Dreams, Reflections*, 194.
179. Singer, *Boundaries of the Soul*, 373.
180. Ibid., 373–75.
181. J. B. Priestley's dedication to *Memories, Dreams, Reflections* by Carl Gustav Jung.
182. *Mirrors of the Soul*, 46.
183. *Al-Funoon* was the first attempt at an exclusively literary and artistic magazine by the Arab immigrant community in New York.
184. Young, *This Man from Lebanon* (1945), 81.
185. *Mirrors of the Soul*, 47, 48.
186. Ibid., 50.
187. K. G. to M. H., May 27, 1913, Chapel Hill papers.
188. K. G. to M. H., May 27, 1913, Chapel Hill papers.
189. K. G. to M. H., June 10, 1913, Chapel Hill papers. Ameen Rihani and Najeeb Diab attended the First Arab Congress in Paris, and some commentators have raised the question whether because of divergent political views Rihani and Gibran became estranged – a question that still remains unresolved (Ameen Albert Rihani, quoted in Bushrui and Nutlak (eds), *In Memory of Kahlil Gibran*, 93–97).
190. *B.P.*, 128–29.
191. Ibid., 129.
192. Ibid., 134.
193. Ibid., 100.
194. K. G. to M. H., July 10, 1913, Chapel Hill papers.

195. *The Prophet*, 112.
196. K. G. to M. H., June 21, 1918, Chapel Hill papers.
197. *B.P.*, 129.
198. Ibid., 125.
199. Ibid., 139.
200. Ibid., 142.
201. Ibid., 143.
202. Sept. 3, 1913, Chapel Hill papers, quoted in J. and K. Gibran, *Life and World*, 256–57.
203. *B.P.*, 136.
204. Ibid., 136–37.
205. Ibid., 148.
206. These lines, after much revision, were later to form part of his first English work, *The Madman: His Parables and Poems*, which he had begun writing in 1911 and published in 1918.
207. *B.P.*, 168.
208. Ibid., 61.
209. M. H. to K. G., April 19, 1913, Chapel Hill papers.
210. M. H. to K. G., April 19, 1913, Chapel Hill papers.
211. *B.P.*, 164.
212. Ibid., 165.
213. Ibid., 168.
214. Ibid., 168, 169.
215. *New York Times*, March 29, 1914, vol. 2, quoted in May, *The End of American Innocence*, 302–03.
216. Bergson promised to pose for Gibran in Paris (*B.P.*, 120).
217. May, *The End of American Innocence*.
218. Ibid., 222–23.
219. Brooks, *America's Coming of Age*, 164.
220. In a letter to Kahlil dated October 2, 1912, Mary refers to the artist's "unfinished portrait" of Fredericka Walling (*B.P.*, 96).
221. M. H. to K. G., Dec. 7, 1913, Chapel Hill papers.
222. K. G. to M. H., Nov. 4, 1913, Chapel Hill papers.
223. K. G. to M. H., Jan. 7, 1914, Chapel Hill papers.
224. K. G. to M. H., Jan. 19, 1914, Chapel Hill papers.
225. K. G. to M. H., Feb. 1, 1914, Chapel Hill papers.
226. J. and K. Gibran, *Life and World*, 247.
227. K. G. to M. H., March 8, 1914, Chapel Hill papers.
228. Gibran actually met Tagore in December 1916.
229. K. G. to M. H., March 8, 1914, Chapel Hill papers.
230. K. G. to M. H., March 8, 1914, Chapel Hill papers.
231. K. G. to M. H., Oct. 31, 1911, Chapel Hill papers.
232. K. G. to M. H., Nov. 1, 1914, Chapel Hill papers.
233. *A Tear and a Smile*, 23.
234. Ibid., v.
235. The title *A Tear and a Smile* was probably consciously borrowed from William Blake's lines: "What to others a trifle appears, Fills me full of smiles or tears" (*Blake*, 817).
236. Naimy, *A Biography*, 126.
237. Bushrui and al-Kuzbari (eds.), *Gibran: Love Letters*, 32.
238. Naimy, "Mind and Thought," 59.
239. *A Tear and a Smile*, 31.

240. Ibid., 189.
241. In Islam the sea represents infinitive divine wisdom.
242. *A Tear and a Smile*, 4.
243. Ibid., 75.
244. Ibid., 61.
245. Ibid., 153, 156.
246. Ibid., 73.
247. El-Hage, "William Blake and Kahlil Gibran," 45; Ghougassian, *Wings of Thought*, 41.
248. *A Tear and a Smile*, 4.
249. Ibid., 5.
250. Ibid., 6.
251. Shelley's opening verse in his "Ode To the West Wind" is similar in mood to Gibran's "Autumn" (*A Tear and a Smile*, 7): O wild West Wind, thou breath of Autumn's being, Thou, from whose unseen presence the leaves dead Are driven, like ghosts from an enchanter fleeing . . . (Hutchinson (ed.), *Shelley*, 160).
252. *A Tear and a Smile*, 7.
253. Ibid., 8.
254. Ibid., 193.
255. Muhi'l-Din ibn 'Arabi (1165–1240), the most celebrated Sufi poet of Islam and the greatest promoter of the unity of religion in Arabic poetry.
256. Quoted in Shah, *The Sufis*, 145.
257. Hawi, *Kahlil Gibran*, 159.
258. Zeno (333–263 B.C.E.), founder of Stoicism.
259. Porphyry (ca. 232–305 C.E.), a pupil of Plotinus.
260. *A Tear and a Smile*, 192.
261. Ibid., 37.
262. "The Poet," in Bushrui, *Introduction*, 36–37.
263. *A Tear and a Smile*, 41.
264. *B.P.*, 189–90.
265. Ibid., 190–91.
266. Ibid., 174.
267. K. G. to M. H., July 22, 1914, Chapel Hill papers.
268. K. G. to M. H., August 7, 1914, Chapel Hill papers.
269. In June 1912, Mary first mentions *The Madman*, reporting that "*The Madman* grows" (*B.P.*, 86).
270. *B.P.*, 150.
271. K. G. to M. H., Sept. 20, 1914, Chapel Hill papers.
272. M. H. to K. G., Sept. 30, 1914, Chapel Hill papers.
273. *B.P.*, 216.
274. K. G. to M. H., Dec. 19, 1909, Chapel Hill papers.
275. *B.P.*, 147.
276. Young, *This Man from Lebanon* (1945), 126.
277. *B.P.*, 190.
278. Ibid., 48.
279. Ibid., 216.
280. K. G. to M. H., Dec. 6, 1914, Chapel Hill papers.
281. K. G. to M. H., Dec. 13, 1914, Chapel Hill papers.

7. THE MADMAN

1. Charles H. Caffin, in the *American*, Dec. 21, 1914, quoted in Young, *This Man from Lebanon* (1981), 70–71.
2. *New York Times*, Dec. 27, 1914, section 5, 11.
3. *Evening Post*, Dec. 26, 1914, 12.
4. *Sun*, Dec. 20, 1914, 2.
5. *Evening Sun*, Dec. 28, 1914, 8.
6. Rose O'Neill bought *The Great Solitude* for $2,500, the Mortens *Nebula* for $1,200, Julia Ellswood Ford *Silence* for $1,000, *The Elements* was sold to a Mrs. Gibson for $1,000, and *Ghosts* to the portrait painter Cecilia Beaux for $700.
7. *Sun*, April 1, 1917, section 5, 12.
8. *B.P.*, 188.
9. K. G. to M. H., Jan. 11, 1915, Chapel Hill papers.
10. M. H. to K. G., Jan. 12, 1915, Chapel Hill papers.
11. "To Albert Pinkham Ryder," quoted in J. and K. Gibran, *Life and World*, 280.
12. *B.P.*, 232.
13. Ibid., 232.
14. K. G. to M. H., Feb. 9, 1915, Chapel Hill papers.
15. K. G. to M. H., Feb. 9, 1915, Chapel Hill papers.
16. *B.P.*, 234.
17. Ibid., 243–44.
18. Ibid., 243.
19. Quoted in Chilvers (ed.), *Oxford Dictionary of Art*, 415.
20. *B.P.*, 334.
21. Ibid., 243.
22. April 11, 1915, Chapel Hill papers, quoted in J. and K. Gibran, *Life and World*, 283.
23. K. G. to M. H., Jan. 11, 1915, Chapel Hill papers.
24. K. G. to M. H., March 14, 1915, Chapel Hill papers.
25. K. G. to M. H., April 23, 1915, Chapel Hill papers.
26. K. G. to M. H., April 25, 1915, Chapel Hill papers.
27. K. G. to M. H., Jan. 28, 1915, Chapel Hill papers.
28. *B.P.*, 182.
29. K. G. to M. H., March 16, 1915, Chapel Hill papers.
30. *B.P.*, 81.
31. Ibid., 360.
32. Ibid., 307.
33. Yeats, *Essays*, 492.
34. *B.P.*, 360.
35. K. G. to M. H., March 14, 1915, Chapel Hill papers.
36. K. G. to M. H., April 9, 1916, Chapel Hill papers.
37. *B.P.*, 235.
38. Chapel Hill papers, June 1915, quoted in J. and K. Gibran, *Life and World*, 283.
39. *B.P.*, 249.
40. "The Perfect World" was later published in 1918 in *The Madman: His Parables and Poems* (1918); quoted in Heinemann edition (1971), 71.
41. June 3, 1915, Chapel Hill papers, quoted in J. and K. Gibran, *Life and World*, 284.
42. The pieces they worked on for *The Madman* included "The Wise Dog," "The Two Hermits," and "On Giving and Taking" (June 11, 1915, Chapel Hill papers, quoted in J. and K. Gibran, *Life and World*, 284).

43. *The Earth Gods* was published in March 1931, a month before Gibran died.
44. K. G. to M. H., July 17, 1915, Chapel Hill papers.
45. June 20, 1915, Chapel Hill papers, quoted in J. and K. Gibran, *Life and World*, 285.
46. *B.P.*, 256.
47. M. H. to K. G., July 1915, Chapel Hill papers.
48. K. G. to M. H., Aug. 2, 1915, Chapel Hill papers.
49. K. G. to M. H., Aug. 20, 1915, Chapel Hill papers.
50. K. G. to M. H., Sept. 10, 1915, Chapel Hill papers.
51. Hitti, *Lebanon in History*, 484.
52. Ibid., 485.
53. It has since been acknowledged by historians that many more people would have died if it had not been for emigrants' remittances which reached over $250 million in the final war years (ibid., 486).
54. K. G. to M. H., Dec. 9, 1915, Chapel Hill papers.
55. M. H. to K. G., Oct. 3, 1915, Chapel Hill papers.
56. K. G. to M. H., Oct. 6, 1915, Chapel Hill papers.
57. K. G. to M. H., Dec. 9, 1915, Chapel Hill papers.
58. *B.P.*, 281.
59. Ibid., 283.
60. *The Madman*, 61.
61. *B.P.*, 385.
62. Ibid., 398.
63. M. H. to K. G., Nov. 21, 1915, Chapel Hill papers.
64. M. H. to K. G., Nov. 21, 1915, Chapel Hill papers.
65. *The Madman*, 11–12.
66. *B.P.*, 269.
67. Ibid., 306.
68. Ibid., 266.
69. Ibid., 267.
70. Ibid., 274.
71. *The Madman*, 9–10.
72. K. G. to M. H., Jan. 12, 1917, Chapel Hill papers.
73. *The Madman*, 10.
74. K. G. to M. H., March 1, 1916, Chapel Hill papers.
75. These writers included Naseeb Arida, Abdul Massih Haddad, Najeeb Diab, Elias Sabagh, and Wadi Bahout. *B.P.*, 269–70.
76. K. G. to M. H., May 26, 1916, Chapel Hill papers.
77. Between 1895 and 1915, Turkish soldiers systematically slaughtered more than a million Armenians and deported others into the north Syrian desert where they died of starvation. Only some 100,000 survived.
78. *B.P.*, 276.
79. K. G. to M. H., May 29, 1916, Chapel Hill papers.
80. K. G. to M. H., June 29, 1916, Chapel Hill papers.
81. K. G. to M. H., July 7, 1916, Chapel Hill papers.
82. Hitti, *Lebanon in History*, 483–86.
83. This letter, from Gibran to Ameen Rihani, is unpublished and undated and written on the Syrian–Mount Lebanon Relief Committee's official writing paper, quoted in Hawi, *Kahlil Gibran*, 106.
84. Oct. 5, 1916, Chapel Hill papers, quoted in J. and K. Gibran, *Life and World*, 294.
85. *A Treasury*, 339–45.

86. *Seven Arts*, November 1916, 52–53.

87. The first issue of *Seven Arts* in November 1916 saw the publication of Gibran's "Night and the Madman," followed by "The Greater Sea" in December, "The Astronomer" and "On Giving and Taking" in January 1917, and "The Seven Selves" in February: "Night and the Madman," 1 (Nov. 1916), 32–33; "The Greater Sea," 1 (Dec. 1916), 133–34; "The Astronomer" and "On Giving and Taking," 1 (Jan. 1917), 236–37; "The Seven Selves," 1 (Feb. 1917), 345.

88. M. H. to K. G., Nov. 2, 1916, Chapel Hill papers.

89. K. G. to M. H., Nov. 5, 1916, Chapel Hill papers.

90. *B.P.*, 280.

91. Alice Raphael Eckstein, "On The Art of Kahlil Gibran," in Bushrui, *Introduction*, 101.

92. Kahlil Gibran to Anthony Bashir, November 10, 1925, coll. of the late Metropolitan Antony Bashir, now the Antiochan Orthodox Christian archdiocese of North America, letter quoted in J. and K. Gibran, *Life and World*, 431–32, footnoted on 445.

93. Ouspensky, *Tertium Organum*, 207.

94. Feb. 3, 1917, Chapel Hill papers, quoted in J. and K. Gibran, *Life and World*, 300. One of these visitors was later identified as Marie El-Khoury.

95. K. G. to M. H., April 20, 1917, Chapel Hill papers.

96. Quoted in May, *The End of American Innocence*, 384.

97. *New York Times*, March 3, 1917, 6; April 1, 1917, 2; April 2, 1917, 1.

98. Quoted in May, *The End of American Innocence*, 385.

99. K. G. to M. H., March 18, 1917, Chapel Hill papers.

100. *B.P.*, 208.

101. M. H. to K. G., April 18, 1917, Chapel Hill papers.

102. M. H. to K. G., April 22, 1917, Chapel Hill papers.

103. *Sunday Herald*, April 22, 1917, 5.

104. The executive committee of the League of Liberation included Elia Abu Madey, Najeeb Diab, Abdul Massih Haddad, and Naseeb Arida.

105. Letter to Theodore Roosevelt, reel 271, Roosevelt Collection, Harvard, quoted in J. and K. Gibran, *Life and World*, 304.

106. K. G. to M. H., Jan. 3, 1917, Chapel Hill papers.

107. *Seven Arts*, which began in September 1916, closed in October 1917 due to financial problems.

108. Williams, *Autobiography*, 158.

109. Charlotte Teller to Mary Haskell, June 2, 1918, quoted in J. and K. Gibran, *Life and World*, 305.

110. M. H. to K. G., June 26, 1918, Chapel Hill papers.

111. K. G. to M. H., Dec. 22, 1917, Chapel Hill papers.

112. Dec. 26, 1917, Chapel Hill papers, quoted in J. and K. Gibran, *Life and World*, 306.

113. *B.P.*, 207.

114. Dec. 26, 1917, Chapel Hill papers, quoted in J. and K. Gibran, *Life and World*, 306.

115. Ibid., 402, 294. Church tradition supports Gibran in this belief: for a time, in the early church, the birthday of Jesus was celebrated on January 6, which became the feast of the Magi when the official birthday was changed to December 25, already celebrated in the Roman empire as the birthday of Sol Invictus and Mithras. Originally January 6 was celebrated as the date of Jesus' baptism (Gilbert, *Magi*, 216, 229).

116. K. G. to M. H., Feb. 26, 1918, Chapel Hill papers.

117. *B.P.*, 311.

118. K. G. to M. H., Feb. 5, 1918, Chapel Hill papers.

119. M. H. journal, May 6, 1918, Chapel Hill papers.

120. *B.P.*, 264.
121. *B.P.*, 85.
122. *B.P.*, 264.
123. *B.P.*, 329.
124. Ibid., 344.
125. M. H. to K. G., June 20, 1918, Chapel Hill papers.
126. *B.P.*, 355.
127. *A Self-Portrait* (1972), 46.
128. *B.P.*, 401, 428.
129. *Publisher's Weekly*, July 3, 1915, 10.
130. May, *The End of American Innocence*, 291–92.
131. *The Madman*, 47–48.
132. Nadeem Naimy, "Kahlil Gibran: His Poetry and Thought," in Bushrui and Gotch (eds.), *Gibran of Lebanon: New Papers*, 35–36.
133. *The Madman*, 8.
134. *A Self-Portrait* (1974), 55.
135. *B.P.*, 316–17.
136. Shah, *The Sufis*, 392. "'The madman' is also sometimes known in Sufic tradition as the 'crazed saint', perhaps the ultimate exemplar of indirect teaching, achieving his results by oblique action. His students suspect the nature of this activity in proportion to their degree, but the activity of the crazed saint remains incomprehensible to outsiders" (Scott, *People of the Secret*, 228).
137. Attar of Nishapur, "The Heart," quoted in Shah, *The Way of the Sufi*, 69.
138. Ibid., 183.
139. Plato wrote: "The men whom he dements God uses as his ministers" (Plato, *Ion*, 534 D, quoted in Perry (ed.), *Traditional Wisdom*, 642).
140. Boehme, *Supersensual Life*, 258.
141. *A Midsummer Night's Dream*, act V, scene 1, lines 7, 8.
142. *Blake*, 538.
143. *Persona* has been derived from *personare*, "to sound through" – the mask being literally the mouthpiece of the cosmic essence, which is manifested through it. See Burckhardt, *Mirror of the Intellect*, 149.
144. *The Madman*, 7–8.
145. Ibid., 54.
146. Ibid., 11–13.
147. Ibid., 15–16.
148. Ibid., 18–19.
149. Ibid., 43–45.
150. Ibid., 33–35.
151. Ibid., 38.
152. Quoted in Hawi, *Kahlil Gibran*, 198.
153. *The Madman*, 71–73.
154. "Sentences of the Khajagan," quoted in Shah, *The Way of the Sufi*, 164.
155. *The Madman*, 21–23.
156. The parable also has Sufi tendencies in its treatment of the idea of inner development, whereby the seeker has to pass through seven stages of preparation before objective understanding can be realized. These stages are sometimes referred to in Sufi thought as "men," representing degrees of the transmutation of consciousness. One of the most significant phenomena of these seven stages is the realization that the individual, who, mistakenly believing that he had a coherent personality, begins to learn through

specific exercises that in fact he possesses a multiple and changing personality, the multiple selves of Gibran's parable (see Shah, *The Sufis*, 394).

157. *The Madman*, 59–60.

158. Gibran wrote to Mary Haskell in February 1912 of "the Great Sea which we call God" (*B.P.*, 61).

159. *The Madman*, 57.

160. Ibid., 57.

161. Ibid., 14.

162. Ibid., 44.

163. Ibid., 35.

164. *The Garden of the Prophet* (1931), 21.

165. Otto, *Parables*, 48–49.

166. Howard Willard Cook, *Sun*, Dec. 15, 1918, 4.

167. *The Dial*, 65, Nov. 30, 1918, 510, quoted in full in Bushrui and al-Kuzbari (eds.), *Gibran: Love Letters*, 16.

168. *Evening Post*, Feb. 1, 1919, 6.

169. *B.P.*, 318.

170. Gibran liked Tagore, but felt that his work did not express "a world-consciousness," and the two men also differed in their views about God (*B.P.*, 283, 356).

171. Gollomb, "An Arabian Poet," 1, 10.

172. Wilkinson (ed.), *New Voices*, 95.

173. *The Nation*, 107, Dec. 28, 1918, 812.

174. Harriet Monroe, *Poetry*, 14, Aug. 1919, 278–79.

175. *The Dial*, undated, in Bushrui and al-Kuzbari (eds.), *Gibran: Love Letters*, 16.

176. February 7, 1919, in ibid., 7.

177. Ibid., 29, 30.

178. *The Procession*, 55.

179. All Bibles or sacred codes have been the causes of the following Errors:

    1. That Man has two real existing principles: Viz: a Body & a Soul.

    2. That Energy, call'd Evil, is alone from the Body; & that Reason, call'd Good, is alone from the Soul.

    3. That God will torment Man in Eternity for following his Energies.

But the following Contraries to these are True:

    1. Man has no Body distinct from his Soul; for that call'd Body is a portion of Soul discern'd by the five Senses, the chief inlets of Soul in this age.

    2. Energy is the only life, and is from the Body; and Reason is the bound or outward circumference of Energy.

    3. Energy is Eternal Delight.

    Blake, 149.

180. *The Procession*, 66.

181. Ibid., 71.

182.   Hell is a city much like London –
        A populous and a smoky city;
        There are all sorts of people undone,
        And there is little or no fun done;
        Small justice shown, and still less pity.

"Peter Bell the Third," Part the Third, I, lines 147–51, in Hutchinson (ed.), *Shelley*, 350.

183. *The Procession*, 72.

184. "The Tables Turned: An Evening Scene on the Same Subject," lines 21–24, Wordsworth, *Works*, 481.

185. *Blake*, 210.

186. *The Procession*, 74.

187. *B.P.*, 327.

188. Ibid., 339. In the 1970s, the musicians the Rahbani brothers and Fayruz, the leading female singer in Lebanon and the Arab world, made sections of this poem one of the most popular Arabic songs of the last twenty-five years.

189. Ziadah, "al-Mawakib," 874–81.

190. Farroukh, "Khayal Jubran," 27–28. It is unfortunate, however, that the English translation by George Kheirallah completely failed to reproduce the rhythm and music of the Arabic original.

191. Bushrui and al-Kuzbari (eds.), *Gibran: Love Letters*, 12–14.

192. *B.P.*, 320.

193. The design for the school ring depicted an open hand holding a rose: "or rather a flower growing in an open hand" (Chapel Hill papers).

194. Parables written at the time were published in 1920 in *The Forerunner*.

195. K. G. to M. H., Nov. 17, 1918, Chapel Hill papers.

196. K. G. to M. H., Nov. 27, 1918, Chapel Hill papers.

197. These huge reparations included a war indemnity which would take fifty years to pay, the loss of German colonies, air force, most of its fleet and army, and over thirteen percent of its territory (though most of its territorial losses could be justified by the principle of self-determination).

198. K. G. to M. H., Dec. 17, 1918, Chapel Hill papers.

199. Ibid., 604.

200. July 25, 1919, in Bushrui and al-Kuzbari (eds.), *Gibran: Love Letters*, 17.

201. Ibid., 23.

202. Alice Raphael, "On the Art of Kahlil Gibran," introduction to *Twenty Drawings*, i–xvii, in Bushrui, *Introduction*, 95–96.

203. Alice Raphael's married name was Eckstein.

204. Raphael, "On the Art of Kahlil Gibran," 101.

205. Ibid., 102.

206. The drawing on the first page of *Twenty Drawings*, "Towards the Infinite," portrays the artist's mother Kamileh, "at the last moment of her life over here and the first moment of her life over there" (Bushrui and al-Kuzbari (eds.), *Gibran: Love Letters*, 31).

207. Raphael, "On the Art of Kahlil Gibran," 105–06.

208. Jan. 28, 1920, in Bushrui and al-Kuzbari (eds.), *Gibran: Love Letters*.

209. Ibid., 2.

210. K. G. to M. H., May 10, 1910, Chapel Hill papers.

211. "On Music," in Bushrui, *Introduction*, 13.

212. Bettina von Arnim, *Goethe's Correspondence with a Child*, vol. 2, 206–16, quoted in Godwin, *Music, Mysticism and Magic*, 201.

213. *The Nation*, 110, April 10, 1920, 485–86.

214. This book, *The Forerunner*, was originally called "al-Mustawhid" ("The Lonely Man": Bushrui and al-Kuzbari (eds.), *Gibran: Love Letters*, 23).

215. *B.P.*, 323.

216. Nov. 9, 1919, in Bushrui and al-Kuzbari (eds.), *Gibran: Love Letters*, 23.

217. A copy of the invitation to this exhibition was sent to May on November 15, 1919 (ibid., 25).

218. A copy of this invitation was sent to May Ziadah on November 30, 1919 (ibid., 27).

219. Ibid., 34.

220. *B.P.*, 324–25.
221. Ibid., 329.
222. Ibid., 325.
223. Ibid., 326.
224. Ibid., 329.
225. Ibid., 339.
226. Ibid., 345–46.

8. A LITERARY MOVEMENT IS BORN

1. *B.P.*, 335.
2. Naimy had reviewed Gibran's *The Broken Wings* in *al-Funoon* in 1913.
3. Sept. 14, 1919, in *A Self-Portrait* (1972), 38.
4. Quoted in Nadeem Naimy, *Mikhail Naimy*, 187.
5. Naimy, *Sab'un*, vol. 2, 119.
6. Naimy, *A Biography*, 156.
7. Ibid., 154–56.
8. A *Hadith* is a saying of the Prophet Muhammad, as distinguished from the *Qur'an*, which is the word of God.
9. A better translation of this *Hadith* is:

   "There lies under the throne of God treasures, the keys to which are the tongues of poets."

10. The two other members were Ameen Rihani and Wadi Bahout.
11. Adham, "Mikhail Naimy," 312.
12. Jayyusi, *Trends and Movements*, 85.
13. Zurayq, "Nasseeb Arida," 77.
14. Najm, *al-Qissah*, 87.
15. Abbud, in *al-Makshuf.*
16. William Catzeflis, intro. to *The Procession.*
17. Naimy, *A Biography*, 157, 158.
18. Jayyusi, *Trends and Movements*, 91–92.
19. Mikhail Naimy Interviews, 1978.
20. Ibid.
21. Ibid.
22. Ibid.
23. Ibid. Rihani was not alone in Arrabitah in accepting the concept of mandates.
24. Ibid.
25. Naimy (Interviews, 1978) thought the donor of the gift may have been a businessman named Saleem Mulouk.
26. From Mikhail Naimy Interviews, 1978.
27. Jayyusi, *Trends and Movements*, 100.
28. *B.P.*, 335.
29. Ibid., 338.
30. The word "al-'awasif" is the plural form of "al-'asifah", meaning "the tempest": for some reason, some translators have used the English singular instead of the more common plural form – "The Tempests". Some critics point out that the influence of Nietzsche is strikingly evident in *al-'Awasif* (*The Tempests*): El-Hage, "William Blake and Kahlil Gibran," 229; Stefan Wild, "Nietzsche and Gibran," in Bushrui and Gotch (eds.), *Gibran of Lebanon: New Papers*, 68, for example, writes that one of the clearest and most often quoted examples of the Nietzschean Gibran is "The Grave Digger";

Moosa, introduction to Huwayyik, *Gibran in Paris* (1976), 25–27.

31. *B.P.*, 343.
32. "The Tempest," in *A Treasury*, 20, 21, 22.
33. Ibid., 26–27.
34. Ibid., 29–30.
35. "Satan," in ibid., 54.
36. Ibid., 46.
37. "Slavery," in ibid., 66, 67.
38. "The Day of my Birth," in *Secrets of the Heart*, 296.
39. "The Grave Digger," in *A Treasury*, 390. Seven years earlier Gibran had said that he was being called the "Grave-Digger" in Syria, in response to his revolutionary Arabic works (*B.P.*, 133).
40. *A Treasury*, 391.
41. Ibid., 390.
42. "The Giants," in *Thoughts and Meditations* (1960), 84.
43. "Narcotics and Dissecting Knives," in ibid., 77–80.
44. "My Countrymen," *Secrets of the Heart*, 133, 134, 135.
45. "Decayed Teeth," in *Thoughts and Meditations* (1961), 27.
46. Hawi, *Kahlil Gibran*, 192.
47. "The Crucified (Written on Good Friday)," in *Secrets of the Heart*, 212, 214, 215.
48. "Eventide of the Feast", in ibid., 226.
49. Gibran told Mary that "Almustafa" in Arabic means "something special, the Chosen and the Beloved, too, really between them both" (*B.P.*, 347). Mikhail Naimy writes: "Almustafa is an Arabic word meaning 'The Chosen.' It is one of Prophet Mohammed's appellations" (*A Biography*, 185).
50. *B.P.*, 356.
51. Ibid., 311.
52. Ibid., 356.
53. December 18, 1920, Chapel Hill papers, quoted in J. and K. Gibran, *Life and World*, 346.
54. Naimy, *A Biography*, 164.
55. Bushrui and al-Kuzbari (eds.), *Gibran: Love Letters*, 40.
56. *B.P.*, 350.
57. Otto, *Parables*, 89–90.
58. *The Forerunner* (1974), 14.
59. Ibid., 1.
60. Ibid., 11.
61. The idea of "longing" is also to be found in Christian mysticism, for example in a classic text, *The Cloud of Unknowing*, the anonymous author writes: "So if you are to stand and not fall, never give up your firm intention: beat away at this cloud of unknowing between you and God with that sharp dart of longing love", 68.
62. *The Forerunner* (1974), 11.
63. Ibid., 13.
64. Ibid., 13–14.
65. Ibid., 14.
66. Ibid., 22–23.
67. Burckhardt, *Mirror of the Intellect*, 118.
68. 1 Corinthians 13:12.
69. Ibn 'Arabi, quoted in Burckhardt, *Mirror of the Intellect*, 121.
70. Meister Eckhart, quoted in ibid., 122.

71. *The Forerunner* (1974), 23.
72. Ibid., 3–7.
73. Ibid., 6.
74. The presence of "the saint" recalls the "crazed saint" of Sufi tradition. For a discussion on the qualities of the "crazed saint" see Scott, *People of the Secret*, 228.
75. *The Forerunner* (1974), 20.
76. Ibid., 46.
77. Birds have been regarded since time immemorial as mediators between heaven and earth, and as embodiments of the immaterial, namely of the soul (Becker (ed.), *Encyclopedia of Symbols*, 41).
78. *The Forerunner* (1974), 31.
79. These words by the great eleventh-century Sufi al-Ghazali were found in a poem he had written in his last illness. Quoted in Lings, *What is Sufism?*, 13.
80. *The Forerunner* (1974), 52.
81. Ibid., 35–37.
82. Ibid., 45.
83. Ibid., 21.
84. Ibid., 8.
85. Ibid., 49.
86. Ibid., 24.
87. Ibid., 27–28.
88. Ibid., 25.
89. Otto, *Parables*, 81.
90. *B.P.*, 391.
91. Ibid., 358, 329.
92. *The Forerunner* (1974), 53.
93. Ibid., 61.
94. *B.P.*, 318.

9. A STRANGE LITTLE BOOK

1. *B.P.*, 357.
2. *Spiritual Sayings*, 70–71.
3. Ibid., 73.
4. Kahlil Gibran to Emile Zaydan, published in *al-Hilal*, 42 (March 1934), 517.
5. Dec. 31, 1922, Chapel Hill papers. A consistent voice of dissent could be found in the Lebanese literary journal *al-Mashriq*: "Who can imagine this poet? Is he a poet or an idiot? He seems childish, empty like his Great Sea . . . In his heart is the irreligious microbe" (*al-Mashriq*, 15 (1912), 315–16; Cheiko, "Bada'i' Jubran Khalil Jubran," 487–93; al-Bustani and Sa'b, "Bayn al-Mashriq," 910–19).
6. Jan. 28, 1920, in Bushrui and al-Kuzbari (eds.), *Gibran: Love Letters*, 29.
7. Nov. 9, 1919, in ibid., 20–21.
8. Nov. 3, 1920, in ibid., 38–39.
9. Naimy, *Sab'un*, vol. 2, 101.
10. *The Book of Mirdad* was first published in Beirut in 1948. In 1954 an English edition appeared in Bombay; in 1962, *The Book of Mirdad* had its first publication in England, and in 1971 a Penguin edition appeared in the U.S.A. In 1984, Naimy was awarded by U.N.E.S.C.O the Baghdad Prize for Literature.
11. Naimy, *Lebanese Prophets*, 8.
12. Naimy, *A Biography*, ix.

13. Ibid., 159–60. First published in Beirut in 1934 and translated into English by Mikhail Naimy in 1950, and published by the Philosophical Library.

14. Moore, Gurdjieff: *The Anatomy of a Myth*, 197.

15. Naimy, *A Biography*, 162–63.

16. Ibid., 166.

17. Bushrui and al-Kuzbari (eds.), *Gibran: Love Letters*, 51.

18. Ibid., 51–52.

19. Ibid., 41.

20. *B.P.*, 361.

21. Ibid., 362.

22. Bushrui and al-Kuzbari (eds.), *Gibran: Love Letters*, 31.

23. Naimy, *A Biography*, 171–72.

24. Hujwiri, *Kashf al-Mahjub*, 36.

25. *Sand and Foam* (1996), 85. This aphorism is the last one in the book.

26. *B.P.*, 366.

27. Mikhail Naimy, *Kahlil Gibran*, 193.

28. *B.P.*, 397.

29. Bushrui and al-Kuzbari (eds.), *Gibran: Love Letters*, 13–14, 37.

30. Dec. 30, 1920, Chapel Hill papers, quoted in J. and K. Gibran, *Life and World*, 346.

31. Gibran first mentions *Iram, City of Lofty Pillars* in a letter to May on June 11, 1919 (Bushrui and al-Kuzbari (eds.), *Gibran: Love Letters*, 11).

32. Rabi'a al-'Adawiyya is described by her biographer as "that woman who lost herself in union with the Divine, that one accepted by men as a second spotless Mary" (Smith, *Mystics of Islam*, 10). Although Wolf translates 'Amena al-'Alawiyah as Amena Divine, the authors will use her Arabic title which implies "of the Sublime."

33. *Iram, City of Lofty Pillars*, information given in translator's prologue to *Secrets of the Heart*, 249–53.

34. Ibid., 269–71.

35. Ibid., 271.

36. Ibid., 272.

37. Unity has in all the cosmos no place of manifestation (mazhar) more perfect than thyself, when thou plungest thyself into thine own essence in forgetting all relationship, and when thou seizest thyself with thyself, stripped of thy appearances, so that thou art thyself in thyself and none of the divine Qualities or created attributes (which normally pertain to thee) any longer refer to thee. It is this state of man which is the most perfect place of manifestation for Unity in all existence.

   (Jili, "al-insan al-kamil" ("the universal man"), from Burckhardt, *De l'homme universal*, 44.) 'Abdu'l Karim al-Jili (1366–1428), was a great Sufi metaphysician who taught in Baghdad.

38. Stepaniants, *Sufi Wisdom*, 19.

39. Burckhardt, *Sufi Doctrine*, 79. In the words of a *hadith qudsi* (a "sacred" hadith, the authority of which is asserted by Sufis only): "He who adores Me never ceases to approach Me until I love him and, when I love him I am the hearing by which he hears, the sight by which he sees, the hand with which he grasps and the foot with which he walks."

40. From Ibn 'Arabi's *Wisdom of the Prophets*, quoted in Stepaniants, *Sufi Wisdom*, 16.

41. Ibid., 62.

42. This view is based on the *hadith qudsi* that states that when the prophet David asked God why He had created the world, God answered, "I was a hidden treasure, and I

wanted to be known, so I created the world" (ibid., 17). Each of the divine names reveals one of the divine qualities and together they form a sphere that links the absolute and the sensible world. The divine names are subject to, and dependent on, the former and rulers as regards the latter, for the created world is derived from them; it is their immediate emanation. In the words of Ibn 'Arabi: "We are the fruit of the Divine unconditioned generosity towards the Divine names" (ibid., 17–18).

43. Ibn 'Arabi, *Wisdom of the Prophets*, 86, in ibid., 18.
44. Haydar Ali quoted in ibid., 20.
45. Ibid., 24.
46. In the words of the mystic poet Jami:

> The unique Substance, viewed as absolute and void of all phenomena, all limitations and multiplicity, is the Real (*al-Haqq*). On the other hand, viewed in His aspect of multiplicity and plurality, under which He displays Himself when clothed with phenomena, He is the whole created universe. Therefore the universe is the outward visible expression of the Real, and the Real is the inner unseen reality of the universe.

(Nicholson, *The Mystics of Islam*, 81–82)

47. Stepaniants, *Sufi Wisdom*, 22–23.
48. *Secrets of the Heart*, 273.
49. Ibid., 279.
50. Ibid., 275. The editor of *Secrets of the Heart*, Martin L. Wolf, footnotes this speech thus: "The zealous Christian in the Near East is taught that it is a sin to repeat any prayer belonging to the Islamic religion" (275).
51. Ibid., 280, 286.
52. *B.P.*, 366.
53. In a letter in 1925 to Anthony Bashir (a young Syrian Orthodox priest who translated some of Gibran's Arabic works into English), Gibran named four contemporary titles he felt deserved to be translated into Arabic: *The Treasure of the Humble* by Maurice Maeterlinck, *Folk-lore of the Old Testament* by James George Frazier, *The Dance of Life* by Havelock Ellis, and *Tertium Organum* by P. D. Ouspensky: "These four books are very valuable. I think they are the best that Westerners have written during our time" (K. G. to Bashir, November 10, 1925, collection of the late metropolitan Anthony Bashir, now the Antiochian Orthodox Christian Archdiocese of North America, quoted in J. and K. Gibran, *Life and World*, 432–32).
54. Claude Bragdon, intro. to Ouspensky, *Tertium Organum*, 3.
55. "Vast man": this could be viewed as a reference to the universe or cosmos as being wrapped up within the human soul, as expressed by the Sufi saying, "The universe is a vast man, and man is a small universe" (*The Prophet*, 164).
56. *The Prophet*, 147.
57. Nov. 9, 1919, in Bushrui and al-Kuzbari (eds.), *Gibran: Love Letters*, 23.
58. *B.P.*, 366.
59. Ibid., 368.
60. Ibid., 359.
61. M. H. to K. G., Nov. 10, 1912, Chapel Hill papers.
62. *B.P.*, 289.
63. Ibid., 290.
64. Aug. 12, 1921, Chapel Hill papers.
65. *B.P.*, 378.
66. *A Self-Portrait* (1972), 65.

67. *B.P.*, 381.

68. Ibid., 383–84.

69. December 2, 1923, in Bushrui and al-Kuzbari (eds.), *Gibran: Love Letters*. Gibran was so perplexed by the attitudes of Western medicine that he wrote to May Ziadah: "What do you say to our writing a book on modern medicine?" (ibid., 71).

70. Naimy, *A Biography*, 166.

71. *B.P.*, 387.

72. Ibid., 415.

73. May 9, 1922, Chapel Hill papers, quoted in J. and K. Gibran, *Life and World*, 359.

74. *B.P.*, 388.

75. Ibid., 373.

76. Ibid., 392.

77. Ibid., 396.

78. Nov. 12, 1922, Chapel Hill papers, quoted in J. and K. Gibran, *Life and World*, 362.

79. *B.P.*, 395, 396.

80. Ibid.

81. Ibid., 394.

82. Twelve of the paintings appeared in *The Prophet*, others appeared in *Jesus, the Son of Man* and *The Wanderer*.

83. *B.P.*, 397–98.

84. "Parables and prose poems like (these) . . . will have all the unpopularity of sermons outside the pulpit" (*Poetry*, 18, April 1921, 40–41).

85. Dec. 31, 1922, Chapel Hill papers, quoted in J. and K. Gibran, *Life and World*, 363.

86. *B.P.*, 402.

87. Ibid., 404.

88. Jan. 2, 1923, Chapel Hill papers.

89. K.G. to M.H., April 30, 1923, Chapel Hill papers. Gibran asked Mary to return the galley proofs of *The Prophet* directly to Alfred A. Knopf, 220 West 42nd St., New York.

90. Also known as *Best Things and Masterpieces*, published in Cairo, in which he included his own sketches (drawn from imagination when he was seventeen) of some of the greatest Arab philosophers and poets such as Ibn Sina (Avicenna), Al-Ghazali, al-Khansa, Ibn al-'Arabi, Abu Nuwas, Ibn al-Muqafa' and others.

91. Ibn Sina (980–1037 C.E.), known to the West as Avicenna, was born near Bokhara in Central Asia. From the age of sixteen this precocious youth served as a physician to several rulers in Persia. Ibn Sina's canon of medicine established him as the leading medical authority in Islam and was used as a definitive text throughout the universities of Europe.

92. Al-Ghazali (1058–1111 C.E.), known to medieval Europe as Algazel, has often been compared to Thomas Aquinas and his monumental *Ihya 'Ulum al-Din* to Aquinas 's *Summa Theologica*. Combining the spiritual awareness of a mystic and the critical intellect of the philosopher he made noteworthy contributions to both theology and metaphysics.

93. Ibn al-Farid (1182–1235 C.E.), the supreme master of mystical odes, was born in Cairo. A devoutly religious youth, his hour of illumination occurred on the Hajj to Mecca. Many of his odes celebrate the hills and valleys around the holy city, scenes endeared by the visions and ecstasies they recalled to his mind. After fifteen years he returned to Cairo where he wrote his exquisite verse, living in the al-Azhar mosque.

94. Some of these aphorisms formed the basis of his English work *Sand and Foam*, which was published in 1926.

95. These poems include "Solitude and Seclusion" (*al-Wahdad wa al-Infirad*); "The Sea"

(*al-Bahr*); "Handful of Beach Sand" (*Hafnah min Rimal al-Shati*); "The Sayings of the Brook" (*Ma Taqul al-Saqiyah*); "For Heaven's Sake My Heart!" (*Billahi Ya Qalbi*); "The Robin" (*al-Shahrour*); "The Great Sea" (*al-Bahr al-'Azam*); "The Seven Reprimands" (*Al-Marahel al-Sab'*): "During a Year not Registered in History" (*Fi-Sanaten Iamum Takun Qat fi al-Tarikh*); trans. Joseph Sheban in *Mirrors of the Soul*, 66–83.

96. *Mirrors of the Soul*, 58.

97. Naimy, *A Biography*, 194.

98. M. H. to K. G., Oct. 2, 1923, Chapel Hill papers.

99. Naimy, "A Strange Little Book," 10–15, quoted in Bushrui, *Introduction*, 149.

100. *B.P.*, 417.

101. Nov. 26, 1923, Chapel Hill papers, quoted in J. and K. Gibran, *Life and World*, 371. Three years after Gibran's death, in 1936, some of his works were performed in a choreographic mime entitled *Office Drawn from the Rhythms of Kahlil Gibran*, 1936. This mime was performed at St. Mark's-in-the-Bouwerie, an Episcopal church in New York. (Otto, *Parables*, 64).

102. Letter to the queen of Romania, 1927. Copy in the possession of authors.

103. Ibid.

104. Passage from *Aramco World*, quoted in Bushrui, *Introduction*, 152.

105. Naimy, "A Strange Little Book," quoted in Bushrui, *Introduction* (1990), 153. Quotation from *The Prophet*, 114.

106. "A Strange Little Book," in Bushrui, *Introduction* (1970), 152.

107. The book sales of *The Prophet* during these years are recorded thus: 8,109 in 1934, 12,539 in 1935, 13,411 in 1937, 14,472 in 1940, 15,911 in 1941, 22,471 in 1942, and in the following five years, 43,564, 65,263, 91,400, 74,897, and 56,822 respectively. Knopf reflected: "The message of *The Prophet* is a solacing one – and the frightening state of the world in recent decades has apparently created a grateful public for it" (*Portrait of a Publisher*, vol. 2, 96). By 1944 it was Knopf's second best seller (60,000 copies) after John Hersey's *A Bell for Adamo*. In 1957, the millionth copy was sold and by 1965 the book had passed the 2.5 million mark. By 1970 *The Prophet* was continuing to sell at the rate of approximately 7,000 a week, its total sales having grown to more than 4 million copies in America alone.

108. Adams, "Speaking of Books," 2.

109. The same integrity was to characterize all of the many subsequent Knopf editions, which may therefore be regarded as definitive. Gibran's manuscripts and typescripts contain several interesting corrections and deletions in his own hand, apparently made not long before publication, some of which are quoted in *The Prophet*; and in Shehadi, *A Prophet in the Making*, a book based on manuscript pages of *The Madman*, *The Forerunner*, *The Prophet*, and *The Earth Gods*, including four hitherto unpublished manuscripts: "Lullaby," "The Last Guest," "Untitled," and "Poverty & Sunday Aphorisms."

110. Five years before the publication of *The Prophet*, Russell had published *The Candle of Vision*, one of the classics of modern Western mysticism. W. B. Yeats described his work as having "a more disembodied ecstasy than any poetry of our time" (*A Book of Irish Verse*, xxix).

111. Russell, *The Living Torch*, 168–69, quoted in Bushrui and Munro (eds.), *Essays and Introductions*, 31.

112. *Sand and Foam*, 31.

113. *The Prophet*, trans. and intro. Sarwat Okasha (1959), quoted in Bushrui and Munro (eds.), *Essays and Introductions*, 159–60.

114. *The Prophet*, 72.

115. Ibid.
116. Ibid., 155.
117. Ibid., 67.
118. Ibid., 93.
119. Ibid., 150.
120. Ibid., 75–76.
121. This idea was expressed by the great German dramatist and poet Friedrich Schiller, who wrote:

> "Truth is not something that can be received from outside, like the actuality or the sensuous existence of things; it is something that the intellectual faculty produces spontaneously, in its freedom."

(Schiller, *On the Aesthetic Education of Man* (1954), 108–09).

122. *The Prophet*, 104, 105.
123. Ibid., 130.
124. Ibid., 103. "God-self": the almighty toward whom all souls yearn; "pygmy": Gibran spells "pigmy" – a symbolic reference to youth, immaturity, and innocence. See also "Behold the Child among his new-born blisses A six years' Darling of a pigmy size!" in Wordsworth, 589, *Ode: Intimations of Immortality from Recollections of early Childhood.*
125. *The Prophet*, 125.
126. Quoted in Nassar, "Cultural Discontinuity in the works of Kahlil Gibran," in his *Essays: Critical and Metacritical*, 95.
127. *The Prophet*, 128.
128. Ibid., 140.
129. Nietzsche, *Thus Spake Zarathustra*, 39.
130. Stefan Wild, "Nietzsche and Gibran," in Bushrui and Gotch (eds.), *Gibran of Lebanon: New Papers*, 70.
131. Claude Bragdon in "Gibran a Modern Prophet from Lebanon," in his *Merely Players*, quoted in Bushrui and Munro (eds.), *Essays and Introductions*, 25.
132. *B.P.*, 389.
133. Quoted in Bushrui and Munro (eds.), *Essays and Introductions*, 25.
134. Ibid.
135. Claude Bragdon, quoted in ibid., 23.
136. *Jesus, the Son of Man* was first published by Knopf in 1928, three years before Gibran's death.
137. *B.P.*, 363.
138. Ibid., 349.
139. Ibid., 208, 389.
140. July 30, 1917, Chapel Hill papers, quoted in J. and K. Gibran, *Life and World*, 313.
141. *The Prophet*, 137.
142. Song of Solomon 2:10–12 and 3:3.
143. *The Prophet*, 95.
144. Matthew 23:37.
145. *The Prophet*, 132.
146. Quoted in Bushrui, *Kahlil Gibran of Lebanon*, 55.
147. *The Prophet*, 132.
148. These three figures were Ibn Sina (Avicenna), Ibn al-Farid, and al-Ghazali. Gibran also wrote an Arabic poem entitled "The Sufi," of which the following is an approximate translation:

To God the praise be; Neither gold nor silver Have we.
No movable And immovable property. Yoke-companion none.
Nor offspring. And Without lineage Through the earth
Which stretches wide, As a phantom we traverse
Whom no one can perceive Save in whose twin orbs
The phantom hides. If we laugh, Distress lurks in time,
And if we weep Behind it joy lies. We are but a spirit!
Should you say to us: "How wondrous!" Then forthright we reply:
"By heaven! Wonder dwells In your own Veil of clay."

(Orfalea and Elmusa (eds.), *Grape Leaves*, 34–35. The Arabic original has never been published)

149. Arberry, *Sufism*, 101.
150. *The Prophet*, 116, 148.
151. Stevenson (ed.), *The Poems of William Blake*, 288.
152. *Blake*, 264. Many parallels are to be found in Sufi mystical theology and Blake's work (Raine, "Blake: The Poet as Prophet," 68–69).
153. *The Prophet*, 104.
154. Pickthall, *The Glorious Qur'án*, 98.
155. In one of Gibran's notebooks, dated 1912, about two hundred of Muhammad's sayings or translations are to be found (Hawi, *Kahlil Gibran*, 274), highlighting the influence of Islam on his writings.
156. Nadeem Naimy, "Kahlil Gibran: His Poetry and Thought," in Bushrui and Gotch (eds.), *Gibran of Lebanon: New Papers*, 47.
157. The three types of journey, according to Ibn 'Arabi, are away from God, toward God, and in God. A journey away from God could be one with a purpose such as reward or punishment, the journey of a fallen angel or one turning away in shame or disobedience, or a mission to humankind. Such journeys are dangerous unless carried out under the direction of the Almighty, as are journeys toward God, of which the classic types are undertaken by those who do not worship one God or who think He is not the sole Creator; or, alternatively, it is an impeccable, God-guided journey. Examples of journeys in God, carrying no rewards but still dangerous, are the rational journey of philosophers and others likely to lose their way without a guide, or the journey of prophets or apostles (Yusuf Ibish, "Ibn Arabi's Theory of Journeying", in Ibish and Marculescu (eds.), *Contemplation and Action*, 206–07, 209–19).
158. Ibid., 210–11.
159. Ibid., 211.
160. Mikhail Naimy, "Gibran at His Peak," in Bushrui and Gotch (eds.), *Gibran of Lebanon: New Papers*, 3–4.
161. Bushrui, intro. to *The Prophet*, 61.
162. *B.P.*, 412.
163. Naimy, *A Biography*, 191–93, wrote that the "Creative Hand" represents

an out-stretched hand, sensitive, powerful, graceful, beautifully sculpted, and with an open eye in the middle of it that seems to see all things. Around the eye is a cyclone-like whirl of wings. Around the whirling wings is a dark abyss heaving with chaotic shadows and fringed with a chain of human bodies. That is the hand of God. It sees as it touches, and imagines as it sees. It imagines forms before it creates them, then touches chaos and out of it makes all forms to issue as by magic. In drawing that hand Gibran's memory may have been carried back to the *Hand of God* by Rodin. The two may have something in common in so far only as the basic idea of creation is concerned, but they are vastly different in conception and execution.

> The rest of the drawings in the book . . . are all deeply symbolic and very carefully executed . . . [and] without exception bespeak the grandeur of the imagination that conceived them and the wonderful sensitiveness of the hand that gave them form.

164. This definition of a parable is given in Otto, *Parables*, 91, 92.
165. Raphael, "On the Art of Kahlil Gibran," introduction to *Twenty Drawings*, i–xviii, quoted in Bushrui, *Introduction* (1970), 98.
166. *Sand and Foam*, 83.
167. Naimy, *A Biography*, 58. Some critics (e.g. Bragdon, *Merely Players*), perceived that Gibran's paintings have a "strikingly Leonardesque quality."
168. June 11, 1919, in Bushrui and al-Kuzbari (eds.), *Gibran: Love Letters*, 11.
169. Barbara Young, "The Many-Sidedness of Gibran", in Bushrui, *Introduction* (1970), 112–13.
170. Naimy, *A Biography*, 224.
171. *B.P.*, 343.
172. Naimy, *A Biography*, 163.
173. Otto, *Parables*, 102.
174. Matthew Arnold in his poem "Dover Beach" poignantly captured the existential *angst* of our modern refusal to heed these eternal harmonies:

> The sea of faith
> Was once, too, at the full, and round earth's shore
> Lay like the folds of a bright girdle furl'd;
> But now I only hear
> Its melancholy, long, withdrawing roar,
> Retreating to the breath
> Of the night-wind down the vast edges drear
> And naked shingles of the world.
> Ah, love, let us be true
> To one another! for the world, which seems
> To lie before us like a land of dreams,
> So various, so beautiful, so new,
> Hath really neither joy, nor love, nor light,
> Nor certitude, nor peace, nor help for pain;
> And we are here as on a darkling plain
> Swept with confused alarms of struggle and flight,
> Where ignorant armies clash by night.

(*The Poems of Matthew Arnold*, 402)

175. K. G. to M. H., Dec. 19, 1915, Chapel Hill papers.
176. The words are those of John Donne, quoted in Isaacs, *Twentieth-Century Literature*, 50.
177. Schiller, *Education of Man* (1985), 53.
178. Jung, *Collected Works*, vol. 18, para. 9.
179. "The Tempest," in *A Treasury*, 20.
180. Dec. 3, 1923, in Bushrui and al-Kuzbari (eds.), *Gibran: Love Letters*, 73.
181. Mikhail Naimy, "Gibran at his Peak," in Bushrui and Gotch (eds.), *Gibran of Lebanon: New Papers*, 9.
182. May 30, 1922, Chapel Hill papers, quoted in J. and K. Gibran, *Life and World*, 360.
183. Dec. 3, 1923, at midnight, in Bushrui and al-Kuzbari (eds.), *Gibran: Love Letters*, 73.

10. THE MASTER POET

1. December 2, 1923, in Bushrui and al-Kuzbari (eds.), *Gibran: Love Letters*, 71.
2. *Sand and Foam*, 41.
3. *B.P.*, 422.
4. October 5, 1923, in Bushrui and al-Kuzbari (eds.), *Gibran: Love Letters*, 59.
5. *B.P.*, 423.
6. Ibid., 304.
7. Robert Hillyer, intro. to *A Tear and a Smile* (1994), xii–xiii.
8. Bragdon, "Modern Prophet from Lebanon", in *Merely Players*, quoted in Bushrui and Munro (eds.), 28.
9. Bercovici, *Around the World*; repr. in "The Syrian Quarter," *The Century Magazine*, 86 (July 1924), 354.
10. Bragdon, *More Lives*, 271.
11. Kahlil Gibran to Witter Bynner, April 14, 1925, Harvard College Library.
12. Rihani, *Jibran Hayyan wa Maytan*, 463; Abu-Madi, "Jibran Taht Mabadi' al-Nu'ayma," 22.
13. Hawi, *Kahlil Gibran*, 67.
14. Karam Mulhim Karam, "Sha'ir yatwi Ajnihatah," *Jibran Hayyan*, 453–54, quoted in Hawi, *Kahlil Gibran*, 69.
15. K. G. to M. H., Sept. 4, 1924, Chapel Hill papers.
16. These meetings with Galsworthy, Chesterton, and Dunsany are verified in *B.P.*, 429. John Galsworthy (1867–1933) wrote the *Forsythe Saga* and won the Nobel prize for literature in 1932. Gilbert Keith Chesterton (1874–1936) wrote a very popular volume of stories about Father Brown the priest-detective. Edward John Moreton Dunsany (1878–1957) was closely associated with W. B. Yeats and the Irish Revival.
17. José Clemente Orozco (1883–1949) was one of a trio of politically committed fresco painters. The other great muralists were David Alfaro Siqueiros (1896–1974) and Diego Rivera (1886–1957), whose revolutionary works unified the divergent cultural roots of their country's history to the demands of its national revolutionary present and, in the opinion of many, created the first great example of post-colonial art.
18. The so-called Delphic Group consisted of a group of artists and writers involved with oriental mystery religions (J. and K. Gibran, *Life and World*, 392).
19. Reed in *Orozco*, quoted in J. and K. Gibran, *Life and World*, 392.
20. April 6, 1921, in Bushrui and al-Kuzbari (eds.), *Gibran: Love Letters*, 48.
21. Letter from Kahlil Gibran to Mariita Lawson, Sept. 26, 1921, in Hunayn, *Rasa'il Jubran*.
22. Ibid., June 22, 1920.
23. Ibid., May 26, 1920; Aug. 14, 1920.
24. *B.P.*, 422.
25. Dec. 1–3, 1923, in Bushrui and al-Kuzbari (eds.), *Gibran: Love Letters*, 69, 72.
26. K. G. to M. H., Oct. 3, 1924, Chapel Hill papers.
27. Naimy, *A Biography*, 197–8.
28. Ibid., 197.
29. *The Prophet*, 106.
30. Naimy, *A Biography*, 197.
31. *B.P.*, 423–24.
32. Young, *This Man from Lebanon* (1945), ix.
33. J. and K. Gibran, *Life and World*, 382.

34. *This Man from Lebanon* was published by Knopf, and although revealing some fascinating aspects of Gibran's character, cannot be regarded as always factually correct.
35. K. G. to M. H., July 8, 1925, Chapel Hill papers.
36. Bushrui and al-Kuzbari (eds.), *Gibran: Love Letters*, xvii.
37. July 22, 1921, Chapel Hill papers.
38. Syud Hussein, editorial, *The (New) Orient*, 2, quoted in J. and K. Gibran, *Life and World*, 382.
39. Naimy, *A Biography*, 198.
40. Mikhail Naimy, "Gibran at his Peak," address given at the opening of the Gibran International Festival, 1970, quoted in Bushrui and Gotch (eds.), *Gibran of Lebanon: New Papers*, 8.
41. Gibran had first mentioned the play *Lazarus* on April 26, 1914 (J. and K. Gibran, *Life and World*, 383–84). These plays first appeared in print in 1972 and 1983 respectively.
42. Gibran to Mr. Smith, May 22, 1926, quoted in ibid., 384.
43. *B.P.*, 344.
44. Seven – a holy number yielded by adding the basic number of the masculine, three, and the basic number of the feminine, four. It is the number of the planets in antiquity (Sun, Moon, Jupiter, Venus, Mercury, Mars, and Saturn), and the number of the days of the week that the planet names bear, as well as the number of days of an individual phase of the moon. In Buddhism there are seven different heavens, and the Qur'an too speaks of "seven heavens" (Suras 2:27; 23:17; 67:3; 78:12). The Chinese saw the seven stars of Ursa Major in connection with seven openings of the body and seven openings of the human heart. Among the Babylonians, one also encounters a regard for seven: the "evil seven," a group of demons that usually appear together, and the "seven winds." In Greece, seven, which was sacred to Apollo and others, played an important role; the seven gates of Thebes, the seven sons of Helios, the seven wise men etc. (Becker [ed.], *Encyclopedia of Symbols)*. Various myths such as the Seven Sleepers appear in Syriac, Coptic, Arabic, Ethiopian, and Armenian Christian literature and in the Qur'an (Hastings [ed.], *Encyclopedia of Religion and Ethics*, vol. 11). In biblical literature the use of the number seven suggests a peculiar regard for it. It appears first at the record of creation and is found in the law regarding feasts, the consecration of priests and altars, defilement, and the sprinkling of blood and oil. Of persons in sevens are sons, chamberlains, maidens, wise men, poor men, women, deacons; also angels, spirits, and devils. Of things in sevens – animals, ears of corn, altars, pillars, streams, eyes, stars and seals. Seven times is connected with bowing, punishment, praising God, restoration, and forgiveness. Seven was also used as a round number, and as sevenfold, in the sense of frequently or fully (Buckland and Williams [eds.], *Universal Bible Dictionary*). In the Bahá'í writings, Bahá'u'lláh speaks of the "Seven Valleys" or "The stages that mark the wayfarer's journey from the abode of dust to the heavenly homeland" (Bahá'u'lláh, *Seven Valleys*, 4).
45. In some of his earlier works, particularly *The Madman*, Gibran's attachment to the number seven is evident: the madman has seven masks stolen (p. 7); his seven selves whisper to each other (p. 21); and he passes seven personalities in his search for "the Greater Sea" (p. 58).
46. *Sand and Foam*, 78. This aphorism is perhaps an echo of the "sealed book" in the book of Revelation (5:1), which has "seven seals."
47. *Sand and Foam*, 30.
48. Ibid., 81.
49. Ibid., 10.
50. Shah, *The Sufis*, 394.
51. Naimy, *A Biography*, 207.

52. *Sand and Foam*, 20.
53. Ibid., 9.
54. Ibid., 12.
55. Ibid., 14.
56. Ibid., 15.
57. Ibid., 25.
58. Ibid., 29.
59. Ibid., 31.
60. Ibid., 60.
61. Some of these aphorisms and wise sayings can be found in *al-Badayi' wa'l-Tarayif* (*Beautiful and Rare Sayings*), published in 1923.
62. *Sand and Foam*, 28.
63. Ibid., 34.
64. Ibid., 66.
65. Ibid., 73.
66. Ibid., 42.
67. Ibid., 81.
68. Kahlil Gibran to Mariita Lawson, May 19, 1920, in Hunayn, *Rasa'il Jubran*, 142.
69. "Sand and Foam," *Transcript* (Boston), December 1926, quoted in Hawi, *Kahlil Gibran*, 233.
70. *Spiritual Sayings*, 22.
71. Feb. 26, 1924, in Bushrui and al-Kuzbari (eds.), *Gibran: Love Letters*, 81.
72. A Self-Portrait (1972), 83.
73. *Sand and Foam*, 84.
74. K.G. to M. H. April 29, 1909, Chapel Hill papers.
75. Naimy, *A Biography*, 20.
76. K. G. to M. H., March 25, 1908, Chapel Hill papers.
77. *B.P.*, 409.
78. Ernst Renan (1822–92): French philologist, historian, and essayist. His *Vie de Jesus* (1863) combines a critical examination of the gospel narratives with an imaginative presentation of the figure of Christ – a portrayal that "earned him both fame and persecution" in his lifetime (Drabble [ed.], *Oxford Companion to English Literature*).
79. Quoted in J. and K. Gibran, *Life and World*, 385.
80. *B.P.*, 363, 294.
81. Ibid., 258.
82. Ibid., 362.
83. Ibid., 93.
84. Letter from Witter Bynner to Lorraine M. George, Santa Fe, February 13, 1941, in *The Works of Witter Bynner*, 167.
85. Gibran encapsulated his ambivalence toward institutionalized religion in *Sand and Foam* (p. 77): "Once every hundred years Jesus of Nazareth meets Jesus of the Christians in a garden among the hills of Lebanon. And they talk long; and each time Jesus of Nazareth goes away saying to Jesus of the Christians, 'My friend, I fear we shall never, never agree.'"
86. *B.P.*, 349.
87. Ibid., 318.
88. "Resurrection," in *Voice of the Master* (1960), 88–92.
89. "When I meditated upon Jesus I always saw Him either as an infant in the manger seeing His mother Mary's face for the first time, or staring from the crucifix at His mother's face for the last time" (*Spiritual Sayings* [1963], 27).
90. In "The Crucified" Gibran writes: "Jesus was not sent here to teach the people to build

magnificent churches and temples . . . He came to make the human heart a temple, and the soul an altar, and the mind a priest" (*Secrets of the Heart* [1992], 215).

91. In "Khalil the Heretic" Gibran writes of the priest: "He is a hypocrite whom the faithful girded with a fine crucifix which he held above their heads as a sharp sword" (*Spirits Rebellious,* 103).

92. *B.P.,* 363.

93. "The Crucified," in *Secrets of the Heart,* 214.

94. "Eventide of the Feast," in ibid., 226.

95. *B.P.,* 338.

96. Ibid., 340.

97. J. and K. Gibran, *Life and World,* 384.

98. Young, *This Man from Lebanon* (1945), 102.

99. Naimy, *A Biography,* 208.

100. Gail, *Other People, Other Places,* 228.

101. Honnold (ed.), *Vignettes,* 158.

102. Talk delivered at reception at Metropolitan Temple, Seventh Avenue and Fourteenth Street, New York, by 'Abdu'l-Bahá, May 28, 1912, in *Promulgation of Universal Peace,* 151.

103. Talk delivered at meeting of International Peace Forum, Grace Methodist Episcopal Church, West 104 Street, New York, by 'Abdu'l Bahá, May 12, 1912, in ibid., 122, 121.

104. Talk delivered at Earl Hall, Columbia University, New York, by 'Abdu'l-Bahá, April 19, 1912, in ibid., 32.

105. Talk delivered at Central Congregational Church, Brooklyn, New York, by 'Abdu'l-Bahá, June 16, 1912, in ibid., 199, 200.

106. Talk delivered at Hotel Sacramento, California, by 'Abdu'l-Bahá, Oct. 25, 1912, in ibid., 375.

107. Talk delivered at the Central Congregational Church, Hancock Street, Brooklyn, New York, by 'Abdu'l-Bahá, June 16, 1912, in ibid., 200, 201, 202.

108. "A Poet's Voice," in *A Tear and a Smile* (1994), 192.

109. Talk delivered at Green Acre, Eliot, Maine, by 'Abdu'l-Bahá, Aug. 17, 1912, in *Promulgation of Universal Peace,* 266.

110. K. G. to M. H., April 16, 1912, Chapel Hill papers.

111. Talk delivered at Green Acre, Eliot, Maine, by 'Abdu'l-Bahá, Aug. 17, 1912, in *Promulgation of Universal Peace,* 262–63.

112. *A Self-Portrait* (1972), 84.

113. Young, *This Man from Lebanon* (1945), 102–103.

114. Both John Haynes Holmes, the former minister of the Community Church in New York (quoted in J. and K. Gibran, *Life and World,* 390), and Claude Bragdon (in "Modern Prophet from Lebanon," *Merely Players,* 144) compare Gibran's work with Browning's.

115. Some scholars, such as Joseph Ghougassian, argue that the exegesis, the thinking, and deeds of Gibran's Jesus concur with Christ's personality as depicted by the four evangelists (*Wings of Thought,* 221).

116. *Jesus, the Son of Man,* 42, 43.

117. Ibid., 4.

118. This view is supported by Joseph Ghougassian in *Wings of Thought,* 221.

119. Some leading New Testament scholars believe that a Christology built on the concept of the "Son of Man" would have solved the endless controversies that dominated Christological debates for so long: "If a modern theologian would have undertaken to

build a Christology entirely on the New Testament idea of the Son of Man not only would such a Christology be entirely orientated toward the New Testament and go back to Jesus' self-designation; it would also have the advantage of putting the logically insoluble problem of the two natures of Christ on a level where the solution becomes visible: the pre-existent Son of Man, who is with God at the very beginning and exists with him as his image, is *by his very nature* divine Man. From this point of view the whole toilsome discussion which dominated the earlier Christological controversies actually becomes superfluous" (Cullman, *Christology*, 137, 192; Cullman's influential thesis was delivered at the Zenos Lectures (1955) at the McCormick Theological Seminary in Chicago).

120. The idea of the divine original man can also be found among the Mandeans and Manicheans, as well as in the cult of Attis.

121. Daniel 7:13, 14. This eschatological dimension is also evident in the parables of chapters 37–71; in the book of Enoch and in Ezra 7:28 and 13:22.

122. Matthew 25:31. Other key eschatological sayings in the gospels are to be found in Luke 17:22 ff.

123. Matthew 25:32.

124. Mark 10:45.

125. Mark 8:31. All biblical quotations are from the Authorized Version of the Bible. Although the Suffering Servant and the Son of Man already existed in Judaism, Jesus' combination of precisely these titles was something completely new. He brought together, in his own person, both a declaration of exultation – the Son of Man – and the expression of the deepest humility – the Suffering Servant of God. Even if there had been a concept of a suffering Messiah in Judaism, suffering was in no way synonymous with the Son of Man coming in all his glory on the clouds of heaven. The connection between the Son of Man and Servant of God in Ezra and in Enoch are of a formal nature and do not allude to suffering. The Son of Man, who comes out of the clouds, does not become incarnate in humanity nor does he assume the form of the Servant (Cullmann, *Christology*, 144, 161). By designating himself the title therefore, Jesus, in a unique act, was able to unite the two apparently contradictory tasks in his self-consciousness and express this unity in his life and teaching.

126. *Jesus, the Son of Man*, 42, 43.

127. Mikhail Naimy's book on Christ, entitled *Min Wahy al-Massih*, was published in Beirut in 1974.

128. Naimy, *A Biography*, 209–10.

129. *Jesus, the Son of Man*, 60.

130. Ibid., 190.

131. Ibid., 2.

132. Ibid., 60.

133. Ibid., 97.

134. Ibid., 102.

135. Ibid., 107.

136. Ibid., 133.

137. Ibid., 8.

138. Ibid., 158.

139. Ibid., 159.

140. Ibid., 64.

141. Ibid., 13.

142. Ibid., 153.

143. Ibid., 68.

144. Ibid., 168.
145. Ibid., 136.
146. Ibid., 35.
147. Ibid., 36.
148. Ibid., 182.
149. Ibid., 183.
150. Ibid., 24.
151. Ibid., 46.
152. Ibid., 45.
153. Ibid., 182.
154. Ibid., 168.
155. Ibid., 114, 115.
156. Ibid., 117.
157. Ibid., 67.
158. Ibid., 93.
159. Ibid., 68.
160. Ibid., 10.
161. Ibid., 48. Gibran once told Mary that if he had had to make his living as a "labourer," he would have been a carpenter (*B.P.*, 137).
162. *Jesus, the Son of Man*, 78.
163. Ibid.,
164. Ibid., 89.
165. Ibid., 171.
166. Ibid., 10.
167. Ibid., 30.
168. Ibid., 70.
169. Ibid., 162.
170. Ibid., 167.
171. *B.P.*, 413, 286.
172. 'Abdu'l-Bahá, *Paris Talks*, 161.
173. *Jesus, the Son of Man*, 26.
174. Mary Magdalene, never recognized as an apostle by the orthodox, is depicted in the Gospel of Mary as the one favored with visions and insights that far surpass Peter's. *The Dialogue of the Savior* praises her not only as a visionary, but as an apostle who exceeds all the rest. She is the "woman who knew the All" (*Dialogue of the Savior* 139: 12–13, Nag Hammadi Library, 235, New York, 1977). One group of gnostic sources claim to have received a secret tradition from Jesus through James and through Mary Magdalene. Members of this group prayed to both the divine Father and Mother: "From Thee, Father, and through Thee, Mother, the two immortal names, Parents of the divine being, and thou, dweller in heaven, humanity, of the mighty name" (Hippolytus, *Refutationis Omnium Haeresium* 5:6; see Pagels, *The Gnostic Gospels*, 22, 49).
175. Talk delivered at women's suffragette meeting, Metropolitan Temple, New York, by 'Abdu'l-Bahá, May 20, 1912, in *Promulgation of Universal Peace*, 134.
176. *Jesus, the Son of Man*, 15. Gibran told Mary on June 16, 1923 that he thought it significant that a tremendous number of names in his life "begin with M" (*B.P.*, 413).
177. *Jesus, the Son of Man*, 12, 13.
178. Ibid., 14–15.
179. Ibid., 15.
180. In *Nymphs of the Valley* the heroine, Martha, is forced into a life of prostitution in

Beirut. In *Sand and Foam* (p. 77) he writes: "You may sit at your window watching the passers-by. And watching you may see a nun walking toward your right hand, and a prostitute toward your left hand. And you may say in your innocence, 'How noble is the one and how ignoble is the other.' But should you close your eyes and listen awhile you would hear a voice whispering in the ether, 'One seeks me in prayer, and the other in pain. And in the spirit of each there is a bower for my spirit.'"

181. *Jesus, the Son of Man*, 146.
182. Ibid., 203–204.
183. Ibid., 209, 214–15.
184. Naimy, *A Biography*, 62.
185. *Jesus, the Son of Man*, 80.
186. Ibid., 215.
187. Talk delivered at 309 West Seventy-eighth Street, New York, by 'Abdu'l-Bahá, June 17, 1912, in *Promulgation of Universal Peace*, 204.
188. *Jesus, the Son of Man*, 16–17.
189. Ibid., 37.
190. Ibid., 54.
191. Ibid.
192. Authors' expression.
193. *B.P.*, 207.
194. *Jesus, the Son of Man*, 119, 120.
195. Ibid., 120, 121.
196. Ibid., 135.
197. Ibid., 139.
198. Ibid., 172.
199. Ibid., 191–92.
200. Ibid., 205.
201. I weep for Adonais – he is dead!
   O weep for Adonais! though our tears
   Thaw not the frost which binds so dear a head!

   Hutchinson (ed.), *Shelley*, 432

202. Frazer, *The Golden Bough*, 454–57.
203. In *Jerusalem* Blake has Jesus saying: "I am not a God afar off, I am a brother and friend. Within your bosoms I reside, and you reside in me" (*Jerusalem*, in *Blake*, 622); and in *The Everlasting Gospel*, Blake's views reflect Gibran's own perceptions of Jesus:

   This is the Race that Jesus ran:
   Humble to God, Haughty to Man,
   Cursing the Rulers before the People
   Even to the temple's highest Steeple;
   And when he Humbled himself to God,
   Then descended the Cruel Rod.
   "If thou humblest thyself, thou humblest me;
   "Thou also dwell'st in Eternity.
   "Thou art a Man, God is no more,
   "Thy own humanity learn to adore,
   "For that is my Spirit of Life,
   "Awake, arise to Spiritual Strife.

   (*The Everlasting Gospel*, in *Blake*, 752–53)

204. *The Everlasting Gospel*, in *Blake*, 750.
205. "A Vision of The Last Judgment," in ibid., 615.
206. *Spiritual Sayings* (1963), 46.
207. *The Everlasting Gospel*, in *Blake*, 749.
208. *Jerusalem*, in ibid., 716–17.
209. Ibid., 621.
210. "Another's Sorrow," in ibid., 122.
211. "The Marriage of Heaven and Hell," in ibid., 158.
212. *The Everlasting Gospel*, in ibid. 750.
213. Annotations to Watson, ibid., 389.
214. D. H. Lawrence, whose last book, *Apocalypse*, was written in 1929 and was an interpretation of the book of Revelation, wrote of the Bible: "The Bible is a book that has been temporarily killed for us by having its meaning arbitrarily fixed. We know it so thoroughly, in its superficial or popular meaning, that it is dead, it gives us nothing any more" (Lawrence, *Apocalypse*, 3).
215. Jenkins, *Christianity*, 66–67.
216. Kahlil Gibran to Mariita Lawson, September 8, 1926.
217. J. and K. Gibran, *Life and World*, 388.
218. *A Self-Portrait* (1972), 80.
219. Naimy, "A Strange Little Book," 15.
220. The exact nature of this political office is unknown and apart from Gibran's reference to the affair (*B.P.*, 438) no other supporting documentary evidence can be found.
221. *B.P.*, 438.
222. J. and K. Gibran, *Life and World*, 389.
223. Wilson, "Jesus was the supreme poet." In the article Wilson discusses *Jesus, the Son of Man* and a book by Walter Russell Bowie entitled *The Master* which was published in the same year (1928).
224. *Manchester Guardian* review quoted in Young, *This Man from Lebanon* (1945), 109–10.
225. Bragdon, "A Modern Prophet from Lebanon," in *Merely Players*, 143–44.
226. John Haynes Holmes' review is quoted in Young, *This Man from Lebanon* (1945), 110, and in *Jesus, the Son of Man* (1928).
227. *Springfield Union* review quoted in Young, *This Man from Lebanon* (1945), 36–37.
228. *B.P.*, 438.
229. *A Self-Portrait* (1972), 85.
230. Kahlil Gibran to Mariita Lawson, August 7, 1928.
231. Ibid., April 6, 1927.
232. *A Self-Portrait* (1972), 86.
233. Bragdon, *More Lives*, 272.
234. *A Self-Portrait* (1972), 86. He also expressed a similar desire to Mary Haskell on May 16, 1929, when he wrote: "My book on Shakespeare is still a thing of the mind" (*B.P.*, 439, and Otto (ed.), *Love Letters*, 670).
235. *A Self-Portrait* (1972), 62.

11. THE RETURN OF THE WANDERER

1. Guests at his forty-sixth birthday included members of the Delphic Group; members of the New York Craftsman's Poetry Group, headed by Elizabeth Crittenden Percy; Judge Richard Campbell, patron of the Abbey Theatre Players; Syud Hussein, editor of the *New Orient*; the poets Estelle Duclo and Van Noppen; the critics José Juan

Tablada and Claude Bragdon; and Dr. Demetrios Callimachos (J. and K. Gibran, *Life and World*, 393).

2. Reed, *Orozco*, 66, 102–105.

3. Hitti, "Gibran's Place and "Influence," 31–33. A commemorative anthology, *al-Sanabil (The Spikes of Grain)*, was prepared for the occasion.

4. *A Self-Portrait* (1972), 89–90.

5. Naimy, *A Biography*, 218.

6. After being completed by Barbara Young, it was published in 1933, but critics doubted its literary value. (Bushrui and al-Kuzbari (eds.), *Gibran: Love Letters*, xi.) Hawi thought that Barbara Young may "have included pieces by Gibran which did not properly belong" to *The Garden of the Prophet* (Hawi, *Kahlil Gibran*, 240).

7. Naimy, *A Biography*, 218.

8. *B.P.*, 439.

9. Feb. 24, 1911, Chapel Hill papers. Quoted in J. and K. Gibran, *Life and World*, 394.

10. Quoted in J. and K. Gibran, *Life and World*, 394. Barbara Young in *This Man from Lebanon* (1945, 113) claimed that, "in 1914–1915, he had written perhaps two-thirds of the book," but some scholars (Hawi, *Kahlil Gibran*, 237) believe that Young was "not particularly devoted to accuracy where dates were concerned." By April 1916 Gibran and Mary were referring to the three gods as "the three *Giants*" (*B.P.*, 270).

11. John Keats (1795–1821) began *Hyperion* in 1818, abandoning it a year later just two years before his death. Hawi found references to Keats's work in Gibran's notebooks of 1904 (Hawi, *Kahlil Gibran*, 175). Gibran wrote a poem about Keats entitled "Bihurouf min Nar" ("With Letters of Fire") which was published in *A Tear and a Smile*.

12. John Keats in *Hyperion: Book 1*, in Drabble (ed.), *The Oxford Anthology of English Literature*, 505.

13. *The Earth Gods* (1962), 3.

14. Keats, *Hyperion*, in Drabble (ed.), *The Oxford Anthology of English Literature*, 504.

15. 'Abdul-Hai, *Tradition*, 146–47.

16. This knowledge is referred to in ibid., 146, and documented in many of Mary Haskell's journal entries.

17. Young, *This Man from Lebanon* (1945), 169.

18. 'Abdul-Hai, *Tradition*, 146.

19. Young, *This Man from Lebanon* (1945), 169.

20. *B.P.*, 258. In Gibran's last work too (*The Wanderer*), his doubts can be detected in the parable "The Two Poems," in which the "greatest poem yet written in Greek", an "invocation to Zeus the Supreme", although remembered "in libraries and in the cells of scholars" is "neither loved nor read" (*The Wanderer* [1995] 60).

21. Bushrui and al-Kuzbari (eds.), *Gibran: Love Letters*, 11.

22. *The Earth Gods*, 5.

23. Ibid., 25.

24. The third god, although a similar figure to the youth in *al-Mawakib* (*The Procession*), views love not as universal and pantheistic but particular: the love between man and woman (Hawi, *Kahlil Gibran*, 238).

25. *The Earth Gods*, 37.

26. Ghougassian, *Wings of Thought*, 45.

27. *The Earth Gods*, 13.

28. Ibid., 38.

29. Ibid., 40.

30. For Gibran, like the Chaldeans he so respected, three was sacred number (*B.P.*, 344). Three is

> the basis of numerous systems and ordering schemes; thus, Christianity, for example, has the three virtues of faith, love, and hope, and alchemy has the 3 basic principles of Sulphur, Salt and Quicksilver, etc. Divine triumvirates are known in many religions, for example in Egypt (Isis, Osiris, Horus), in Hinduism (Brahma, Vishnu, Shiva), etc. Such divine triumvirates often appear in conjunction with Heaven, Earth and Air (which binds them together). In contrast to this, Christianity has a triune God who is often envisaged as being a unity of three persons (a trinity). As the number of fulfilment of a self-contained entirety, 3 is frequently encountered in fairy tales as the number of tests that one must withstand or riddles that one must solve. (Becker (ed.), *Encyclopedia of Symbols*, 298)

> At the root of all ancient traditions is the teaching of the law of three principles or three forces – which states that for any effective manifestation, three forces have to combine in an appropriate relationship: an active force (force of intention), a passive force (force of opposition), and a reconciling force. Humanity is seen as an image of the world, created by the same laws that create and govern the world: "The action of the three forces and the moment of entry of the third force may be discovered in all manifestations of our psychic life; in all the phenomena of the life of human communities; of humanity as a whole; and in all the phenomena of nature around us" – on whatever scale and in whatever world it may take place, from molecular to cosmic phenomena (Ouspensky, *Cosmological Lectures*, 7–9).

31. *This Man from Lebanon* (1945), 113.
32. The prosody in *The Earth Gods* is often ponderous:

> Now I will rise and strip me of time and space,
> And I will dance in that field untrodden,
> And the dancer's feet will move with my feet;
> And I will sing in that higher air,
> And a human voice will throb within my voice."

(*The Earth Gods*, 40)

> Here the device of repetition, which Gibran had so often used before to such telling effect, merely holds up the verse. The fourth line in particular is an example of the vapid generalizing that can so easily beset "ethereal poetry."

33. Hawi, *Kahlil Gibran,* 239. The Sufi concept of the 'Perfect Man' (*al-insan al-kamil*) is paralleled in other spiritual traditions and is derived from Jewish mysticism.
34. *The Everlasting Gospel,* in *Blake,* 750.
35. *The Earth Gods,* 39.
36. Young, *This Man from Lebanon* (1945), 112.
37. *B.P.,* 229.
38. *A Self-Portrait* (1972), 90.
39. Gibran never lived to see these parables published; they were finally published as *The Wanderer* in 1932 by Knopf.
40. *B.P.,* 440.
41. K.G. to M.H., Nov. 8, 1929, Chapel Hill papers.
42. *A Self-Portrait* (1972), 88.
43. Letter from Felix Farris to Gibran, in ibid., 91.
44. Idella Purnell, "Gift for Mimicry Harms Poet," review of English edition of Mikhail Naimy's biography, *Los Angeles Daily News,* Nov. 4, 1950, p. 9.
45. Her coded entries of this time included "L.1," "L-1-2", "8L-62-P3-PH.4," which she later explained as: "The pencilled cap. Letters and numerals atop of pp. are a code to

record work with K. Gibran's mss" (in July 12–Aug 2, 1930, in Chapel Hill papers quoted in J. and K. Gibran, *Life and World,* 396).

46. Naimy, *A Biography,* 209.
47. "Song of the Wave," in *A Tear and a Smile,* 177.
48. *The Prophet,* 114.
49. *B.P.,* 225.
50. The titles are those given by Annie Salem Otto in *Parables;* the interpretations are those of the present authors.
51. *The Earth Gods,* 31.
52. *A Self-Portrait* (1972), 89.
53. J. and K. Gibran, *Life and World,* 396–37. Kahlil wrote to Mary Haskell on November 21, 1930 telling her that Marianna was now living at 281 Forest Hills St., Jamaica Plains, Mass. (*B.P.,* 441). Marianna lived a simple existence until 1968 when illness forced her into a nursing home where she died in her eighty-eighth year on March 28, 1972 (J. and K. Gibran, *Life and World,* 421).
54. J. and K. Gibran, *Life and World,* 397.
55. Gibran's work continues to become more universal than ever and it is estimated that it has been translated into more than thirty languages.
56. Naimy, *A Biography,* 216.
57. *The Wanderer,* 3.
58. K. G. to M. H., March 16, 1931, Chapel Hill papers.
59. Hawi, *Kahlil Gibran,* 239.
60. May 30, 1922, Chapel Hill papers. Gibran's message of hope and healing never seemed to wane or waver.
61. *The Wanderer,* 3.
62. Ibid., 86.
63. *B.P.,* 204.
64. Ibid., 270.
65. Ibid., 150.
66. *The Wanderer,* 38.
67. Ibid., 37.
68. Ibid., 7.
69. Nadeem Naimy, "Kahlil Gibran: His Poetry and Thought", in Bushrui and Gotch (eds.), *Gibran of Lebanon: New Papers,* 35–36.
70. *The Prophet,* 92.
71. *The Wanderer,* 12.
72. Ibid., 46.
73. Ibid., 39.
74. Ibid., 43.
75. Ibid., 26.
76. Ibid., 78.
77. Ibid., 84.
78. Gibran like his contemporary T. S. Eliot felt the "river within." T. S. Eliot writes: "The river is within us, the sea is all about us", in *Four Quartets* ("The Dry Salvages," 1:15), 25; and in "Ash Wednesday":

> Sister, mother
> And spirit of the river, spirit of the sea,
> Suffer me not to be separated
> And let my cry come unto Thee.

79. *The Wanderer*, 82–83. "The sea," "River," "ocean," "cloud," "rain," and "mist" are key symbols for Gibran in both his Arabic and English works, for example: The sea representing the great spirit or greater self; a boundless drop to a boundless ocean – the self yearning to return to its source; mist: mystery and eternity.

80. *The Wanderer*, 7.

81. Ibid., 13.

82. Naimy, *A Biography*, 217.

83. Ibid., 219.

84. Ibid.

85. In a letter to J. and K. Gibran, Gertrude Stein claimed that before the end of his life Gibran asked her to marry him (September 3, 1975, quoted in J. and K. Gibran, *Life and World*, 432).

86. Ibid.

87. Isaac Horowitz translated *The Prophet* into Hebrew according to Gertrude Stein in ibid., 433.

88. Gertrude Stein, letter to J. and K. Gibran, November 7, 1977. Extracts quoted in ibid. 433.

89. *A Self-Portrait* (1972), 93.

90. *B.P.*, 365.

91. Naimy, *A Biography*, 222.

92. Ibid., 40–41.

93. Ibid., 227.

94. *B.P.*, 442.

95. Jayyusi, *Trends and Movements*, 94–95.

96. *The Prophet*, 90–91.

97. *B.P.*, 443.

98. Ibid., 444.

99. Ibid., 445.

100. "The Last Days of Gibran", 21.

101. *B.P.*, 6.

102. Young, "Gibran's Funeral," 23–25.

103. Naimy, *A Biography*, 264.

104. *B.P.*, 447–48.

105. Ibid., 448.

106. *The Prophet*, 154.

EPILOGUE

1. Yousef Sarkis, *Jami'al Tasanif al-Haditha*, Cairo, Sarkis Library, 1927, vol. I.

2. Yousef Sarkis, *Mu'am al Maltbo'at*, Cairo, Sarkis Library, 1928–29.

3. Yousef Ass'ad Daghir, *Masader al-Dirasah al-Adabiyah*, Sidon, al-Mokhalles Printing Press, 1956.

4. Ameen Khalid, *Muhawalat-fi Darsi Jubran*, Beirut, al-Maba'a al-Katholikiah, 1933.

5. Shukrallah Al-Jurr, *Nabi Orphalese*, Brazil, Matba'at al-Andalus, 1939.

6. Jameel Jabr, *Jurbran Siratuhu, Adabuhu, Falsafatuhu wa Rasmuhu*, Beirut, Rihani, 1958.

7. Mikhail Naimy, *Jubran Khalil Jubran: Hayatuhu, Mawtuhu, Adabuhu, Fannuhu*, Beirut, Dar Sader wa Beirut, 1934.

8. Mikhail Naimy interviewed in 1978 said: "I wrote my book on Gibran from a personal perspective. This is how I saw him and this is what I have recorded" (Mikhail Naimy Interviews, 1978).

9. Khalil S. Hawi, *Kahlil Gibran: His Background, Character and Works*, Beirut, American University of Beirut, 1963 (repr. London, Third World Centre for Research and Publication, 1982).

10. Suheil Bushrui (ed.), *An Introduction to Kahlil Gibran*, Gibran International Festival, May 23–30, 1970, Beirut, Dar el-Mashreq.

11. Suheil Bushrui, *Kahlil Gibran: A Bibliography* (of English and Arabic Publications), Beirut, Centenary Publications, 1983.

12. Department of English, American University of Beirut, Prospectus 1973–74, pp. 16–17.

13. Translated from the Arabic by Suheil Bushrui and Salma H. al-Kuzbari. Translations also exist in French, German, Italian, and Spanish.

14. Suheil Bushrui and Paul Gotch (eds.), *Gibran of Lebanon: New Papers*, Beirut, Librairie du Liban, 1975.

15. Salma Khadra Jayyusi, *Trends and Movements in Modern Arabic Poetry*, Leiden, E. J. Brill, 1977, 91.

16. William Shehadi, *Kahlil Gibran: A Prophet in the Making; Manuscript Pages of* The Madman, The Forerunner, The Prophet, The Earth Gods *and Four Hitherto Unpublished Manuscripts: Lullaby, The Last Guest, Untitled, Poverty and Sundry Aphorisms*, Beirut, the American Univeristy of Beirut, 1991. The late William Shehadi began his work on these manuscripts assisted substantially by Suheil Bushrui as co-editor. The fighting in Lebanon in the 1980s prevented the continuation of the joint editorial work and the book was completed by Dr. Shehadi himself.

17. Kahlil Gibran is the poet's cousin and namesake.

18. Wahib Kayrouz, *'Alam Jubran al-Rassam*, Beirut, Gibran National Committee, 1982.

19. Wahib Kayrouz, *'Alam Jubran al-Fikri*, Beirut, Bisharia, 1984, 2 vols.

20. *In Memory of Kahlil Gibran: The First Colloquium on Gibran Studies*, collected, edited and introduced by Suheil B. Bushrui and Albert Mutlak, Librarie du Liban, 1981.

21. The exhibition illustrates selected aspects of the life and work of Kahlil Gibran. It consists of over 100 photographs, with commentary, suitably reproduced for public display, of people, places, and events in the poet's lifetime and also of reproductions of some of Gibran's paintings, drawings, and sketches. The material includes a number of rare photographs, and the collection brought together here is unique. The selected passages and photographs illustrate comprehensively both the range of Gibran's work and, for the English reader, its peculiar quality, at once exotic and familiar. The exhibition sets the poet in the context of his life, his native land and the travels, spiritual as well as geographic, that shaped his genius.

22. President Kerr, in inter-office correspondence with Professor Suheil Bushrui dated March 5, 1983 stated: "The Deans and I are unanimously enthusiastic" in their announcement of plans for a Gibran chair.

23. *"The Prophet" by Kahlil Gibran, A Musical Interpretation featuring Richard Harris*, Atlantic Recording Corporation of New York, 1974.

24. Neil Lawson Baker, *A Prayer for Lebanon: The Gibran Bronzes* (privately printed brochure).

25. Letter from Jimmy Carter to William Baroody, chairman and president, the Kahlil Gibran Centennial Foundation, Washington D.C.; May 24, 1991, published in *The Kahlil Gibran Memorial Garden: A Gift to the People of the United States of America* (catalogue), 1991.

26. *The Prophet: Introduction and Annotations*, ed. Suheil Bushrui, Oxford, Oneworld, 1995.

27. *Il Profeta*, introduzione e traduzione a cura di Suheil Bushrui, Milan, Biblioteca Universale Rizzoli, 1993.

28. Robert Bouquins, *Les oeuvres complètes de Kahlil Gibran*, Laffont, 1997.

29. *The Books of the Century*, Waterstones in association with Channel 4, September 1996.

Bibliography

WORKS BY KAHLIL GIBRAN

Works in Arabic

al-'Ajnihah al-Mutakassirah (*The Broken Wings*), New York, Mir'at al-Gharb, 1912
'Ara'is al-Muruj (*Nymphs of the Valley*), New York, al-Mohajer, 1908
al-'Arwah al-Mutamarridah (*Spirits Rebellious*), New York, al-Mohajer, 1906
al-'Awasif (*The Tempests*), Cairo, al-Hilal, 1920
al-Badayi' wa Taray'if (*Beautiful and Rare Sayings*), Cairo, Maktabti al-'Arb, 1925
Dam'ah wa Ibtisamah (*A Tear and a Smile*), New York, Mir'at al-Gharb, 1914
al-Mawakib (*The Procession*), New York, Mir'at al-Gharb, 1919

Works written in English

The Earth Gods, New York, Alfred A. Knopf, 1931; London, Heinemann, 1962 (references
   in notes are to 1962 edition)
The Forerunner: His Parables and Poems, New York, Alfred A. Knopf, 1920; London,
   Heinemann, 1963, 1974 (references in notes are to 1974 edition)
The Garden of the Prophet, New York, Alfred A. Knopf, 1931, 1933; London, Heinemann,
   1954
Jesus, the Son of Man: His Words and his Deeds as Told and Recorded by Those who Knew him,
   New York, Alfred A. Knopf, 1928; London, Heinemann, 1954; Oxford, Oneworld,
   1993 (references in notes are to 1993 edition)
Kahlil Gibran, a Prophet in the Making: Manuscript Pages of The Madman, The Forerunner,
   The Prophet, *and* The Earth Gods, *and Four Hitherto Unpublished Manuscripts: Lullaby,
   The Last Guest, Untitled, Poverty and Sundry Aphorisms*, ed. W. Shehadi, Beirut,
   American University of Beirut, 1991
Lazarus and his Beloved: A One-Act Play, ed. and intro. by the author's cousin and namesake,
   Kahlil Gibran, and his wife, Jean Gibran, Greenwich, CT, New York Philosophical
   Society, 1973; London, Heinemann, 1973
The Madman: His Parables and Poems, New York, Alfred A. Knopf, 1918; London,
   Heinemann, 1946, 1963, 1971 (references in notes are to 1946 edition)
The Prophet, New York, Alfred A. Knopf, 1923; London, Heinemann, 1926; *The Prophet:
   Introduction and Annotations*, ed. S. B. Bushrui, Oxford, Oneworld, 1991, 1995, 1997
   (references in notes are to 1995 edition)
The Prophet, trans. S. Okasha (into Arabic), Cairo, Dar al-Maaref, 1959
Prophet, Madman, Wanderer (slightly abridged anthology), London, Penguin, 1995
Sand and Foam, New York, Alfred A. Knopf, 1926, 1996; London, Heinemann, 1927, 1954
   (references in notes are to 1996 edition)

The Wanderer: His Parables and his Sayings, New York, Alfred A. Knopf, 1932, 1995; London, Heinemann, 1965 (references in notes are to 1995 edition)

Works translated from Arabic

Beautiful and Rare Sayings, Cairo, Makrabet al-Gharb, 1923

The Beloved: Reflections on the Path of the Heart, trans. J. Walbridge, Ashland, White Cloud Press, 1994

Between Night and Morn: A Special Selection, trans. A. R. Ferris, New York, Wisdom Library, 1972

The Broken Wings, trans. A. R. Ferris, New York, Citadel Press, 1957, 1989; London, Heinemann, 1959; New York, Wisdom Library, 1972

The Eye of the Prophet, trans. from the French by M. Crosland, from a translation by M. Dahdah, London, Souvenir Press, 1995

The Kahlil Gibran Reader: Inspirational Writings, Secaucus, Carol Publishing Group, 1995

Mirrors of the Soul, trans. and with biographical notes by J. Sheban, New York, Philosophical Library, 1965; New York, First Carol, 1992 (references in notes are to 1992 edition)

Nymphs of the Valley, trans. H. M. Nahmad, New York, Alfred A. Knopf, 1948; London, Heinemann, 1948

The Life of Kahlil Gibran and his Procession, ed., trans., and with a biographical sketch by G. Kheirallah, New York, Arab-American Press, 1947; New York, Wisdom Library, 1958

Prophecies of Love: Reflections from the Heart, selected by J. Clardy, Kansas City, Hallmark Cards Inc., 1971

Prose Poems, trans. A. Ghareeb, New York, Alfred A. Knopf, 1934; London, Heinemann, 1964

A Second Treasury of Kahlil Gibran, ed. M. L. Wolf and trans. A. R. Ferris, New York, Citadel Press, 1962

Secrets of the Heart, ed. M. L. Wolf, trans. A. R. Ferris, New York, Philosophical Library, 1947; New York, Signet, 1965; New York, First Carol, 1992 (references in the notes are to 1992 edition)

Spirit Brides, trans. J. R. I. Cole, Santa Cruz, White Cloud Press, 1993

Spirits Rebellious, trans. H. M. Nahmad, New York, Alfred A. Knopf, 1948; London, Heinemann, 1949, 1964 (references in notes are to 1949 edition)

Spiritual Sayings, ed. and trans. A. R. Ferris, New York, Bantam, 1970; London, Heinemann, 1962, 1974 (references in notes are to 1974 edition)

The Storm: Stories and Prose Poems, trans. J. Walbridge, Santa Cruz, White Cloud Press, 1993

A Tear and a Smile, trans. H. M. Nahmad, intro. R. Hillyer, New York, Alfred A. Knopf, 1950, 1994; London, Heinemann, 1950 (references in notes are to 1994 edition)

Tears and Laughter, trans. A. R. Ferris, New York, Philosophical Library, 1947; New York, First Carol, 1990 (references in notes are to 1990 edition)

A Third Treasury of Kahlil Gibran, ed. A. D. Sherfan, Secaucus, Citadel Press, 1975

Thoughts and Meditations, trans. A. R. Ferris, New York, Citadel Press, 1961; London, Heinemann, 1960, 1961, 1973

The Treasured Writings of Kahlil Gibran, Secaucus, Castle, 1985

A Treasury of Kahlil Gibran, ed. M. L. Wolf, trans. A. R. Ferris, New York, Citadel Press, 1951; London, Heinemann, 1974; London, Mandarin, 1991, 1994 (references in notes are to 1991 edition)

The Vision: Reflections on the Way of the Soul, trans. J. R. I. Cole, Ashland, White Cloud Press, 1994

The Voice of Kahlil Gibran: ed. R. Waterfield, London, Penguin, 1995

The Voice of the Master, trans. A. R. Ferris, New York, Citadel Press, 1963; London,

Heinemann, 1960, 1973
The Wisdom of Gibran: Aphorisms and Maxims, ed. and trans. J. Sheban, New York, Philosophical Library, 1966

Art works

Drawing and Watercolors by Kahlil Gibran (1883–1931) December 2–21, New York, M. Knoedler & Co., 1946
An Introduction to the Art of Kahlil Gibran, Alpine Fine Arts Collection, 1991
Sculpture: Kahlil Gibran, foreword by E. H. Turner, Boston, Bartlet Press, 1970
Twenty Drawings, intro. A. Raphael, New York, Alfred A. Knopf, 1919

Short writings (articles and poems) published in Syrian World *(New York)*

"On the Art of Writing," 4, 9, May 1930, 26
"Critics," 2, 10, April 1928, 34
"The Deeper Pain," 6, 3, November 1931, 10
"Defeat" (poem), 3, 7, January 1929, 23
"Fame" (trans. A. Ghareeb), 3, 10, April 1929, 28
"Freedom and Slavery" (poem), 6, 6, February 1932, 43
"Gibran's Message to Young Americans of Syrian Origin" (repr. from the first issue of *Syrian World*), 5, 8, April 1931, 44–45
"On Giving and Taking," 4, 7, March 1930, 32
"On Giving and Taking," 5, 2, October 1930, 38
"The Great Longing," 3, 8, February 1929, 8
"Greatness," 5, 1, September 1930, 41
"The Great Recurrence," 6, 4, December 1931, 12–14
"On Hatred," 4, 10, June 1930, 28
"Helpfulness," 4, 8, April 1930, 13
"I Wandered among the Mountains," in Syrian Folk Songs, 1, 2, May 1927, 11
"The King of Aradus," 3, 3, September 1928, 17
"Love" (poem), 2, 12, June 1928, 11
"A Man from Lebanon Nineteen Centuries Afterward," 3, 5, November 1928, 21–26
"A Marvel and a Riddle," 5, 5, January 1931, 18
"O Mother Mine" (Moulaya), in Syrian Folk Songs, 1, 9, March 1927, 13
"Night" (trans. A. Ghareeb), 3, 6, December 1928, 10–12
"Out of my Deeper Heart," 3, 11, May 1929, 14
"Past and Future," 5, 6, February 1931, 40
"The Plutocrat," 3, 4, October 1928, 10
"Reflections on Love," 6, 2, October 1931, 44
"Revelation" (trans. A. Ghareeb), 5, 10, June 1931, 24–25
"Said a Blade of Grass," 2, 9, March 1928, 11
"The Saint," 3, 9, March 1929, 9
"Song," 5, 4, December 1930, 13
"Speech and Silence," 5, 7, March 1931, 36
"Three Maiden Lovers," in Syrian Folk Songs, 2, 2, August 1927, 13
"The Two Hermits," 2, 4, October 1927, 10
"The Two Learned Men," 4, 5, January 1930, 29
"War," 2, 7, January 1928, 5
"War and the Small Nations," 2, 11, May 1928, 23
When my Sorrow was Born," 2, 6, December 1927, 18
"To Young Americans of Syrian Origin," 1, 1, July 1926, 4–5

"Youth and Age," 1, 6, December 1926, 3–5

LETTERS

Hilu, V. (ed. and arr.), *Beloved Prophet: The Love Letters of Kahlil Gibran and Mary Haskell and her Private Journal*, New York, Alfred A. Knopf, 1972 (in notes *B.P.*)

Bushrui, S. B. and S. H. al-Kuzbari (eds. and trans.), *Blue Flame: The Love Letters of Kahlil Gibran and May Ziadah*, Harlow, Longman, 1983

Bushrui, S. B. and S. H. al-Kuzbari (eds. and trans.), *Gibran: Love Letters*, Oxford, Oneworld, 1995 (rev. ed. of *Blue Flame*)

Chapel Hill papers (Minis family papers), in the Southern Historical Collection, University of North Carolina at Chapel Hill, item #2725, 1948 (includes correspondence of Mary Elizabeth [Haskell] Minis from and about Kahlil Gibran)

I Care about your Happiness: Quotations from the Love Letters of Kahlil Gibran and Mary Haskell, selected by S. P. Schutz and N. Hoffman, Boulder, Blue Mountain Arts, 1976

Otto, A. S. (ed. and arr.), *The Love Letters of Kahlil Gibran and Mary Haskell*, Houston, Annie Salem Otto, 1964

Unpublished Gibran Letters to Ameen Rihani, trans. S. B. Bushrui, Beirut, Rihani House for the World Lebanese Cultural Union, 1972

BIOGRAPHY AND CRITICISM

Works wholly devoted to Gibran

Bushrui, S. B., *Kahlil Gibran: A Bibliography*, Beirut, Centenary Publications, 1983

Bushrui, S. B., *Kahlil Gibran: An Introductory Survey of his Life and his Work*, Ibadan, University of Ibadan Press, 1966

Bushrui, S. B., *Kahlil Gibran of Lebanon: A Re-evaluation of the Life and Work of the Author of* The Prophet, Gerrards Cross, C. Smythe, 1987

Bushrui, S. B. (ed.), *An Introduction to Kahlil Gibran* (Gibran International Festival, May 23–30, 1970), Beirut, Dar el-Mashreq, 1970, 1990

Bushrui, S. B., J. M. Munro, M. Smith, and S. A. Hamdeh, *A Poet and his Country: Gibran's Lebanon*, Beirut, Middle East Press Inc., 1970

Bushrui, S. B. and P. Gotch (eds.), *Gibran of Lebanon: New Papers*, Beirut, Librairie du Liban, 1975

Bushrui, S. B. and J. M. Munro (eds.), *Kahlil Gibran: Essays and Introductions*, Beirut, Rihani House, 1970

Bushrui, S. B. and A. Mutlak (eds.), *In Memory of Kahlil Gibran: The First Colloquium on Gibran Studies*, Beirut, Librairie du Liban, 1981

Daoudi, M. S., *The Meaning of Kahlil Gibran*, Secaucus, Citadel Press, 1982

Ghougassian, J. P., *Kahlil Gibran: Wings of Thought: The People's Philosopher*, New York, Philosophical Library, 1973

Gibran, J. and K. Gibran, *Kahlil Gibran: His Life and World*, Boston, New York Graphic Society, 1974; New York, Avenel Books, 1981; New York, Interlink Books, 1991 (references in notes are to 1981 edition)

Gibran, Kahlil, *Kahlil Gibran: A Self-Portrait* (includes fifty letters), ed. and trans. A. R. Ferris, London, Heinemann, 1960, 1972, 1974 (references in notes are to 1974 edition)

Guraieb, A., "Jubran Khalil Jubran," *al-Haris*, 8, 1931

Hawi, K. S., *Khalil Gibran: His Background, Character and Works* (includes four letters), Beirut, American University of Beirut, 1963; Beirut, Arab Institute for Research and Publishing, 1972; London, Third World Centre for Research and Publication, 1982

(references in notes are to 1972 edition)

Huwayik, Y., *Gibran in Paris*, trans. and intro. M. Moosa, New York, Popular Library, 1976

Kahlil Gibran: Essays and Introductions (anthology of criticism compiled for the Gibran International Festival, May 23–30, 1970), Beirut, Rihani House, 1970

Naimy, M., *Kahlil Gibran: A Biography*, New York, Philosophical Library, 1950, 1975, 1985 (references in notes are to 1950 edition)

Naimy, M., *Kahlil Gibran: His Life and his Work* (includes twenty-seven letters written to the author), Beirut, Khayat, 1964; Beirut, Naufal, 1974 (references in notes are to 1974 edition)

Otto, A. S., *The Art of Kahlil Gibran* (includes four letters), Port Arthur, Hinds Printing Company, 1965

Otto, A. S., *The Parables of Kahlil Gibran: An Interpretation of his Writings and his Art*, New York, Citadel Press, 1963

Rihani, A., *In Memory of Kahlil Gibran: The First Colloquium on Gibran Studies*, Beirut, Librairie de Liban, 1981

Shehadi, W., *Kahlil Gibran: Writer, Poet, Artist*, Washington, D.C., A.D.C. Research Institute, A.D.C. issue paper no. 12, 1985

Sherfan, A. D., *Kahlil Gibran: The Nature of Love*, New York, Philosophical Library, 1971

Waterfield, R. (ed.), *The Voice of Kahlil Gibran: An Anthology*, London, Arkana, 1995

Young, B., *This Man from Lebanon: A Study of Kahlil Gibran*, New York, privately printed by the Syrian American Press, 1931; New York, Alfred A. Knopf, 1945, 1981

Theses

El-Hage, G. N., "William Blake and Kahlil Gibran: Poets of Prophetic Vision," Ph.D. thesis, State University of New York at Binghampton, 1980; published in *Dahesh Voice*, 2, 1, June 1996

Etre, B. G., "The Influence of Lebanese Culture on the Writings of Kahlil Gibran," M.A. thesis, Makato State College, 1970

Hanna, S. ibn Salim, "An Arab Expatriate in America: Kahlil Gibran in his American Setting," Ph.D. thesis, Indiana University, 1973

Miller, N. C., "Prophet or Madman: The Enigma of Kahlil Gibran," M.A. thesis, University of Texas at El Paso, 1954

Ross, M. J., "The Writings of Kahlil Gibran," M.A. thesis, University of Texas, 1948

Salter, M., "Kahlil Gibran, *The Prophet*," M.A. thesis, Miami University, 1968

Takla, S. B., "Women Characters in the Work of Kahlil Gibran," Beirut, Lebanese University, 1970

Wright, N. M., "Gibran Kahlil Gibran: Poet, Painter and Philosopher," M.A. thesis, University of New Hampshire, 1938

Works devoting some attention to Gibran's work or life

Bercovici, K., *Around the World*, New York, Century, 1924

Bragdon, C., *Merely Players*, New York, Alfred A. Knopf, 1929

Bragdon, C., *More Lives than One*, New York, Alfred A. Knopf, 1937

Brockelmann, C., "Die moderne arabische Litteratur," *Geschichte der arabischen Litteratur* (dritter Supplementband), Leiden, E. J. Brill, 1942

Bynner, W., "Kahlil the Gibranite," in *The Borzoi*, New York, Alfred A. Knopf, 1925

Hooglund, E. J. (ed.), *Crossing the Waters: Arab-Speaking Immigrants to the United States before 1940*, Washington, D.C. and London, Smithsonian Institution Press, 1987 (includes chap. by J. and K. Gibran, "The Symbolic Quest of Kahlil Gibran: The Arab as Artist in America")

Jayyusi, S. K., *Trends and Movements in Modern Arabic Poetry*, 2 vols., Leiden, E. J. Brill, 1977

Khemiri, T. and G. Kampffmeyer, *Leaders in Contemporary Arabic Literature*, London, Trubner, 1930

Knopf, A. A., *Portrait of a Publisher 1915–1965: Reminiscences and Reflections*, 2 vols., New York, Typophiles, 1965

Knopf, A. A., *Some Random Recollections: An Informal Talk Made at the Grolier Club*, New York, Typophiles, 1949

Nahas, J., *Seventy-eight and Still Musing: Observations and Reflections: With Personal Reminiscences of Gibran as I Knew him*, Hicksville, N.Y., Exposition Press, 1974

Naimy, N. N., *The Lebanese Prophets of New York*, Beirut, American University of Beirut, 1985

Naimy, N. N., *Mikhail Naimy: An Introduction*, Beirut, American University of Beirut, faculty of arts and sciences, Oriental Series no. 47, 1967

Nassar, E. P., *Essays: Critical and Metacritical*, Rutherford, N.J., Fairleigh Dickinson University Press, Associated University Presses, 1983

Nassar, E. P., *Wind of the Land: Two Prose Poems*, Detroit, Association of Arab-American University Graduates, A.A.U.G. monograph series no. 11, 1979

Pilpel, H. and T. Zavin, *Rights and Writers*, New York, Dutton, 1960

Poetry Criticism, vol. 9, Detroit, Gale Research, Inc., 1994

Reed, A., *Orozco*, New York, Oxford University Press, 1956

Russell, G. W. (AE), *The Living Torch*, New York, Macmillan, 1938

ESSAYS, ARTICLES, AND REVIEWS IN MAGAZINES AND NEWSPAPERS

'Abbud, M., in *al-Makshuf*, 3, Beirut, 1937

Amyuni, M. T., "William Shehadi, *Kahlil Gibran, a Prophet in the Making*" (review), *Middle East Studies Association Bulletin*, 28, 1, July 1994, 138

Bacon, B. W., "Jesus and his Interpreters," *New Republic*, 57, 734, December 26, 1928, 69

Beder, A., "The Spirit of Gibran" (poem), *Syrian World*, 5, 9, May 1931, 18

Benet, W. R., "Round about Parnassus," *Saturday Review of Literature*, 7, 36, March 28, 1931, 696

Benet, W. R., "Round about Parnassus," *Saturday Review of Literature*, 8, 24, January 2, 1932, 428

Booklist, 16, April 1920, 231 (review of *Twenty Drawings*)

Booklist, 27, September 1931, 19 (review of *The Earth Gods*)

Booklist, 28, March 1932, 301 (review of *The Wanderer*)

Booklist, 45, June 1949, 357 (review of *Tears and Laughter*)

Bookman, 42, December 20, 1920, 347 (review of *The Forerunner*)

Boston Evening Transcript, January 25, 1919, 9 (review of *The Madman*)

Boston Evening Transcript, November 3, 1920, 6 (review of *The Forerunner*)

Boston Evening Transcript, December 1928, 1 (review of *Jesus, the Son of Man*)

Boston Evening Transcript, April 29, 1931, 2 (review of *The Earth Gods*)

Boston Evening Transcript, March 9, 1932, 2 (review of *The Wanderer*)

Bragdon, C., "Gibran Lives," *Syrian World*, 5, 8, April 1931, 18

Bulletin from Virginia Kirkus Bookshop Service, 16, January 15, 1948, 44 (review of *Nymphs of the Valley*)

Bulletin from Virginia Kirkus Bookshop Service, 17, December 15, 1949, 685 (review of *A Tear and a Smile*)

Bushrui, S. B., "Gibran and the Cedars," *al-Kulliyah*, Summer 1973, 10–12

Bushrui, S. B., "Gibran of Lebanon: The Fiftieth Anniversary of his Passing in 1931," *Lebanon 81*, 29, March–April 1981

Bushrui, S. B., "Kahlil Gibran, Poet of Ecology," *Resurgence*, 176, May/June 1996

Bushrui, S. B., "Kahlil the Heretic on Liberty: A New Translation with a Note," *al-Kulliyah*, Summer 1969, 12–14

Canadian Forum, 27, March 1948, 286 (review of *Secrets of the Heart*)

Chapin, L., "Another Side of Gibran," *Christian Science Monitor*, February 7, 1973, 17

Christian Century, 65, February 4, 1948, 144 (review of *Secrets of the Heart*)

Churchman, 163, July 1949, 16 (review of *Tears and Laughter*)

Coblentz, S. A., "Gibran's Companion to *The Prophet*," *New York Times Book Review*, 39, June 10, 1934, 23

Cooley, J. K., "A Man with a Flair in his Soul," *Christian Science Monitor*, June 4, 1970, 19

Cooley, J. K., "Fifteen Years of Mounting Sales," *Publishers' Weekly*, 133, April 2, 1938, 1451–52

Cournas, J., "The Story of a Life-ist," *New York Times Book Review*, 50, January 14, 1945, 2

Crozer Quarterly, 26, July 1949, 286 (review of *Tears and Laughter*)

Dempsey, D., "Improvement," *New York Times Book Review*, November 23, 1952, 8

Edwards, D., "The Artist Gibran," *Syrian World*, 6, 7, April 1932, 34–36

Elridge, P., "Gibran's Jesus," *New York Evening Post*, November 24, 1928

Ethics, 58, April 1948, 228 (review of *Secrets of the Heart*)

"Four New Books of Poetry," *New York Times Book Review*, 36, 20, May 17, 1931, 23

al-Ghurayyib, K., "Dhikrayat Jubran, al-Rihani, Rustum, Mukarzil, al-Ghurayyib," *Awraq Lubnaniyah*, January 1958, 6–10

"Gibran Kahlil Gibran," *Syrian World*, 5, 8, April 1931, 18

"Gibran a Year After," *Syrian World*, 6, 7, April 1932, 26–33

Gollomb, J. "An Arabian Poet in New York," *New York Evening Post*, March 29, 1919, book section, pp. 1–100

Hanna, S., "Gibran and Whitman: Their Literary Dialogue," *Literature East and West*, December 7, 1968, 174–98

Hitti, P. K., "Tributes to Gibran, Gibran's Place and Influence in Modern Arabic Literature," *Syrian World*, 3, 8, February 1929, 30–32

Journal of Philosophy, 45, February 26, 1948, 137 (review of *Secrets of the Heart*)

Kanjer, S., "But is it not Strange that even Elephants will Yield and that *The Prophet* is Still Popular?" *Il Por Time*, June 25, 1972, 8–9

"The Kahlil Gibran Museum Re-opens in Lebanon," *The Middle East*, 250, 1995, 48

"The Last Days of Gibran," *Syrian World*, 5, April 1931, 21

Lecerf, J., "Djabran Kahlil Djabran et les origines de la prose poétique moderne," *Orient*, 3, 1957, 7–14

Library Journal, 72, September 15, 1947, 1266 (review of *Secrets of the Heart*)

Library Journal, 73, February 15, 1948, 331 (review of *Nymphs of the Valley*)

Literary Review, February 5, 1927, 14 (review of *Sand and Foam*)

Lively, P., "*Kahlil Gibran*, by Jean Gibran and Kahlil Gibran," *The Spectator*, 269, July 25, 1992, 28

Luxner, L., "A Garden for Gibran," *Aramco World*, 41, 2, March 1990, 2

Malarkey, J., "The Vision and Message of Kahlil Gibran: A Centenary Assessment," *Middle East Studies Association*, 1983

Metz, H., "In Perspective: Memories of Gibran," *Provicence Journal*, March 14, 1973

Mokarzel, S. A., "Gibran's Tears," *Syrian World*, 3, 8, February 1929, 32–33

Mullin, G., "Blake and Gibran," *Nation*, 110, April 10, 1920, 485

Naimy, M., "The Gift of Genius," *Lotus: Afro-Asian Writing*, 18, 1973, 68–80

Naimy, M., "A Strange Little Book," *Aramco World*, 15, 6, November–December 1964, 10–17

Naimy, N., "The Mind and Thought of Kahlil Gibran," *Journal of Arabic Literature*, 5, 1974, 55–71

Nation, 107, December 28, 1918, 812 (review of *The Madman*)

New York Call, November 24, 1918, 6 (review of *The Madman*)

New York Evening Post, February 1, 1919, 6 (review of *The Madman*)

New York Herald Tribune Books, May 22, 1927, 12 (review of *Sand and Foam*)

New York Herald Tribune Books, December 2, 1928, 6 (review of *Jesus, the Son of Man*)

New York Herald Tribune Books, May 3, 1931, 23 (review of *The Earth Gods*)

New York Herald Tribune Books, February 7, 1932, 10 (review of *The Wanderer*)

New York Herald Tribune Books, November 19, 1933, 28 (review of *The Garden of the Prophet*)

New York Times Book Review, April 18, 1948, 27 (review of *Nymphs of the Valley*)

New York Times Book Review, July 25, 1948, 19 (review of *Secrets of the Heart*)

New York Times Book Review, April 3, 1949, 7 (review of *Tears and Laughter*)

New York Times Book Review, February 19, 1950, 5 (review of *A Tear and a Smile*)

North American Review, 226, December 1928 (review of *Jesus, the Son of Man*)

"Notes on *The Madman*," *The Dial*, 65, December 30, 1918, 778

"Notes on *Sand and Foam*," *The Dial*, 83, September 1927, 265

"Notes on *Sand and Foam*," *Times Literary Supplement*, 1314, April 17, 1927, 253

"Philosophy of Work," *Journal of the National Educational Association* (Washington), 18, June 1929, 182

Poetry, 18, April 1921, 40–41 (review of *The Forerunner*)

"Profits from the Prophet," *Il Por Time*, May 15, 1972, 30

"Prophet from Bisherri," *Time*, 45, 4, January 22, 1945, 98ff.

Ross, N. W., "*Beloved Prophet: The Love Letters of Kahlil Gibran and Mary Haskell and her Private Journal*," *Saturday Review*, April 15, 1972, 68 (review of *Beloved Prophet*)

Ruskin, G. M., "On First Viewing Gibran's *The Prophet*" (poem), *Syrian World*, 6, 7, April 1932, 33

Saal, R. W., "Speaking of Books: *The Prophet*," *New York Times Book Review*, May 16, 1965, 2

Saal, R. W., "Tributes to Gibran . . . at the Hotel McAlpin in New York . . . on the Occasion of the Twenty-fifth Anniversary of the Publication of his First Literary Work," *Syrian World*, 3, 9, February 1929, 29–33

San Francisco Chronicle, June 13, 1948, 20 (review of *Secrets of the Heart*)

San Francisco Chronicle, September 1929, 21 (review of *Tears and Laughter*)

San Francisco Chronicle, March 5, 1950, 18 (review of *A Tear and a Smile*)

Saturday Review of Literature, 10, 19, November 25, 1933, 296 (review of *The Garden of the Prophet*)

Saturday Review of Literature, 33, May 20, 1950, 21 (review of *A Tear and a Smile*)

"Son of Man," *Pictorial Review* (New York), 36, December 1934, 15

"Spirit of the Worker," *Journal of the National Education Association* (Washington), 38, May 1949, 332

"Spirits Rebellious," *The Examiner*, September 24, 1949

Springfield Republican, June 12, 1949, 7 (C) (review of *Tears and Laughter*)

Springfield Republican, April 18, 13 (A) (review of *Twenty Drawings*)

"A Syrian Humanist," *New York Evening Post*, February 5, 1926

Syrian World, 6, 5, January 1932, 42 (review of *The Wanderer*)

Times Literary Supplement, January 8, 1949, 21 (review of *Nymphs of the Valley*)

Tracy, W., "A Land, a Poet, a Festival," *Aramco World*, July–August 1970, 4–7

Turner, S., "Gibran Kahlil: Tales of a Levantine Guru," *Saturday Review*, March 13, 1971, 54–55

Wilson, P. W., "Jesus was the Supreme Poet," *New York Times Book Review*, December 23, 1928, 18 (review of *Jesus, the Son of Man*)

Woerheide, C., "William Shehadi, *Kahlil Gibran, a Prophet in the Making*" (review), *International Journal of Middle East Studies*, 26, 4, November 1994, 744–46

Young, B., "Gibran" (poem), *Syrian World*, 3, 8, February 1929, 32

Young, B., "Gibran's Funeral in Boston," *Syrian World*, 5, 8, April 1931, 23–25

Young, B., "The Son of Man," *Pictorial Review*, 36, December 1934, 15

Young, B., "I Would Build a City," *Aramco World*, April 1954, 4–5

Ziadah, M., "al-Mawakib," *al-Hilal*, 22, 1919, 874–81

RECORDINGS

The Prophet, New York, Atlantic Recording Corporation, 1974 (a musical interpretation featuring Richard Harris; music composed by Arif Marding; one stereo record with the following selection from *The Prophet*: 1 "The Coming of the Ship," "On Love," "On Marriage," "On Children," Trilogy from *The Prophet* [Love, Marriage, Children; "On Living," "On Eating and Drinking," "On Clothes," "On Work"; 2 "On Crime and Punishment," "On Laws," "On Teaching and Self-Knowledge," "On Friendship," "On Pleasure," "Theme from *The Prophet*" ["Pleasure is a Freedom Song"], "On Religion," "On Death," "The Farewell"), S.D., 18120

The Kahlil Gibran Companion, read by Stephen Lang, New York, Random House Audio Publishing, 1995

Shahid, Irfan, "Gibran in the Anglo-Saxon World," in *Arab and American Relations Past, Present, and Future*, recorded at the Library of Congress Seminar for the Near East Section, Washington, D.C., 1995

POCHETTE

The World of Kahlil Gibran, SLD recording and Gibran National Committee, 1971, with Neil Bratton, Mouna Bassili, Maureen O'Brien, John Bassili (two records with the following selections: *Jesus, the Son of Man*, "A Wisdom in Galilee," "Mary Magdalene," "A Man from Lebanon," "The Woman of Byblos"; *The Garden of the Prophet*, "Beyond Death," "Pity the Nation," "O Mist my Sister"; *Sand and Foam*, "Aphorisms and Parables," "Message to the Lebanese in America"; *The Prophet*, "On Love," "On Children," "On Freedom," "On Pleasure," "On Death," "Farewell"; *The Madman*, "God")

EXHIBITIONS

Gibran Photographic Exhibition, organized and assembled by S. B. Bushrui, Gibran International Festival, Beirut, May 23–30, 1970

Kahlil Gibran International Exhibition, organized and assembled by S. B. Bushrui for the Gibran National Committee and the American University of Beirut, Beirut, August 2–15, 1972

Saroyan, A., *Kahlil Gibran: Paintings and Drawnings 1905–1930*, New York, Vrej Bahoomian Gallery, May 25–June 25, 1989

The World of Kahlil Gibran: A Pictorial Record of his Life and Work, ed. and assembled with biographical notes by S. B. Bushrui, Paris, U.N.E.S.C.O. Palace, March 19–22, 1996

WORKS IN LANGUAGES OTHER THAN ENGLISH

French

WORKS BY KAHLIL GIBRAN

Le fou, trans. A. Chahine, Paris, Editions Asfar, 1990
Le jardin de prophète et Le sable et l'écume, trans. J. Lévy, Paris, Editions du Chêne, 1995
Jésus fils de l'homme, trans. J.-P. Dahdah, Paris, Albin Michel, 1996
Lettres d'amour: Lettres d'amour de Kahlil Gibran à May Ziadah, trans. C. Carme and A. Derouet from a translation by S. B. Bushrui and S. H. al-Kuzbari, Orsay, Librairie de Medicis, 1996
Merveilles et Processions, trans. J.-P. Dahdah, Paris, Albin Michel, 1996
L'oeil du prophète, anthology arr. J.-P. Dahdah, Paris, Albin Michel, 1991
Les oeuvres complètes de Kahlil Gibran, coll. Bouquins, Paris, Robert Laffont, forthcoming
Le prophète, trans. M. de Smedt, Paris, Albin Michel, 1990
Le prophète, preface by Adonis, trans. A. Wade Minkowski, Monaco, Gallimard, 1992
Le prophète, trans. S. Stétié, Paris, Naufal, 1992
Le prophète, preface by A. Maalouf, trans. J. Lévy, Paris, Le Livre de Poche, 1993
Le prophète, trans. and commentary J.-P. Dahdah, Paris, Editions du Rocher, 1993
Le prophète, trans. G. Villeneuve, Paris, Editions Mille et une Nuits, 1994
Le prophète, trans. and commentary J.-P. Dahdah, Paris, J'ai Lu, 1995
Le prophète et Le jardin du prophète, trans. C. Aboussouan and C. Dubois, Paris, Editions du Seuil, 1992
Le sable et l'écume, trans. J.-P. Dahdah, Paris, Albin Michel, 1990
Visions du prophète, anthology arr. J.-P. Dahdah, Paris, Editions du Rocher, 1995

WORKS ON GIBRAN

Dahdah, J.-P., *Kahlil Gibran: une biographie,* Albin Michel, 1994 (Prix France-Liban)
Dahdah, J.-P., "Kahlil Gibran: poète de la sagesse," *Revue Question De,* 83, Albin Michel, 1990
Naaman, A., "Du Côté du 14 avenue du Maine" (Gibran in Paris), *Arabies,* Paris, October 1993, 47–51
Zogheib, Henri, "Le phénomène Gibran aux Etats-Unis," *Arabies,* Paris, October 1993, 52–55

Italian

WORKS BY KAHLIL GIBRAN

Le Ali infante, ed. S. B. Bushrui and I. Farinelli, Recco, Insieme Gruppo Editoriale, 1992
Letter d'amore, intro. and commentary S. B. Bushrui and S. al-Kuzbari, Milan, San Paolo, 1996
Il profeta, intro. and commentary S. B. Bushrui, Milan, Biblioteca Universale Rizzoli, 1993

BOOKS ON GIBRAN

Bushrui, S. B., *Gibran del Libano,* trans. Isabella Farinelli, Ricco, Insieme Gruppo Editoriale, 1987, Orsay, Librairie de Medicis, 1996

GENERAL BIBLIOGRAPHY

'Abbud, M., *Juddud wa Qudama': Dirasat wa Naqd wa Munaqashat*, Beirut, Dar al-Thaqafah li al-Tiba' ah wa al-Nashr wa al-Tawzi, 1954

'Abbud, M., *Ruwwad al-Nahdah al-Hadithah*, Beirut, n.p., 1952

'Abdu'l-Bahá, *Paris Talks: Addresses Given by 'Abdu'l-Bahá in Paris in 1911–1912*, 11th ed., London, Bahá'í Publishing Trust, 1979

'Abdu'l-Bahá, *The Promulgation of Universal Peace: Talks Delivered by 'Abdu'l-Bahá during his Visit to the United States and Canada in 1912*, Wilmette, Bahá'í Publishing Trust, 1982

'Abdul-Hai, M., *Tradition and English and American Influence in Arabic Romantic Poetry: A Study in Comparative Literature*, published for the Middle East Centre, St. Antony's College Oxford, London, Ithaca Press, 1982

Abu-Madi, I., "Jibran Taht Mabadi' al-Nu'ayma," *al-Samir*, 18, 1935

Ackroyd, P., *T. S. Eliot*, London, Penguin, 1993

Adams, J. D., "Speaking of Books," *New York Times Book Review*, September 29, 1957

Adham, I., "Mikhail Naimy," *al-Hadith* magazine, Aleppo, 1940

Arberry, A. J., *Sufism*, London, George Allen & Unwin, 1950

Badron, M. and M. Cooke (eds.), *A Century of Arab Feminist Writing*, London, Virago, 1990

Bahá'u'lláh, *The Seven Valleys and the Four Valleys*, trans. M. Gail, Wilmette, Bahá'í Publishing Trust, 1986

Baker, C. H. (ed.), *Josephine Preston Peabody, Diary and Letters*, Boston, Houghton Mifflin, 1927

Bates, J. L., *The United States 1898–1928*, New York, McGraw-Hill, 1976

Beard, R. and L. C. Berlowitz (eds.), *Greenwich Village: Culture and Counterculture*, published for the Museum of the City of New York, New Brunswick, Rutgers University Press, 1993

Becker, U. (ed.), *Element Encyclopedia of Symbols*, Brisbane, Element, 1994

Beer, J., *Blake's Visionary Universe*, Manchester, Manchester University Press, 1969

Bender, T., *New York Intellect*, New York, Alfred A. Knopf, 1987

Benjamin, W., *Paris, capitale du XIXe siècle*, Paris, 1989

Bennett, J. G., *Gurdjieff: Making a New World*, London, Turnstone, 1976

Blake, W., *The Marriage of Heaven and Hell*, reproduction of original, with intro. and commentary by G. Keynes, London, Oxford University Press, 1975

Blake, W., *Songs of Innocence & of Experience*, London, Folio Society, 1992

Bloom, H., and L. Tring (eds.), *Romantic Poetry and Prose*, London, Oxford University Press, 1973

Boehme, J., *Supersensual Life*, London and New York, Everyman, 1912–1934

The Bookman, September 1911

Boullata, I. J., "Gibran in the Diaries of Josephine Preston Peabody," *al-Arabiyya*, 10, Spring 1977

Bramley, S., *Leonardo: The Artist and the Man*, trans. S. Reynolds, London, Michael Joseph, 1992

Brooks, V. W., *America's Coming of Age*, New York, B. W. Huebsch, 1915

Brooks, V. W., *New England: Indian Summer*, New York, E. P. Dutton, 1940

Brown, C. M., *The Romantic Imagination*, Cambridge, MA, Harvard University Press, 1949

Browne, E. G., *A Literary History of Persia*, London, Cambridge University Press, 1956

Buckland, A. R. and A. L. Williams (eds.), *The Universal Bible Dictionary*, London, Lutterworth, 1914

Burckhardt, T., *An Introduction to Sufi Doctrine*, trans. D. M. Matheson, Wellingborough, Thorson, 1976

Burckhardt, T., *De l'homme universal*, Lyon, P. Derain, 1953

Burckhardt, T., *Mirror of the Intellect: Essays on Traditional Science and Sacred Art*, ed. and trans. W. Stoddart, Cambridge, Quinta Essentia, 1987

Bushrui, S. B., "Arab–American Cultural Relations in the Twentieth Century: The Thought and Work of Ameen Rihani," address given at the Library of Congress, 1990

Bushrui, S. B. (ed.), *Anglo-Irish Literature in Lebanon and the Arab World*, triennial report, 1970–73, Cork, International Association for the Study of Anglo-Irish Literature, 1973

al-Bustani, B., *Udaba' al-'Arab fi al-Andalos wa 'Asr al-Inbi'ath*, 4th imp., Beirut, 1958

al-Bustani, F. and E. S'ab, "Bayn al-Mashriq wa al-Saih," *al-Mashriq*, 21, 1923

Bynner, W., *The Works of Witter Bynner: Selected Letters*, ed. and intro. J. Kraft, New York, Farrar, Strauss, Giroux, 1981

Capra, F., *The Tao of Physics: An Exploration of the Parallels between Modern Physics and Eastern Mysticism*, London, Flamingo, 1989

Cheikho, L., *al-Adab al-'Arabiyyah fi al-Qarn al-Tasi' 'Ashar*, Beirut, n.p., 1924–26, 2 vols. in 1

Cheikho, L., "Bada'i' Jubran Khalil Jubran wa Tara'ifuh," *al-Mashriq*, 21, 1923

Chilvers, I. (ed.), *The Concise Oxford Dictionary of Art and Artists*, Oxford, Oxford University Press, 1990

Christie-Murray, D., *Reincarnation*, London, David & Charles, 1981

The Cloud of Unknowing, London, Penguin, 1961

Cobban, Helena, *The Making of Modern Lebanon*, London, Hutchinson, 1985

Coleridge, S. T., *The Poems of Coleridge*, London, John Lane

Copies of the Original Letters from the Army of General Bonaparte in Egypt, Intercepted by the Fleet under the Command of Admiral Lord Nelson (English translation), London, 1798, vol. 1

Coward, D., "Renan's Religion," *Times Literary Supplement*, March 28, 1997

Cullman, O., *The Christology of the New Testament*, trans. S. C. Guthrie and C. A. M. Hall, London, SCM, 1973

Curtie, M., *The Growth of American Thought*, New York, Harper, 1943

Daghir, Y. A., *Masader al-Dirasah al-Adabiyah*, Sidon, al-Mokhalles Printing Press, 1956

Davidson, J., *The Robe of Glory: An Ancient Parable of the Soul*, Shaftesbury, Element, 1992

Davies, O. (ed.), *Meister Eckhart: Selected Writings*, London, Penguin, 1994

Davis, M., *William Blake: A New Kind of Man*, London, Paul Elek, 1977

De la Tour du Pin, P., *The Dedicated Life in Poetry*, intro. S. Spender, London, Harvill Press, 1948

De Man, P. (ed.), *Selected Poetry of Keats*, New York, New American Library, 1966

Drabble, M. (ed.), *The Oxford Anthology of English Literature: Romantic Poetry and Prose*, Oxford, Oxford University Press, 1973

Drabble, M. (ed.), *The Oxford Companion to English Literature*, Oxford, Oxford University Press, 1985

The Dramatic Works of Denis Johnson, Gerrard's Cross, Colin Smythe, 1979, vol. 2

El Hage, George, *Dahesh Voice*, 1996

Eliot, T. S., *Four Quartets*, London, Faber & Faber, 1943

Eliot, T. S., *The Use of Poetry and the Use of Criticism*, London, 1933

Emerson, R. W., *Selected Essays*, Harmondsworth, Penguin, 1985

Evans, G. B. (ed.), *The Riverside Shakespeare*, Boston, Houghton Mifflin, 1974

Farroukh, O., "Khayal Jubran fi Manthumatih," *al-Amali*, 1, 35, 1939, 27–28

Ferguson, J., *Encyclopaedia of Mysticism*, London, Thames & Hudson, 1976

Forkroads: A Journal of Ethnic-American Literature, Spring 1996

Foucault, M., *Madness and Civilization: A History of Insanity in the Age of Reason*, trans. R.

Howard, London, Random House, 1967

Fox, M., *Original Blessing*, Santa Fe, Bear & Co., 1983

Frazer, J. G., *The Golden Bough*, abridged ed., London, 1957, vol. 1

Gad, C. J. B., *The Man and his Works*, New York, Moffat Yard, 1920

Gail, M., *Other People, Other Places*, Oxford, George Ronald, 1982

Gallup, D. (ed.), *Flowers of Friendship*, New York, Alfred A. Knopf, 1953

George, H., *Progress and Poverty*, New York, Appleton, 1879

Gibb, H. A. R., *Modern Trends in Islam*, Chicago, Chicago University Press, 1947

Gibb, H. A. R., "Studies in Contemporary Arabic Literature," *Bulletin of the School of Oriental and African Studies*, 4, 1927–28

Gilbert, A. G., *Magi*, London, Bloomsbury, 1996

Godwin, J., *Music, Mysticism and Magic*, New York, Arkana, 1987

Gombrich, E. H., *The Story of Art*, London, Phaidon, 1978

Grimsley, R., *The Philosophy of Rousseau*, Oxford, Oxford University Press, 1973

Haim, Sylvia Gourgi, *Arab Nationalism*, Berkeley, University of California Press, 1962

Handlin, O., *Boston's Immigrants*, Cambridge, MA, Harvard University Press, 1979

Hane, J., *W. B. Yeats*, London, Macmillan, 1965

Hartley, A. (ed.), *The Penguin Book of French Verse*, Harmondsworth, Penguin, 1977

Hastings, J. (ed.), *The Encyclopedia of Religion and Ethics*, Edinburgh, T. & T. Clark, 1920

Hemmings, F. W. J., *Culture and Society in France, 1848–1898*, London, Batsford, 1971

Hemmings, F. W. J. and R. J. Niess (eds.), *Emile Zola*, Geneva, Salon, 1959

Henn, T. R., "The Bible in Relation to the Study of English Literature today," *Hermathena*, Dublin University Review no. C, 1965

Hinnells, J. (ed.), *The Penguin Dictionary of Religions*, Harmondsworth, Penguin, 1984

Hitti, P. K., *Lebanon in History from Earliest Times to the Present*, London, Macmillan, 1957

Hitti, P. K., *The Arabs: A Short History*, London, Macmillan, 1968

Hoagland, D. R., "In Praise of John Muir," *On Nature*, San Francisco, North Point Press, 1986

Hollingdale, R. J., *Nietzsche: The Man and his Philosophy*, London, Routledge & Kegan Paul, 1965

Honnold, A. (ed.), *Vignettes from the Life of 'Abdu'l-Bahá*, Oxford, George Ronald, 1982

Hourani, A., *Arabic Thought in the Liberal Age 1798–1939*, Cambridge, Cambridge University Press, 1962

Hourani, A. and N. Shehadi (eds.), *The Lebanese in the World: A Century of Emigration*, London, Centre for Lebanese Studies in association with I. B. Tauris, 1992

Howells, W. D., *Literature and Life*, New York, Harper & Brothers, 1902

Hujwiri, U. J., *Kashf al-Mahjub*, trans. R. A. Nicholson, London, Luzac, 1911–1959

Hunayn, R., *Rasa'il Jubran al-Ta'ihah*, Beirut, Naufal, 1983

Hutchinson, T. (ed.), *Shelley: Complete Poetical Works*, Oxford, Oxford University Press, 1905, 1970

Ibish, Y. and Marculescu, I. (eds.), *Contemplation and Action in World Religions*, Seattle and London, University of Washington Press, 1977–78

Ibn al-'Arabi, M., *The Tarjuman-al-Ashwaq: A Collection of Mystical Odes*, trans. R. A. Nicholson, London, Theosophical Publishing House, 1978

Inge, W. R., *Studies of English Mystics: St Margaret's Lectures 1905*, London, John Murray, 1907

Isaacs, J., *An Assessment of Twentieth-century Literature*, London, Secker & Warburg, 1951

Ishaq, A., *al-Durar: A Selection from his Works*, ed. and coll. A. Ishaq, Beirut, n.p., 1909

Jabr, J., *Jibran, Siratuh, Adabuhu, Falsafatuhu wa Rasmuhu*, Beirut, Rihani, 1958

Jacobs, A., *A New Dictionary of Music*, Harmondsworth, Penguin, 1968

Jenkins, J., *Examining Religions: Christianity*, Oxford, Heinemann, 1995

Johnson, D., *The Dramatic Works of Denis Johnson*, vol. 2, Gerrard's Cross, Colin Smythe, 1979

Jung, C. G., *Collected Works*, ed. H. Read, M. Fordham, and G. Adler, trans. R. F. C. Hull, Princeton, Princeton University Press, 1967

Jung, C. G., *Jung: Selected Writings*, intro. A. Storr, London, Fontana, 1983

Jung, C. G., *Memories, Dreams, Reflections*, London, Collins, 1982

al-Jurr, S., *Nabi Orphalese*, São Paolo, Matba'at al-Andalus, 1939

Kaufmann, W., *Nietzsche: Philosopher, Psychologist, Antichrist*, Princeton, Princeton University Press, 1974

Kayrouz, W., *'Alam Jubran al-Fikri*, 2 vols., Beirut, Bisharia, 1984

Kayrouz, W., *'Alam Jubran al-Rassam*, Beirut, Gibran National Committee, 1982

Keynes, G. (ed.), *Blake: Complete Writings with Variant Readings*, Oxford, Oxford University Press, 1959, 1972 (in notes *Blake*; references in notes are to 1972 edition)

Khalid, A., *Muhawalat-fi Darsi Jubran*, Beirut, al-Maba'a al-Katholikiah, 1933

King, U., *Towards a New Mysticism*, London, Collins, 1980

Kipling, R., *Sixty Poems*, London, Hodder & Stoughton, 1939

Kripalani, K., *Gandhi: A Life*, New Delhi, Longman, 1968

Kronick, J. G., *American Poetics of History: From Emerson to the Moderns*, Louisiana, Louisiana State University Press, 1984

Lassky, V., *The Mystical Theology of the Eastern Church*, London, James Clark & Co., 1957

Lawrence, D. H., *Apocalypse*, Cambridge Edition, Granada, 1981

Lebanon and the World in the 1980s, University of Maryland, Center for International Development, 1983

Leicht, H., *History of the World's Art*, London, Spring Books, 1963

Lewis, B., *The Arabs in History*, London, George Allen & Unwin, 1981

Lings, M., *What is Sufism?* London, George Allen & Unwin, 1981

Maeterlinck, M., *The Treasure of the Humble*, London, George Allen, 1897

al-Majmu'a al-Kamila li Mu'alafat Jubran Khalil Jubran, 2 vols., ed. and intro. M. Naimy, Beirut, Dar Sader and Dar Beirut, 1961

Marrash, F., *Ghabat al-Haqq*, ed. and rev. with intro. 'Abd al-Masih Intaki, Cairo, n.p., 1922

May, H. F., *The End of American Innocence: A Study of the First Years of our Own Time: 1912–1917*, London, Jonathan Cape, 1959

McDowall, D., *Lebanon: A Conflict of Minorities*, London, Minority Rights Group, 1996

McNulty, F. H., "Mahjar Literature: An Annotated Bibliography of Literary Criticism and Bibliography in Western Languages," *Mundus Arabicus*, 1, 1981

Miller, L. B., "Engines, Marbles, and Canvases: The Centennial Exposition of 1876," in *Lectures 1972–1973*, Indianapolis, Indians Historical Society, 1973

Monroe, H., *Poetry*, 14, New York, August 1919

Moore, G. (ed.), *The Penguin Book of American Verse*, London, Penguin, 1954

Moore, J., *Gurdjieff: The Anatomy of a Myth*, Shaftesbury, Element, 1991

Murphy, W., *Prodigal Father: The Life of John Butler Yeats (1839–1922)*, Ithaca, Cornell University Press, 1978

Naimy, M., *The Book of Mirdad*, Beirut, Sader, 1948

Naimy, M., "Fajr al-'Amal Ba'da Layl al-Ya's," *al-Funoon*, 1, July 1913, 50–70

Naimy, M., *Jubran Khalil Jubran: Hayatuhu, Mawtuhu, Adabuhu, Fannuhu*, Beirut, Dar Sader wa Beirut, 1934

Naimy, M., *Min Wahy al-Massih*, Beirut, Naufal, 1974

Naimy, M., *Sab'un Hikayat 'Umr*, 3 vols., Beirut, Sader, 1959–60

Najm, M., *al-Qissah fi al-Adab al-'Arabi al-Hadith*, Cairo, Dar Misr al-Tiba'ah, 1952 al-Naqqash, M., *Arazat Lubnan (Cedar Tree of Lebanon)*, intro. N. al-Naqqash, Beirut, n.p., 1869

Nicholson, R. A., *A Literary History of the Arabs*, Cambridge, Cambridge University Press, 1930

Nicholson, R. A., *Studies in Islamic Mysticism*, Cambridge, Cambridge University Press, 1921

Nicholson, R. A., *The Mystics of Islam*, London, Routledge & Kegan Paul, 1914, 1974

Nietzsche, F., *Thus Spake Zarathustra*, trans. R. J. Hollingdale, Harmondsworth, Penguin, 1969

Nugent, W. T. K., *From Centennial to World War: American Society, 1876–1917*, Indianapolis, Bobbs-Merrill, 1977

O'Connor, U., *Biographers and the Art of Biography*, London, Quartet, 1993

Orfalea, G. and S. Elmusa (eds.), *Grape Leaves: A Century of Arab American Poetry*, trans. A. Ghareeb, Salt Lake City, University of Utah Press, 1988

Osborne, H. (ed.), *The Oxford Companion to Art*, Oxford, Clarendon Press, 1970

Ouspensky, P. D., *The Cosmology of Man's Possible Evolution: The Cosmological Lectures, 1934–1940*, Shaftesbury, Agora, 1989

Ouspensky, P. D., *A New Model of the Universe*, London, Routledge Kegan Paul, 1931

Ouspensky, P. D., *Tertium Organum: A Key to the Enigmas of the World*, trans. N. Bessaraboff and C. Bragdon, London, Routledge & Kegan Paul, 1970

Pagels, E., *The Gnostic Gospels*, London, Weidenfeld & Nicolson, 1977

Parrish, S. M., "Currents of the Nineties in Boston and London: Fred Holland Day, Louise Imogen Guiney and their Circle," unpublished Ph.D. thesis, Harvard University, 1954

Perry, W. N. (ed.), *A Treasury of Traditional Wisdom*, Bedfont, Perennial Books, 1981

Pickthall, M., *The Meaning of the Glorious Qur'an*, London, al-Furqan, n.d.

The Poems of Matthew Arnold, 1840–1867, intro. A. Quiller-Couch, London, Oxford University Press, 1922

Prendergast, C., *Paris and the Nineteenth Century*, Oxford, Blackwell, 1992

Purnell, I., "Gift for Mimicry Harms Poet," review of English ed. of Mikhail Naimy's biography, *Los Angeles Daily News*, November 4, 1950

Raine, K., "Blake: The Poet as Prophet," in S. B. Bushrui (ed.), *Essays and Studies 1982*, London, John Murray, 1982

Raine, K., *Blake and the New Age*, London, George Allen & Unwin, 1979

Raphael, A. P., *Goethe and the Philosopher's Stone*, New York, Garrett, 1965

Reincarnation: An East–West Anthology, New York, Julian Press, 1967

Rihani, A., *Aina Tajid Amin al-Rihani*, Beirut, Rihani House, 1979

Rihani, A., *The Book of Khalid*, New York, Dodd, Mead & Co., 1911

Rihani, A., *A Chant of Mystics and Other Poems*, ed. S. B. Bushrui and J. Munro, Beirut, Rihani House, 1970

Rihani, A., *Jibran Hayyan wa Maytan, Majmu'ah Tashtamil 'ala Mukhtarat mimma Katab was Rasam Jibran Khalil Jibran, wa mimma Qila fihi*, ed. and intro. H. Mas'ud, São Paolo, n.p., 1932

Rihani, A., *Nubza fith-Thawra el-Faransiya*, al-Hoda, n.p., 1902

Rihani, A., *The Path of Vision*, Beirut, Rihani House, 1970

Rihani, A., *Rasa'il Amin al-Rihani*, Beirut, Rihani House, 1959

Riis, J. A., *How the Other Half Lives*, New York, Dover, 1970

Rilke, R. M., *Selected Poems*, trans. and intro. J. B. Leishman, Harmondsworth, Penguin, 1964

Roman, J., *Paris 1890s*, London, Prentice Hall, 1963

The Rubaiyat of Omar Khayyam, trans. E. Fitzgerald, intro. L. Housman, London, Collins, n.d.

Russell, G. (AE), *The Candle of Vision*, Sturminster Newton, Prism, 1990

Russell, G. (AE), *The Living Torch*, New York, Macmillan, 1938

Salem, L. A., "The Sanctity of Seven," *Dahesh Voice*, 2, 4, March 1997

Salibi, K. S., *The Modern History of Lebanon*, London, Weidenfeld & Nicolson, 1965

Sarkis, Y., *Jami'al Tasanif al-Haditha*, Cairo, Sarkis Library, 1927

Sarkis, Y., *Mu'jam al-Maltbo'at*, Cairo, Sarkis Library, 1928–29, vol. 1

Schenk, H. G., *The Mind of the European Romantics*, Oxford, Oxford University Press, 1979

Schiller, F., *On the Aesthetic Education of Man*, trans. R. Snell, London, Routledge & Kegan Paul, 1954

Schiller, F., *On the Aesthetic Education of Man*, trans. E. M. Wilkinson and L. A. Willoughby, Oxford, Clarendon Press, 1985

Scott, E., *The People of the Secret*, London, Octagon, 1983

Shah, I., *The Sufis*, trans. R. A. Nicholson, intro. R. Graves, London, Jonathan Cape, 1969

Shah, I., *Tales of the Dervishes*, London, Jonathan Cape, 1967

Shah, I., *The Way of the Sufi*, London, Penguin, 1974

Shah, I., *Wisdom of the Idiots*, London, Octagon, 1970

Sheldrake, R., *The Rebirth of Nature*, London, Rider, 1990

Shoghi Effendi, *God Passes By*, Wilmette, Bahá'í Publishing Trust, 1979

Shoghi Effendi, *The Promised Day is Come*, Wilmette, Bahá'í Publishing Committee, 1941

Singer, J., *Boundaries of the Soul: The Practice of Jung's Psychology*, Sturminster Newton, Prism, 1994

Smith, M., *Readings from the Mystics of Islam*, London, Luzac & Co., 1992

Spiller, R. E., W. Thorp, T. H. Johnson, and H. S. Canby (eds.), *Literary History of the United States*, New York, Macmillan, 1962

Stepaniants, M. T., *Sufi Wisdom*, New York, State University of New York Press, 1994

Stevenson, W. H. (ed.), *The Poems of William Blake* text by D. B. Erdman, London, Longman, 1971

Stewart, R. J., *The Spiritual Dimension of Music*, Vermont, Destiny Books, 1990

Stoddart, W., *Sufism: The Mystical Doctrines as Methods of Islam*, Wellingborough, Aquarian Press, 1976

Sullivan, J. U. N., *Beethoven: His Spiritual Development*, London, Unwin, 1964

Tagore, R., *Selected Poems*, trans. W. Radice, London, Penguin, 1985

Thomas, K., *Man and the Natural World*, Harmondsworth, Penguin, 1984

Thompson, J., *'Abdu'l-Bahá, the Center of the Covenant*, Wilmette, 1948

Thompson, J., *The Diary of Juliet Thompson*, Los Angeles, Kalimát Press, 1983

Thoreau, H. D., *The Maine Woods*, London, Penguin, 1988

Trobridge, G., *Emanuel Swedenborg: His Life, Teachings and Influence*, London, Frederick Warne & Co., n.d.

Underhill, E., *The Essentials of Mysticism*, Oxford, Oneworld, 1995

The Upanishads, trans. Swami Prabhavananda and F. Manchester, Southern California, Vedanta Society, 1948

Upshall, M. (ed.), *The Hutchinson Encyclopedia*, Oxford, Helicon, 1993

Van der Post, L., *Jung and the Story of our Time*, Harmondsworth, Penguin, 1979

Vigny, A. de, *Paris, oeuvres complètes*, Paris, Pléiade, 1950

Virtue's Household Physician, London, Virtue, 1950, vol. 1

Warner, R. (ed.), *Encyclopedia of World Mythology*, London, Peerage Books, 1975

Watt, W. M. (trans.), *The Faith and Practice of al-Ghazali*, Oxford, Oneworld, 1994

Weston, J. L., *From Ritual to Romance*, New York, Doubleday, 1957

Whitman, W., *Leaves of Grass, by Walt Whitman, Including a Facsimile Autobiography Variorum, Readings of the Poems and a Department of Gathered Leaves*, London, Siegle

Hill & Co., 1907

Whitman, W., "I Sing the Body Electric," London, Phoenix, 1996

Whitman, W., *Song of Myself,* London, Penguin, 1986

Whitman, W., *The Complete Poems,* London, Penguin, 1986

Wilber, K., *The Holographic Paradigm and Other Paradoxes,* Boulder, Shambhala, 1982

Wilkinson, M. M. (ed.), *New Voices,* rev. ed., New York, Macmillan, 1929

Williams, W. C., *The Autobiography of William Carlos Williams,* New York, New Directions Books, 1951

Witcutt, W. P., *Blake: A Psychological Study,* London, Hollis & Carter, 1946

Woledge, B., Brereton, G., and Hartley, A. (eds.), *The Penguin Book of French Verse,* Harmondsworth, Penguin, 1975

Women, Voice of the Oppressed, Association for the Liberty of Culture and Women's Human Rights International Association, 1996

Woods, R., "The Poor in Great Cities," *Wellesley Prelude,* 7 May 14, 1892

Wordsworth, W., *The Works of William Wordsworth,* Wordsworth Poetry Library, Ware, Wordsworth Editions, 1994

Yeats, W. B. (ed.), *A Book of Irish Verse,* London, Methuen, 1900

Yeats, W. B., *Essays,* London, Macmillan, 1924

Yeats, W. B., *The Poets,* London, J. M. Dent, 1990

Yeats, W. B. (ed.), *The Poems of William Blake,* London, Routledge & Kegan Paul, 1905

Zinn, H., *A People's History of the United States,* London, Longman, 1980

Zurayq, Q., "Nasseeb Arida," *al-Adib,* Beirut, 8, 1946

Index